# THE
# ANTI-SLAVERY MOVEMENT
# IN ENGLAND

## A STUDY IN ENGLISH
## HUMANITARIANISM

By

FRANK J. KLINGBERG

ARCHON BOOKS
1968

[YALE HISTORICAL PUBLICATIONS. MISCELLANY XVII]

LIBRARY OF CONGRESS CATALOG CARD NUMBER: 68-26924
PRINTED IN THE UNITED STATES OF AMERICA

TO

ELIZABETH WYSOR KLINGBERG

# PREFACE

The British anti-slavery crusade, covering approximately the years from 1770 to 1833, is an outstanding development of a general humanitarian movement. Beginning in the second quarter of the eighteenth century, this movement expressed itself in many different ways. Churches and schools were built, hospitals were established, missionaries were sent to the ends of the earth, the criminal code was revised, prisons and prison discipline were humanized, better poor laws were enacted, labor legislation was begun, the Roman Catholics were emancipated, parliament was reformed, and a swelling chorus of voices was raised in behalf of the brown men of Asia and the black men of Africa and America.

The emancipation of the British slaves in 1833 was the result of a half century of unparalleled effort. The campaign is a first instance of an appeal to public opinion by means of all the modern agencies of publicity; lecture, pamphlet, newspaper, and bill board. It is the first example of the open participation of women in a contest. So well intrenched, however, was negro slavery in the modern world that it lived on in full vigor for more than another generation after British emancipation.

In the present study no effort has been made to carry the account beyond legal emancipation in 1833, nor to tell the story of the anti-slavery struggle in France, the United States, or other countries. The subject ramifies in all directions. It is related to the striking decline of the West Indies, the growth of cane sugar in non-British territory, the development of the beet sugar industry, and the shifting of the British Empire from the West Indies to India. Many allied topics need detailed inquiry, such as, the financial history of the slave trade, the diplomatic negotiations for abolition, the British navy as an agent in the suppression of the illicit slave traffic, the importation of Hindu laborers into the West Indies and South Africa, and the diversion of British shipping from carrying negroes to transporting European emigrants. Some of these studies are projected; others are under way. This volume is primarily a chronicle of the change in public opinion which once favored and built up the slave system by robbery, war, diplomacy, and the careful investment of capital and skillful management, and then in turn used all the resources of statesmanship and all the arts of public appeal to pronounce slavery a crime and an economic mistake.

This study, which in its original form was a doctoral dissertation, was begun at the University of Kansas at the suggestion of Professor Wilbur C. Abbott, and was continued at Yale University under the direction of Professor Charles M. Andrews. To both of these men I am indebted for suggestions and advice. Professor Andrews read the entire manuscript with the utmost care, and, with characteristic generosity, offered me invaluable counsel and criticism. It is a pleasure to express my gratitude to him. Professor Frank Melvin of the University of Kansas gave the manuscript a painstaking and scholarly reading, and, from his ample knowledge of the period, indicated many modifications. My colleague, Professor William A. Morris, has supported me with generous words of encouragement and has been most helpful in his hints. Another colleague, Dr. Margaret S. Carhart, has saved me from numerous slips and found many opportunities for amendment. My indebtedness to her is great.

Valuable gleanings from their own researches have been given me by Professor Chauncey B. Tinker of Yale University, by Dr. Lois Whitney of Goucher College, by Professor Ronald S. Crane of Northwestern University, and by Professor Cecil A. Moore of the University of Minnesota. These specialists in the eighteenth century have permitted me to incorporate into my book material from their discoveries. I gratefully acknowledge their contributions and thank them for their interest.

The University of California has generously enabled me to have researches made in London and to avail myself of the rich stores of anti-slavery material deposited in the libraries of this country. Every library to which application was made allowed borrowings from its archives. The list of my obligations includes practically every large library in the United States. My thanks are due to the officials of these institutions for their ready assistance in searching for and making their materials available. Only a few can be named: The Yale University Library, The Harvard University Library, The Boston Public Library, The Boston Athenaeum, The New York Public Library, The Columbia University Library, The Peabody Institute Library, The Johns Hopkins University Library, The Library of Congress, The John Crerar Library, The Newberry Library, The University of Chicago Library, The Oberlin College Library, The Henry E. Huntington Library and Art Gallery, The Leland Stanford Junior University Library, and the University of California Library. My thanks would be incomplete without special reference to Mr. Everett R. Perry, Mr. Albert C. Read, Miss Susanna B. Ott, and Miss Laura C. Cooley, officials of the Los Angeles Public Library, for their zeal in securing materials for me.

Professor R. Coupland's excellent *Wilberforce: A Narrative* appeared when this study was practically completed. The fine biography of another humanitarian leader, *Lord Shaftesbury,* by J. L. and Barbara Hammond, became available at about the same time. These studies suggest biographies of other eminent humanitarian leaders.

F. J. K.

University of California,
   Southern Branch,
      December 15, 1924.

# CONTENTS

# CHAPTER I

## NEW WORLDS AND NEGRO SLAVERY

During the heroic age of discovery and exploration the Portuguese and the Spaniards brought four continents into the stream of European life.[1] The imaginary islands of the western seas were replaced by two real continents with groups of tropical islands nestling between them. The harbors of the dimly known continents of Africa and Asia became ports of call for the vessels of European mariners. Such places as the Guinea coast, Sofala, Aden, Goa, Calicut, and Macao were added to European geographical knowledge. And off to the southeast of Asia were the rich Spice Islands, the stepping stones to the forbidding continent of Australia.

The Portuguese spent most of the fifteenth century in pushing down the west coast of Africa, settling the nearby groups of Atlantic islands, and noting for future use the vast negro labor supplies of the Guinea coast. Finally, in 1487-1488, knowledge of the all-sea route to the fabled riches of the Orient, so well described by Marco Polo, was completed. Diaz rounded the southern end of Africa by sea, and Covilham journeyed by land and by sea across the Indian Ocean to Calicut and as far down the east coast of Africa as Sofala.

Although the all-sea route to the East was no longer a

[1] Western Asia and northern Africa were always closely connected with Europe and with each other. From time to time explorers went to India and to China. Both Christianity and Mohammedanism were to be found south of the Sahara and northern Africa became Arabic in culture. In earlier ages Asiatic peoples had doubtless migrated into Africa, changed the racial character of the negroes, and modified their languages. See Carl Meinhof, ''Native Languages in Africa,'' *The Living Age*, 318, 31-55.

mystery, a decade passed by before Vasco da Gama sailed on his memorable voyage from Lisbon to Calicut. In 1500, Cabral, by swinging far out to the west, gave the Portuguese direct knowledge of South America as well as of Africa and Asia.[2] The old commercial empires of Italians in the Mediterranean, of Arabs on the Indian Ocean and its arms, and of Chinese on both sides of the straits of Malacca were quickly superseded by an all-Portuguese empire extending from Lisbon in Europe around the coast of Africa to southern and western Asia with its outlying islands. And in the western world south of the mouth of the Amazon, the neglected settlements of Brazil slowly developed.

In the meantime, the Spaniards discovered the two American continents and the many West Indian islands. On these, "the stepping stones to the Great Western continent, nearly every colonizing nation has set its foot."[3] On one of these Columbus landed, and during his four voyages he visited many of the islands as well as both continents.[4] The first permanent settlement he planted in Santo Domingo in 1493. The Spaniards soon found that they had encountered a vast continental obstruction, which lay between them and the East, just as Africa separated the Portuguese from their goal. A whole generation was to pass before Magellan carried out the design of Columbus, and reached the East by sailing west, and thus gave the Spaniards their claim to the Philippines.

[2] The Portuguese with possessions both in Africa and in America became leading slave traders during the eighteenth and nineteenth centuries. They claimed Brazil both by papal assignments and Cabral's discovery.

[3] C. P. Lucas, *A Historical Geography of the British Colonies* (second edition, Oxford, 1905), II, 3.

[4] It is worth noting that Columbus discovered all the groups of the present British West Indian islands except Barbadoes, which seems to have been first seen by the Portuguese.

By the time Magellan's ship returned to Spain, each Iberian power had circumvented its obstacles, and was rapidly staking out its empire. The Portuguese had tapped the riches of the Asiatic civilizations by way of the Cape of Good Hope. The Spaniards, on the other hand, could follow either the route mapped out for them by Magellan and thread their way through the straits he navigated, or go over the Isthmus of Panama crossed by Balboa as early as 1513. Each power was handicapped in reaching the rich Spice Islands by a narrow neck of land which has been cut in modern times, and today Europe and Eastern Asia are thousands of miles nearer to each other, whether the route is east by Suez or west by Panama.

Conditions in the East and in the West were vastly different. In the former were centres of civilization with industrial skill and commercial enterprise. Millions of people were ready to ship their products to the European market. A steady flow of economic goods could be taken for granted. The labor supply was adept and ample. In the West, on the other hand, the Spaniards found that the Indians, for the most part, were in an inferior state of civilization with primitive economic abilities. If the Spaniard and the other Europeans were to gain wealth in the Americas, it was necessary to make the Indians into miners or farmers, to settle the lands with immigrants, or to introduce an African labor supply. The Indian population, particularly in the West Indies, quickly perished when brought into contact with white men and put at hard work. As a means of saving the Indians and adding to the number of laborers, negroes were brought from the West Coast of Africa, and the Americas became the recipients of the two great streams of immigrants; white men from Europe destined primarily, but by no means exclusively, for the temperate

zones, and negroes flowing in a steady stream into the
tropics to grow the tropical products which Europeans
most desired—tobacco, sugar, coffee, rice, cotton, indigo,
pimento, and the like.

Fertile lands in the American tropics were abundant;
capital and managing ability could be imported from
Europe when not available on the spot; and an abundant
supply of laborers was just across the Atlantic. "The
West Indies . . . lie over against West Africa," says
Sir Charles Lucas, "their tropical heat and tropical
products called for a black population."[5] The negroes,
who had been discovered half a century before America
was found, could be hunted in their warm lands, which
became a great game preserve for labor, and brought
across the Atlantic to the work fields of the West. The
demand in Europe was for tropical products wherewith
to supplement the abundant home-grown food stuffs of
the temperate zone. As the Crusaders centuries earlier
hurried to the eastern end of the Mediterranean for the
spices of the East Indies, so the Europeans now spread
their sails for the rich Asiatic and American lands.

Before the development of the West Indies is sketched,
a brief description of them is necessary. Cuba, Haiti,
Jamaica, and Porto Rico form the Greater Antilles, and
the semicircle of smaller islands to the east, the Lesser
Antilles, which, in the words of Froude, "Stand like a
string of jewels round the neck of the Caribbean Sea."[6]
These islands extend in a curved chain from Florida to
the northern coast of South America and vary in size
from Cuba, the largest, which is about the size of the
state of New York, to dots of but a few acres in extent.
Beginning with the Bahamas in the north, they end with
Trinidad off the coast of Venezuela. Cuba with one side

5 C. P. Lucas, *A Historical Geography of the British Colonies*, II, 3.
6 J. A. Froude, *The English in the West Indies*, p. 30.

helps to enclose the Gulf of Mexico, while with the other it partly forms the Caribbean Sea.

The islands are partly of coral formation and partly volcanic in origin. Some of the almost land-locked harbors are obviously the craters of extinct volcanoes, and occasionally a volcano bursts into life and rains destruction over a whole island. During certain seasons of the year many of the islands are subject to violent hurricanes. Tropical diseases, such as yellow fever, have visited the islands again and again. Despite these handicaps of a tropical climate and the destructive powers of hurricanes and earthquakes, Europeans developed the West Indies.

For about a century Spain was left in almost undisputed possession of the American Mediterranean. This age has been summarized by Froude: "Strange scenes streamed across my memory, and a shadowy procession of great figures who have printed their names in history. Columbus, and Cortez, Vasco Nuñez, and Las Casas; the millions of innocent Indians who, according to Las Casas, were destroyed out of the islands, the Spanish grinding them to death in their gold mines; the black swarms who were poured in to take their place, and the frightful story of the slave trade.'"[7]

Then England, France, and Holland entered the field. First, they came as pirates taking possession of some of the smaller islands which Spain had passed by. "Adventurers, buccaneers, corsairs, privateers, call them by what name we will," says Froude, "stand as extraordinary but characteristic figures on the stage of history, disowned or acknowledged by their sovereign as suited diplomatic convenience. The outlawed pirate of one year was promoted the next to be a governor and his country's

[7] J. A. Froude, *The English in the West Indies*, p. 27.

representative. In those waters the men were formed
and trained who drove the Armada through the Channel
into wreck and ruin. In those waters, in the centuries
which followed, France and England fought for the ocean
empire, and England won it—won it on the day when her
own politicians' hearts had failed them, and all the
powers of the world had combined to humiliate her, and
Rodney shattered the French fleet, saved Gibraltar, and
avenged Yorktown. If ever the naval exploits of this
country are done into an epic poem—and since the Iliad
there has been no subject better fitted for such treatment
or better deserving it—the West Indies will be the scene
of the most brilliant cantos."[8] The American Mediterranean was one of the world's great stakes of diplomacy,
a cockpit in which the fate of empires was decided. From
1689 to 1815 it was a major battle zone of the second Hundred Years' War between England and France. In 1782,
when Rodney won his famous victory over De Grasse
and reëstablished British sea power in America, Barbadoes, Bahamas, Bermuda, St. Lucia, and Jamaica alone
remained in English hands. Nelson received his early
training in the West Indies, married his unhappy wife
there, and hunted Villeneuve among the islands in the
campaign which ended at Trafalgar. The islands vied
with each other in erecting monuments to his memory.

The history of the continental colonies is closely tied
up with that of the Caribbean Sea. When the great staple
crops such as sugar destroyed diversified agriculture,
many white colonists left the islands and migrated to the
continent. The importance of the islands for many years
was so great that before 1757 the British postal system
made more ample provision for the islands than for the
mainland. Revenue measures such as the Stamp Act ap-

[8] J. A. Froude, *The English in the West Indies*, p. 10.

plied to the West Indies as well as to the mainland. Schemes of resistance were devised not only by the thirteen but by all the colonies from Canada to Jamaica. A lively commerce existed between the islands and the mainland, and British attempts to aid the former helped to bring on the American Revolution,[9] while British determination to punish the thirteen revolted States after the Revolution helped to increase West Indian distress.[10] The small island of Nevis gave us our ablest finance minister, Alexander Hamilton. Napoleon's failure in Haiti together with the renewal of the war with England caused the cession of Louisiana to the United States, which has become the great economic and political power of this region of the world.

The fact that the British West India colonies had but a small white population is of profound significance. The demand for sugar was so tremendous that the plantation system replaced the small farmers, leaving the islands in the possession of white planters, a few white laborers, some free negroes and mulattoes, and hosts of slaves. This situation made the colonists dependent on the mother country for defence and for keeping the ocean highways open for food supplies. Revolt during the eighteenth century was never anything more than an academic question, because the fear of foreign conquest and of slave insurrections made it necessary to station regiments and war vessels in the islands; hence the mere threat of the removal of these imperial forces was sufficient to still the talk of white rebellion.

England was the home of the West Indian. There he returned at the earliest moment when he could desert his

[9] F. W. Pitman, *The Development of the British West Indies, passim.*
[10] H. C. Bell, ''Studies in the Trade Relations of the British West Indies and North America, 1783-1793,'' in the *English Historical Review,* XXXI, 429-441, July, 1916.

plantation; thus he created the problem of absenteeism. On the American continent a sturdy white population, deeply rooted in the soil, regarded the new land as a permanent home. The settlement in the temperate zone was a true colony with all of its institutions adapted to a large, permanent white population, such as family life, churches, schools, and colleges; the tropical island colony was a commercial enterprise. A temperate climate and a stable society spelled progress in one instance; a torrid climate accompanied by hurricanes, earthquakes, tidal waves, and fevers created danger and uncertainty in the other. The maker of the United States lived on his farm or plantation; the landlord of the English West Indies was quite often an absentee living in England.[11]

These islands in the western seas stirred the imaginations, filled the purses, and wrecked the careers of men, as have the gold and the diamond and the oil fields of later ages. Not only were great riches taken from their fields but much of the wealth gathered in Mexico, in Perú, and even in the Orient was loaded on galleons which passed the islands on the voyage to Spain. Nestled among the islands were pirates of every nation, forming a great international brotherhood for plunder. So well known was this world that when Daniel Defoe told the immortal story of Robinson Crusoe, he could think of no more fitting scene than the West Indies and placed his hero there on an island near the mouth of the Orinoco close to Trinidad. The business of Robinson Crusoe was naturally that of a slave trader who, while on his way from Brazil to Africa, was shipwrecked.[12] The story of Friday, moreover, is of more than literary interest, as the drawing of

[11] For a good brief contrast between the West Indies and the mainland, see F. W. Pitman, *The Development of the British West Indies*, pp. 1-41.

[12] Paul Dottin, ''L'Isle de Robinson'' in *Mercure de France*, November 15, 1922, vol. 160, 112-119.

this character illustrates the English conception of the savage. Great as was the genius of Defoe, he was unable to paint a real savage, but made Friday an Englishman. A century later negro slaves were popularly invested with many of the qualities of Englishmen, and their emancipation was founded on this psychological assumption. The anti-slavery leaders argued that the negro had the same wants and desires as white men and that as a freedman he would at once work as much or more than as a slave. The other side vigorously denied all such assumptions.

The development of the British West Indies is a fascinating story. After a period of piracy and buccaneering against the Spaniards actual English colonization began. The Spaniards were in possession of the four large islands and held many strategic points on the mainland. Many of the smaller islands, however, were totally unoccupied by Europeans, and to these went not only the English, but the Dutch, the French, and the Danes. St. Christopher was settled in 1623; Barbadoes, which was totally uninhabited except as it had been stocked by the Portuguese with swine, was colonized in 1624-1625; Nevis in 1628; Antigua in 1632; Montserrat in the same year; Anguilla in 1650; and Jamaica, the only large British West Indian island, was wrested from the Spaniards in 1655 after an attack on Santo Domingo had failed. Settlement of the Bahamas began at New Providence in 1666, the Virgin Islands were conquered in 1672, and British colonization for that century ended with the acquisition of Turks Island in 1678.

The first half of the eighteenth century slipped away without any new British acquisitions, but, during the Seven Years' War, Dominica was conquered in 1761; St. Vincent and St. Lucia in 1762, while several captured islands, such as Cuba and Guadeloupe, were returned to

Spain and France. Permanent occupation of Trinidad dates from 1797; of British Honduras from 1798; of Tobago from 1803; and of British Guiana from the same year.[13] The small islands vary in size from 32 square miles for Montserrat to 166 for Barbadoes. The only fairly large places are Trinidad, 1,754 square miles, or half again as large as Rhode Island; British Honduras, 7,562 square miles; Jamaica, 4,286 square miles, or about the size of Connecticut; the Bahamas, 4,466 square miles, and British Guiana, 100,000. The British West Indies, "though they include tracts on the mainland in British Honduras and British Guiana, are on the whole a collection of island dependencies."[14]

For the development of these islands hordes of negroes were required. While it is not possible to determine the exact number of slaves who were torn away from the shores of Africa and planted on the sugar, cotton, coffee, and tobacco plantations of the new world, probably for long periods of time more negroes were brought from Africa than Europeans from Europe. This statement suggests the astounding proportions of the slave trade. From 1680 to 1786 the total importation of slaves into the British colonies alone has been estimated at 2,130,000 or an annual average of 20,095.[15] The general tendency

[13] For tables of information regarding the British West Indies, see C. P. Lucas, *A Historical Geography of the British Colonies*, II, 2, and F. W. Pitman, *The Development of the British West Indies*, opposite page 1.

[14] C. P. Lucas, *A Historical Geography of the British Colonies*, II, 3.

[15] Bryan Edwards, *History of the British West Indies* (second edition, London, 1794), II, 55. It has been estimated that at the beginning of the nineteenth century, England held 800,000 slaves in her colonies; France, 250,000; Denmark, 27,000; Spain and Portugal, 600,000; Holland, 50,000; Sweden, 600; there were also about 2,000,000 slaves in Brazil and about 900,000 in the United States. This was the basis for the demand for the slave trade and in this trade other nations were extensively engaged. *Cf.* Augustin Cochin, in Lalor, *Cyclopedia of Political Science, Political Economy, and of Political History of the United States* (New York, 1890), III, 723.

was for the trade to increase, and at different times after the middle of the eighteenth century it ran over the 100,-000 mark annually. In 1786 it was estimated that 104,100 slaves were exported from Africa, while in the period after the American Revolution the annual number was given as 74,000.[16]

A brief description of the African races and of the strange traffic by which the population of one continent was whisked across the Atlantic in the traders' vessels and transplanted into the tropical fields of the western world is necessary in order to understand the struggle for abolition. The Portuguese in their hardy effort to trade with Africa and to reach India by the all-sea route came in contact with the negro areas of Africa, and began the slave trade a half century before Columbus.[17] Northern Africa is Mediterranean, and belongs to Europe or to Asia. At the time of the Portuguese expansion it was Berber and Arab in race and Mohammedan in religion. It therefore did not contain many negro slaves, but rather supplied them by the Arab penetration of Africa to the south of the Sahara desert. Here the negro tribes were to be found, mostly north of the equator. Farther south were the Bantu tribes, whose characteristics made them less valuable as slaves.

Before the discoveries of Columbus, then, the slave trade was in full swing with the Portuguese established along the coast of the Gulf of Guinea, ''upon whose

16 F. W. Pitman, *The Development of the British West Indies*, p. 70. In 1788, Robert Norris of Liverpool estimated the number at 74,200 divided as follows: English 38,000; French 20,000; Portuguese 10,000; Dutch 4,000; Danes 2,000; Macpherson in his *Annals of Commerce* states that in 1768 about 97,000 negroes were taken, of which the British carried 60,000. Bryan Edwards, *History of the British West Indies*, II, 57, accepts the estimate of Norris.

17 James Bandinel, *Some Account of the Trade in Slaves from Africa as Connected with Europe and America*, p. 14.

shores the vast fan-shaped hinterland poured its exiles along converging lines." During the sixteenth century the Portuguese largely monopolized the trade. They were followed by the Dutch, who were commercially supreme during the first half of the seventeenth century.[18] A conflict with England running through the middle years of this century and a longer struggle with France made the Dutch commercial empire tributary to the English and elevated the French as the chief rival of England. In the field of politics this change showed itself in the coming of William of Orange to England as king and marked the beginning of the series of wars from 1689 to 1815.

Naturally a monopoly of the "game preserve" of labor, as the African hunting grounds have been well named, was a much coveted stake of diplomacy. For the Spaniards, living up to the terms of the papal demarcation line, had never taken possession of any part of Africa, and so were not in a position to supply themselves with slaves.[19] In 1701 the French were assigned the Asiento, or contract for supplying the Spanish colonies with slaves. In the world-wide struggle for colonial and commercial supremacy it seemed that Louis XIV might win. After this lucrative commerce had fallen into his hands, he might well hope that Frenchmen would be able to penetrate the vast Spanish Empire and make it a colony of French business enterprise.

The next war, however, turned the tide against Louis, while events marched more fortunately for his rival. The Methuen Treaty in 1703 made Portugal an economic vassal of England, the Union of Scotland and England in

---

[18] C. P. Lucas, *A Historical Geography of the British Colonies*, II, 66.

[19] James Bandinel, *Some Account of the Trade in Slaves from Africa*, pp. 63-64. From 1769 for some years Spain assigned the privileges of the Asiento to her own subjects. During the sixty years from 1580 to 1640 the Portuguese empire was in Spanish hands.

1707 brought Scottish commercial genius into partnership with that of England, and the Peace of Utrecht in 1713 secured to England so many concessions that she had all the substance of victory, while the aged Louis sank into his grave with its mere shadow. Chief among the English gains was the Asiento as well as the right to break into the Spanish commercial monopoly by sending a ship annually to the Isthmus of Panama for trade.[20] Spain thus began to follow Portugal into economic inferiority to the rising insular power. In England this slave trade victory was celebrated as a commercial triumph.

During the century that the trade was still to be legal, the English exploited their victory to the utmost. Originally London and Bristol were the chief trading centres, but by leaps and bounds Liverpool outdistanced her rivals until she was the one outstanding slave carrier of the world, so that it was said that the city was built on the bones of African slaves. During the last sixteen months before the trade was abolished Liverpool alone sent out one hundred and eighty-five ships for the African trade, capable of carrying about 50,000 slaves at a profit of over thirty per cent on the investment.[21] So profitable was this traffic that independent traders broke down the monopoly companies which were organized from time to time.[22]

The French followed hard on the heels of the English both as slave traders and sugar growers. In a marvel-

[20] James Bandinel, *op. cit.*, pp. 57-62. For a good discussion of the importance assigned to the West Indies as well as to the slave trade see William Cunningham, *Growth of English Industry and Commerce in Modern Times* (Cambridge, 1912), II, part I, 474-479. The terms of the Asientos with France and with England are given on page 475, footnote 4.

[21] Gomer Williams, *History of the Liverpool Privateers . . . with an Account of the Liverpool Slave Trade*, p. 678.

[22] F. W. Pitman, *The Development of the British West Indies*, pp. 64-67.

ously short time they developed the fertile island of Hispaniola, so that Adam Smith in his *Wealth of Nations* published in 1776 said, "It is now the most important of the sugar colonies of the West Indies and its produce is said to be greater than that of all the English sugar colonies put together."[23] While the English stood first in the slave trade, the French led all others in their genius for using slave labor. Out of the capital produced by slave labor the French built up their rich West Indian empire, while the English imported much of their capital from the home country. The wealth of Hispaniola just before the catastrophe of the French Revolution is stated by Leroy-Beaulieu: "Santo Domingo became the greatest producer of sugar in the world. Its exports rose from 11,000 livres tournois in 1711 to 193,000,000 in 1788 or nearly £8,000,000, sterling; it was almost double the actual exportation from Jamaica, calculated in money, it was more than double calculated in quantity, its commerce employed 1000 ships and 15,000 French sailors."[24] Into all of these colonies, English and Dutch, Danish and French, this incessant stream of black labor was fed. The brutality of the slave catcher in Africa, the horrors of the passage across the Atlantic on tropic seas known as the "middle passage," the deaths on slave plantations, all went on almost unheeded while European vied with European to catch the slaves, to carry them to the plantations, and to drive them on to the production of sugar, tobacco, indigo, rice, and other products of the plantation. Throughout the West Indies the cry was for more slaves, and the trader was criticized for bringing so few to the markets and selling them for such a high price.

The homeland of the negroes was practically unknown

23 Adam Smith, *Wealth of Nations* (Cannan edition), II, 73.

24 Paul Leroy-Beaulieu, *De la Colonisation chez les Peuples Modernes* (sixième édition, Paris, 1908), I, 167-168.

to Europeans. Northern or Roman Africa alone has a history. Africa was largely unexplored until well into the nineteenth century. About the year 1800 white explorers were just beginning to penetrate the interior.[25] When the anti-slavery movement began, the region south of the Sahara was peopled by the negro and Bantu tribes, who have left no written record of the past, no monuments commemorating great deeds, and no sagas handed down from generation to generation. Compared with most of the European and Asiatic peoples, the negroes were strikingly backward. Art, science, and literature were almost entirely undeveloped among them. In the eighteenth century the comparative study of the races of mankind was in its infancy. There was no body of accepted fact to which people could appeal; in consequence, the widest differences of opinion were expressed on negro character, the possibilities of civilizing Africa, and all kindred subjects. Opinion of the negro varied from regarding him on the one hand as the superior of the white man, and on the other as little more than an ape.[26]

[25] Between 1768 and 1773 James Bruce entered Abyssinia and found the source of the Blue Nile. His work led to the formation of the African Association in 1788 for the exploration of the unknown parts of Africa. In 1795 the Association sent out Mungo Park, who explored the Middle Niger, and in 1805 on a second expedition he crossed by land to the upper waters of this river and attempted to sail down to its mouth but was drowned at Bussa. The first scientific explorer was Heinrich Barth, who, in the service of the English, spent four years in the middle of the nineteenth century in the exploration of the heart of Africa in the vicinity of Lake Chad, the Niger, and Tripoli. Livingstone began his work in South Africa about the same time.

[26] English opinion in the seventeenth and early eighteenth centuries was generally quite unfavorable to the negro. Godwin in his *Negro's and Indian's Advocate* (1680), pp. 13, 14, 43, felt it necessary to argue the question of the African as a human being, "methinks the consideration of the shape and figure of our negro's Bodies, their Limbs and Members, their Voice and Countenance in all things according with other Men's; together their Risibility and Discourse (Man's peculiar Faculties) should be a sufficient conviction." And again, "They make them the Posterity of

Despite a century and a half of investigation and of study the sharpest differences of opinion still exist. A few statements from recent writers will, however, reveal some generally accepted facts. An extremely unfavorable view is that of the Englishman, Meredith Townsend, who says: "None of the black races, whether negro or Australian, have shown within the historic time the capacity to develop civilization. They have never passed the boundaries of their own habitats as conquerors, and never exercised the smallest influence over people not black. They have never founded a stone city, have never built a ship, have never produced a literature, have never suggested a creed. . . . It is said that the negro is buried in the most 'massive' of the four continents, and has been, so to speak, lost to humanity; but he was always on the Nile, the immediate road to the Mediterranean, and in West and East Africa, he was on the sea. Africa is probably more fertile, and almost certainly richer than Asia, and is pierced by rivers as mighty, and some of them at least as navigable. What could a singularly healthy race, armed with a constitution which resists the sun and defies malaria, wish for better than to be seated on the Nile, or the Congo, or the Niger, in numbers amply sufficient to execute any needed work, from the cutting of forests and the making of roads up to the building of cities? How was the negro more secluded than the Peruvians; or why was he 'shut up' worse than the Tartar of Samarcand, who one day shook himself, gave up all tribal feuds, and, from the Sea of Okhotsk to the Baltic and southward to the Nerbudda, mastered the world? . . . The negro went by himself far beyond the Australian savage. He learned

that unhappy son of Noah, who they say, was together with his whole family and Race cursed by his father. . . . For from thence, as occasion shall offer they'll infer their negro's Brutality; justifie their reduction of him under bondage; . . .''

the use of fire, the fact that sown grain will grow, the value of shelter, the use of the bow and the canoe, the good of clothes; but there to all appearances he stopped, unable, until stimulated by another race like the Arab, to advance another step.''[27]

The white man is proud of his past and never attempts to conceal his slow ascent from savagery and serfdom. But Mr. Townsend tends to minimize the geographical handicaps from which the negro suffered. His isolation was almost complete. Europeans explored the Americas long before they mastered Africa. Africa is largely an elevated plateau from which the rivers break into the lowlands, creating serious waterfall obstructions and impeding communication. South America, for example, could be penetrated by way of the Amazon and La Plata river systems, but white men found the penetration of Africa extremely difficult.

Mr. Ulrich Bonnell Phillips has given a fairer statement of the hindrance of the African environment. ''Of all regions of extensive habitation,'' he says, ''equatorial Africa is the worst. The climate is not only monotonously hot, but for the greater part of each year is excessively moist. Periodic rains bring deluge and periodic tornadoes play havoc. . . . The general dank heat stimulates vegetable growth in every scale from mildew to mahogany trees, and multiplies the members of the animal kingdom, be they mosquitos, elephants or boa constrictors. . . . For mankind life is at once easy and hard. Food of a sort may often be had for the plucking, and raiment is needless; but aside from the menace of the elements human life is endangered by beasts and reptiles in the forest, crocodiles and hippopotami in the rivers, and sharks in the sea, and existence is made a burden to all but the

27 Meredith Townsend, Asia and Europe, pp. 92, 356-358.

happy-hearted by plagues of insects and parasites. . . .
Endurance through generations has given the people
large immunity from the effects of hook-worm and malaria, but not from the indigenous diseases, kraw-kraw,
yaws, and elephantiasis, nor of course from dysentery
and smallpox which the Europeans introduced. Yet robust health is fairly common, and where health prevails
there is generally happiness, for the negroes have that
within their nature. They could not thrive in Guinea without their temperament.''[28] Such qualities of physical endurance and temperament made the negro a good slave.
The Spaniards estimated early that one negro could do
the work of four Indians.[29]

Negro Africa consisted of numerous tribes which were
often at war with each other, and among which the Arab
slave trader moved uneasily. To the destruction of life
by civil war must be added the human sacrifices demanded by religion and witchcraft. And lastly, in later
years, to the large Arab slave traffic was added that of
the Christians, who were probably responsible for carrying 12,000,000 negroes out of the continent, and who, in
the process, caused an equal number to be sacrificed.[30]
Such a toll of destruction might well have meant the de-
population of the continent, but instead there are something like 120,000,000 negro peoples in Africa today,
while in the western world live about 25,000,000 descend-
ants of former slaves.

[28] Ulrich B. Phillips, *American Negro Slavery*, pp. 3-5. Phillips has
given the first scholarly presentation of American negro slavery. All students of any phase of the subject are heavily indebted to him for this excellent work.

[29] Herrera, *Historia General*, dec. I, lib. IX, cap. 5; dec. II, lib. II, cap.
8.

[30] W. E. B. Du Bois, ''The Negro in America,'' in *The Encyclopedia
Americana*, XX, 47, estimates that the slave trade cost Africa 100,000,000
lives.

The fact that there were many different tribes of varying degrees of abilities and in somewhat different stages
of development was well recognized by the slave traders,
who were often instructed to load their vessels with a
certain kind of blacks who would bring higher prices.
The fact that certain of the tribes were better looking,
more intelligent, and more civilized than others was
partly responsible for the good opinion of negroes held
by anti-slavery leaders. By citing the most backward
tribes, on the other hand, it was possible to paint a dark
picture. Cannibalism and native slavery were fairly common, but the form of slavery among Africans was rather
mild, as there was but little hard work. In many parts of
Africa a man could live by merely stretching out his hand
for food, and cruel labor was uncalled for. Mr. Jerome
Dowd remarks, "A consideration of all facts seems to
justify the conclusion that the lot of the slaves of this
zone was a fortunate and happy one as compared to that
of slaves in more advanced societies. The more intense
labor of the slaves among civilized people and the consequent greater restraints and exactions imposed by the
master, cause breaches of discipline which furnish provo-
cations to ill-treatment and overwork. . . . [But] the savage master does not place so much value upon time and
labor and hence does not rush his slaves, and second . . .
savage masters do not draw such tight class distinctions."³¹

The differences between the negroes and Bantus are
partly linguistic and partly physical. All the Bantu tribes
of southern and central Africa speak dialects of one language, while the negroes have many separate languages.
The Bantus seem to be negroes with an admixture of
Hamitic blood. There is now general agreement on the

³¹ Jerome Dowd, *The Negro Races*, I, 100-101.

physical characteristics of the negroes. They have very dark-brown skin, "black crisp hair, which is flat on section, a relatively long head, with flat, broad nose and projecting jaws with thick everted lips. In stature they are tall, with long arms and slender legs."[32]

Naturally there is less agreement on the mental characteristics of negroes. A general opinion is that the primitive negro has the mind of a child, is normally good-natured and cheerful, impressionable, and has a dog-like fidelity. He is capable of becoming a craftsman of considerable skill.[33] It was precisely the ability to receive training in iron work, weaving, and carving as well as to learn the rudiments of agriculture that made the negro valuable as a slave either in Africa or in America.

The very qualities which have made the negro the world's premium slave were noted by Azurara, the earliest chronicler of Guinea. After observing the first cargo of captives, he wrote of the differences between negroes and Moors: "First, that after they had come to this land of Portugal, they never more tried to fly, but rather in time forgot all about their own country, as soon as they began to taste the good things of this one; secondly, that they were very loyal and obedient servants, without malice; thirdly, that they were not so inclined to lechery as the others; fourthly, that after they began to use clothing they were for the most part fond of display, so that they took great delight in robes of showy colours, and such was their love of finery, that they picked up the rags that fell from the coats of other people of the country and sewed them on to their garments, taking great pleasure in these, as though it were matter of some greater perfection. And what was still better, as I have already said,

---

[32] Article on "The Negro" in *The New International Encyclopedia*, XVI, 693-694.

[33] Article on "The Negro" in *The Encyclopedia Britannica*, XIX, 345.

they turned themselves with a good will into the path of
the true faith, in which after they had entered, they received true belief, and in this same they died.'"[34]

In this statement is found the combination of traits
which so long delighted the white man: an equal facility
on the part of the negro in becoming a good servant and
a good Christian. And for the benefits of religion he was
to enter a life of servitude, until that day when a changed
moral feeling and new economic condition forced the annihilation of slavery.

[34] Gomez Eannes de Azurara, *Chronicle of the Discovery and Conquest
of Guinea*, translated by C. R. Beazley and E. P. Prestage, in the Hakluyt
Society *Publications*, XCV, 85.

# CHAPTER II

## THE FORMATION OF PUBLIC OPINION IN GREAT BRITAIN AGAINST SLAVERY AND THE SLAVE TRADE. THE NEW DETERMINANT: HUMANITARIANISM. EMANCIPATION OF THE SLAVES IN GREAT BRITAIN

The great change in opinion on the justice and expediency of the slave trade which occurred during the course of the one hundred years from 1713 to 1815 has been well stated by Baines: "So totally different was the feeling which then prevailed on this subject that whilst the article of the treaty of Vienna, denouncing the African slave trade, was regarded as the noblest article of the great pacification of 1815, the article of the treaty of Utrecht, giving England the privilege of importing negroes into the Spanish possessions in America as well as into her own, was regarded as one of the greatest triumphs of the pacification of 1713."[1]

The elder Pitt was still a champion of the slave trade; the younger Pitt struggled to have it abolished. In fact, we may well say that on this question the century after the peace of Utrecht can be divided into two parts; the first fifty years are characterized by stray voices raised in opposition but without any effective steps against either the slave trade or slavery. The second half century is characterized by active, organized opposition leading to emancipation in England in 1772 and in Scotland in

[1] Quoted from Gomer Williams, *History of the Liverpool Privateers . . . with an Account of the Liverpool Slave Trade*, p. 470.

1778, to the destruction of the trade in 1806 and 1807, and to the attempts to secure universal abolition at the congress of Vienna. During the first period, the British legislature encouraged the trade, the legal authorities declared in its favor. During the second period, the courts outlawed slavery in the British Isles and parliament made slave trading a felony with the penalty of deportation, and later it was declared a capital crime, certainly an astounding revolution.

This right-about change of opinion in the course of one hundred years, when analyzed, reveals the radical forces at work in society. During the fifty years following the peace of Utrecht in 1713, government was absolutely in the hands of the old middle class—the aristocracy. The kings, who had formerly intervened occasionally between rich and poor, had virtually abdicated. The new middle classes were not yet powerful enough to fight the aristocracy. Public opinion could ill make itself felt when debates were reported at best inadequately and newspapers were scarce. Taste was formed by the same aristocratic element of society, and men of letters, as in the case of Swift, had to depend on rich patrons or on the support of government.

The dynamic spirit of the eighteenth century showed itself in literary and scientific activity; the novel was developed by Richardson and Fielding; geological collections were made and the first professorship of geology was established at Cambridge; biological work of importance was done, and museums were founded, including the British Museum; antiquarians began to enlarge their explorations into English documents, thus laying the foundation for genuine historical research; ancient buildings were studied for their art, leading to the revival of Gothic architecture. Gray and Johnson studied the history of English literature; Priestley and Cavendish laid the foundations of chemistry; Hume wrote an excellent connected history of England. The idea of the continuity of history was developed and, instead of the dead past, there grew up the concept of the living past, expounded by such master historians as Robertson and Gibbon, as well as Hume. The able exponent of continuity, Edmund Burke, in his old age became so opposed to change that the French Revolution easily made him the outstanding European conservative.

The achievements in the fields of science and literature are equaled if not surpassed by the progress in industry and agriculture. Invention followed hard on the heels of invention. Where formerly men toiled by hand, the steam engine drove machines. More ships plowed the ocean highways. Where but one blade of grass had grown before there were now literally two or more. Such marvelous advances were made in live-stock breeding that the animals of the end of the century bore little resemblance to their inferior ancestors.[2]

Such rapid economic changes created a country of many new-rich men and multitudes of poor. The capitalist and laborer classes became more clearly marked in English society than they had been before. New social problems were created, which demanded settlement.[3] In consequence, discussion raged upon such public questions as the distress and poverty caused by the new industrial system; the hardships created by the new agriculture with its extermination of many of the small farmers; and

[2] For a good treatment of English agriculture see R. E. Prothero (Lord Ernly), *English Farming, Past and Present, passim.*

[3] George Macaulay Trevelyan, *British History in the Nineteenth Century,* pp. xiv-xv, says that Johnson and Burke "thought that the world would remain what they and their fathers had known it. With them, time moved so slowly that they thought it stayed still withal. A very different experience has taught us to perceive that the forms of our civilization are transient as the bubbles on a river."

those phases of over-sea expansion which seemed to pay too little attention to the rights of Asiatics and Africans. The trial of Warren Hastings and the investigation and destruction of the slave system were to be two of the dramatic expressions of this new spirit of inquiry and striving for justice.

Reformers did not devote themselves solely to one cause. The man who was interested in the destruction of the slave trade was generally interested also in better government for India, or in the founding of missionary societies, in teaching the people of England their letters or in prison reform, in wiser poor relief or in hospitals for the sick.[4]

The leaders of the humanitarian causes were not men of Miltonic genius and left no literature comparable with that of the seventeenth century. But, on the other hand, they did not exhaust themselves in religious strife; rather, they devoted their lives and fortunes to the remedying of practical evils. William Wilberforce, probably the most influential of the group, published his creed in a book called *A Practical View,* in which he urged in a somewhat commonplace fashion that it was not enough to be a nominal Christian, and that a real Christian must be distinguished by the magnitude of his good works.[5]

During the reign of George III public propaganda on a large scale became possible for the first time in English

4 Abundant proof of this fact is found in the careers of such men as Sharp, Wilberforce, Brougham, Zachary Macaulay, Buxton, as well as of others.

5 William Wilberforce, *A Practical View of the Prevailing Religious System of Professed Christians in the Higher and Middle Classes, contrasted with Real Christianity.* This was published in April, 1797. Seven thousand five hundred copies were sold in the first six months. By 1824, fifteen editions had been published in England and twenty-five in America. The standard biography of Wilberforce is R. Coupland, *Wilberforce: A Narrative* (Oxford, 1923).

history. New magazines and newspapers were founded to meet the needs of the growing body of readers or to champion a special cause; reporters were freely permitted in parliament so that the great orators of the period, Fox, Burke, Sheridan, Pitt, and others, no longer addressed merely the limited audience within the walls of a house of parliament, but had the wide constituency of the British Isles in mind. Indeed, the fight against the slave trade and against slavery is the first striking example of public campaigning with both sides well organized, well supplied with money, and ably led.[6] Later periods became remarkable for greater variety of reforms advocated at one and the same time. The later public became so large that it could not have one center or one set of interests, but the age of George III had been such that it was possible to focus attention upon but a few questions.

Not only were economic, social, political, and intellectual factors of change at work in eighteenth century England, but new concepts regarding human nature and human perfectibility were developed. Philosophic thinkers taught humanitarianism, started a "back to nature" movement, and intensified the belief in "the noble savage." The anti-slavery crusade was an outgrowth of this humanitarianism and of the idealization of backward peoples, which was so characteristic of mid-century thought. Each of these developments will be briefly considered. The founder of the benevolent school of philosophy in England was Lord Shaftesbury, whose *Characteristics* appeared in 1711. He was opposed to the egoistic philosophy of Hobbes and maintained that "Man is natu-

---

[6] C. E. Fryer in *The American Historical Review*, XXIX, p. 767, says that the mobilization of public opinion in favor of the repeal of the Test and Corporation Acts is an earlier illustration of organized constitutional protest than the agitation against the slave trade.

rally a virtuous being, and is endowed with a 'moral sense' which distinguishes good from evil as spontaneously as the ear distinguishes between harmony and discord. . . . To be good he needs only to be natural.'"[7] The benevolent passions, he argued, far outweigh the selfish ones. The compassionate man is the perfect man; the selfish man is an unnatural monster.

The reign of George I was one of religious decay. Honest churchmen had been driven out of the Anglican church by the political turmoil of the preceding decades; and Walpole had used the church to serve his own ends. The fight between deists and the orthodox still further weakened the church and caused its charitable organizations to suffer. The doctrine that charity returns to the donor a hundredfold became the chief argument of the church in behalf of the downtrodden. Wesley in his *Further Appeal to Men of Reason and Religion* summarized the moral state of England. He denounced "the liberty and effeminacy of the nobility; the widespread immorality; the jobbery of charities; the stupid self-satisfaction of Englishmen; the brutality of the Army; the indolence and preferment humbug of the church—the true cause, as he says, of the contempt of the clergy, 'which had become proverbial.' "[8]

The triumph of the philosophy of Shaftesbury about the year 1725 meant "not merely a revival of social and literary interest in philanthropy, and a revulsion from the moral coarseness of the time, but the replacing of the old prudential argument (namely that charity brings recompense in this world and the next) by a more disin-

[7] C. A. Moore, "Shaftesbury and the Ethical Poets in England, 1700-1760," in *Publications of the Modern Language Association* (1916), XXXI, p. 269.

[8] Leslie Stephen, *English Literature and Society in the Eighteenth Century*, p. 154. The Tract is in John Emory, *The Works of the Rev. John Wesley*, I, 34-175.

terested motive that lent itself to the sentimental belief in natural goodness.[9]

Shaftesbury directly influenced James Thomson, who became the first important humanitarian poet in England. In his *Seasons* (1726-1730) he advocated prison reform, the founding of Georgia, and the establishment of the Foundling Hospital, and he depicted the horrors of the slave trade. Many other writers followed in Thomson's footsteps and in this way deistic humanitarianism became a powerful force in British life. Both Shaftesbury and Thomson might be called "friends of mankind" and fathers of the "cult of humanity."

Bolingbroke and Pope were less inclined to believe in the natural goodness of man and emphasized the need of the conquest of man's nature by reason. But they, too, urged the need for benevolence. The orthodox Christians opposed the deists on religious grounds, and, not to be outdone by them, stressed humanitarianism as a product of true Christianity. The position of the orthodox was best stated in *Night Thoughts* (1742-1745) by Edward Young, who, while he took issue with his opponents that virtue is its own reward, was at pains to point out that kindness and benevolence were taught and practiced by all true believers.[10] The work of such men as the Wesleys and Whitefield gave an added impetus to the growing humanitarian sentiment within the churches. The triumph of humanitarianism in English literature soon became complete, so that Johnson was able to write in 1758, "But no sooner is a new species of misery brought to view, and the design of relieving it proposed than every hand is open to contribute something, every tongue is busied in solicitation and every art of pleasure is em-

[9] Moore, *Publications of the Modern Language Association*, XXXI, 273.

[10] *Ibid.*, p. 310.

ployed for a time in the interest of Virtue.'"[11] The reign of George II, then, was one of a great outpouring of literature in favor of kindness and charity, and one during which the conscience of the nation was educated in preparation for the reforms of the reign of George III. To this new humanitarianism should now be added another contemporary development which contributed to the anti-slavery crusade,—the idealization of backward peoples, the creation of the belief in "the noble savage."[12]

During the middle years of the eighteenth century interest in primitive man was revived largely by a great increase of travel and the publication of travel books. The earlier collections of voyages, such as those of Hakluyt and Pinkerton, were supplemented by the accounts of Cowley, John Cooke, Dampier, Woodes Rogers, John Clipperton, George Shelvocke, Roggewein, Francis Pelsart, Abel Tasman, Anson, Byron, and James Cook.[13] The savage tribes of the age of discovery were viewed somewhat as were the classical heroes of the Golden Age. The prevailing tendency was to attribute to savage man a long list of virtues, although they were occasionally described as brutal. Whatever the Europeans lacked was to be found among the savage men of the corners of the earth, living in a state of human brotherhood. The idealization of the savage may be assigned partly to Las Casas and to the Jesuits, but the tendency was a very old one. In the prevailing thought of the mid-century and in the swarm of new discoveries, this movement became

[11] Moore, *op. cit.*, p. 317.

[12] Miss Lois Whitney, "English Primitive Theories of Epic Origins" in *Modern Philology*, XXI, May, 1924, gives an excellent account of the origin of the ideas regarding primitive people. Chauncey B. Tinker discusses the same subject in *Nature's Simple Plan*. Additional material, including a fine bibliography, is to be found in R. S. Crane's review of Professor Tinker's book in *Modern Language Notes*, XXXIX, No. 5, pp. 291-297.

[13] Whitney, *Modern Philology*, XXI, 370.

far more intense than it had ever been before. The conception of "the happy savage" seems to have developed first in connection with the American Indians. Much was written in praise of their love of country, their bravery, their simple mode of life, and their hospitality. This view of "the noble savage" was easily extended to include the people of the South Sea islands. So strong did the belief in the happiness and goodness of backward peoples become that when Indians, Esquimaux, and South Sea islanders were brought to England, actual contact with them did little to destroy the prevailing enthusiasm.[14] Although a similar friendly conception of the negroes does not seem to have been worked out to such an extent at this time, stray voices were raised in their favor as early as the seventeenth century. Evidently vast stores of favorable sentiment could readily be used in their behalf.

An early opponent of the slave system was Mrs. Aphra Behn. She had lived in Surinam, and wrote a novel, *Oroonoko: or The Royal Slave,* which was published in 1696.[15] It was afterwards dramatized by Southerne, and was well known throughout the eighteenth century. With rare power she describes the nobility of the negro, the brutality of the captain of the slave ship, and the savagery of the white slave owners, who finally chopped the slave to pieces as they burned him to death. Defoe not only made a colored man into a devoted comrade, but he condemned the slave trade in *The Reformation of Manners.* In his *Life of Colonel Jacque* he advocated a better treatment for negroes. If governed by gentler methods,

[14] Enthusiasm continued despite contact with Indians, Esquimaux, South Sea islanders, and negroes. *Ibid., passim;* Tinker, *Nature's Simple Plan, passim.* A fairly large number of negroes lived in Great Britain.

[15] Mrs. Behn, *Histories and Novels* (eighth edition, London, 1735), I, 75-200. Professor Tinker is authority for the statement that a dramatic version of Oroonoko (about 1760) still exists.

he maintained "the negroes would do their work faithfully and cheerfully . . . they would be the same as their Christian servants, except that they would be the more thankful, and humble, and laborious of the two."[16] Pope, Richard Savage, and Shenstone pleaded for backward peoples; Thomson in his *Seasons* drew a terrible picture of a shark following a slave ship:

> "Lured by the scent
> Of steaming crowds, of rank disease, and death,
> Behold, he, rushing, cuts the briny flood,
> Swift as the Gale can bear the ship along;
> And, from the partners of that cruel trade,
> Which spoils unhappy Guinea of her sons,
> Demands his share of prey."[17]

The first persons in England, however, to voice opposition were the Quakers, whose founder, George Fox, as early as 1671, said: "Then as to their blacks or negroes, I desired them (the 'Friends' in Barbadoes) to endeavor to train them up in the fear of God, as well those that were bought with their money as those that were born in their families. . . . I desired also that they would cause their overseers to deal mildly and gently with their Negroes, and not use cruelty toward them, as the manner of some hath been and is, and *that after certain years of servitude they should set them free.*"[18] The position

---

16 Defoe, *Colonel Jacque* (G. A. Aitken's edition), I, 174.

17 *The Poetical Works of James Thomson* (Houghton, Mifflin Company), II, 95, lines 1014 ff. An article by Professor C. A. Moore, "Whig Panegyric Verse, 1700-1760," to appear in *Publications of the Modern Language Association*, contains additional references to the slave system as treated in English poetry.

18 Thomas Hodgkin, *George Fox*, pp. 228-229. George Fox in his *Journal* (Philadelphia, n.d.), p. 642, says, "And friends, be not negligent, but keep up your Negroes' meetings and your family meetings, and have meetings with the Indian kings, and their councils and subjects everywhere, and with others."

taken by Fox was given practical application when, in 1727, the Society of Friends passed a resolution condemning both the slave trade and the ownership of slaves. The exact words were: "It is the sense of the meeting, that the importing of negroes from their native country and relations, by Friends, is not a commendable or allowed practice, and is, therefore, censured by this meeting."[19]

From such a resolution it is evident that the Friends were in part implicated in the traffic, and that it was difficult for some of them to give up a business so lucrative that profits were commonly thirty per cent. Their growing determination to stand apart from it is shown in a series of actions. In 1758 they warned all Quakers against the trade, and in 1761 they excluded from their society all who continued to be active in it. A similar resolution adopted two years later marks the end of the first fifty year period after 1713 and shows how little had been done in England.[20] The slave trade was given up by Quakers, but nothing positive had been said about slavery itself, which had a rather firm foothold even in England, although it is barely possible that no Quakers were slaveholders there. In America, on the other hand, the action of the Quakers was more vigorous. The matter was first brought up by the German Quakers of Germantown, Pennsylvania, 1688. In 1696 the Pennsylvania Quakers advised their members against the slave trade and urged them to bring their negroes to the meetings and to give them all possible religious instruction.[21] By 1754 they had advanced in their views and called the trade "*man stealing*—the only theft which by Mosaic law, was pun-

---

[19] Thomas Clarkson, *History of the Abolition of the Slave Trade* (London, 1839), p. 89.

[20] *Ibid.*, pp. 89-90, 90-91.

[21] *Ibid.*, p. 101.

ished with death;—'He that stealeth a man, and selleth him, or if he be found in his hand, he shall surely be put to death.' '[22]

By means of resolutions of the years 1774 and 1776 all who were concerned in the slave trade or who would not emancipate their slaves, were excluded from membership. The result of this action was that by the year 1780 slavery had almost absolutely disappeared in the Philadelphia Quaker district, and seems to have been given up by all other American Quakers about the same time. It lingered longer in the South.[23]

The agitation in America has a direct bearing on English opinion. An American Quaker, Anthony Benezet, was one of the earliest authorities on the slave trade, and to this writer Thomas Clarkson turned for information when he wrote his essay on the traffic in 1785. Benezet also carried on a correspondence with Granville Sharp, George Whitefield, and John Wesley.[24]

While the Quakers played a memorable part in arousing public opinion against the slave trade and slavery and were the pioneers in emancipating their own slaves, the attack on slavery was supported by numbers of other Christians. As early as 1680 Godwin, an Anglican clergyman, who had lived in Barbadoes, protested against the brutal treatment of negroes in his tract, *The Negro's and Indian's Advocate.* He denounced the slave trade as one for which "*Vengeance* cannot be long expected ere it fall upon the *inhuman Authors.*"[25] About the same time,

[22] Thomas Clarkson, *op. cit.*, pp. 103, 105, 106.
[23] E. R. Turner, *The Negro in Pennsylvania* (1911), pp. 72-77.
[24] Thomas Clarkson, *History of the Abolition of the Slave Trade*, p. 118. Benezet and Sharp not only wrote to each other but abridged each other's work. See Prince Hoare, *Memoirs of Granville Sharp* (London, 1828, second edition), I, 150-153.
[25] Coupland, *Wilberforce*, p. 77. S. H. Swinny, "The Humanitarianism

Richard Baxter, the famous nonconformist divine, declared that slave traders ought to be considered the enemies of mankind. In 1766 Bishop Warburton proclaimed that the traffic was contrary to both divine and human law. From time to time other churchmen raised their voices in sharp protest.

Seventeenth century philosophical thought in England and in France was generally favorable to slavery. But in the eighteenth century this institution fell under the condemnation of both Locke and Montesquieu. The former expressed himself against slavery in emphatic terms: "This freedom from absolute, arbitrary power, is so necessary to, and closely joined with a man's preservation, that he cannot part with it, but by what forfeits his preservation and life together: for a man, not having the power of his own life, cannot, by compact, or his own consent, enslave himself to any one, nor put himself under the absolute, arbitrary power of another, to take his life away, when he pleases. Nobody can give more power than he has himself; and he that cannot take away his own life, cannot give another power over it."[26]

Montesquieu treated the subject of slavery much more fully, and in the fifteenth book of the *Spirit of Laws* he attacked and destroyed the usual arguments in favor of slavery as resting on the right of conquest, the right of the individual to sell himself, the right of the father to sell his child, and the right of the Christian to dominate over the heathen. By a clever turn he reduced the arguments in favor of negro slavery to biting irony. "The Europeans having extirpated the Americans, were obliged to make slaves of the Africans, for clearing such vast tracts of land." "Sugar would be too dear, if the

of the Eighteenth Century and its Results," in *Western Races and the World* (edited by F. S. Marvin, Oxford, 1922), p. 127.

[26] John Locke, *Two Treatises on Government* (1764 edition), bk. II, ch. 4.

plants which produce it were cultivated by any other than slaves.'' ''These creatures are all over black, and with such a flat nose that they can scarcely be pitied.'' ''It is hardly to be believed that God, who is a wise Being, should place a soul, especially a good soul, in such a black, ugly body.'' ''The negroes prefer a glass necklace to that gold which polite nations so highly value: can there be a greater proof of their wanting common sense?'' ''It is impossible for us to suppose these creatures to be men, because, allowing them to be men, a suspicion would follow, that we ourselves are not Christians.''[27]

The works of such men as Locke and Montesquieu were addressed to the higher classes of society and furnished ample ammunition for any one eager to attack the slave system. But at the end of the Seven Years' War in 1763 practically no action had been taken against either the slave trade or slavery. Slavery then existed not only in the British colonies but in Great Britain itself. The slow development of public opinion against slavery was unfortunately matched by the extension of slavery.

The first important step was the vindication of the freedom of the slave in the English and Scottish courts. In view of the fact that there were a fairly large number of negro slaves in Great Britain and that the buying, selling, and transporting of negroes went on there, it seemed wise to one of the remarkable men of the time, Granville Sharp, to get a judicial decision, defining exactly the status of slaves in England. He believed that slavery could not exist there, and so he determined to bring matters to a test. Thus Granville Sharp struck the first genuine blow against the institution. The career of this man

---

[27] M. De Secondat, Baron de Montesquieu, *The Spirit of Laws* (Nugent's translation), bk. XV, ch. 5.

is so important and withal so interesting that it deserves more than passing mention.

Although Granville Sharp was the grandson of an Archbishop of York, he was not trained in the public schools and the university, but spent his youth as an apprentice to a linen-draper. His original Quaker master gave way to a Presbyterian, followed in succession by a Roman Catholic, a Socinian, and a Jew. The young apprentice was transferred with the business from owner to owner. To argue religious beliefs with each of these in turn, Sharp taught himself Greek and Hebrew in addition to carrying on his daily work.[28]

At the end of his seven year apprenticeship, he became an obscure clerk in the ordnance department for the next eighteen years, only to resign when he felt he could not render service against the revolting American colonies. In the meantime he applied himself to many outside things. By careful research he proved that a certain retired tradesman was in fact a member of the nobility and saw him seated among the peers of the realm.[29] He engaged in learned arguments over the book of Ezra. He defeated an unjust claim of one of the nobility to an English forest. He fought a great duel with Samuel Johnson on the subject of the impressment of seamen, calling Johnson's argument "plausible sophistry and important self-sufficiency" and throwing out the Scriptural warning, "Woe to them that call evil good, and good evil."[30]

In 1767, while still a clerk in the ordnance department, he was brought into contact with the case of a negro, Jonathan Strong, who, after having been beaten and abandoned by his master and restored to health by Sharp, was claimed by his former owner, who brought

[28] Prince Hoare, *Memoirs of Granville Sharp* (London, 1820), p. 29.
[29] *Ibid.*, p. 30.
[30] *Ibid.*, p. 169.

suit against Sharp for the recovery of his slave. The lawyers whom Sharp consulted declared that the law was against him and cited the opinion of Yorke and Talbot, formerly attorney-general and solicitor-general, stating that Lord Chief Justice Mansfield agreed with them.[31] Owing to some legal irregularities and the boldness of Sharp in preventing the seizure of the negro, the man was freed without any decision on the main question of the legality of slavery in England.

A good deal of confusion existed at this time as to the validity of slavery in England. In the fifth year of William and Mary the court of common pleas decided that a negro boy was a slave, because negroes are heathens. Chief Justice Sir John Holt of the court of king's bench expressed the opinion, which was apparently not embodied in a decision, that as soon as a negro came to England he became free.[32] This opinion, however, does not seem to have been effective. The resultant uncertainty was such that people having slaves in England applied to Yorke and Talbot for an opinion and were told in 1729 that: "We are of opinion that a slave, by coming from the West Indies into Great Britain or Ireland, either with or without his master, does not become free, and that his master's right and property in him is not thereby determined or varied, and that baptism doth not bestow freedom upon him, or make any alteration in his temporal condition, in these kingdoms. We are also of the opinion that the master may legally compel him to return again to the plantations." Twenty years later on the 19th of October, 1749, Yorke, having become Lord Chancellor Hardwicke, recognized that "trover would lie."[33]

[31] Prince Hoare, *Memoirs of Granville Sharp*, p. 36.
[32] *Dictionary of National Biography*, XXVII, 205.
[33] T. B. and T. J. Howell, *State Trials*, XX, 80, 81, 82.

Sharp applied to lawyers and even to Blackstone for help, but got no satisfaction and conducted his own researches. These he embodied in a pamphlet, *On the injustice and dangerous tendency of tolerating slavery, or even admitting the least claim to private property, in the persons of men, in England.* In this he cited the opinion of Lord Chief Justice Holt, studied the whole subject of villeinage and its abolition, and argued that under the British constitution force could not be used without legal process. He then distributed this pamphlet among the lawyers. Additional cases came up, but no legal decision on the main question was given until the case of the negro Somerset in 1772.[34] It was in the conduct of this case that Granville Sharp won claim to everlasting fame as a great benefactor of mankind. Sir James Stephen describes the case as "above all memorable for the magnanimity of the prosecutor, who though poor and dependent, and immersed in the duties of a toilsome calling, supplied the money, the leisure, the perseverance, and the learning, required for this great controversy, . . . and who, mean as was his education, and humble as were his pursuits, had proved his superiority as a Jurist, on one main branch of the law of England, to some of the most illustrious Judges by whom that law had been administered."[35]

The story of James Somerset was simple enough. Brought to England from Virginia by his master, Charles Stewart, he escaped, and was seized as a slave to be taken to Jamaica for sale. He was taken on board the vessel, *Anne and Mary,* and held in the custody of Captain Knowles. The case was well argued by both sides at three different terms of the court. Chief Justice Mansfield

[34] Prince Hoare, *Memoirs of Granville Sharp,* pp. 37-45.

[35] Sir James Stephen, *Essays in Ecclesiastical Biography* (second edition, London, 1850), II, 317.

counselled that the case be settled by private agreement
or by some arrangement which would make a decision of
the court unnecessary. Delay was due in part to the fact
that the judges were exceedingly reluctant to render a
decision. They were reluctant to emancipate between 14,-
000 and 15,000 slaves worth £50 apiece by means of a
judicial decision. It was the question not merely of destroying £700,000 worth of property, but also of caring
for the freedmen.[36]

The court held that: "The only question is whether the
cause on the return is sufficient? If it is the negro must be
remanded; if it is not, he must be discharged. Accordingly the return states, that [sic] the slave departed and
refused to serve; whereupon he was kept, to be sold
abroad. So high an act of dominion must be recognized
by the law of the country where it was used. The power
of a master over his slave has been extremely different,
in different countries. The state of slavery is of such nature, that it is incapable of being introduced on any reasons, moral or political, but only by positive law, which
preserved its force long after the reasons, occasion, and
time itself from whence it was created, is erased from
memory. It is so odious that nothing can be suffered to
support it, but positive law. Whatever inconveniences,
therefore, may follow from the decision, I cannot say this
case is allowed or approved by the law of England; and
therefore the black must be discharged."[37]

The Somerset case was important, not merely because
it induced some of the ablest legal talent to debate the

---

36 Howell, *State Trials*, XX, 79.

37 This matter is taken from the account in Howell, *State Trials*, XX, 1-
82. Not only had Yorke and Talbot given their opinion but also Lord Chancellor Hardwicke, sitting as chancellor on the 19th of October, 1749, had
recognized that "trover would lie." In other words that a slave could be
recovered by means of judicial action.

question of slavery and called public attention to this subject, but because it set the precedent for a similar decision in Scotland in the Joseph Knight case, decided on January 15, 1778. This decision was made upon a much broader ground than that taken in the Somerset case. The legality of the whole slavery system was pronounced untenable.[38] The verdict of the Scottish judges is so often overshadowed by the Somerset pronouncement that it merits citation: "The Court were of opinion, that the dominion assumed over this negro, under the law of Jamaica, being unjust, could not be supported in this country to any extent; that, therefore the defender had no right to the negro's service for any space of time, nor to send him out of the country against his consent; that the negro was likewise protected under the act of 1701, c. 6 . . . from being sent out of the country against his consent—the judgments of the sheriff were approved of, and the Court remitted the cause *simpliciter.*"[39]

Slavery was thus outlawed from every part of the British Isles. In the beginning Granville Sharp believed that it would be possible to make these decisions apply to the colonies as well. In a letter to Lord North, dated February 18, 1772, while the Somerset case was in process of being decided, Sharp wrote: "I might allege, indeed, that

[38] Boswell's *Life of Johnson* (Hill edition, New York, 1891), III, 241-243, says, "for it went upon a much broader ground than the case of Somerset . . .; being truly the general question, whether a perpetual obligation of service to one master in any mode should be sanctified by the law of a free country."

[39] Howell, *State Trials*, XX, 6, 7. A summary of the act of 1701, p. 21, is: "that no person shall be transported forth of this kingdom, except with his own consent, given before a judge or by legal sentence, under the certification, that any judge or magistrate, who shall give order for such transportation, or any one, who shall so transport another, shall not only be liable in the pecuniary pains of wrongous imprisonment, as declared by the act, but shall lose their offices, and be declared incapable of all public trust."

many of the plantation laws (like every other act which contains anything which is *malum in se*, evil of its own nature), are already *null and void* in themselves; because they want every necessary foundation to render them *valid*, being absolutely contrary to the laws of reason and equity, as well as the laws *of God.*"[40]

The Joseph Knight decision might well lend color to the view that slavery was illegal throughout the empire, but Mansfield in the Somerset case had made it clear in his decision that the emancipation of the slaves in the West Indies would be a matter for parliament.[41] Half a century of conflict lay ahead. Since the destruction of the slave trade and of slavery in the colonies was accomplished by mobilizing public opinion against it, the convictions of leading men of the time were indicative of the coming struggle.

The master of the Literary Club and the literary dictator of the age was Samuel Johnson. On no subject was he more outspoken than on that of the horrors of slavery.[42] However ready he was to follow King George III in opposing the American colonies in their revolt, he was perfectly independent in opposing the government boldly on the subject of slavery. There is good reason to believe that the very matter of slavery made him so ready to

[40] Prince Hoare, *Memoirs of Granville Sharp*, pp. 78-80. The following quotation from the letter to Lord North shows Sharp's boldness and his constant reference to religion: "and I apprehend, my Lord, that there is no instance whatever which requires more *immediate redress* than the present miserable and *deplorable slavery* of Negroes and Indians, as well as white English servants, in our colonies.—I say immediate redress, because, *to be in power*, and to neglect (as life is very uncertain) even a day in endeavoring to put a stop to such monstrous injustice and abandoned wickedness, must necessarily endanger a man's *eternal* welfare, be he ever so great in *temporal* dignity or office."

[41] Mansfield's decision applied only to England and Ireland.

[42] Johnson's Opinions on Slavery are collected in Boswell's *Life of Johnson*, II, 549-551. All the following quotations are from these pages.

write his pamphlet, *Taxation No Tyranny,* in which occurs the expression "How is it that we hear the loudest *yelps* for liberty among the drivers of negroes?" While visiting at Oxford, he caused consternation by offering as his toast, "Here's to the next insurrection in the West Indies."

As early as 1740, while Georgia was being planted, he argued in favor of the natural right of the negroes to liberty and independence. In 1756 he described Jamaica as "a place of great wealth and dreadful wickedness, a den of tyrants and a dungeon of slaves." Three years later he wrote, "Of black men the numbers are too great who are now repining under English cruelty." In telling about the Portuguese, he remarked, "We are openly told that they had the less scruple concerning their treatment of the savage people, because they scarcely considered them as distinct from beasts; and indeed, the practice of all the European nations, and among others of the *English barbarians that cultivate the southern islands of America,* proves that this opinion, however absurd and foolish, however wicked and injurious, still continues to prevail. Interest and pride harden the heart, and it is in vain to dispute against avarice and power." Elsewhere he wrote, "An individual may, indeed, forfeit his liberty by a crime; but he cannot by that crime forfeit the liberty of his children." The discovery of a new region filled him with anxiety, "I do not much wish well to discoveries, for I am always afraid they will end in conquest and robbery."

Johnson's attitude on this question is well shown not only by the notable criticisms quoted above but by the argument he submitted at the time of the Joseph Knight case, by which slavery was abolished in Scotland, the second big step toward emancipation. He concluded his argument as follows: "No man is by nature the property of another; The defendant is, therefore, by nature free; The rights of nature must be some way forfeited before they can justly be taken away: That the defendant has by any act forfeited the rights of nature we require to be proved; and if no proof of such forfeiture can be given, we doubt not but that the justice of the court will declare him free.''[43] For purposes of the argument Johnson was glad in this instance to avail himself of the doctrine of original equality, although at other times he was vehement in denouncing that theory. So interested was Johnson in this case that he offered to subscribe money to aid the negro.

The position taken by James Boswell when he wrote the biography was quite different from that of Johnson. ''To abolish a *status*,'' he said, ''which in all ages God has sanctioned, and man has continued, would not only be *robbery* to an innumerable class of our fellow-subjects; but it would be extreme cruelty to the African Savages, a portion of whom it saves from massacre, or intolerable bondage in their own country, and introduces into a much happier state of life; especially now when their passage to the West Indies and their treatment there is humanely regulated. To abolish that trade would be to 'shut the gates of mercy on mankind.' ''[44]

Among the powerful personalities who stamped themselves upon the age was John Wesley. He was extraordinarily gifted both with tongue and pen, and used all the arts of essay and letter writing, public speaking, and private intercourse to make his ideals prevail with his

---

[43] *Ibid.*, III, 228-231. Johnson had a negro servant, Francis Barber, whom he left well provided with property. The negro was thrifty and refused to contribute to the support of some of Johnson's relatives. John Hawkins in his *Life of Samuel Johnson* (Dublin, 1787), pp. 528 ff., regarded this as ''ill-directed benevolence'' and made contemptuous remarks about the negro.

[44] Boswell's *Life of Johnson*, III, 231-232. Boswell contrasted the condi-

countrymen. His opposition to the slave trade and slavery was that of the leader of a large English population which heard him preach in the open fields throughout his endless itinerary of thousands of miles over the countryside.

In 1772, while the Somerset case was being considered, he wrote: "In returning, I read a very different book published by an honest Quaker, on the execrable sum of all villainies, commonly called the Slave Trade. I read of nothing like it in the Heathen world, whether ancient or modern; and it infinitely exceeds, in every instance of barbarity, whatever Christian slaves suffer in Mohammedan countries."[45] He made a close study of the arguments used in the Somerset case, quoting particularly from Hargrave's argument in favor of the negro.

Two years after this celebrated decision he restated his ideas in a tract called *Thoughts upon Slavery.*[46] In this pamphlet he covers the subject thoroughly in a style that all could understand. While Johnson is often involved in his statements, Wesley is simple and clear. In

tion of English laborers with that of slaves in "'No Abolition of Slavery'" in *The Gentleman's Magazine* (London, 1791), LXI, Part I, 357-358.

> "'Beggars at every corner stand,
> With doleful look and trembling hand;
>
> .    .    .    .    .    .    .
>
> Some share with dogs the half-eat bones
> From dunghills pick'd with weary groans.'"

Strikingly different is the happy lot of the negroes.

> "'No human beings are more gay:
> Of food, clothes, cleanly lodgings sure,
> Each has his property secure;
> Their wives and children are protected;
> In sickness they are not neglected;
> And when old age brings a release,
> Their grateful days they end in peace.'"

[45] John Emory, *The Works of the Reverend John Wesley* (New York, 1825), IV, 366.

[46] *Ibid.*, VI, 278-293.

the first part he discusses the nature of slavery and its beginnings in America. In the second part he treats of the conditions in Africa. When he comes to part three, he launches into the subject of the slave trade with a wealth of information upon all of its manifestations. His method of treatment is well shown in his telling quotation from Anderson, *History of Trade and Commerce;* " 'England supplies her American colonies with negro slaves, amounting in number to about one hundred thousand every year;' that is, so many are taken on board our ships; but at least ten thousand of them die in the voyage; about a fourth part more die at the different islands, in what is called the seasoning. So that at an average, in the passage and seasoning together, thirty thousand die; that is, properly are murdered. O earth, O sea, cover not thou their blood!"[47] Throughout the essay the simple statement of facts is followed by an emotional appeal. In part four he takes up the question of the justice and mercy of slavery. He expresses himself with intense vigor: "Where is the justice of inflicting the severest evils on those that have done us no wrong? of depriving those that never injured us in word or deed, of every comfort of life? of tearing them from their native country, and depriving them of liberty itself, to which an Angolan has the same natural right as an Englishman, and on which he sets as high a value? Yea, where is the justice of taking away the lives of innocent, inoffensive men; murduring thousands of them in their own land, by the hands of their own countrymen; many thousands, year after year, on shipboard, and then casting them like dung into the sea; and tens of thousands in that cruel slavery to which they are so unjustly reduced?"[48]

47 John Emory, *op. cit.,* VI, 284.
48 *Ibid.,* VI, 286.

He then discusses the economic aspects of slave labor, knowing, as did most of the men who came after him, that if he could prove the impolicy of the whole system, his battle would be half won. Statesmen might be unwilling to rid England of what was merely a moral crime, but would be ready to correct a mistake, following out Talleyrand's maxim, "A mistake is worse than a crime." "It is not clear," he says, "that we should have either less money or trade, (only less of that detestable trade of man-stealing,) if there was not a negro in all our islands, or in all English America. It is demonstrable, white men, inured to it by degrees, can work as well as them; and they would do it, were negroes out of the way, and proper encouragement given them."[49]

When Wesley comes in part five to the remedies for this evil, he sees no hope except by a personal appeal to the individuals concerned. In the year 1774 legislative action seemed hopeless, and so he addressed the participants each in turn. To the captain he says: "Immediately quit the horrid trade: at all events, be an honest man."[50] To the merchant: "It is you that induce the African villain to sell his countrymen; and in order thereto, to steal, rob, murder, men, women, and children, without number, by enabling the English villain to pay him for so doing. . . . And is your conscience quite reconciled to this? Does it never reproach you at all?"[51] Last, there is the appeal to the slave owner in these high strung words: " 'The blood of thy brother' (for, whether thou wilt believe it or no, such he is in the sight of Him that made him) 'crieth against thee from the earth,' from the ship and from the waters. . . . Surely it is enough;

[49] John Emory, *op. cit.*, VI, 288-289.
[50] *Ibid.*, VI, 291.
[51] *Ibid.*, VI, 291.

accumulate no more guilt, spill no more blood of the innocent!''[52]

It was, indeed, a threatening day for the whole system of modern negro slavery when the man whom many have called the greatest Englishman of the eighteenth century was thus moved to express himself not only against the slave trade, but also against the institution of slavery itself.

In 1791, when the moral forces of England had gathered themselves together, no longer to attack the trade by personal moral suasion but by decree from the imperial parliament, the last act of this religious leader, four days before his death, was the penning of a letter to Wilberforce on this topic. Shrewd to the end, he foresaw the long bitter fight ahead, and prepared men for defeat and disappointment as well as for ultimate victory. ''I see not,'' he wrote, ''how you can go through your glorious enterprise, in opposing that execrable villany, which is the scandal of religion, of England, and of human nature. Unless God has raised you up for this very thing, you will be worn out by the opposition of men and devils. But, if God be for you, who can be against you? O be not weary in well doing! Go on, in the name of God, and in the power of his might, till even American slavery (the vilest that ever saw the sun) shall vanish away before it.''[53]

Strange as it may seem after reading Wesley's almost unmeasured denunciation of the slave system, the fact remains that men of religion were divided on this subject. Among those who favored slavery was George Whitefield, for a time a worker with Wesley and one of the renowned open air preachers and orators of his time.

[52] John Emory, *op. cit.*, VI, 292.
[53] *Ibid.*, VII, 237.

It is only fair to state, however, that Whitefield died in 1770, two years before the Somerset case was decided and, indeed, before the agitation had become powerful. He went so far in 1748 as to use his influence with the Georgia trustees to have slavery introduced into the new colony,[54] where it had originally been banned. For the support of his orphan asylum he purchased a plantation and slaves in South Carolina, in the belief that it was "impossible for the inhabitants to subsist without the use of slaves."[55] He argued for the lawfulness of slavery on scriptural grounds, thus placing himself in direct opposition to such a deist as Thomas Paine.

When Whitefield heard that the Georgia trustees had voted for slavery, his joy was great. Writing in 1751 from England to a minister in Georgia, he said in part: "Thanks be to God! that the time for favoring that colony seems to be come. Now is the season for us to exert ourselves to the utmost for the good of the poor Ethiopians. . . . As to the lawfulness of keeping slaves, I have no doubt, since I hear of some that were bought with Abraham's money, and some that were born in his house. I, also, cannot help thinking, that some of those servants mentioned by the apostles, in their epistles, were or had been slaves. It is plain that the Gibeonites were doomed to perpetual slavery; and, though liberty is a sweet thing to such as are born free, yet to those who never knew the sweets of it, slavery perhaps may not be so irksome. However this be, it is plain to a demonstration, that hot countries cannot be cultivated without negroes. What a flourishing country might Georgia have been, had the use of them been permitted years ago! How many white people have been destroyed for want of them, and how

[54] L. Tyerman, *The Life of the Rev. George Whitefield* (New York, 1877), II, 205-206.

[55] *Ibid.*, II, 169-170.

many thousands of pounds spent to no purpose at all!
. . . and, though it is true that they are brought in a
wrong way from their native country, and it is a trade
not to be approved of, yet, as it will be carried on
whether we will or not, I should think myself highly favored if I could purchase a good number of them, to make
their lives comfortable, and lay a foundation for breeding up their posterity in the nurture and admonition of
the Lord.''[56]

While moralists such as Whitefield and Wesley were
arguing for or against slavery, a telling blow against the
impolicy and expense of this system of labor was struck
by the founder of modern economic science, Adam Smith,
in his *Wealth of Nations,* which appeared in 1776. "It
appears," he says, ". . . from the experience of all ages
and nations, I believe, that the work done by freemen
comes cheaper in the end than that performed by
slaves.''[57] And again: "the work done by slaves, though
it appears to cost only their maintenance, is in the end
the dearest of any. A person who can acquire no property, can have no other interest but to eat as much, and
to labor as little as possible. Whatever work he does beyond what is sufficient to purchase his own maintenance,
can be squeezed out of him by violence only, and not by
any interest of his own.''[58] He states the item of expense
as follows: "But though the wear and tear of a free servant be equally at the expense of his master, it generally
costs him much less than that of a slave. The fund destined for replacing or repairing, if I may say so, the wear
and tear of a slave is commonly managed by a negligent
master or careless overseer.''[59]

56 L. Tyerman, *op. cit.,* II, 272-273.
57 Adam Smith, *The Wealth of Nations,* I, 83.
58 *Ibid.,* I, 364.
59 *Ibid.,* I, 82.

In fact, though Adam Smith regarded the system of slavery as a most uneconomical one, he was prepared to state that the greater success of the French colonies in the West Indies was due to the better management of their slaves under a more arbitrary government. He holds: "as the profit and success of the cultivation which is carried on by means of cattle, depend very much upon the management of the cattle; so the profit and success of that which is carried on by slaves, must depend equally upon the good management of those slaves; and in the good management of their slaves the French planters, I think it is generally allowed, are superior to the English."[60] The same thought recurs to him: "But the prosperity of the sugar colonies of France has been entirely owing to the good conduct of the colonies, which must therefore have had some superiority over that of the English; and this superiority has been remarked in nothing so much as in the good management of their slaves."[61]

Smith held that only the great profits made from the cultivation of such crops as sugar and tobacco made slavery possible. "The planting of sugar and tobacco can afford," he says, "the expense of slave cultivation. The raising of corn, it seems, in the present times cannot. In the English colonies, of which the principal produce is corn, the far greater part of the work is done by freemen. The late resolution of the Quakers in Pennsylvania to set at liberty all their negro slaves, may satisfy us that their number cannot be very great. Had they made any considerable part of their property, such a revolution could never have been agreed to. In our sugar colonies, on the contrary, the whole work is done by slaves, and in our tobacco colonies a very great part of it. The profits of a sugar-plantation in any of our West Indian colonies are

60 Adam Smith, *op. cit.*, II, 88.
61 *Ibid.*, II, 89.

generally much greater than those of any other cultivation that is known either in Europe or America. And the profits of a tobacco plantation, though inferior to those of sugar, are superior to those of corn as has already been observed.''[62] Apparently Smith leaves out of account the question of whether the sugar and tobacco plantations could have been cultivated, as early or as fully, or indeed cultivated at all, without negro slavery. Whitefield, as was stated above, believed slavery a necessary part of tropical economy. The fact that the younger Pitt studied the works of Adam Smith and regarded him with veneration makes the influence of the Scottish economist fundamental in the struggle for the extirpation of slavery.

The able utilitarian leader, Jeremy Bentham, who was active in many reform movements, especially the reform of criminal law, was an early opponent of slavery. The severe laws in force to keep the slaves submissive would naturally interest keenly a man of his turn of mind. He says: ''Let the colonists reflect upon this: if such a code be necessary, the colonies are a disgrace and an outrage upon humanity; if not necessary, these laws are a disgrace to the colonists themselves.''[63] ''It is not to be disputed that sugar and coffee, and other delicacies, which are the growth of those islands, add considerably to the enjoyments of the people here in Europe; but taking all these circumstances into consideration, if they are only to be obtained by keeping three hundred thousand men in a state in which they cannot be kept but by the terror of such executions: are there any considerations of luxury or enjoyment that can counterbalance such evils?''[64]

[62] Adam Smith, op. cit., I, 365.

[63] The Works of Jeremy Bentham, Principles of Penal Law (John Bowring edition, Edinburgh, 1859), I, 444.

[64] Ibid., I, 444.

Bentham joined hands with Adam Smith in attacking the economic foundation of slavery, holding that a freeman did produce more than a slave: "Two circumstances concur in diminishing the produce of slaves: the absence of the stimulus of reward, and the insecurity of their condition. It is easily perceived, that the fear of punishment is little likely to draw from a labourer all the industry of which he is capable, all the work that he can furnish. Fear leads him to hide his powers, rather than to show them; to remain below rather than to surpass himself. By a work of supererogation, he would prepare punishment for himself: he would only raise the measure of his ordinary duties by displaying superior capacity."[65]

Bentham, however, is not satisfied with the general statement of the case, but, as was always his habit, goes on to refine the matter more fully and clearly under three heads as follows:

"1. It is not true that the day-labourer has not the motive of reward. The most skilful and the most active are better paid than others: those who distinguish themselves are always preferred for the most lucrative employments: here, then, is a real reward which accompanies all their efforts.

"2. The free labourer has his point of honor as well as others. In a free country, shame attaches to the character of an idle or unskilful workman; and in this respect the eyes of his companions are so many helpers to those of the master: this punishment of the popular sanction is inflicted upon a multitude of occasions, by judges who have no interest in sparing it.

"3. Whatever appears to the day-labourer as a gain, is a certain gain; everything which he acquires is his

[65] *The Works of Jeremy Bentham, Principles of the Civil Code*, I, 345.

own, and no one else has a right to touch it: but we have seen that there is no real security for the slave."[66] It is unnecessary to add to this evidence the further statement that Bentham was an opponent of slavery from every standpoint. In conclusion it need only be said that he regarded all laws for the amelioration of the lot of slaves as of slight value. His comment is, "that, in the West India colonies, a freeman . . . could enjoy the benefit, such as it was, of committing at pleasure all manner of enormities, short of murder, on the bodies of all persons in a state of slavery . . . In some places, by the substitution of a small fine to all other punishment, the licence to add or substitute murder to every other injury is completed."[67] This masterly English reformer seldom wrote anything during his long life without making some comments adverse to slavery.

Thomas Paine, whose life as a powerful radical leader was spent in England, America, and France, published his essay on slavery in Philadelphia in March, 1775. He called attention to the anomaly of striving for freedom and maintaining slavery at the same time. "That some desperate wretches," he said, "should be willing to steal and enslave men by violence and murder for gain, is rather lamentable than strange. But that many civilized, nay christianized people should approve, and be concerned in the savage practice, is surprising; and still persist, though it has so often been proved contrary to the light of nature, to every principle of justice and Humanity, and even good policy, by a succession of eminent men, and several late publications."[68] The actual contents

66 The Works of Jeremy Bentham, Principles of the Civil Code, I, 345-346. Bentham did not know negro psychology and character and so his argument is based largely upon his observations of Englishmen.

67 Ibid., View of the Rationale of Evidence, VI, 86-87.

68 The men cited by Paine show that even as early as 1775 there was in

of the pamphlet are not unusual. Paine commented on the ordinary items of civil war in Africa, the middle passage, the seasoning in the West Indies, and the like. He quotes Baxter approvingly that *"the Slave Traders should be called Devils, rather than Christians: and that it is a heinous crime to buy them."*[69] "Certainly one may," he says, "with as much reason and decency, plead for murder, robbery, lewdness, and barbarity, as for this practice. They are not more contrary to the natural dictates of Conscience and feelings of Humanity; nay, they are all comprehended in it." He continues, "the gain of that trade has been pursued in opposition to the Redeemer's cause, and the happiness of men: Are we not, therefore, bound in duty to him and to them to repair these injuries, as far as possible, by taking some proper measures to instruct, not only the slaves here, but the Africans in their own countries." That this writing had a decided effect is shown by the fact that about a month later the first American Anti-slavery Society was formed in Philadelphia.[70] Paine at different times busied himself, as did others, with practical schemes for the gradual emancipation of all American slaves.

In addition to the opponents of slavery mentioned a number of other prominent men attacked slavery. Dr. William Robertson, both in his *History of America* and in his *Charles the Fifth*,[71] declared slavery contrary to humanity and to the teachings of Christianity. He held, too, that Christianity had been responsible for the de-

England an extensive and rapidly growing literature dealing with the slave trade and slavery.

[69] *The Writings of Thomas Paine* (Conway edition, New York, 1894-1895), I, 4 ff.

[70] See Moncure Daniel Conway, *The Life of Thomas Paine* (New York, 1893), I, 41 ff.

[71] William Robertson, *The History of the Reign of the Emperor Charles the Fifth* (Prescott edition, Philadelphia, 1902), I, 264-268.

struction of slavery in Western Europe, and from this the thought naturally followed that slavery ought to be abolished among all Christian peoples.

Dr. Paley in his *Moral Philosophy* severely condemned the slave system, saying: "But necessity is pretended, the name under which every enormity is attempted to be justified; and after all, what is necessity? It has never been proved that the land could not be cultivated there, as it is here, by hired servants. It is said, that it could not be cultivated with quite the same conveniency and cheapness, as by the labour of slaves; by which means, a pound of sugar, which the planter now sells for sixpence, could not be afforded under sixpence-halfpenny—and this is the necessity!"[72] Paley's work was adopted as a textbook in some of the English colleges and was widely read throughout the country.

Two celebrated Frenchmen entered the field of discussion at the time of the American Revolution, Raynal and Condorcet. The former delivered a long and passionate attack, which aroused the keenest sympathy for the negroes and resentment against their oppressors. Over two hundred pages of his *Histoire des deux Indes* were devoted to the slave system.[73] "It was that book," Morley says, "which brought the lower races finally within the pale of right and duty in the common opinion of France." The work was so popular that several translations into English were made between 1776 and 1783, and thus a vast storehouse of ammunition was placed at the disposal of the abolition leaders.[74] Raynal discussed the natural

[72] William Paley, *Complete Works* (New York, 1824), III, 146 ff. Thomas Clarkson, *History of the Abolition of the Slave Trade*, p. 79.

[73] Abbé Raynal, *A Philosophical and Political History of the Settlements and Trade of the Europeans in the East and West Indies* (Justamond's translation), V, bk. XI, 140-455.

[74] Swinney, *Western Races and the World*, p. 130. It is, of course, needless to say that the work of Raynal does not bear close modern criticism.

resources, climate, and the inhabitants of Africa as well as the slave trade and slavery.

One or two brief quotations will make clear the vigor of Raynal's writings. "But these Negroes, say they, are a race of men born for slavery; their dispositions are narrow, treacherous, and wicked; they themselves allow the superiority of our understandings, and almost acknowledge the justice of our authority. The minds of the Negroes are contracted; because slavery destroys all the springs of the soul. They are wicked; but not sufficiently so with you. They are treacherous; because they are under no obligation to speak truth to their tyrants. They acknowledge the superiority of our understandings, because we have perpetuated their ignorance; they allow the justice of our authority, because we have abused their weakness. As it was impossible for us to maintain our superiority by force, we have, by a criminal policy, had recourse to cunning. We have almost persuaded them that they were a singular species, born only for dependence, for subjection, for labour, and for chastisement. We have neglected nothing that might tend to degrade these unfortunate people, and we have afterwards upbraided them for their meanness."[75]

Raynal includes the negroes in the brotherhood of man in this striking sentence: "One common Father, an immortal soul, a future state of felicity, such is thy true glory, and such likewise is theirs."[76]

The other French creator of English public opinion in this early period was Condorcet, whose anonymous pamphlet appeared in 1781. He attacked the slave system more systematically than had Raynal.[77] But whatever

[75] Abbé Raynal, *A Philosophical and Political History of the Settlements and Trade of the Europeans in the East and West Indies*, V, 298.

[76] *Ibid.*, V, 299.

[77] Condorcet, *Réflexions sur l'esclavage des nègres* (1781).

part Frenchmen played in the attack on slavery, the movement was really English in character. From the time of George Fox, the Quaker religious leader, on the one hand, and John Locke, the philosophical thinker, on the other, a body of literature had been steadily growing against human bondage.[78]

By the year 1783 powerful leaders in religion, literature, economics, law, and government had done much to awaken the public conscience. Slowly the ignorance regarding the slave system was being dispelled; the powerful economic arguments in favor of slavery were being questioned. The hope began to be expressed that England and France, by walking shoulder to shoulder, might be able to exterminate the traffic without either taking an advantage of the other in maritime affairs. But the American Revolution, into which France was soon drawn, made either legislative or diplomatic action impossible. During the war the slave trade declined along with other commerce. Johnson disliked the Americans because slavery existed among them. But they in turn inserted a ringing charge in an unpublished draft of the Declaration of Independence[79] against George III as an encourager of the slave trade. Franklin expressed himself with much vigor at the time of the Somerset case by writing from London in 1772 of "the hypocrisy of this country which encourages such a detestable commerce by laws for promoting the Guinea trade; while it piqued itself on its virtue, love of liberty, and the equity of its courts in setting free a single negro." The separation of the colonies with their slaves from the empire undoubtedly made emancipation in the remainder easier in 1833. The

[78] No effort has been made in this study to treat French opinion except as incidental to what was going on in England.

[79] Carl Becker, *The Declaration of Independence* (New York, 1922), pp. 212-216.

abolition of the slave trade, however, would have become effective sooner, if the two countries had remained together under the British flag, thus preventing the later enormous illicit trade when pirate ships sought refuge first under one flag and then under the other. It was relatively easy to abolish slavery in the British Isles where there was an abundance of free labor, but in the colonies slavery was regarded as vital for the production of economic goods, as important at that time as the production of steel or oil in our own age.

The humanitarian forces were destined to suffer many defeats in their long battle against the slave system. The destruction of slavery in Great Britain by judicial decisions was the first great victory. Of the Somerset case Lord Stowell said in 1827: "Thus fell a system confirmed by a practice which had obtained, without exception, ever since the institution of slavery in the colonies, and had likewise been supported by the general practice of this nation, and by the public establishment of its Government. . . . The suddenness of this convulsion almost puts one in mind of what is mentioned by an eminent author, on a very different occasion, in Roman History: . . . 'The People of Rome suddenly became quite another people.' "[80]

[80] *West Indian Reporter*, No. IX, 165, Dec. 1827.

# CHAPTER III

## THE ATTACK ON THE SLAVE TRADE 1783-1793. AGGRESSIVE HUMANITARIANISM

The slave trade, checked by the American Revolution when all commerce was seriously crippled, revived after the Peace of 1783. Liverpool, its chief center, tended to monopolize the traffic. Indeed about half of the whole African slave trade seems to have been carried on in Liverpool ships.[1] Accompanying the revival of the trade, was the revival of active opposition to it. The growing mass of literature against it, written from the seventeenth century on, began to affect public opinion widely. A careful study of the evidence makes clear the fact that the discussion had reached the ears of thousands; only a few concrete cases of atrocities were needed to make the issue a serious political one. Granville Sharp was still the most active among the agitators, and, when the case of the slave ship *Zong* came up for trial, he secured the attendance of a shorthand reporter to take down the evidence, which he circulated over the kingdom. The captain of the *Zong*, finding many of his cargo of slaves ill, held counsel with some of his men as to what was to be done. If the slaves died of sickness, the loss would fall upon the owners, including the captain of the vessel; if they were thrown overboard to save the ship, the loss would have to be borne by the underwriters. The motive alleged was a shortage of water, but this was disproved at the trial. Two trials were held to decide who should bear the loss

---

[1] Gomer Williams, *History of the Liverpool Privateers . . . with an Account of the Liverpool Slave Trade*, pp. 495, 679.

of the one hundred and thirty-two slaves thrown overboard into the sea. Although the verdicts differed, both
brought out the appalling nature of the action.

Sharp sent complete details of the case to the lords
commissioners of the Admiralty, asking that the men who
threw the negroes overboard be punished for murder.[2]
He also reviewed the case in a letter to the Duke of Port-
land, first lord of the Treasury,[3] stating that eleven years
before he had asked Lord North to abolish both the slave
trade and slavery. The government again refused to act,
but public opinion was profoundly stirred by the incident, "As a proof of the extreme depravity which the
Slave Trade introduces amongst those that become inured to it . . ."[4]

James Ramsay, a new man, now came upon the scene;
as a member of the navy and as a rector in the islands, he
had had much practical experience with slavery. In 1784
he was induced to publish *An Essay on the Treatment
and Conversion of African Slaves in the British Sugar
Colonies.* This essay struck a fresh note and, coming from
a man so recently active in the islands and with such inti-
mate knowledge of the facts, it opened up the whole field

[2] Prince Hoare, *Memoirs of Granville Sharp* (London, 1828, 2 vols.), I,
361 ff., and II, appendix VIII, pp. xxvi-xxxiii. Date of letters, July 2, 1783.

[3] *Ibid.,* I, 360-361. Date of letters, July 18, 1783.

[4] *Ibid.,* I, 359. One of the lawyers at the trial, Heywood, said, "That the
present is a *new* cause, is allowed on all hands; and I hope, for the honour
of humanity and mankind in general, it will be the *last.* That, in point of
importance, it is the greatest that ever came before this Court, cannot be
disputed. We are not now merely defending the under-writers from the dam-
ages obtained against them: I cannot help thinking that my friends who
came before me, and myself, on this occasion, appear as counsel for millions
of mankind, and the cause of humanity in general." "Lord Mansfield also
appears to have weighed the same point very strictly.—'The matter,' he
said, 'left to the jury was, *whether it was from necessity;* for they had no
doubt (*though it shocks one very much*) that the case of slaves was the
same as if horses had been thrown overboard. It is a very shocking case.' ''

of controversy and drew fire at once from the opposition. The extreme hostility which he encountered materially shortened his life. Mr. Molyneux, the chief enemy of Ramsay, announced his death in these words, "Ramsay is dead—I have killed him."[5]

Ramsay presented nearly all the arguments used against the slave trade and slavery in succeeding years. His friendship with Clarkson, Sharp, Sir Charles Middleton, and Wilberforce made it possible for him to use his first-hand information with the fullest effect. Nearly all the numerous men and women in England who knew the hardships of slave labor refused to testify against it, either because they were economically interested in its maintenance or because they feared the animus of the "slave power." Friends of the slave system were found in all ranks of English society. During the whole of the anti-slavery crusade only three men with first-hand knowledge of West Indian slavery were conspicuous in the fight, James Ramsay, James Stephen, and Zachary Macaulay; and of these Ramsay was the earliest. His book appeared about the time (1784) that Stephen went to the islands. Personal information about slave conditions was invaluable, if people were to be interested in the subject. On the way home on board ship Ramsay told his fellow passengers, Sir Charles Middleton and his wife, about conditions in the islands, and they became converts to anti-slavery projects.[6]

In his book, Ramsay indicted English West Indian slavery as the most cruel practiced by any nation. He asserted that the French gave their negroes more food, more holidays, more religious instruction, more private property, and in general more humane treatment than

[5] R. I. and S. Wilberforce, *Life of William Wilberforce,* I, p. 235, cited hereafter as *Life of Wilberforce.*

[6] *Ibid.,* I, 143 ff.

did the English. This testimony supported the view of
Adam Smith and carried conviction because of the great
mass of detail given as to the exact amount of weekly
food permitted, the annual allowance of scanty clothing,
of quack medicines, the scrap of salt beef at Christmas,
and the like. The French encouraged their slaves to
marry and respected a marriage once made by efforts to
keep the family together and to settle it on a small tract
of land with a few domestic animals, goats or a hog, and
chickens. In this way the slave was started on the road to
self-respect and honesty, and took the first steps in civilization.[7] The French planters, too, were generally resident in the islands, a fact of immense benefit to the slaves,
as the owner raised his own provisions and lived in a
family style on the plantation with his slaves assembled
about him, free from the ambition of retiring to Europe
and therefore of overworking his dependents in order to
pile up a hasty fortune.

Ramsay contrasted the French with the English, ''An
English planter if out of debt, must run away to England,
which he calls his home, where generally lost to every
useful purpose in life, he vies with the nobility in ex-
travagance, and expence, while his attorney, and manager, are obliged to overwork, and pinch, his poor slaves,
to keep up, or increase the usual remittances. . . .''[8] The
English planters were in debt, and had virtually sold
themselves to English mortgagees, while the French improved their estates out of the produce of their own soil.
Borrowed money was, in the opinion of Ramsay, a cause
of ruin for the English planter[9] on whose land slavery
was described as growing steadily more severe. High

---

[7] James Ramsay, *An Essay on the Treatment and Conversion of African
Slaves in the British Sugar Colonies*, pp. 45-47.

[8] *Ibid.*, p. 48.

[9] *Ibid.*, p. 50.

prices for sugar and heavy debts had induced the English planter to sacrifice all the private plots or provision grounds of slaves and also the grass lands for sugar growing. This confiscation made the food problem more serious and in addition forced the hated burden of gathering grass for the domestic animals upon the overworked and underfed slaves.[10] Ramsay's detailed pictures of slave life and his exact description of their huts, their meals, their care when sick or old,[11] are more convincing because they are not wholly dark. The exact economy of the plantation with its hours of work and its regimented slaves preceded or followed by the overseer with whip in hand,[12] presented itself clearly to the English reader, who knew little of the storied plantation society outside of fiction or the counting house. He cited a number of instances of good management of slaves,[13] and declared that under kind masters the physical condition of the slaves was superior to that of the laborers in England.[14]

[10] James Ramsay, *op. cit.*, pp. 68-69. The author maintained that within a period of less than thirty years the annual expense of running a plantation had been more than doubled. In order to send out two or three more cakes of sugar an expense of hundreds of pounds in provisions to slaves, in oats to horses, and in keeping up the stock of slaves and cattle was incurred. Often the very fertility of an island as in the case of St. Christopher caused such a craze for sugar growing that the slaves were neglected and cruelly over driven. Ramsay's knowledge of slavery was mostly obtained in St. Christopher.

[11] *Ibid.*, pp. 67-70. Ramsay says, p. 71, that married managers are much needed, particularly because the wives take good care of the children and of pregnant women. Women well treated would bear and rear enough children to keep up the population of the plantations.

[12] *Ibid.*, p. 59, described the work of the slaves: ''The discipline of a sugar plantation is as exact as that of a regiment: at four o'clock in the morning the plantation bell rings to call the slaves into the field. Their work is to manure, dig, and hoe, plow the ground, to plant, weed, and cut the cane, to bring it in to the mill, to have the juice expressed and boiled into sugar.''

[13] *Ibid.*, p. 86.          [14] *Ibid.*, pp. 78, 79.

In Ramsay's opinion the only successful missionaries in the islands were the Moravians, whose success was based on unending toil, patience, and clever adaptation of their religious teachings to the weakness and ignorance of the negroes.[15] While admitting his own failure to improve the negroes and insisting that he made them worse by indulgent treatment, he believed in the capacity of the negroes for improvement. He outlined a comprehensive plan, embodying religious education,[16] special protective laws, the appointment of official protectors to whom a slave could appeal, the punishment of cruel masters, the encouragement of marriage, the regulation of food, clothing, and rest, the assignment of task work, the assurance of homes and garden plots, the granting of self-government in minor matters, and the adoption of a plan for manumission. Such a program was intended to prepare the slaves for far distant emancipation.[17] This program differed but little from that advocated by the anti-slavery leaders forty years later.

To show the negro character as one affected by other motives than fear and as susceptible of improvement, Ramsay related a story of a negro named Quashi. The tale illustrates, in the literary phrases and noble conduct

[15] James Ramsay, *op. cit.*, pp. 140-143. The results obtained were declared to be ''a considerable degree of religious knowledge, an orderly behavior, a neatness in their persons and clothing, a sobriety in their carriage, a sensibility in their manner, a diligence and faithfulness in their stations, industry and method in their own little matters, an humility and piety in their conversation, an universal unimpeded honesty in their conduct.'' In Antigua alone there were 2,000 Moravian Christian slaves.

[16] *Ibid.*, pp. 227-233. The author wished a minister of the Established Church for each 3,000 inhabitants, a school in every parish, and special devotional exercises and songs adapted to the needs and capacities of the slaves. ''Negroes, who are well treated and in spirits, sing at work.''

[17] *Ibid.*, pp. 241-246. On p. 241, the purpose is stated to make them subject to the *penalties* of the law, but also *entitled* to its *security* and leave them under the *management* of a master but protected from his *barbarity*.

attributed to the slave, the idealization of primitive races common at the time. This man was extremely proud of the fact that his skin had never been marked by the whip,[18] a distinction so uncommon that it was greatly prized. He had grown up as a playmate of his master and had always been trusted, but one day his master because of some suspicion ordered a flogging with the cart whip.[19] "Quashi dreaded this mortal wound to his honour" and slipped away unnoticed, intending as the custom was, to get a neighboring planter to intercede for him on a feast day. Etiquette forbade the master to overlook a fault unless a "protector" interceded, which procedure allowed him to overlook his command. Before the slave could get any one to intercede for him, he encountered his master and a struggle ensued in which at the end Quashi was victorious, and, drawing a knife over his helpless victim, who lay in dreadful expectation, he said, " 'Master, I was bred up with you as a child; I was your play-mate when a boy, I have loved you as myself; your interest has been my study; I am innocent of the cause of your suspicion; had I been guilty my attachment to you might have pleaded for me. Yet you have condemned me to punishment, of which I must ever have borne the disgraceful marks; thus only can I avoid them!' " With these words he drew the knife with all his strength across his own

[18] James Ramsay, *op. cit.*, p. 213. "A negro, who has grown up to manhood, without undergoing a solemn cart-whipping, as some by good chance will, . . . takes pride in what he calls the smoothness of his skin, its being unrazed by the whip; and he would be at more pains, and use more diligence to escape such a cart-whipping, than many of our lower sort would use to shun the gallows."

[19] *Ibid.*, p. 64, gives this account of the cart whip or cattle whip, the same instrument that was used to drive mules: "This instrument in the hands of a skillful driver, cuts out flakes of skin and flesh with every stroke; and the wretch, in this mangled condition is turned out to work in dry or wet weather, which last, now and then, brings on the cramp, and ends his sufferings and slavery together."

throat, and fell down dead without a groan, on his "master, bathing him in his blood.'"[20]

Punishment for small offences was severe. "Canebreaking," or eating the stalks of cane for juice, was a common cause of punishment. One of the witnesses before a parliament committee stated that the whip belonged so much to the atmosphere of the West Indies that every child, white or black, who was asked to do a task, demanded a whip before he could set at it. The planter party declared that the whip was a mere badge of authority, and that the overseer sometimes preceded his men, instead of driving them from the rear.

The slave question, then, was no longer merely a topic for philosophical speculation. Philosophers had written essays upon the nature of man, literary men had pleaded for greater benevolence and kindness, bishops had eloquently appealed to religious considerations of brotherly love, the Quakers had withdrawn from the iniquity, but these formed, after all, a relatively small religious body. Upon the whole, the powerful slave interests had until 1784 felt safe in avoiding controversy.

The time was ripe for organized effort. The first people to realize this were the Quakers themselves, who appointed a committee to work for the abolition of the slave trade by means of tracts and the press. In 1783 they presented a petition to parliament for its destruction.[21] In

---

[20] James Ramsay, *op. cit.*, pp. 212-215.

[21] *Parliamentary History*, XXIII, 1026. *House of Commons Journals*, XXXIX, 487. Lord North in a few words expressed his warm admiration of the Quaker body and his sympathy with the object of their petition, but declared that the trade had become in some measure necessary to every nation in Europe, and that it would be next to an impossibility to induce them to give it up. *Parliamentary History*, XXIII, 1026-1027. Two years later, in 1785, the inhabitants of Bridgewater petitioned for the destruction of the slave traffic but quite without effect. Ten years earlier, in 1775 and 1776, the question had been brought up without result.

1784 they prepared twelve thousand copies of a written statement called *The Case of Our Fellow-creatures, the oppressed Africans, respectfully recommended to the serious Consideration of the Legislature of Great Britain, by the people called Quakers.* The next year they circulated a book by Anthony Bezenet on the condition of the negro slaves in the British colonies. In 1786 Thomas Clarkson began his efforts toward the annihilation of the slave system by publishing his essay *Is it lawful to make men slaves against their will?;* the next year William Wilberforce announced publicly that he would champion the cause in parliament, and at the same time the Society for the Abolition of the Slave Trade was formed in London with Sharp as president.

The attack upon the slave system having been determined upon, all possible help was enlisted. Ramsay, who for several years had fought almost alone, now found himself one of many. William Cowper, the poet of the Evangelical party, William Blake, the sentimentalist poet, and John Newton, the ex-slave trader and pietist, all joined in the battle. The narration of the attack upon the slave trade must be delayed to indicate the special contribution of each of these persons.

The African race had the support of Cowper, whose work as a reformer is characterized by intense zeal. The friend of John Newton, the ex-slave trader and a founder of Evangelicalism, Cowper wrote a number of separate poems on the subject of slavery, and in *The Task* (1785) attacked the abuses of the day, including the slave system.[22]

This poem for a period of years was more widely

[22] For an excellent statement on the development of English sentimentalism during the eighteenth century see, *English Poets of the Eighteenth Century* (edited by Ernest Bernbaum, New York, 1918), introduction, pp. xvii to xxviii.

known than any other of the time. The lines describing man's inhumanity were in popular literary fashion:

> Oh for a lodge in some vast wilderness,
> Some boundless contiguity of shade,
> Where rumour of oppression and deceit,
> Of unsuccessful or successful war,
> Might never reach me more! My ear is pained,
> My soul is sick, with every day's report
> Of wrong and outrage with which earth is filled.

Another line describes the negro as a brother, and as an Englishman with a black skin according to the popular view:

> He finds his fellow guilty of a skin
> Not coloured like his own . . .[23]

His best appeal comes in the familiar summons to his countrymen:

> I would not have a slave to till my ground,
> To carry me, to fan me while I sleep,
> And tremble when I wake, for all the wealth
> That sinews bought and sold have ever earned.
> No: dear as freedom is, and in my heart's
> Just estimation prized above all price,
> I had much rather be myself the slave
> And wear the bonds than fasten them on him.
> We have no slaves at home: then why abroad?
> And they themselves, once ferried o'er the wave
> That parts us, are emancipate and loosed.
> Slaves cannot breathe in England; if their lungs
> Receive our air, that moment they are free:
> They touch our country and their shackles fall.

---

[23] *The Poems of William Cowper* (edited by J. C. Bailey, London, 1905), "The Task," book II, ll. 1-7, 12-13.

That's noble, and bespeaks a nation proud
And jealous of the blessing. Spread it then,
And let it circulate through every vein
Of all your empire; that where Britain's power
Is felt, mankind may feel her mercy too.[24]

"For the rest, the book [book six of *The Task*] is, perhaps, the most striking evidence of the way in which
Cowper half perceived and half created the humanitarian
reforms which were to be brought about by the generation that was growing up at his death. Few poets have
had more direct influence. He must not, of course, be
given the credit of what was mainly accomplished by a
great religious movement; but . . . the Evangelicals
owed a great deal to the poet who carried their doctrines
into places not to be reached by a preacher's voice. . . .
If the debtors are no longer imprisoned, if India is no
longer oppressed, if public schools are no longer places
of barbarism and terror, if slaves are free, and animals
protected from cruelty both by opinion and law, our
gratitude must not forget that Cowper pleaded for them
all in what was the most popular poem of its day.'"[25]

The influence of such verse was formidable enough to
start rumors attacking Cowper. He was quoted as being
in favor of the slave trade party because he refused to
deny himself sugar and rum. Again, it was reported that
he had changed his mind on the slave trade after reading
an account of African conditions, to the effect that, before the commencement of the traffic, the negroes, multiplying prodigiously, had been obliged to devour each
other.[26]

Contemplation of the subject of slavery depressed

[24] *The Poems of William Cowper*, book II, ll. 29 ff.
[25] *Ibid.*, introduction, p. li.
[26] Thomas Wright, *The Correspondence of William Cowper* (London,
1904), IV, 190-191.

Cowper and in a letter to his friend, John Newton, he despaired of reform, ending with the remark ''such arguments as Pharaoh might have used to justify his destruction of the Israelites, substituting only sugar for bricks, may lie ready for our use also; but I think we can find no better.'' In a letter to the Rev. Mr. Bagot he expressed his determination not to degrade poetry by writing further descriptions of slavery. His imagination allowed him to contemplate scenes of horror created by God, but not those created by men.[27]

The feeling for the common man and for a simple society is to be found in the works of Burns and William Blake. The latter was the supreme sentimentalist of the century. ''To him every atom of the cosmos was literally spiritual and holy; the divine and the human, the soul and the flesh were absolutely one. . . . He hymned the sanctity of animal life; even the tiger, conventionally an incarnation of cruelty, was a glorious creature of divine mould; to slay or cage a beast was, the 'Auguries of Innocence' protested, to incur anathema.''[28] Blake revealed his opinion of the negro in ''The Little Black Boy'' (1787), saying in the first stanza:

> My mother bore me in the southern wild,
> And I am black, but O! my soul is white;
> White as an angel is the English child,
> But I am black, as if bereav'd of light.[29]

It was most fitting that an ex-slave trader should be one of the chief leaders in the crusade against the traffic in negroes. John Newton (1727-1807), English divine, hymn writer, and a founder of Evangelicalism, illustrates the amazing changes in English sentiment within

[27] Thomas Wright, *op. cit.*, IV, 281-282.

[28] Ernest Bernbaum, *English Poets of the Eighteenth Century*, p. xxxvii.

[29] *The Poetical Works of William Blake* (edited by John Sampson, London, 1914), p. 68.

the span of a lifetime. In early life, he deserted from the navy, helped one or two factors in securing slaves on the coast of Africa, and became the captain of a slaver. Even after he acknowledged himself under deep religious influence, he continued this career and read the religious service to the crew on board a vessel carrying a cargo of negroes, with the conviction that his business was part of the divine plan. By slow degrees he became a most active opponent of the traffic and testified, wrote, and preached against it. He influenced Cowper, Hannah More, and Wilberforce, and rejoiced to live long enough to see the business of his youth abolished by act of parliament.

As significant as the change in Newton's career was the frankness with which he, in a public confession, apologized for his share in the slave trade. "If my testimony should not be necessary or serviceable, yet, perhaps, I am bound in conscience to take shame to myself by a public confession, which, however sincere, comes too late to prevent or repair the misery and mischief to which I have formerly been accessory."[30] Illness had interrupted his voyages to Africa. "Thus I was unexpectedly freed from this disagreeable service. . . . I think I should have quitted it sooner, had I considered it as I do now, to be unlawful and wrong. But I never had a scruple upon this head at the time; nor was such a thought once suggested to me by any friend. What I did I did ignorantly; considering it as the line of life which divine providence had allotted me, and having no concern in point of conscience, but to treat the slaves while under my care, with as much humanity as a regard to my own safety would admit."[31]

[30] Rev. John Newton, "Thoughts upon the African Slave Trade" (1788), in *The Works of the Rev. John Newton* (New Haven, 1824), IV, 533.
[31] *Ibid.*, IV, 534.

He estimated that of a total of eight thousand seamen, who were engaged in the slave trade in one year, fifteen hundred, or one-fifth, were lost by sickness and brutality.[32] From his own observation he knew that the character of the business naturally made for extreme brutality. Holding the slaves down, and punishing for insurrection, gradually accustomed traders to cruelty. To illustrate the effects of long familiarity with cruelty he related the case of a mate who threw a child overboard because it moaned at night in its mother's arms and kept him awake.[33] In trading with the natives it was the custom to rob and despoil them in every conceivable way. "Not an article that is capable of diminution or adulteration is delivered genuine, or entire," he declared.[34] The spirits were diluted with water, false heads were put into kegs and barrels, the linen and cotton cloths were opened and two or three yards cut from the middle. The English had come to be regarded upon the coast as consummate villains. "When I have charged a black with unfairness and dishonesty, he has answered, if able to clear himself, with an air of disdain, 'What! do you think I am a white man?' "[35]

Newton believed that most of the slaves were captives of the native wars, and that most of these wars would cease when Europeans stopped offering to exchange goods for slaves. He estimated that in addition to the hundred thousand slaves exported annually, at least as many more were killed in war. Of the losses of life at sea, he thought an average between the more successful and unsuccessful voyages, including all contingencies, would be one-fourth mortality of the whole purchase.[36] The cargo of a vessel of approximately a hundred tons was expected to purchase from two hundred and twenty

[32] Rev. John Newton, *op. cit.*, IV, 538.    [33] *Ibid.*, IV, 539.
[34] *Ibid.*, IV, 542.    [35] *Ibid.*, IV, 543.    [36] *Ibid.*, IV, 545.

to two hundred and fifty slaves. The consignee of one of his cargoes at Antigua told him that calculations as exact as possible had been made to determine which was the more saving method of managing slaves, whether by moderate care to prolong their lives or by straining their strength to the utmost to use them up and replace them by new purchases. The latter method was determined to be the cheaper, and in the island of Antigua, a slave seldom lived more than nine years.[37]

The formation of the Abolition Society in 1787[38] made up of nine Quakers, and Clarkson, Sharp, and one other, with Wilberforce as chief adviser, was the initial step for a parliamentary battle. The decision to strike at the slave trade and not at slavery was made at one of the early meetings of the organization. Granville Sharp, alone among the ten present, favored making slavery an issue also,[39] but the others agreed that an immediate attempt to emancipate the slaves would be futile. An attack on slavery as well as on the slave trade would have resulted in fatal opposition, while an attack on the former alone would have left the slave trade intact to be carried on for the benefit of all non-British possessions. However, this decision need not obscure the fact that both issues were part and parcel of the same system. The later history of the agitation showed that, as long as there was slavery, a very substantial slave trade was inevitable. Slavery called for a supply of new slaves; the slave trade was one of the means of obtaining them.

[37] Rev. John Newton, *op. cit.*, IV, 548-549.

[38] This committee reminds one of the national committee of one of our political parties. The character and size of the committee varied from time to time. An amazing amount of work was done. Tracts and books were printed and circulated. Clarkson's work was directed, people were interviewed, petitions were drawn up, and evidence was prepared for presentation to parliament.

[39] Prince Hoare, *Memoirs of Granville Sharp*, II, 234-235.

There was, however, some validity in the view that the abolition of the trade, by diminishing the supply, would cause owners from motives of self-interest to treat their slaves better and to protect to some extent the women and children.[40] A final motive for the particular program of reform was the unwillingness of the British government to force measures upon the colonial legislatures. The memory of the American Revolution was still vivid. The slave trade could be abolished by parliament as unquestionably within its jurisdiction. Emancipation would be a direct overruling of the West Indian colonial legislatures.

The English campaign turned upon the settlement of several delicate questions. The cruelty and the impolicy of the slave trade had to be established; evidence of a convincing kind that the value of the West Indies would not be destroyed had to be gathered. In these efforts to

[40] The severity of negro slavery in the British West Indies exceeded that in the United States very decidedly. Despite the fact that there was a fair amount of illicit slave trade into the United States, there is a good deal of evidence to show that the increase of negroes was greater under slavery in the United States than since emancipation. In fact, the negro race is not increasing so rapidly as it once did. This seems to support the contention of the South that the physical lot of the slave was better than that of the freedman. The following table on the "Distribution of Negroes in the United States" was prepared by W. F. Willcox:

| Slavery | Per Cent of increase of Negroes | Per Cent of increase of Whites | Ratio of increase of Negroes to increase of Whites—100 |
|---|---|---|---|
| 1800-1820 | 76.8 | 82.7 | 93 |
| 1820-1840 | 62.2 | 80.5 | 77 |
| 1840-1860 | 54.6 | 89.7 | 61 |
| Freedom |  |  |  |
| 1860-1880 | 48.2 | 61.2 | 79 |
| 1880-1900 | 34.2 | 53.9 | 64 |
| 1900-1920 | 18.4 | 41.9 | 44 |

This table is found in "Eugenics in Race and State," Second International Congress of Eugenics, II, 166-174.

convince the country and parliament, Clarkson became the indefatigable field agent of the reformers, Wilberforce the parliamentary leader, and the younger Pitt, the prime minister, the powerful friend of the movement in its early stages. A host of new workers appeared upon the scene, taking the place of those who had died after a lifetime of work, and of others who had changed sides. It is hardly too much to say that for almost two generations from 1787 to 1833 the anti-slavery propaganda had the support of a large proportion if not of a majority of the people of England. The agitation lasted so long that father and son united their forces, as in the case of the Stephens and the Macaulays. The two best-known leaders, Clarkson and Wilberforce, however, lived through the period from the beginning of serious parliamentary action until success was reached.

Clarkson's father was a clergyman and the son graduated at St. John's College, Cambridge. He was to follow his father's profession and was ordained a deacon. His interest in the subject of slavery was aroused by Dr. Peckard, the vice-chancellor, who preached a sermon against the traffic in 1784, and in the next year announced, for the Latin essay of the senior bachelor of arts, the subject, *Anne liceat invitos in servitutem dare?* (Is it right to make slaves of others against their will?) Clarkson, having won a prize the year before, felt it particularly incumbent on him to win again. He found it difficult to get the information he wished until he happened to learn of Anthony Benezet's *Historical Account of Guinea,* which in turn introduced him to the leading authorities on Africa. Clarkson's sensitive, indeed morbid, nature can be seen in the passage in which he describes his feelings while writing the essay. "But no person," he says, "can tell the severe trial which the writing of it proved to me. I had expected pleasure from the invention of the arguments, from the arrangement of them, from the putting of them together, and from the thought, in the interim, that I was engaged in an innocent contest for literary honours. But all my pleasure was damped by the facts which were now continually before me. It was but one gloomy subject from morning to night. In the daytime I was uneasy. In the night I had little rest. I sometimes never closed my eyelids for grief. . . . I always slept with a candle in my room, that I might rise out of bed and put down such thoughts as might occur to me in the night, if I judged them valuable, conceiving that no arguments of any moment should be lost in so great a cause.'"[41]

The matter continued to absorb his thoughts, and soon he asked himself whether he could not render some practical service to the negroes. Naturally, his first thought was to translate the prize essay from Latin into English and to enlarge it as he went along. In searching for a publisher, he became acquainted with William Dillwyn and other Quakers, as well as with such men as Granville Sharp and James Ramsay. They gladly helped him to publish the essay in 1786,[42] and the work was quickly distributed among leading men. The author met Sir Charles Middleton, who had already been won over by James Ramsay; he met John Newton; he learned that Bishop Porteus, soon to become Bishop of London, would champion the cause in the church and in the House of Lords. He interviewed some of the members of parliament and

[41] Thomas Clarkson, *History of the Abolition of the African Slave Trade*, pp. 137, 138. Obviously Clarkson was a man of quite a different temperament from John Newton.

[42] *Ibid.*, pp. 140-142. The title of the work is, *An Essay on the Slavery and Commerce of the Human Species, particularly the African, translated from a Latin Dissertation, which was honoured with the First Prize in the University of Cambridge, for the year 1785, with Additions.*

came into contact with William Wilberforce.[43] Clarkson says of him: "On my first interview with him, he stated frankly, that the subject had often employed his thoughts, and that it was near his heart. . . . On learning my intention to devote myself to the cause, he paid me many handsome compliments. He then desired me to call upon him often, and to acquaint myself with his progress from time to time. He expressed also his willingness to afford me any assistance in his power in the prosecution of my pursuits."[44] In other words, Wilberforce had found an ideal ally.

As a collector of evidence Clarkson has probably never been equaled. No fact was too small for him to neglect; no task too tedious for his patience; no undertaking too hopeless for him to attempt. At the peril of his life, he visited ships, carefully measuring their storage space; he crossed the Severn on a stormy night in pursuit of witnesses, a risk which perhaps no other man in the kingdom would have taken.[45] He searched the ships of port after port to look for a single man, whose name he did not even know, and found him on the three hundred and seventeenth ship he visited.[46] At enormous personal peril he braved the wrath of the slave dealers of Bristol and Liverpool, and barely escaped being purposely crowded off the end of a pier to certain death. He brought to justice a number of captains who had brutally used members of their crews. He went over the shipmasters' rolls, tracing the fate of twenty thousand seamen, until he proved conclusively that the trade was not the nursery of seamen but their grave. He collected specimens of the natural products of Africa to show that a purely natural commerce with that continent would be

---

[43] Thomas Clarkson, *History of the Abolition of the African Slave Trade*, pp. 143-155.
[44] *Ibid.*, p. 155.    [45] *Ibid.*, pp. 250 ff.    [46] *Ibid.*, pp. 408-410.

better than the European slave trading.[47] Evidence, painstaking evidence, is what he sought, and he was shrewd enough not to make any mistake, realizing that if he were caught in a few errors, however slight, the whole body of his facts would be questioned. For his exhibits he secured handcuffs, leg-shackles, mouth-openers for forced feeding, and all the implements of the trade.[48]

Liverpool was so identified with the traffic that, while it was easy enough to get evidence privately, no one was willing to come out into the open and brave the wrath of his fellow townsmen. The stake of Liverpool in this commerce has been well stated by Ramsay Muir: "Not only did it employ nearly one-fourth of the total tonnage of the port; not only did it engage the capital of over one hundred of the town's principal merchants; but many hundreds of humbler citizens were enriched by it. 'Almost every order of people,' says a Liverpool writer in 1795, 'is interested in a Guinea cargo. . . . He who cannot send a bale, will send a bandbox. . . . It is well known that many of the small vessels that import about an hundred slaves are fitted out by attorneys, drapers, ropers, grocers, tallow-chandlers, barbers, tailors, etc.,' of whom 'some have one-eighth, some a fifteenth, some a thirty-second' share. An army of sailors, who got better pay on these ships than on any other; a host of shipwrights, ship's chandlers, manufacturers of chains and implements, whose livelihood depended upon the trade, all equally resented attacks upon it. It had flooded Liverpool with wealth, which invigorated every industry, provided the capital for docks, enriched and employed the mills of Lancashire, and afforded the means for opening out new and ever new lines of trade. Beyond a doubt it was the slave trade which raised Liverpool from a

---

47 Thomas Clarkson, *op. cit.*, pp. 197, 214, 273.
48 *Ibid.*, pp. 222-224.

struggling port to be one of the richest and most prosperous trading centres of the world.'"[49] So powerful was the pressure exerted on men that they sometimes even changed sides. The most discouraging case in Clarkson's experience was that of a man named Norris, who had given him much evidence against the trade, but who later appeared before the Privy Council as one of its chief defenders. The new material Clarkson had gathered he embodied in an essay on the *Impolicy of the Slave Trade.*[50]

In the meantime, Wilberforce and Pitt had arranged for a hearing before the Privy Council committee. The report of the council, submitted to parliament in April, 1789, was simply a collection of evidence, presented by the contending parties. The materials were grouped in six sections: (1) on the civilization of West Africa and how slaves are made; (2) on "the manner of carrying slaves to the West Indies"; (3) on the treatment of slaves on the plantations; (4) on the extent of the trade and population, slave and free, of the West Indies; (5) (6) on the slave trade and slavery as practiced by other nations. An impartial man, reading the report, would instantly have condemned the trade. The most convincing witness on the question of how slaves were obtained was a traveler, Dr. Andrew Spaarman, professor of physic at Stockholm, who gave this evidence: "When the kings of the country want slaves for the purchase of goods, they send their horsemen in the night to the villages to make as many slaves as they can. In the neighbourhood of Goree he saw one of these expeditions. The King of Barbessia came to him in the night to tell him that he

[49] Ramsay Muir, *A History of Liverpool,* pp. 194-195.
[50] Thomas Clarkson, *History of the Abolition of the African Slave Trade,* pp. 225-227, 275, 319. Norris had even outlined to Clarkson a scheme of duties against the slave trade and a plan for encouraging a legitimate commerce with Africa.

was going to send out a party to make slaves as he wanted brandy to encourage his officers. In the course of the conversation, the King became so intoxicated with madeira by Dr. Spaarman's bedside that he was carried away speechless. Dr. Spaarman saw the party set out and saw them return with some slaves they had made. They conceal part of those they make on these occasions in order to enhance the price.'"[51]

Pitt, although already interested and eager to avail himself of Clarkson's knowledge, did not reveal his previous information but drew out Clarkson, giving the latter the impression that he himself knew little about the topic. The most impressive bit of evidence submitted was the muster rolls of the seamen engaged in the slave trade, showing the very high mortality. Grenville was less reserved than Pitt, and therefore seemed to Clarkson to be better informed.[52]

The collection of evidence went on unceasingly for several years. Often, after traveling between fifty and one hundred miles to get a witness, the indefatigable Clarkson would be disappointed. One instance must suffice: "I have heard him, a surgeon, describe scenes of misery which he had witnessed, and on the relation of which he himself almost wept. But mark the issue again. 'I am a surgeon,' says he; 'through that window you see a spacious house. It is occupied by a West Indian. The medical attendance upon his family is of considerable importance to the temporal interests of mine. If I give you my evidence I lose his patronage. At the house above him lives an East Indian. The two families are connected: I fear, if I lose the support of one I shall lose that of the

51 *Report of the Lords of the Committee of Council,* etc., 1789; R. Coupland, *Wilberforce,* pp. 116-117.

52 Thomas Clarkson, *History of the Abolition of the African Slave Trade,* pp. 272-274.

other also; but I will give you privately all the intelligence in my power.' "[53]

William Wilberforce inherited great wealth and assured social position. He early showed striking ability and developed a genius for friendship. Possessed of the qualities that made for eighteenth century leadership, he moved on terms of intimacy with the younger Pitt, Charles James Fox, Edmund Burke, Castlereagh, Canning, and Wellington. In his various country homes, where Pitt frequently went to spend the night as his guest, even in the absence of the host, were planned those philanthropies and religious movements which abolished the slave trade and slavery, put Bibles in the hands of hundreds of thousands, taught other hosts their letters, and sent missionaries to the ends of the earth. With the gift of parliamentary eloquence and real capacity for statesmanship, he devoted himself primarily not to general politics but to humanitarian causes. He and his friends worked for human betterment with a zeal and a success which might well arouse the envy of a great religious order. Though probably the closest friend of the younger Pitt, he never allied himself with any political party, but founded "the party of no party men," known in derision as "The Saints." The aim of these men was to promote by all sorts of reforms their ideals as to the brotherhood of man.

In personality Wilberforce was joyous, witty, and gracious. He held his friends so spellbound that many of them were not aware that he was lacking in originality and creative imagination, and that he found close application to work difficult and burdensome. Although he worked long hours and allowed his house to become a hotel, filled with statesmen and friends, he was accused

[53] Thomas Clarkson, *op. cit.*, p. 334.

of "busy indolence," lack of system, indecision, and a love for the small gossip of political life. While he produced several books, his *Practical View*, which, despite its dullness, went through about twenty editions on each side of the Atlantic, was forced to completion through the diligence of the women of his household, who jotted down important phrases as they fell from his lips, and, by bringing the book continually before him, caused it to be finished.[54] Accompanying his vivacity and wit was a considerable degree of sarcastic power, shrewdness, and knowledge of the world. Yet he was so genial and kindly that "he might have passed for the brother of any man, and for the lover of every woman, with whom he conversed."[55]

He was born in Hull in 1759. As a child he was weak and delicate. As a man he never became robust, and in early manhood, in endeavoring to overcome his suffering, he acquired the opium habit. Upon the death of his father when he was nine years old, he came under the influence of an aunt, who was a follower of Whitefield and a supporter of the Evangelical movement. His mother was unwilling to have him become a "Methodist," and after two years took him home to Hull and encouraged him to lead a normal joyous boy's life. In his eighteenth year he entered St. John's College, Cambridge, where he became acquainted with the younger Pitt and other able young men, but did not distinguish himself as a student.

After college Wilberforce joined in the fashionable life of London and at the clubs met Fox, Sheridan, and

---

[54] Sir James Stephen, *Essays in Ecclesiastical Biography*, II, 223-224, says, "he never held, nor could ever have attained to a place among philosophers or poets, and . . . nature had not formed him for patient inquiry, suspended judgment, or for faith in the glorious unrealities of fiction . . . his name would scarcely have descended to posterity if he had devoted himself to any other than an active life."

[55] *Ibid.*, II, 216.

Windham, and cemented his friendship with Pitt. A political career was a natural choice for such a young man, and in 1780 he entered parliament for Hull. Four years later he was returned for the county of York, in the bitter campaign which gave Pitt his majority in the House of Commons. In the meantime, religious introspection absorbed him. In 1784, accompanied by his mother and the Rev. Isaac Milner, an old friend and schoolfellow, he took a trip to Nice. The young men read and studied together Doddridge's *Rise and Progress of Religion*. A little later they read the Greek Testament, with the result that Wilberforce felt a conviction of sin, much to the alarm of his mother, who feared he might become a religious fanatic. He gradually worked himself into a state of religious peace, but his constant introspection throughout life has probably, as Lecky says, a suggestion of morbidness in it. Inclination to withdraw from the world he was prevented from yielding to by the thought of the numerous reforms that were needed and by the conviction that it was the duty of a Christian to lead in such movements.

During the same year, 1784, Wilberforce founded a society for the reformation of manners.[56] Meanwhile, his interest in the West Indian slaves developed rapidly. He gathered information from the slaveholding merchants in London, and he discussed the question of slavery with Grenville and Pitt. The latter was reluctant to see such an able, powerful, and weathy supporter withdraw into seclusion, and perceived clearly that a definite task would provide a channel for Wilberforce's religious zeal and keep him in active life in parliament for many years. He, therefore, suggested an immediate attack on the slave trade as a suitable undertaking. "Pitt recommended me," said Wilberforce, "to undertake its con-

[56] *Manners* is used in the sense of *morals*.

duct, as a subject suited to my character and talents. At
length, I well remember, after a conversation in the open
air, at the root of an old tree at Holwood, just above the
steep descent into the vale of Keston, I resolved to give
notice on a fit occasion in the House of Commons of my
intention to bring the subject forward."[57] It might be
said that the two men, under the tree still called Wilberforce oak, sealed the fate of slavery and the slave trade
in modern times. It was thought best for Wilberforce not
to become a member of the abolition committee, but to
work in harmony and coöperation with it. In fact, he
greatly influenced the affairs of the committee from this
time on. Granville Sharp expressed the usual opinion of
him when he said: "His position as member for the largest county, the great influence of his personal connections, added to an amiable and unblemished character,
secure every advantage to the cause."[58]

When the time came to hear evidence before the Privy
Council, Wilberforce was ill and was ordered away to
Bath. So serious was the situation that the London committee discussed finding another leader if Wilberforce
should give the word, but the latter had provided one in
the prime minister himself. Toward the end of 1788 Wilberforce returned to London, and in May of the next
year, he brought forward his motion on the subject in the
House of Commons. Although still weak, he spoke for
over three hours with such effect that no less a judge
than Edmund Burke declared "that the House, the nation, and Europe, were under great and serious obligations to the hon. gentleman for having brought forward
the subject in a manner the most masterly, impressive,
and eloquent. The principles were so well laid down, and
supported with so much force and order, that it equalled

[57] R. I. and S. Wilberforce, *Life of Wilberforce*, I, 150-151.
[58] *Ibid.*, I, 153.

anything he had heard in modern times, and was not perhaps to be surpassed in the remains of Grecian eloquence."[59] Porteus, Bishop of London, wrote: "It is with heart-felt satisfaction I acquaint you that Mr. Wilberforce yesterday opened the important subject of the Slave Trade in the House of Commons, in one of the ablest and most eloquent speeches that was ever heard in that or any other place. It continued upwards of three hours, and made a sensible and powerful impression upon the House. He was supported in the noblest manner by Mr. Pitt, Mr. Burke, and Mr. Fox, who all agreed in declaring that the Slave Trade was the disgrace and opprobium of this country, and that nothing but entire abolition could cure so monstrous an evil. It was a glorious night for this country."[60]

The supporters of the slave trade, in their many petitions[61] and speeches, argued that the trade was necessary to the further development of the West Indies, upon which the security of Britain, the strength of its navy, and the permanence of its manufactures so greatly depended; that agriculture could not be carried on there without slaves; that the trade had been guaranteed and even encouraged by a large number of acts of parliament, on the good faith of which many men had invested their fortunes in the islands;[62] that even if Great Britain

[59] R. I. and S. Wilberforce, *op. cit.*, I, 219. Pitt stated that an inquiry was being made by the Privy Council and that until that was finished nothing would be done. Fox regretted that the inquiry was not by the House of Commons and declared himself ready to vote for the abolition of the traffic. In this he was supported by Burke but opposed by several representatives of the slave interests. *Parliamentary History*, XXVII, 495-506.

[60] R. I. and S. Wilberforce, *Life of Wilberforce*, I, 220.

[61] *House of Commons Journals*, XLIV, 351 ff. and 380 ff.

[62] Encouraged by charters granted in 1662 and 1672 to the African Company, and by *Statutes* 15 Car. II, c. 7; 22 and 23 Car. II, c. 26; 7 and 8 Will. III, c. 22; 9 and 10 Will. III c. 26; 3 and 4 Anne, c. 3; 6 Geo. II, c. 13; 12 Geo. II, c. 30; 5 Geo. III, c. 44; 23 Geo. III, c. 65; 27 Geo. III,

abolished the trade, it would be vigorously carried on by her rivals, who eagerly sought it; that the trade, instead of being abolished, ought to receive the encouragement of parliament in the face of fierce foreign competition; and finally, that the propositions were unjust because they would take away private property without compensation.[63]

Wilberforce, in his speech, gave a complete and clear outline of the policy he intended to follow, set forth all the horrors of the traffic, and answered all arguments which had been made, or were likely to be made, by his opponents.[64] He based his arguments primarily on the report of the Privy Council, but he defended his position on moral grounds as well, and contended that even if it were shown that the abolition of the trade would lead to more or less disaster, he would urge it, nevertheless; for the trade was detrimental to Africa as a whole. The horrors of the "middle passage" were beyond comprehension,—twelve and one-half per cent perished in the passage, four and one-half per cent died on shore before the day of sailing, and one-third more died during the "seasoning."[65] Abolition would not be ruinous to the islands, for with better care the natural increase of the negroes would be sufficient to supply the demands of labor, and improvement in the physical and moral condition of the slaves would begin.[66] The ships and capital engaged in the trade could find other employment. As more sailors died in this trade in one year than in all other trades in two years, it was a detriment to the navy. Abolition of the traffic would probably not be opposed by

c. 27; to promote and secure loans. 5 Geo. II, c. 7; 13 Geo. III, c. 14; 14 Geo. III, c. 79.

[63] *House of Commons Journals*, XLIV, 351 ff. and 380 ff.

[64] *Parliamentary History*, XXVIII, 41 ff.

[65] *Ibid.*, 41 ff.

[66] See Macpherson, *Annals of Commerce*, IV, 150.

foreign nations; rather they were likely to join in its suppression. In France the sentiment against it was strong; the king was favorable to abolition, and Necker had already pledged himself.[67] The trade was of such a nature that abolition and not regulation was the only remedy. Pitt and Fox supported Wilberforce and believed that the coöperation of foreign nations might be secured, and that Great Britain was powerful enough to protect her islands from illicit trade.[68]

This first great debate illustrates the nature of the fight against the slave system which was to go on until the slaves were emancipated in 1833. If eloquence could have killed the slave trade, this first debate would have done so. Indeed, the masters of the art of eloquence, among the greatest of modern times, exerted themselves almost without ceasing. Sometimes they were feebly answered by argument; sometimes they were merely overwhelmed in the voting; sometimes they won in the House of Commons only to suffer a crushing defeat in the Lords. Or again the powerful West Indies interest would ask for the taking of additional evidence, thereby delaying the question for a year.

Abolition could not be made a government measure because Pitt's cabinet was divided and so were his supporters in both houses. That, too, was the situation in the Whig party, where Burke and Fox argued and voted against the traffic, but other Whigs favored it. The hope was to win by reason and argument enough men in both parties to carry abolition. Although the debating ability of the adherents of the slave trade was far inferior to that of its enemies, members of parliament were so bound by inherent conservatism that they were quite un-

[67] W. E. H. Lecky, *History of England in the Eighteenth Century* (New York, 1878), VI, 292.
[68] *Parliamentary History*, XXVIII, 41-71.

willing to vote the extinction of a traffic which had been encouraged for a century. The taking of evidence by the House of Commons might throw more light upon the subject, and would certainly cause delay. Thus the very fact that the trade had hosts of defenders was a sufficient reason for postponing the question until a later time.

Early in 1790 Wilberforce, in order to speed up matters, carried a motion[69] to examine witnesses before a special committee of the House and on this he acted, ably aided by William Smith. The amount of work done was enormous. Long hours of hard work daily were his lot, because it was exceedingly difficult to keep men from misrepresenting the facts of such a subject either willfully or unconsciously. When not working on the committee, he busied himself with the collection and examination of other masses of evidence, until his health threatened to give way again. At one time it even seemed as if only the West Indian side of the question would be presented before the committee.[70]

After the evidence before the select committee of the House of Commons had been taken, another parliamentary battle was in order in the spring of 1791. An election had been held, and Pitt was somewhat stronger in parliament, but he was still unable to make abolition a govern-

[69] *Parliamentary History*, XXVIII, 311-315.

[70] R. I. and S. Wilberforce, *Life of Wilberforce*, I, 265 ff. ''Mr. Wilberforce and Mr. Babington,'' writes a friend from Yoxall Lodge, ''have never appeared downstairs since we came, except to take a hasty dinner, and for half an hour after we have supped: the Slave Trade now occupies them nine hours daily. Mr. Babington told me last night, that he had 1400 folio pages to read, to detect the contradictions, and to collect the answers which corroborate Mr. W's assertions in his speeches: these, with more than 2000 pages to be abridged, must be done within a fortnight. They talk of sitting up one night in each week to accomplish it.'' At different times, Wilberforce, religious as he was, even violated Sunday by working on business in regard to the slave trade. *Ibid.*, I, 282-290.

ment measure. When finally in April, 1791, all was ready for the first big test vote, the signs were by no means favorable. At this stage John Wesley made his last contribution by warning Wilberforce that the fight would be a long and bitter one. Every preparation had been made. Wilberforce's dinners and lunches with statesmen, abolition leaders, and those interested in other humanitarian causes made his life not one round of pleasure but one long season of toil.[71]

The effects that would be produced by the abolition of the slave trade were partly at least a matter of opinion. The abolitionists tried to establish their case so that it would be convincing enough to win the people of the British Isles and, if possible, the planters in the West Indies as well. All of the facts or possibilities presented by the abolitionists, the supporters of the trade denied. The people who would be most adversely affected were the Guinea merchants,[72] and they were able to rally practically the whole body of West Indian planters, whether resident in the islands or in England. This opposition was most formidable. It is only necessary to recall the fact that in 1798 the younger Pitt estimated that the income derived from the West Indies was greater than that from the whole of the rest of the empire including Ireland.[73] Moreover, what was deemed to be a direct attack

[71] R. I. and S. Wilberforce, *op. cit.*, I, 265. Note such entries as these: "7th, Walked about after breakfast with Pitt and Grenville." "17th, Hoare, Samson, Wedgwood, Granville Sharpe, Clarkson, Henry Thornton, and Whitbread dined with me."

[72] The profits made in the slave trade are commonly stated as over thirty per cent. See *ante*, p. 13. Moreover, the London merchant, who made advances to the West India planter, always obtained ample security and handsome profits, even when the planter suffered heavy losses.

[73] G. M. Trevelyan, *British History in the Nineteenth Century*, p. 88. The statement reads, "Pitt, in proposing the income tax of 1798, calculated that, of the incomes enjoyed in Great Britain, those derived from the West Indies

on one species of property was bound to rouse much symthy in other commercial men. Once let it be established, so ran the argument, that the British legislature could annihilate property by vote, and no property would be safe. When the time for the battle of 1791 arrived, a friend wrote Wilberforce: "From the complexion of yesterday it appears to me that you will not make effectual progress this year. The moment they bring a single man to your bar they arrest you completely for this session. Immediate abolition will not go down in our House, and gradual will be stifled in the other."[74]

The arguments of the three great leaders were directed toward the same goal. The principal point Wilberforce made was that in several islands the natural increase of the negro population was already sufficient to keep up the slave population.[75] Pitt directed his efforts to proving the same point, using Jamaica as an example. Fox compared the argument that if England withdrew from the trade other nations would take it up, to that of a robber who robs to keep others from robbing, as others will rob anyway, and perhaps more cruelly.[76]

The result of the battle on the motion of April, 1791, was a defeat by a vote of 163 to 88, in the words of Wilberforce: "Tuesday, 19th Resumed debate and badly beat."[77] As before, talent and oratory were in the minority; silent effective votes in the majority. Striking passages abound in the speeches. "But on every view," said Wilberforce, "it becomes Great Britain to be forward in the work. One-half of this guilty commerce has

very much surpassed those derived from Ireland and from all the rest of the world outside the British Isles."

[74] R. I. and S. Wilberforce, *Life of Wilberforce*, I, 294-295.

[75] *Parliamentary History*, XXIX, 250-262.

[76] *Ibid.*, 335 ff., 354 ff.

[77] R. I. and S. Wilberforce, *Life of Wilberforce*, I, 298; *Parliamentary History*, XXIX, 459.

been conducted by her subjects, and as we have been great in crime let us be early in repentance. There will be a day of retribution wherein we shall have to give account of all the talents, faculties, and opportunities which have been intrusted to us. Let it not appear that our superior power has been employed to oppress our fellow-creatures, and our superior light to darken the creation of our God.''[78]

The heroic efforts of the great debaters, then, were as unavailing in 1791 as they had been two years before. No convincing arguments were made by the opposition, but it was plain that the majority of the members of the house had decided in favor of the trade. The property rights of the Guinea merchant and the West Indian planter were not to be overridden even at the request of the prime minister and the orators of the Whig opposition. One of the majority put the case clearly for his side. ''The leaders, it is true,'' he said, ''are for Abolition. But the minor orators, the dwarfs, the pygmies, will, I trust, this day carry the question against them. The property of the West Indians is at stake; and though men may be generous with their own property, they should not be so with the property of others.''[79]

[78] R. I. and S. Wilberforce, *Life of Wilberforce*, I, 299.

[79] *Parliamentary History*, XXVIII, 311-315, 711-714; XXIX, 250-359. The general effect of the French Revolution on English life is stated in R. I. and S. Wilberforce, *Life of Wilberforce*, I, 261. ''When I entered life,'' Mr. Wilberforce wrote, ''it is astonishing how general was the disposition to seize upon church property. I mixed with very various circles, and I could hardly go into any company where there was not a clergyman present without hearing some such measure proposed. I am convinced that if the public feeling had not been altered by our seeing how soon every other kind of plunder followed the destruction of tithes in France, our clergy would by this time have lost their property.'' The comment made by Horace Walpole on this vote is interesting: ''The abolition of the slave trade has been rejected by the House of Commons, though Mr. Pitt and Mr. Fox united earnestly to carry it: but commerce chinked its purse, and the sound is generally prevalent with the majority; and humanity's tears,

In Santo Domingo a revolution had already broken out which was marked by horrible reprisals of the blacks againsts the whites. The abolitionists held that the condition in Santo Domingo was one of the best arguments against new importations of unruly blacks, while their opponents maintained that the destruction of the trade would lead to revolt, as the negroes would feel that they had no chance of being relieved of their heavy burdens by new arrivals.

The year 1792 opened with promise. Until the large adverse vote Wilberforce had frowned upon the plan of the London committee to organize committees of correspondence similar to those of the American Revolution, and thus to bring the utmost pressure upon the members of the House of Commons by means of aroused public opinion. Now he changed his tactics on the ground that plans to stir up the country were justified "by that vote of the House of Commons on the Slave Trade question, which proved above all things the extremely low ebb of real principle there."[80] He urged Clarkson and Dr. Dickson to tour the counties, spreading copies of an *Abstract of the Evidence* given before the Commons and *The substance of the late Debate*.[81] He was incessant in urging his helpers on: "I wish you and all other county labourers to consider yourselves not as having concluded, but as only beginning your work: it is on the general impression and feeling of the nation we must rely, rather than on the political conscience of the House of Commons. So let the flame be fanned continually, and may it please

and eloquences figures and arguments had no more effect than on those patrons of liberty, the National Assembly in France; who, while they proclaim the rights of men, did not choose to admit the sable moiety of mankind to a participation of those benefits." Letter to Miss Mary Berry, 1791, in Walpole's *Letters* (Toynbee edition, Oxford, 1903), XIV, 418.

[80] R. I. and S. Wilberforce, *Life of Wilberforce*, I, 334.

[81] *Ibid.*, I, 300.

God, in whose hands are the hearts of all men, to bless
our endeavours.'"[82] To a supporter in his own county,
Yorkshire, he wrote: "You can judge how far a respectable county meeting could be convened for the purpose
of petitioning parliament for the Abolition. Were Yorkshire but to open the path, other counties I am persuaded
would crowd in after it, and gladly follow in its train.
Pray turn this over in your mind, and remember only
there is little room for delay.'"[83]

Instructions, advice, encouragement, flew in all directions. Now it was a hint how to approach a powerful
member of the nobility and get his support, or again,
how to win an influential person or at least to persuade
him to remain neutral. Political as well as moral reasons
were to be used. "The terms of your petition ought to be
such as to allow of a man's signing it who rather recoils
from the idea of immediate Abolition. It might not be
amiss if you could, some way or other, make the proposal
of moving or seconding to Ryder through a respectable
channel in the county, as well as through a private
friend; (though I really believe *he* will be found ready to
respond to the chord of friendship); but if his father
were to see reason to believe, that his coming forward
would be likely to attach him Wedgwood, and all the
Abolitionists in Staffordshire, it might operate wonderfully. I will endeavor to stave off the day of discussion
till the middle of March, by way of giving time for the
fermenting matter to work. Do not mistake my term
'stave,' I will keep to my day when it is once named.'"[84]

Wilberforce had good reason to hold to his decision,
because the embers of the French Revolution had set the

---

[82] R. I. and S. Wilberforce, *op. cit.*, I, 334.
[83] *Ibid.*, I, 334-335. Pride in his own large county, Yorkshire, was sufficient to cause him to speak of other counties as "countylings."
[84] *Ibid.*, I, 337.

island of Santo Domingo on fire, thus giving a new argument against abolition to the people of England, already badly frightened by the events that were happening in Paris. From the beginning, Edmund Burke, that relentless foe of the Revolution, had warned Englishmen against the dangers of French infection. Without the French Revolution the slave trade might have been abolished before the year 1795, but the West India interest soon saw its opportunity to frighten friends of this reform.

The alarm regarding Santo Domingo struck all the higher classes and included even Pitt.[85] What made matters more serious was that George III now changed sides. Up to this time the feeling of the king had been revealed when he whispered to Wilberforce at the levee, "How go on your black clients, Mr. Wilberforce?"[86] From this time forth all opponents, including members of the cabinet, could count on the support of the persistent king, who for a generation was able to bend any minister to his own purpose.[87]

The situation in April, 1792, then, was characterized by widespread sympathy for abolition on the one hand and by a powerful and growing opposition on the other.[88] Pitt, though he had tried to dissuade Wilberforce, rallied to his friend in the debate and made what is generally regarded as the greatest speech of his career.[89] Fox, Grey, and Windham agreed on the power of the speech, and a

[85] R. I. and S. Wilberforce, *op. cit.*, I, 341. "The insincerity of my heart has been shamefully evinced to me today, when I could hardly bring myself to do my duty and please God at the expense (as I suspect it will turn out) of my cordiality with Pitt, or rather his with me."

[86] *Ibid.*, I, 344.

[87] Lecky, *England in the Eighteenth Century*, VI, 284.

[88] In 1792 a total of 519 petitions were presented. *Parliamentary History*, XXIX, 1055-1058.

[89] *Ibid.*, 1133-1158.

motion for gradual abolition was carried by a vote of 238 to 85. The fatal word "gradual" was overlooked for the time being;[90] after bitter arguments and several divisions, it was interpreted to mean January 1, 1796.[91] When the bill was introduced in the House of Lords, that body decided to hear evidence of their own, and thus postponed any settlement until the ensuing session.[92]

The trade had lost many of its open defenders who resorted to the policy of delay. By an adroit policy of delay, however, the people interested in the trade preserved it for half a generation. The two ablest supporters of the slave trade in the House of Commons were members of the cabinet, Jenkinson and Dundas, who did not defend the slave trade as such, but worked for delay. The former had proposed to render abolition unnecessary by ameliorating the lot of the slaves in the islands; his motion was lost. Dundas had urged the insertion of the word "gradually" in place of "immediately," and this had been adopted. Pitt had endeavored to bridge the gap between the contestants by showing that abolition would not be followed by the disasters which its opponents predicted, because the negro population, under better treatment consequent on fresh labor supplies being cut off, would increase fast enough to supply the demands of labor.[93]

Before another year had passed England and France were engaged in the great duel which lasted for a score of years and postponed most reform movements for over a generation. Interest in the horrors of the "middle pas-

[90] R. I. and S. Wilberforce, *Life of Wilberforce*, I, 345-346.

[91] *Ibid.*, I, 349. The vote was 161 to 121 against the date Jan. 1, 1795, and 151 to 132 in favor of Jan. 1, 1796. The vote for Jan. 1, 1793, was lost by 158 to 109. *Parliamentary History*, XXIX, 1213, 1273, 1292, 1293.

[92] *House of Lords Journals*, XXXIX, 404.

[93] *Parliamentary History*, XXIX, 1158.

sage'' naturally sank when from the other side of the English channel armed Frenchmen were eagerly gazing toward England. The younger Pitt early turned his attention to the possibility of conquering the French West India Islands. Under such circumstances the slave trade flourished.

## CHAPTER IV

## WAR, REACTION, AND THE GROWTH OF THE SLAVE POWER. ABOLITION AS AN INTERNATIONAL QUESTION. THE DESTRUCTION OF SANTO DOMINGO

Three objects were always in the minds of the abolitionists at one and the same time: the destruction of the slave trade, foreign as well as British; the amelioration of slavery in the West Indies; and the civilization of Africa. Attempts to secure the universal abolition of the slave trade by treaty were made as soon as the active organized agitation began in England in 1787. As has been stated above, hostility against it was stirring in France and America as well as in England. During the period of the first crusade in Great Britain, well known Frenchmen were waging a contest in France. In 1788, *Les Amis des Noirs* was organized with Condorcet and La Layette among its members; and within a short time such men as Mirabeau, Brissot, Necker, Sieyès, and the Abbé Grégoire became supporters of abolition. Under such leaders it was not unreasonable to hope that French and English abolition could be attained at the same time. Quite naturally, then, the first thought in England, when the question came to the front as one of political importance, was to ask France to join in the destruction of the traffic. Many Englishmen felt that if England gave up the traffic, it would merely fall into the hands of France, Spain, and Portugal, and thus England would make a sacrifice in behalf of her commercial rivals and possible enemies without in any way stopping the trade.

Pitt gave the matter early attention.[1] In the fall of 1787, Wilberforce was permitted to write to Eden, the British minister at Paris, that Pitt was intensely interested in this question and that success could be attained much more easily if France were to join in a settlement. Early in November Pitt himself wrote Eden to urge France "to discontinue the villainous traffic now carried on in Africa." In December he sent to Eden, who was about to take up the post at Madrid, another message as follows:

"Mr. Wilberforce has communicated to me your last letter respecting the African business. The more I reflect upon it, the more anxious and impatient I am that the business should be brought as speedily as possible to a point; that, if the real difficulties of it can be overcome, it may not suffer from the prejudices and interested objections which will multiply during the discussion. Of course it cannot yet be ripe for any official communication; and when you transmit the memorandum, which I see you were to draw up, I hope it will be quite secret for the present. If you see any chance of success in France, I hope you will lay your ground as soon as possible with a view to Spain also. I am considering what to do in Holland, but the course of business there makes the secrecy, which is necessary at least for a time, more difficult."[2]

The French government expressed its sympathy with the cause,[3] but was unwilling to commit itself lest it surrender its trade in slaves to the British in case British abolition should fail. When Necker came to power in France, Pitt was encouraged to hope for success, because Necker had been a vigorous opponent of the trade, but he

---

[1] Rose, *William Pitt and National Revival*, p. 459.

[2] *Ibid.*, p. 459-460; R. I. and S. Wilberforce, *Life of Wilberforce*, I, 155-157.

[3] Rose, *William Pitt and National Revival*, p. 460.

too refused to do anything. Spain also refused to act, so that the English abolitionists were at the beginning forced to proceed without hope of foreign aid. The most effective argument that could be used by their opponents remained in force.

The first defeat of abolition in 1789 caused the English abolitionists to send Clarkson to France to coöperate with the French party. He was received in a friendly manner and was able to pour the results of his investigations into the ears of his French allies. Even Louis XVI read the essay on the *Impolicy of the Slave Trade*. But the enemies of abolition were as strong in France as in England, and Clarkson found, after he had worked for six months, that nothing had been accomplished and that he was being denounced as a British spy. Civil war in France and in the West Indies soon produced a great reaction in England. Thus matters remained until the outbreak of the war with France early in 1793. The fact must not be lost sight of, however, that the English abolitionists could never rest until the slave trade had been abolished by all nations. They were outraged quite as much by the foreign as by the British slave trade. Consequently, they brought forward the matter of universal abolition on all occasions when there seemed any prospect of success.

The French Revolution affected the question of abolition in a number of different ways, some of which have been mentioned. Strange as it may seem, France helped to delay abolition in England at first because she would not give up the trade. Later when, as a part of her revolutionary legislation, she did abolish it and slavery also, Englishmen were frightened and confirmed in their support of the slave system. Led by Burke, the reactionaries in England stamped as Jacobin all reform movements, including the abolition of the slave traffic. Consequently, such men as Pitt and Fox, as well as Wilberforce, were obliged to spend their time arguing, not that the slave trade was a crime, but rather that its abolition was not a radical French doctrine but a good English one.

Another effect produced was insurrection in the French West Indies, particularly in Santo Domingo, and the speedy destruction of the world's greatest sugar colony. This tragedy meant a startling increase in the prices of sugar and the sudden prosperity of the British sugar islands. However powerful the economic interests defending the slave trade had been, they now became much more powerful. Moreover, with increased prices for sugar went higher prices for slaves and the consequent encouragement and increase of the slave trade. A little later when the British had made themselves masters of the seas and of many of the French, Dutch, and Spanish islands, they found themselves almost the world's sole slave carriers and the masters of most of the sugar producing areas. Under these circumstances the amount of British capital devoted to the maintenance of the slave system was increased and all chances of immediate abolition were destroyed.

The story of the port of Liverpool gives a clear idea of the strength of the interests which were able, aided by the war, to continue the slave trade for twenty years after the first organized assault was made upon it, that is, from 1787 to 1807. Ramsay Muir has told of the magnitude of the slave interests in this one city: "In the eleven years from 1783 to 1793, 878 round trips were made by Liverpool slaving ships. They carried 303,737 slaves from Africa to the West Indies; and sold them for £15,186,850. Deducting agents' commissions and incidental expenses, the total amount remitted to Liverpool came to over twelve millions and a quarter sterling. Not all this, of course, was profit; the cost of the cargoes sent out to Africa as purchase for the slaves has still to be deducted, as well as the cost of the maintenance of the ships. But even after these deductions have been made, the total profits amounted to over thirty per cent; or an average of nearly £300,000 *per annum* during the whole period under consideration."[4]

These were the profits of but one leg of the journey. In the West Indies the holds of the vessels were loaded with sugar, coffee, rum, tobacco, and other products which yielded huge profits. Lastly, there were the profits made out of the trip from Liverpool to Africa, where the cheapest commodities of the most inferior grades were exchanged for slaves at enormous profits, and that completed the immense triangle of gains.

An interesting question in connection with the abolition of the slave trade early in the next century is, whether or not the war made the commerce of the port of Liverpool less and less, in percentage at least, a slave trade commerce, so that the people of the city as a whole were more ready to give it up.

In 1792, the tonnage of the Liverpool ships engaged in the African trade was about one-twelfth of the whole tonnage which entered the port, while in 1807 the African tonnage formed approximately a twenty-fourth part of the total.[5] The steady commercial growth of the city is seen in its swelling tonnage of 112,000 in 1780; 224,000 in 1796; 611,190 in 1811; 1,225,313 in 1827.[6] Despite the

---

[4] Ramsay Muir, *A History of Liverpool*, p. 193. On page 184 Muir says, "By the middle of the eighteenth century Liverpool was fairly launched upon this iniquitous traffic, the most lucrative the world has ever seen."

[5] Gomer Williams, *History of Liverpool Privateers and . . . an Account of the Liverpool Slave Trade*, pp. 614, 620-622, 678. Ramsay Muir has a good sketch of John Newton, pp. 199-201, and a picture and sketch of Hugh Crow, the last slave trade captain to sail from Liverpool before the abolition became effective in 1807, pp. 201-202.

[6] *Ibid.*, p. 622.

fact that the abolition of the slave trade produced a slight setback, a city with such commercial momentum quickly recovered from the loss of a relatively small part of its expanding commerce.

The slave insurrection in the French islands is very important in the anti-slavery struggle. The inhabitants of the French West Indies watched anxiously the transformation of society in France. Insurrection in the islands soon followed and, as a result, Santo Domingo was lost to France. It soon became apparent that the slaves might take matters into their own hands, declare themselves free, and thus settle the whole negro problem. The excitement of the revolution in France naturally spread with great rapidity to the islands. First, it aroused the interest of white planters, both those resident in France and those in the islands; then it reached the mulattoes of both regions; and finally, it inflamed the negroes, particularly those in Santo Domingo. The upheaval resulted, in the end, in the destruction of the French-organized economic life of the island, the eradication of all the white population, and such scenes of bloodshed as the world has seldom seen. Undoubtedly the planters made a mistake by asking for a representation in the national assembly of France, because by so doing they raised the question of who should vote in the islands, brought on a struggle with the mulattoes, and caused the different assemblies of France to pursue a course which meant disaster for all concerned, including the slaves themselves, even though they were eventually freed.[7] In short, by the end of the year 1791, the most flourishing French colony was a wreck.

[7] The transfer of Dundas to the War Office in 1794 gave the conduct of military operations and the handling of colonial problems to the chief enemy of abolition. J. W. Fortescue, *History of the British Army*, IV, part I, 71-72. Rose, *William Pitt and the Great War*, pp. 219-249. T. Lothrop Stoddard,

The French changed their position on the colonies so often, and so mismanaged even the emancipation of the slaves that with them all was quickly lost. When blow on blow was struck against the lives and properties of the white inhabitants of Santo Domingo by the assemblies of France, and when the governments of France sent out commissioners who used the blacks against the whites, all bonds of sympathy with the home land were loosened, and in desperation the white inhabitants appealed for protection to the rulers of Jamaica and even to Pitt himself. When war was declared early in 1793, the prospect of capturing the rich French islands appealed to Pitt and he decided to seize and hold them as a just compensation for England's efforts in the war.

In 1789 the population of French Santo Domingo was estimated at 40,000 whites, 60,000 mulattoes, and about 500,000 negro slaves. Its exports of sugar, coffee, and cotton were valued at over £7,500,000, or more by a third than those of all the British West Indies combined. A great Gibraltar-like fortress, Mole St. Nicholas, stood sentinel over this part of the West Indies and cities such as Port-au-Prince and Cap Français were rivals of Spanish Havana and the pride of the mother country.[8] The destruction of such a valuable possession was an almost unheard of catastrophe and the British were welcomed by a large part of the whites as saviours of their lives and fortunes. Under such conditions the Mole St. Nicholas fell without a blow. Reinforcements were sent from England late in 1793 under Sir John Jervis and Sir

The French Revolution in San Domingo, passim. In his speech of 1792 Pitt brought out the fact that most insurrections were caused by negroes recently from Africa. Abolition of the slave trade would cut off the supply of the most dangerous negroes and make the lot of the slaves better. Several of the leaders of the revolt in Santo Domingo were from Africa.

[8] For this and following, see Rose, Pitt and the Great War, pp. 219-249; J. W. Fortescue, History of the British Army, IV, part I, 327-328.

Charles Grey. These took Martinique, St. Lucia, Guadeloupe, Marie Galante, and the Saintes. In June, 1794, a detachment from Mole St. Nicholas captured Port-au-Prince with rich spoils of cannon, ships, and cargoes. Other places had been captured earlier, so that by the autumn of 1794 the British were in possession of all of the French islands except Guadeloupe, which the French had recaptured. Disease and slave insurrections, however, quickly thinned the garrisons, and while there was booty at first, holding the islands soon became a very expensive business. The Spanish part of Santo Domingo served as a retreat for all opponents.[9] Other forces were sent out under Abercromby. War with Spain was not declared until October, 1796, but the effect was soon seen in Santo Domingo, where the British were forced to withdraw into Mole St. Nicholas. On January 1, 1798, the British forces evacuated the island without difficulty by making an agreement with the negro chief, Toussaint. They then sailed away leaving him in possession. Neither the British nor the French were ever able to recover Santo Domingo. The island became the home of two negro republics. Some of the other French islands were held by the British, however, and Trinidad was captured from the Spaniards.[10]

In defence of Pitt's decision to conquer the French West Indies it may be said that not only would Britain be able to recoup herself for her sacrifices in the war, but she hoped to prevent the insurrection and chaos of the

[9] J. W. Fortescue, *History of the British Army*, IV, part I, *passim*. It should be noted that the British were never in full possession of the French part of the island. There was the greatest internal confusion among French whites, mulattoes, negroes, and the English.

[10] *Ibid.*, IV, part I, 545-565; Rose, *William Pitt and the Great War*, pp. 219-249, *passim*. Fortescue, IV, *passim*, gives an excellent account of the situation in the West Indies and the loss of the British army. The work is much more than a military account.

French islands from spreading to her own. There was some real danger that the English islands would follow the French to destruction. To conquer and hold these French islands, then, would be to save the richest part of the British empire and enlarge it at the same time. Pitt hoped that a wise policy of checking the importation of savages from the Congo would make the British islands easier to hold and that a definite amelioration in the lot of the slaves would make them more loyal. All students of the subject agree that the failure of this policy caused great losses to Great Britain, in that it made France the friend of the slaves and later freedmen, and necessitated large British forces in the West Indies where the troops speedily fell victims to tropical diseases.

The losses of the British troops were frightful and Fortescue shows that the disasters of these expeditions so damaged the British army that it was not rebuilt until the time of Wellington. The influence of the slave trade in causing this loss is stated by Rose as follows: "The lapse of the question of abolition in the years 1795-6 was a public misfortune; for the slaves, despairing of justice from England, turned to France. For the good of the cause they murdered men, women or children, with equal indifference; and when hunted down, died with the cry *Vive la République*. Here was our chief difficulty in the West Indies. Owing to the refusal of Parliament to limit the supply of slaves or to alleviate their condition, we had to deal with myriads of blacks, exasperated by their former hardships, hoping everything from France, and able to support climatic changes which dealt havoc to the raw English levies. In truth, the success of the West Indian expeditions depended on other factors besides military and medical skill. It turned on political and humanitarian motives that were scouted at Westminster. The French Jacobins stole many a march on the

English governing classes; and in declaring the negro to be the equal of the white man they nearly wrecked Britain's possessions in the West Indies."[11]

The efforts of the English abolitionists were by no means confined to securing the legal outlawry of the slave trade. Pending abolition, it was thought imperative to pass an act proportioning according to the tonnage the number of captives that could be crowded on a vessel. In 1788, Sir William Dolben brought in such a bill for increasing the comfort of the slaves in British ships.[12] This measure was strenuously opposed, but Pitt was determined to carry it, and declared that if the trade could not be regulated, he would vote for its abolition as "shocking to humanity, abominable to be carried on by any country, and which reflected the greatest dishonour on the British Senate and the British nation." He added that the measure should become operative from that day, June 10th.[13] In the House of Lords, Pitt was opposed on this measure by some of the members of his own cabinet, which drew from him the statement that if the bill failed he and they would not remain in the same cabinet. After great effort on the part of the supporters of the bill, it passed by a majority of two votes. Pitt was so moved that he forced the king to keep parliament in session until the bill became a law.[14]

Another achievement was the organization of the Sierra Leone Company to carry on lawful commerce with Africa and to develop the civilization of that continent, as well as to find a refuge for the slaves freed by judicial decisions in Great Britain in 1772 and 1778 and for the slaves carried off during the American Revolution and

---

[11] Rose, *William Pitt and the Great War*, p. 238.
[12] *Parliamentary History*, XXVII, 573 ff.
[13] *Ibid.*, 598.
[14] *Ibid.*, 638-649; J. Holland Rose, *Pitt and National Revival*, p. 462.

landed in Nova Scotia and elsewhere. Defeáted on the
slave trade issue in 1791, the men turned to this problem
under the leadership of Henry Thornton, a member of
the Evangelical party, a humanitarian leader, and one
of the substantial bankers of England.[15] Thornton's
great variety of philanthropic interests illustrates the
typical activities of the "Clapham Sect"[16] of which he
was an influential member. His father, John Thornton,
regularly gave away £2,000 or £3,000 every year, supporting the first generation of Evangelicals, buying advow-
sons in order to appoint deserving clergymen to the liv-
ings, and circulating Bibles and religious books all over
the world. At the time when Cowper was mentally sick,
Thornton doubled his annuity of £200; in return Cowper
described his benefactor in *Charity*. The son inherited his
father's devotion to philanthropy. Until his marriage in
1796 he gave away six-sevenths of his annual profits of
about £10,000 per year; and thereafter he donated one-
third. He spent £20,000 in paying a debt of honor, although not legally bound to do so; he paid a graduated
income tax though not required to do so by law; gave
£600 to Hannah More for schools, and supported other
schools as well.

Thornton was connected with Wilberforce by the marriage of near relatives and when he bought a home at
Battersea Rise upon Clapham Common, Wilberforce

15 R. I. and S. Wilberforce, *Life of Wilberforce*, I, 305-308. A colony
had been established at Sierra Leone in 1787; in 1789 the settlement was
temporarily destroyed. When the Sierra Leone Company was formed the
colony was reorganized. In 1792, John Clarkson, brother of Thomas Clarkson, arrived with one thousand freedmen from Nova Scotia.

16 For a discussion of the "Clapham Sect" see Sir James Stephen,
*Essays in Ecclesiastical Biography*. This name was applied to the small
group of wealthy and powerful Evangelicals who clustered around Wilberforce at Clapham. They have been described as, "Sober, self-complacent
and narrow-minded . . . full of a sincere zeal for good causes." Ramsay
Muir, *A Short History of the British Commonwealth*, II, 221.

shared in the establishment until his own marriage in 1797. The library of this house was the meeting place for the "Clapham Sect," the centre of many activities. Thornton, as chairman of the Sierra Leone Company, formed the company, secured the capital, drew up the constitution, selected the governor, sent out the settlers, and transferred the colony to the government in 1807. This difficult project consumed the capital of £240,000. Thornton lost £2,000 or £3,000 but held he was a gainer in other ways. He was first treasurer of the Society of Missions to Africa and the East, organized in 1799, which soon became the Church Missionary Society. He was also first treasurer of the British and Foreign Bible Society.[17]

When men of such character and business ability as Thornton devoted themselves to proving that slavery was not only cruel but contrary to the teachings of Christianity, the turtle dinners given by the West Indian planters and the votes from the rotten boroughs bought by their funds must in the end prove useless. Not only did the founding of Sierra Leone absorb much of the time of these men, but it brought actively into the contest a man who ranks with Wilberforce as a supporter of the negro race, Zachary Macaulay, the father of Thomas Babington Macaulay, the historian.

Macaulay, who had been an overseer in Jamaica, became disgusted with slavery and returned to England. He was chosen as a man well fitted to aid in the establishment of the new Sierra Leone settlement in Africa. This was plundered by a French fleet in 1794, while he was governor. He gained first-hand knowledge of the slave trade by crossing the Atlantic on a slaver.

With revolution, reaction, and insurrection raging, and

[17] *Dictionary of National Biography*, article on Henry Thornton.

with Pitt determined to make good English losses by conquests in the Caribbean, Wilberforce was able to keep the subject of abolition alive in parliament after 1792. But the next ten years were a time of great discouragement. Public agitation was practically out of the question. The London Abolition Society ceased to have any influence and seldom met. Clarkson, on account of illness, had to retire from the conflict, and such new recruits as James Stephen, Zachary Macaulay, and Henry Brougham were only beginning their work. The important thing was to keep the matter alive, and this the abolitionists were able to do. They hoped to gain a decisive victory by securing universal abolition when peace was made with France. As it turned out, however, they were able to achieve their end by a change in political and economic conditions which divided the West Indian leaders and paved the way for abolition. As early as 1794, some of the opponents of abolition were alarmed at a slave trade, which was building up the former French islands as rivals of the old English islands and threatening the price of sugar by permanently admitting these newly conquered islands within the British tariff wall. They realized that the products of the two countries would be competitors in the English market and that this competition would endanger the prosperity of the older possessions. When this danger was fully perceived and Fox came into office, the slave trade was doomed.

Various unsuccessful efforts to secure action by parliament were made in 1793.[18] Wilberforce proposed a

---

[18] The negro question had supporters and opponents in both parties. When Pitt reconstructed his cabinet by taking in some of the Whigs he had to make concessions on the slave trade. G. M. Trevelyan, *Lord Grey of the Reform Bill*, p. 55. Wilberforce moved the further consideration of the abolition of the slave trade but this was lost by 61 to 53 votes. *Parliamentary History*, L, 514.

measure to keep British slave traders from supplying foreigners with slaves, but it failed.[19] The situation in the House of Lords was, in fact, quite hopeless. Led by members of the royal family and several members of the cabinet, the opposition to any worth-while measure was overwhelming. In 1794 Wilberforce got through the Commons his bill to stop the supply of slaves to foreigners, but it was thrown out in the Lords.[20] For several years after 1792, owing to the war and to the activity of enemy cruisers, the slave trade fell off,[21] but when British maritime supremacy was reëstablished the traffic revived. Not only did the war make discussion of abolition more difficult, but the friendship of Pitt and Wilberforce was threatened by their disagreement about the necessity of war.[22] The former went into the war thinking that a stable peace could be secured after some easy victories. The latter felt that the entrance of Great Britain into the war was unnecessary and that greater efforts should have been made to remain out of it, particularly by assuring the French that the British had no intention of meddling in the internal affairs of their country. Wil-

---

[19] R. I. and S. Wilberforce, *Life of Wilberforce*, II, 23.

[20] Rose, *William Pitt and National Revival*, p. 474.

[21] Pitt stated that "Since this trade had actually ceased of itself on account of the war, the motion was but to prevent its revival." *Parliamentary History*, XXX, 1443-1444. The bill passed the Commons on the second reading by a vote of 56 to 38, but was lost in the Lords by a vote of 43 to 4. *Ibid.*, XXXI, 469-470.

[22] The war destroyed the possibility of appealing to public opinion. Nearly all the most ardent French sympathizers were in favor of the abolition of the traffic. One man wrote that "I do not imagine that we could meet with twenty persons in Hull at present who would sign a petition, that are not republicans. People connect democratical principles with the Abolition of the Slave Trade, and will not hear it mentioned. This is, I hear, precisely the case in Norfolk." R. I. and S. Wilberforce, *Life of Wilberforce*, II, 18. The London Society for the abolition of the slave trade became almost useless. It seldom met in 1794, twice a year in 1795, 1796 and 1797, and then not at all until May, 1804. *Ibid.*, II, 19.

berforce, too, having a less optimistic temperament, felt that the longer the war was continued the greater would be the victories, but that they would be French victories. In 1795, Wilberforce endeavored to obtain a law to carry into effect Dundas's amendment of 1792, namely, that abolition should become effective on January 1, 1796. Dundas, however, now came forward with another amendment, providing that gradual abolition should take place sometime after the conclusion of peace, and, despite the opposition of Pitt and Wilberforce, he carried the day by a vote of seventy-eight to sixty-one.[23] In the debate Wilberforce admitted that the West Indies were in a dangerous state, but ascribed this situation to the fact that 100,000 negroes had been imported since 1792, thus greatly increasing the inequality between the whites and blacks.[24] He criticized the Lords who, in three years, had devoted only fourteen days to the examination of this most important subject.[25] Fox and Pitt warmly supported him. Pitt argued that it was "incumbent upon a British legislature to show, by its conduct, the contrast between the wild, spurious, and imaginary tenets of the 'Rights of Man,' and the genuine principles of practical justice and rational liberty. It was incumbent upon the house to take the speediest measures to heal the wounds which humanity has suffered from the prosecution of the slave trade, and thereby to disarm the Jacobins of their most dangerous engine of attack, and provide for the country the surest and most effectual means of safety."[26]

The next year, 1796, things looked more promising; a bill was carried in the Commons only to be lost by four votes on the third reading.[27] Wilberforce noted with a sad heart that enough of his supporters were present at

[23] *Parliamentary History,* XXXI, 1345.
[24] *Ibid.,* 1323 ff.    [25] *Ibid.,* 1331-1332.    [26] *Ibid.,* 1342 ff.
[27] *Ibid.,* XXXII, 737-763, 862-902.

the opera to have carried the bill.[28] If Pitt had not given up hope of carrying the measure after the defeat in 1792, he certainly lost all hope after 1796. The coming of peace and with it a new order of things was at this time the only hope for the success of any reform movement.

The session of 1797 was naturally indifferent to the measure because the war was going badly, distress stalked through the land, allies were falling away, mutiny in the fleet was rife, and a financial panic was raging. At this stage, by means of an address to the crown, the proposal was made that the governors of the colonies should urge the colonial assemblies to improve the lot of the slaves by reform measures so that the slave trade would no longer be necessary to keep up the supply. This measure Pitt urged Wilberforce to accept, but on the latter's refusal Pitt as usual argued on the abolition side; the measure was carried by a majority of over thirty votes.[29] About this time, too, Windham changed sides and became an enemy of abolition, and Bryan Edwards, the historian of the British West Indies, entered parliament and further strengthened the slave trade forces.[30]

The possibility of peace with France in 1797 offered an opportunity to try to come to an agreement with that country on the slave trade, but Pitt for some reason did not introduce the subject. James Stephen, one of the ablest abolitionists, felt there might be a reversal of ac-

[28] R. I. and S. Wilberforce, *Life of Wilberforce*, II, 142. *Parliamentary History*, XXXIII, 251-294. The vote was 74 to 70.

[29] *House of Commons Journal*, LII, 461; R. I. and S. Wilberforce, *Life of Wilberforce*, II, 196. Wilberforce's entry is: ''Discussed about Ellis's motion, till very late—much hurt—Pitt wanted me to close with it modified, but when I would not, stood stiffly by me.''

[30] R. I. and S. Wilberforce, *Life of Wilberforce*, II, 196, 277. *Parliamentary History*, XXXIII, 569-576, 1410 ff. The open support of Canning appeared in May, 1797, and the open hostility of Windham first appeared in April, 1798.

tion in France whose slaves, having been emancipated, were in danger of being reënslaved.[31] Naturally Wilberforce exerted himself to get the negro question taken up, and wrote Pitt as follows: "I must honestly say, I never was so much hurt since I knew you as at your not receiving and encouraging this proposal, which even Lord Liverpool himself ought to have approved on the ground on which he used to oppose. Do, my dear Pitt, I entreat you reconsider the matter, I am persuaded of your zeal in this cause, when, amidst the multitude of matters which force themselves on you more pressingly, it can obtain a hearing; but I regret that you have so been drawn off from it."[32]

During the years 1798 and 1799 some constructive action was taken by those interested in the West Indies to relieve the slave trade and slavery of some of its worst features. The address requesting the colonial legislatures to ameliorate the lot of slaves was one such measure. An act of George II, which authorized the sale of slaves at the suit of their master's creditors, was repealed, and an act was passed securing a greater height between the decks of slave ships, and giving bounties to masters and surgeons if losses on the voyage from Africa were small.[33] In this same year, 1799, another effort was made by Wilberforce to get action in the House of Commons. He was ably supported by a new recruit, George Canning, who called attention to the fact that, under the resolution of 1797, the legislatures of the colonies had done nothing worth while and prophesied that they would do nothing. He attacked the trade not only by straight argument but by means of biting irony. Despite

31 R. I. and S. Wilberforce, *Life of Wilberforce*, II, 224.

32 Letter is in Rose, *William Pitt and National Revival*, p. 476.

33 28 George III, c. 54. Compare with 29 George III, c. 66; 38 George III, c. 88.

this effort the motion was lost by a vote of eighty-two to seventy-four.[34]

When Wilberforce and Canning failed again to secure abolition, Henry Thornton made an attempt to get the slave trade restricted to certain parts of Africa because the very existence of the Sierra Leone settlement was constantly threatened by slave raiders. This bill passed the Commons by small majorities in very thin houses. When introduced into the Lords, it was defeated by a vote of sixty-eight to sixty-one, despite the vigorous support given it there by Dr. Horsley, Bishop of Rochester,[35] who denounced all those who would pretend that the slave trade had Scriptural sanction.

Pitt's hope and enthusiasm in the cause were gone. He continued to speak in its favor, but many of his best friends doubted his zeal.[36] A long letter to Pitt from George Canning, a friend of abolition, shows how widespread the distrust of the prime minister was in December, 1799. Canning through the Ellises was in touch with moderate West Indian opinion.[37] The question at issue was whether or not by means of an order in Council the slave trade was to be prohibited to the newly conquered islands. Pitt was so slow in acting that the Ellises and other West Indians decided that he had no intention of doing anything against any part of the slave trade. Pitt resigned before anything was done.

[34] *Parliamentary History*, XXXIV, 518 ff.; Clarkson, *History of the Abolition of the Slave Trade*, pp. 559-560.

[35] *Parliamentary History* XXXIV, 1118-1138; XXXVIII, 1139. Clarkson, *History of the Abolition of the Slave Trade*, pp. 561-562. The latter gives, p. 563, contents, 25; not contents, 32; proxies on each side, 36.

[36] R. I. and S. Wilberforce, *Life of Wilberforce*, II, 225. James Stephen wrote to Wilberforce, "Mr. Pitt unhappily for himself his country and mankind, is not zealous enough in the cause of the negroes, to contend for them as decisively as he ought, in the Cabinet any more than in parliament."

[37] The letter is given in Rose, *Pitt and Napoleon*, pp. 321-324.

From the evidence given above it is clear that the complete abolition of the slave trade was a thing no longer hoped for under the conditions that then obtained. The best evidence of Pitt's sincerity is the fact that neither Wilberforce nor Clarkson ever lost faith in him. The opinion of the latter deserves quotation. After referring to Pitt's early interest and his failure to get France to agree to abolition in 1788, he says: "From this time his efforts were reduced within the boundaries of his own power. As far, however, as he had scope, he exerted them. If we look at him in his parliamentary capacity, it must be acknowledged by all, that he took an active, strenuous, and consistent part, and this year after year, by which he realized his professions. In my own private communications with him, which were frequent, he never failed to give proofs of a similar disposition. I had always free access to him. I had no previous note or letter to write for admission. Whatever papers I wanted, he ordered. He exhibited also in his conversation with me on these occasions marks of a more than ordinary interest in the welfare of the cause. Among the subjects, which were then started, there was one, which was always near his heart. This was the civilization of Africa. He looked upon this great work as a debt due to that continent for the many injuries we have inflicted upon it: and had the abolition succeeded sooner, as in the infancy of his exertions he had hoped, I know he had a plan, suited no doubt to the capaciousness of his own mind, for such establishments in Africa, as he conceived would promote in due meed this important end."[38]

[38] Clarkson, *History of the Abolition of the Slave Trade*, pp. 573-574. But it was during the years 1794 to 1804, when Clarkson had retired because of ill health, that the sincerity of Pitt was most called in question. Also there is the possibility that Clarkson was deceived by the easy access to Pitt and his friendly manner.

The severest indictment of Pitt is that made by Lecky:
"He never, it is true, abandoned the cause; he spoke uni-
formly and eloquently in its favour, but he never would
make it one on which his ministry depended. He suffered
Dundas to take a leading part against the abolition. He
suffered the cause to be defeated year after year by men
who would have never dared to risk his serious displeasure, and he at the same time exerted all his influence with
the abolitionists to induce them to abstain from pressing
the question.

"This, however, was not all. From the beginning of the
war, the complete naval ascendancy of England almost
annihilated the slave trade to the French and Dutch colonies, and when these colonies passed into the possession
of England the momentous question arose whether the
trade which had so long been suspended should be suffered to revive. It was in the power of Pitt by an Order
of Council to prevent it, but he refused to take this
course. It was a political and commercial object to
strengthen these new acquisitions, and as they had so
long been prevented from supplying themselves with
negroes they were ready to take more than usual. The
result was that, in consequence of the British conquests
and under the shelter of the British flag, the slave trade
became more active than ever. Wilberforce declared, in
January 1802, that it had been 'carried, especially of late
years, to a greater extent than at any former period of
our history.' English capital flowed largely into it. It
was computed that under his administration the English
slave trade more than doubled, and that the number of
negroes imported annually in English ships rose from
25,000 to 57,000.'"[39]

Pitt's honesty is supported by J. Holland Rose, who

[39] Lecky, *England in the Eighteenth Century*, V, 64-66.

practically agrees with Clarkson that the many forms of
opposition made it impossible in such an era of strain
and stress for the prime minister to succeed in any part
of his reform policy. Possibly even the issuance of an
order in Council, so eloquently pleaded for by Canning
and Wilberforce, was beyond the power of the minister.[40]

[40] Rose, *William Pitt and National Revival*, pp. 477-479. The *Minutes* of
the West India Committee of Planters and Merchants, such as those for the
years 1787-1807, outline the various activities of this body. The defence of
the slave trade against the abolitionists was but one item. The protection
of cargoes of merchandise in the harbors of Great Britain by means of a
special police and on the high seas by naval convoys were especially urgent
matters. Problems of a sugar scarcity or a ruinous surplus were constant.
A levy on West Indian produce, varying from one pence to twelve pence per
cask of sugar and proportional amounts on other crops, was made for the
protection of the large interests involved.

# CHAPTER V

## THE ABOLITION OF THE BRITISH SLAVE TRADE

The opening of the new century found enthusiasm for the cause of abolition at a low ebb. Instead of being abolished, the trade was being carried on more vigorously than ever before. Where formerly the British carried in their ships something like half of the negroes, they now had driven their competitors off the seas and transported nearly all of the African levies. Wilberforce's call to his countrymen to be earliest in repentence as they had been greatest in crime was answered merely by their becoming still greater in crime.

This was, however, but the darkness before the dawn. Several changes were taking place which would eventually make the abolition of the traffic much easier. The Act of Union with Ireland, while it failed to give Roman Catholic Emancipation to the Irish and thus intensified the Irish problem, had brought one hundred new representatives into the British parliament. These new members could generally be counted on to vote for the abolition of the slave trade, because they had neither a traditional nor an economic interest in it; besides, having problems of their own to bring before parliament, they tended to ally themselves with the English reformers.[1]

Among the supporters of the slave trade itself certain economic changes were making new currents of thought. For one thing, the trade had had a fifteen year lease of

[1] David Macpherson, *Annals of Commerce*, IV, 141, 154.

life and certainly every planter who needed to stock up with labor was having ample time to do so. Moreover, the planters were divided by the old question of the return of the islands to the French and Dutch rivals, which Canning discussed in his letter to Pitt. Even if the conquered islands were to remain British, they would still be the rivals of the old islands in the English and European market.[2] The question arose among them as to whether the slave trade was or was not carried on primarily for the benefit of their future rivals. Were not the planters of the old British Islands merely championing a trade for the benefit of their new competitors? This division in West Indian opinion appeared at least as early as 1794, when the bill for the abolition of the foreign slave trade was supported by Vaughan and Barham, who called upon their fellows to support a humane bill which was in no way adverse to their interests.[3]

In the new century the abolition movement was also aided by the restoration of settled government in France. The Jacobin terror which had lasted from 1793 to 1799 could not maintain its full intensity when Napoleon Bonaparte became first consul and a few years later assumed the title of emperor. For a new French monarchy had replaced the old, although based on quite a different social order. The French were now so far removed from dangerous Jacobin principles that they were soon ready to revive both the slave trade and slavery.

Much time was spent in fruitless negotiations with the West Indians. The year 1800 was largely consumed in an effort to bring about the suspension of the slave trade for a term of from five to seven years by agreement. But by June 6th, Wilberforce reported the disappointment of

2 *Parliamentary Debates*, II, 461-463.

3 *Parliamentary History*, XXX, 1446, 1447, February 25, 1794; R. I. and S. Wilberforce, *Life of Wilberforce*, II, 49.

his party: "I have suffered great chagrin on the subject of the Slave Trade. Pitt listened too easily to the assurance of several of the principal of the West Indian proprietors, who declared themselves willing to support a suspension for five years, till at length, when we hoped all was going on prosperously, a public meeting of the West Indian body, at which a strong anti-abolition spirit was manifested, shook the resolution of our timid converts, and all, except Sir William Young turned round.''⁴ Pitt promised to issue an order in Council to stop the importation of negroes into the new settlements, into which three-fourths of the slaves were sent. In order to induce the planters to accept this measure, Wilberforce instructed James Stephen, one of the ablest anti-slavery investigators, to obtain the numbers of slaves imported into the new colonies for a number of years past. "It is an argument," he wrote, "to be pressed on those who are unassailable by higher principles, that the British ought not to invest much capital in colonies, which may probably have to be surrendered on the return of peace.''⁵ Before anything could be done, Pitt fell from power and Addington became prime minister. The latter refused to inject the slave trade question into the Amiens peace negotiations with France and refused to prevent the importation of negroes onto the vacant lands of Trinidad.⁶

While the peace of Amiens lasted, attention was at-

⁴ R. I. and S. Wilberforce, *Life of Wilberforce*, II, 368. Letter to the Rev. T. Gisborne, June 6, 1800. Wilberforce stated that negroes had risen in price from £76 to £120 per head. West India Committee of Planters and Merchants, *Minutes*, May 2, 1800.

⁵ R. I. and S. Wilberforce, *Life of Wilberforce*, II, 377-378.

⁶ *Parliamentary History*, XXXVI, 442-445, 854-882; R. I. and S. Wilberforce, *Life of Wilberforce*, II, 369-370; III, 37 ff. Wilberforce estimated, p. 37, that the clearing of the new lands "would take near a million of human beings!" Canning suggested that it would take something like 250,-000 negroes to cultivate Trinidad. *Parliamentary History*, XXXVI, 865.

tracted to Napoleon Bonaparte's attempt to reconquer Santo Domingo. British opinion was largely in his favor.[7] It was at this stage of English history that James Stephen published *The Crisis of the Sugar Colonies,* arguing against the recapture of the island. The government, however, favored the French reconquest, stating that British interest was concerned in the success of the expedition and that "Whatever persons might have thought before they must think this now."[8] British merchants were busily engaged in helping Bonaparte in the reconquest of Santo Domingo. The abolitionists planned to stop this practice,[9] but the renewal of the war with France made any other action unnecessary and also delayed the abolition question for the year 1803.

The prospects for the year 1804 were bright. Selfish economic reasons for abolition were slowly gaining ground among the West Indians themselves, some of whom again approached the abolition leaders with the plan of suspending the slave trade for three or five years.[10] "They have not the assurance," Wilberforce commented, "to pretend to be influenced by any principles of justice, (this is literally true) but merely by a sense of interest. The soil of Demarara, Berbice, and

[7] R. I. and S. Wilberforce, *Life of Wilberforce,* III, 42. Wilberforce notes, March 20, 1802, "News of French fleet's arrival in West Indies. Resisted by Toussaint's order. Massacre of whites in Guadaloupe reported. All people siding with Buonaparte and wishing his arms success over Toussaint's as the only way of preventing Black empire in the West Indies. Stephen's contrary system, I believe, right in the main."

[8] *Ibid.,* III, 47, 48, 50; *Parliamentary History,* XXXVI, 881. The Nova Scotia negroes in Sierra Leone rebelled.

[9] R. I. and S. Wilberforce, *Life of Wilberforce,* III, 85.

[10] *Ibid.,* III, 163, 164. Barham, an able West Indian, said in debate: "at this time the colonists were less disposed to enter on such a trade. Their profits were not one-third of what they used to be, and their temptations to speculation were consequently curtailed. There would besides be less inducement to wish the importation of fresh negroes, when that importation was at best only tolerated." *Parliamentary Debates,* II, 463.

Surinam, is so fertile that an acre will produce as much as three (generally speaking) in our old islands. There is also in them an inexhaustible store of untilled land, fit for sugar. Consequently the proprietors of estates, knowing that the demand for sugar is not even now greater than the supply, are afraid lest they should be in the situation of the owners of an old and deep mine, who are ruined by the discovery of some other where the ore can be obtained almost on the surface.'"[11]

This opportunity was one not to be neglected, and so Wilberforce decided to ask Addington to introduce the matter of suspension, saying in mild sarcasm, he "will be the sober, practical man, in opposition to the wild enthusiasts who are for total Abolition."[12] Wilberforce accordingly wrote, calling his attention to the subject, but the prime minister declined to act. The West Indians, on their part, had miscalculated opinion among themselves, for at a meeting at the London Tavern, on May 17th, the proposal for suspension was rejected in favor of the motion of Lyon, the agent for Jamaica, "that every legal and proper step should be taken to oppose the progress of any Bill which may be brought into parliament either to suspend or abolish the Slave Trade."[13] The fear was that once suspended the trade would be killed forever.[14] There was not the slightest doubt, however, that economic motives had divided the planters, and that numbers of them were in favor of the abolition of the trade.

Great Britain was temporarily at peace with France and the Irish were ready to show their humanity by voting for abolition. An Irish dinner was held, at which thirty-three or thirty-four Irish were present, Wilberforce's health was toasted, and then all of them went and voted for abolition with the result that the first reading

11 R. I. and S. Wilberforce, *Life of Wilberforce*, III, 164.
12 *Ibid.*, III, 165.   13 *Ibid.*, III, 166.   14 *Ibid.*, III, 167.

was carried one hundred and twenty-four to forty-nine.[15]
The large vote was something of a surprise. The change
of position has been summarized: "Its supporters were
now as overwhelming in numbers as they had always
been in argument. From that night the issue of the question was clear."[16]
Congratulations poured in from all sides. The one time
slave trader and leader of the Evangelical party, John
Newton, wrote that though he was within two months of
his eightieth year, the prospect of the accomplishment of
this task "will give me daily satisfaction so long as my
declining faculties are preserved."[17] The leader of the
Utilitarians, Jeremy Bentham, said: "I sympathize with
your now happily promising exertions in behalf of the
race of innocents, whose lot it has hitherto been to be
made the subject matter of depredation for the purpose
of being treated worse than the authors of such crimes
are treated, for those crimes, in other places."[18]

Victory, however, was far from being assured in the
Commons. On the second reading Castlereagh and Windham spoke against the measure, and little was said in its
favor; the victory, however, was one hundred and two to

[15] R. I. and S. Wilberforce, *op. cit.*, III, 168. Before introducing his motion for general abolition Wilberforce had arranged for a meeting between
a West Indian moderate and Pitt in the hope that the trade might be suspended by agreement. The result was failure. "My conversation with Milli-
gan," wrote Pitt, "amounted only to this, that he and other sensible West
Indians wished for the suppression; but the great majority would oppose
it, many from adherence to former opinion, and more from the fear that if
once suspended the Trade could never be revived. In this state, and having
had no time to settle any thing with any part of the Cabinet, I see no use
in moving suspension, . . ." West India Committee of Planters and Merchants, *Minutes*, May 17, 29, and June 5, 1804.

[16] R. I. and S. Wilberforce, *Life of Wilberforce*, III, 169. Date May 30,
1804. Abolition of slave trade passed the Commons in 1792 and 1796. The
Irish by no means remained unanimous in their support.

[17] *Ibid.*, III, 169.

[18] *Ibid.*, III, 170.

forty-four.[19] Meantime preparations were begun for the vote on the third reading. The opponents made an effort to confuse Wilberforce by charging that he had not read the great mass of papers recently presented to the House. He retorted that he always familiarized himself immediately with all of the material available.[20] It was difficult to keep the abolition forces united. Some of the Irish threatened to leave London and had to be urged to remain; others of them had been won over to the other side. Castlereagh remained firm in his opposition, but hinted that the time had come when Dundas ought to support abolition; Pitt was of but little help. The bill, however, passed the third reading by sixty-nine to thirty-three.[21] The session was so far advanced, however, that after conferring with Grenville and Bishop Porteus and the many friends of the measure, it was decided not to attempt to get the approval of the Lords at that time and risk defeat.[22]

Much could be done without complete abolition and the group determined to try again to get the slave trade to the conquered colonies abolished. When Wilberforce saw Pitt, July 3, 1804, he was assured, as he had been several years before, that this trade could and would be stopped by royal proclamation, and, after a consultation with his

[19] *Parliamentary Debates*, II, 543-558. On page 557, the vote is given as 100 to 42. R. I. and S. Wilberforce, *Life of Wilberforce*, III, 174.

[20] *Parliamentary Debates*, II, 544, 545; R. I. and S. Wilberforce, *Life of Wilberforce*, III, 175, 176. Debate of June, 1804.

[21] *Parliamentary Debates*, II, 871; Stanhope, *Life of Pitt* (second edition, 1862), IV, 202. Vote given is 69 to 33 in *Parliamentary Debates;* 99 to 33 in *Life of Wilberforce*, III, 178.

[22] R. I. and S. Wilberforce, *Life of Wilberforce*, III, 180. Pitt had taken the matter up in the cabinet which had voted for delay. It was agreed ''that the subject to be hung up till next year, on the ground that the examination of evidence indispensable.'' Wilberforce was bitterly disappointed: ''I own it quite lowers my spirits to see all my hopes for this year at once blasted, yet *I can't help myself.*'' *Ibid.*, III, 180-181.

chief supporters, he agreed to accept this promise.[23] The matter was delayed for over a year. Wilberforce recorded this observation in reporting to interested friends: "I saw certain significant winks and shrugs, as if I was taken in by Pitt, and was too credulous and soft, etc. . . ."[24] The order was finally issued by the active enemy of abolition, Lord Castlereagh, September 13, 1805. "This is preventing the importation of a vast number of poor creatures," comments Wilberforce, "who would otherwise, as in the last war, have been the victims of our great capitalists."[25] The old British islands were henceforth the sole markets for slaves carried in British ships.

The plan for the campaign that was to lead to complete victory included the writing of several pamphlets or books on the different aspects of the African question to reinform the people of England and members of parliament. Wilberforce planned to tell the African part; Clarkson and Lord Muncaster, author of the *Historical Sketches,* were asked to help him. Stephen was working on the West Indies.[26] The year 1805 brought another defeat in the House of Commons, by a vote of seventy-seven to seventy, which Wilberforce explained as follows: "The Irish members absent, or even turned against us.

[23] R. I. and S. Wilberforce, *op. cit.,* III, 184. Brougham, Grant, Babington, William Smith, Henry Thornton, and Zachary Macaulay were the men present.

[24] *Ibid.,* III, 233.

[25] *Ibid.,* III, 234; Stanhope, *Life of Pitt,* IV, 204. Wilberforce estimated the number of negroes saved in this way at 12,000 or 15,000 per annum and thought that £18,000,000 had been invested in the foreign islands during the war before the peace of Amiens. The long delay in issuing this order in Council might still be explained by West Indian opposition. Better reasons are the slender majority that Pitt had in parliament, which made him reluctant to offend any supporters; the state of his health; and the condition of Europe. His anti-abolitionist colleagues do not seem to have opposed this order.

[26] R. I. and S. Wilberforce, *Life of Wilberforce,* III, 197 ff.

. . . Some Scotch I believe, Who were last year neutral, voted against us. Great canvassing of our enemies, and several of our friends absent through forgetfulness, or accident, or engagements preferred from lukewarmness."[27] Another reason for defeat was that Pitt and Addington had united their political forces and Pitt had to defer to his colleague's well-known opposition to abolition.[28]

But the many long years of hesitation and delay were past. When Fox and Grenville came in as chief ministers, the abolition cause moved rapidly to triumph. Fox had got the Prince of Wales to promise not to oppose abolition and was ready to exert himself in dead earnest to win.[29] A law, replacing the order in Council of the year before, passed both houses without serious trouble. Fox and Grenville felt it impossible to get a bill abolishing the whole trade through the Lords that session, but promised to take it up the next, and in the meantime a general resolution for abolition was to be passed through both houses. In his speech on the resolution, Fox made the oft quoted declaration which is perhaps his most fitting epitaph, "So fully am I impressed with the vast importance and necessity of attaining what will be the object of my motion this night, that if during the almost forty years that I have had the honor of a seat in Parliament, I have been so fortunate as to accomplish that end only, I should think I had done enough and could retire from public life with comfort and the conscious satisfaction that I had done my duty."[30] This resolution declar-

[27] R. I. and S. Wilberforce, *Life of Wilberforce*, III, 212.

[28] *Parliamentary Debates*, III, 641-674.

[29] R. I. and S. Wilberforce, *Life of Wilberforce*, III, 259. The accession of Fox and Grenville to power coincided with the growing opposition to the trade and the increasing division of West Indian opinion.

[30] *The Speeches of Charles James Fox*, VI, 659; *Parliamentary Debates*, VII, 580-581.

ing the slave trade "contrary to the principles of justice, humanity, and sound policy and pledging abolition with all practicable expediency" was duly passed by a vote of one hundred and fourteen to fifteen.[31] Stephen and Wilberforce then suggested a bill to prevent the employment of any new ship in the trade, and this quickly became a law.[32] In other words, the new ministry, while not unanimous in its opposition, was led by men who were ready to proceed to action.

Before anything more could be done Fox died, leaving the bills without his able support. The abolitionists had been disappointed too many times to leave anything to chance. The London committee redoubled its efforts.[33] Evidence was collected to be presented to the Lords if required, and Wilberforce set himself the task of writing an address upon the slave trade to present to the members of parliament, particularly those of the House of Lords, in order "to supply people who wish to come over, with reasons for voting for us."[34] The usual order of procedure was reversed and the bill was introduced in the Lords first, where it was ably managed and fostered by Grenville.[35] Lord St. Vincent, who held with his lost friend, Nelson, that the abolition of the slave trade was a "damned and cursed doctrine, held only by hypocrites," entered his solemn and final protest against this measure of national ruin, and walked out of the house. Nevertheless, it carried by the large vote of one hundred to thirty-six.[36]

31 *Parliamentary Debates*, VII, 603. Vote given in *Debates*, is 114 to 15.

32 46, George III, c. 52.

33 R. I. and S. Wilberforce, *Life of Wilberforce*, III, 271.

34 *Ibid.*, III, 273. The book was finished Jan. 27, 1807, and printed by Jan. 31. *Ibid.*, III, 288.

35 *Ibid.*, III, 293. Wilberforce says no newspaper account of Grenville's speech appeared.

36 *Parliamentary Debates*, VIII, 672, 693; *House of Lords Journals*, XLVI, 55.

As soon as the debate opened in earnest in the Commons, it was apparent that victory was certain. The solicitor-general, Sir Samuel Romilly, brought forth loud cheers by contrasting Napoleon and Wilberforce. "When he looked at the man at the head of the French monarchy," Romilly said, "surrounded as he was with all the pomp of power, and all the pride of victory, distributing kingdoms to his family and principalities to his followers, seeming, when he sat upon his throne to have reached the summit of human ambition and the pinnacle of earthly happiness, and when he followed that man into his closet or to his bed, and considered the pangs with which his solitude must be tortured, and his repose banished, by the recollection of the blood he had spilled, and the oppressions he had committed; and when he compared with those pangs of remorse, the feelings which must accompany his honorable friend [Wilberforce] from that House to his home, after the vote of that night should have confirmed the object of his humane and unceasing labors; when he should retire into the bosom of his happy and delighted family, when he should lay himself down on his bed, reflecting on the innumerable voices that would be raised in every quarter of the world to bless him; how much more pure and permanent felicity must he enjoy, in the consciousness of having preserved so many millions of his fellow-creatures, than the man with whom he had compared him, on the throne to which he had waded through slaughter and oppression!"[37] After the victory of two hundred and eighty-three votes against sixteen, the friends of Wilberforce[38] gathered

[37] *Parliamentary Debates*, VIII, 978-979, 995; *House of Commons Journals*, LXII, 161.

[38] R. I. and S. Wilberforce, *Life of Wilberforce*, III, 298. John Thornton, Heber, Sharp, Macaulay, Grant and Robert Grant, Robert Bird, and William Smith.

around him. " 'Let us make out the names of these sixteen miscreants; I have four of them,' said William
Smith. Mr. Wilberforce . . . looked up hastily from the
note he was writing—'Never mind the miserable 16, let
us think of our glorious 283.' "[39]
The bill after various adventures passed both houses
and received the royal assent as the last act of the government that was going out of office.[40] It was natural for
Wilberforce to express his gratitude in religious phrase-
ology: he says, "How wonderfully the providence of God
has been manifested in the Abolition Bill."[41] Lord Grenville, after the final passing of the bill in the Lords, con-
gratulated that house on having performed "one of the
most glorious acts that had ever been done by any assembly of any nation in the world."[42] But with all of his
unrivalled knowledge of conditions and opinions on both
sides, Wilberforce really does not seem to have been able
to account for the rather sudden triumph of his cause. "I
really cannot account for the fervour," he wrote, "which
happily has taken the place of that fastidious, well-bred
lukewarmness which used to display itself in this subject,
except by supposing it to be produced by that almighty
power which can influence at will the judgment and affections of men."[43]
A long campaign of humanitarianism under able men;
a readjustment of the economic interests of the West
Indians; a growth of industry and commerce so that the
slave trade was of smaller relative importance in the
total commerce of the country, although absolutely

[39] R. I. and S. Wilberforce, *op. cit.*, III, 298; West India Committee,
*Minutes*, Mar. 24, 1807.

[40] 47 George III, Session I, c. 36; *House of Commons Journals*, LXII,
290.

[41] R. I. and S. Wilberforce, *Life of Wilberforce*, III, 304.

[42] *Parliamentary Debates*, IX, 170.

[43] R. I. and S. Wilberforce, *Life of Wilberforce*, III, 304.

greater; the prospect of carrying the commerce on under other flags or illicitly; the example of abolition by other countries; the prospect of gaining universal abolition at the next peace congress; the determination of Fox and Grenville; all these played their part. Without humanitarian leadership, however, there would have been failure.

Indeed, it was most fitting that the British slave trade should have been brought to an end by the coöperation of the three forces which, whenever joined together, made the humanitarian cause triumph. The first was the powerful Evangelical Party led by such men as John Newton, Henry Thornton, James Stephen, Zachary Macaulay, William Cowper, William Wilberforce, and many others. The second force was the reform party not based on religious motives, including such men as Adam Smith, Edmund Burke, Jeremy Bentham, William Pitt, Henry Brougham, and Charles James Fox. The last named statesman, in his life and in his death, showed the wide gulf between him and the Evangelicals. He was a lover of justice and humanity, but drew his main consolation in life out of the ancient authors. Near the end of his life he requested: "Read me the sixth book of Virgil!"[44] The third group was made up of those hard-headed, practical men, who could be appealed to on the ground of "impolicy" from a national point of view and particularly when the "impolicy" was clearly one which affected adversely their own pocketbooks. The fight against the slave system was not over, however; the battle had only just begun.[45]

[44] R. D. O'Leary, "Culture," *The Sewanee Review Quarterly*, XXIII, 13.

[45] The best treatment of the economic motives for abolition is Franz Hochstetter, *Die wirtschaftlichen und politischen Motive für die Abschaffung des britischen Sklavenhandels im Jahre 1806-1807* (Leipzig, 1905).

# CHAPTER VI

## THE STRUGGLE FOR UNIVERSAL ABOLITION OF THE SLAVE TRADE

From 1807 to 1823, every effort was made to secure the general abolition of the slave trade by all the maritime powers and to make the British laws effective so that there would be no illicit trade. By 1823 it had become apparent that none of the three aims of the humanitarian party was being achieved. The slave trade flourished under other flags, the coast of Africa presented all the old scenes, destroying the possibility of civilizing that continent,[1] and the condition of the slaves in the British colonies did not seem to be improved. Accordingly, the abolitionists decided to strike at the root of the evil and begin a campaign against the institution of slavery in the hope that the emancipation of the British slaves would in time be followed by universal emancipation.

For the moment, however, the people of England thought they had secured a great deal in the abolition of their own trade, and it was but natural that a time of rest should follow the exertions of twenty years. Time alone could show what the effects of abolition would be, not only on the prosperity of the country, but also on the condition of the slaves. Only when the abolitionists found that the trade was still being carried on to a great extent were they again aroused.

[1] Wilberforce held that the civilizing of Africa was the most important part of the abolitionist program. See Wilberforce, *Abolition of the Slave Trade, passim.*

At the time the abolition bill was passed, some important men had little faith in the hopes of the abolitionists in regard to the good effects of the suppression of this traffic by parliament. Representatives of this group were Lord Castlereagh and Lord Sidmouth, who had fought the abolition of the trade to the very end on the ground that the abolition act could not be enforced. Their view was that, while much might be done for humanity by regulation, on the coast of Africa, in the "middle passage," and in the West Indies, it was rash beyond measure to prohibit the trade altogether. They believed that the smuggling which must ensue would occasion more misery to the negroes than their race was undergoing at the time.[2]

Others were ready to solve the problem of the enforcement of the abolition act by freeing the slaves in the colonies, and a motion was made for leave to bring in a bill for the gradual emancipation of the slaves in the West Indies. This motion, however, was dropped, as less than forty members were present, a number insufficient for the consideration of any question.[3] Wilberforce was opposed to this motion and declared that such a measure at that time would be injurious to the slaves and ruinous to the colonies. He and his friends were satisfied with what had been gained; their sole aim was the abolition of the slave trade, and not the emancipation of the slaves. These two objects had always been confounded by the enemies of abolition, whereas its friends had always distinguished between them.[4] For several years there was little parliamentary activity. But in 1810, when papers concerning the slave trade were presented to the House of Commons, an address was voted thanking His Majesty for

[2] *Parliamentary Debates*, II, 471, 870; VII, 234, 1144.
[3] *House of Commons Journals*, LXII, 250.
[4] *Parliamentary Debates*, IX, 143, 144.

the efforts made to secure the relinquishment of the trade by foreign nations, and asking him to persevere in the cause, in which his noble efforts had thus far not been successful. The house was surprised and indignant to find that certain persons in the country had continued an illicit trade, and asked that the officers of the navy and the customs officials be ordered to stop this contemptuous practice. A resolution was passed declaring that early in the next session the house would take into consideration such measures as would tend effectively to prevent such daring violations of the law.[5]

The mover of this resolution, Henry Brougham, had early interested himself in colonial questions, and he became one of the most powerful enemies of the slave system in the empire. He was a speaker of such power that he could command the attention of the House of Commons at times when other abolitionists were forced to talk to empty benches. He took up the matter of the illicit trade in a fiery speech. The abolitionists "were aware," he said, "how obstinately such a trade would cling to the soil where it had taken root; they anticipated the difficulties of extirpating a traffic which had entwined itself with so many interests, prejudices, and passions. But I must admit, that although they had forseen, they had considerably underrated those difficulties. They had not made sufficient allowance for the resistance which the real interests of those directly engaged in the trade, and the supposed interests of the colonies, would oppose to the execution of the acts: they had underrated the wickedness of the Slave Trader, and the infatuation of the planter . . . it is now found that this abominable commerce had not completely ceased, even in this country!"[6]

[5] *House of Commons Journals*, LXV, 503.

[6] *Parliamentary Debates*, XVII, 659-660; Brougham, *Speeches of Henry Lord Brougham* (Edinburgh, 1838), II, 20-21.

He reviewed the Spanish slave trade particularly as carried on to Cuba, saying that the average annual importation had risen from 5,840 to 8,600. "This statement," he remarked, "among other things, proves how much the American flag is used in covering the foreign Slave Trade; for, after the commencement of hostilities between Spain and this country, the trade could only have been carried on to a very limited extent in Spanish bottoms; and yet, instead of being checked by the war, it has greatly increased since 1795."[7] He charged that about thirty thousand negroes were carried annually from Africa to Brazil.[8] He stated that the American government was acting in good faith, but that it could not control the activity of its subjects with a limited ocean police. To suppress the trade a mutual right of search with other powers would have to be secured.[9] Until such a time, slaves would be smuggled into the British islands from the Spanish.

The main purpose of Brougham's speech was to expose the British slave trader, who had continued the traffic illicitly. He declared, "that, lurking in some dark corner of the ship, is almost always to be found a hoary slave trader—an experienced captain, who, having been trained up in the slave business from his early years, now accompanies the vessel as a kind of supercargo, and helps her by his wiles, both to escape detection and to push her inquitous adventures."[10] "Once root out the trade," he continued, "and there is little fear of its again springing up. The industry and capital required by it will find out other vents. The labour and ingenuity of the persons engaged in it will seek the different channels which

[7] *Parliamentary Debates*, XVII, 660; Brougham, *Speeches*, II, 21.
[8] *Parliamentary Debates*, XVII, 661; Brougham, *Speeches*, II, 22.
[9] *Parliamentary Debates*, XVII, 664 ff.; Brougham, *Speeches*, II, 23-27.
[10] *Parliamentary Debates*, XVII, 669; Brougham, *Speeches*, II, 31.

will continue open. Some of them will naturally go on the highway, while others will betake themselves to piracy, and the law might in due time, dispose of them.'"[11] Brougham ended by advocating greater zeal on the part of the government to secure the suppression of this traffic and suggested that slave trading be made a felony.[12] The next year this was done, and the punishment was made fourteen years' transportation or imprisonment for five years.[13] But the British slave trade showed such vitality that in 1824 the offence was made capital and so continued until 1837, when the penal code was modified and slave trading became punishable with transportation for life.[14]

Such indictments as that of Brougham, supported as he was by a strong following in parliament and in the country, convinced the government that its political existence was tied up with the difficult problem of universal abolition. Even during the previous year, 1809, an order in Council had been issued assuming the right of search against Portuguese vessels despite an old treaty to the contrary.[15] This was followed in 1810 by a treaty to prevent Portuguese subjects from carrying on the trade in parts of Africa not belonging to them. Sweden agreed to abolish the trade in 1813, and Denmark, which in 1804 had forbidden the importation of negroes into her colonies, agreed in 1814 to prohibit the trade entirely to her subjects.[16] The Dutch government prohibited the trade to its subjects in June, 1815, and two months later agreed

---

11 *Parliamentary Debates*, XVII, 672; Brougham, *Speeches*, II, 34-35.

12 *Parliamentary Debates*, XVII, 674-675; Brougham, *Speeches*, II, 36 ff.

13 51 Geo. III, c. 23.

14 Brougham, *Speeches*, II, 14-15.

15 *Cambridge History of British Foreign Policy*, II, 235.

16 R. I. and S. Wilberforce, *Life of Wilberforce*, IV, 127; *Cambridge History of British Foreign Policy*, II, 236.

to prohibit the trade entirely, including the importation into the Dutch East Indies.[17] In dealing with Portugal the first thought was to get her to give up Bissao in Portuguese Guinea, south of the Gambia River, or, if she was unwilling to surrender it, at least to stop the slave trade there.[18]

Wilberforce and his confederates had a well defined policy in dealing with the British government. They did not oppose it needlessly on ordinary questions because they felt that governments were all much alike anyway, and their main hope was to keep the slave trade before the ministers by private interviews, letters, activity in parliament, and petitions from the country, showing that public opinion was back of them. Wilberforce explained their tactics as follows: "I am persuaded that, besides the particular benefit to be derived in each particular instance from the minister's compliance with our wishes, we serve the cause instead of injuring it by applying to them on all fair occasions, because we show them that our attention is wakefully directed to the subject, and therefore that they also must be awake."[19] So strong a hold did Wilberforce have on the government that the slave trade sections of proposed treaties with foreign powers were submitted to him by Castlereagh for comment. As his sons state, he "was ready to compel the government by friendly violence to insert the stipulations which this cause required."[20] In 1813 he declared that a proposed agreement with Portugal was unacceptable. About this he wrote to James Stephen: "I would, however, treat Lord Castlereagh with great civility; he

[17] *Cambridge History of British Foreign Policy*, II, 236.
[18] R. I. and S. Wilberforce, *Life of Wilberforce*, IV, 19, May 8, 1812. Wilberforce urged Castlereagh to secure Bissao from the Portuguese.
[19] *Ibid.*, IV, 79. Letter to Zachary Macaulay, Nov. 4, 1812.
[20] *Ibid.*, IV, 133. Note the interesting expression "friendly violence."

behaves to us very handsomely; and we must remember that he himself was a high-duty man, and therefore allow for his assigning more efficiency to that proceeding than you or I should do."[21]

The defeat of Napoleon in Russia in 1812, in Germany in 1813, and in France early in 1814, suddenly brought nearer a general conference of the great powers, an opportunity which found the friends of the negroes somewhat unprepared, and caused feverish activity on their part.[22] The plan agreed upon at a meeting of the African Institution was "to give up the Register Bill for the present, and to push for a convention for the general abolition—to present an address to the Crown, to negociate with the foreign powers, and to forward the measure by all means."[23]

Wilberforce wrote a letter to Talleyrand and prepared an address to the czar, Alexander I, appealing to him, that as he had been the chief deliverer of the continent of Europe from despotism he should perform a work of mercy for the continent of Africa.[24] Macaulay was sent to France to aid the cause there.[25] In France all the old *Amis des Noirs* were out of favor, and most of the members of the government did not even understand the intentions of the abolitionists.[26] Wilberforce was so de-

---

[21] R. I. and S. Wilberforce, *op. cit.*, IV, 135, Aug. 28, 1813. High duty was a scheme, often discussed, to have a high import tariff adopted so as to protect the home-grown slave against the cheaper imported man.

[22] *Ibid.*, IV, 177. Wilberforce condemned himself, April 23, 1814, for not "having foreseen this conjuncture, and been prepared with works in all the modern languages against the Slave Trade."

[23] *Ibid.*, IV, 177.

[24] *Ibid.*, IV, 177. People present at this meeting were the usual group. The Duke of Gloucester, Lord Grey, Lord Grenville, Lord Lansdowne, Zachary Macaulay, Henry Thornton, William Smith, James Stephen, Brougham, Mackintosh, and Wilberforce.

[25] *Ibid.*, IV, 180.

[26] *Ibid.*, IV, 186. Macaulay reported, "that when he dined with Malouet,

termined that he said he hoped not a colony would be re-stored to France except on condition that no slaves were to be imported into it.[27]

Castlereagh, who was on the continent personally con-ducting British policy during the period of the overthrow of Napoleon, soon returned to England with the first peace of Paris, which he presented to the House of Com-mons amidst almost universal rejoicing.[28] When the tu-mult had died down, Wilberforce rose and expressed his regret in these words: "calling to mind the arrangements made in it respecting the slave trade, I cannot but con-ceive that I behold in his hand the death warrant of a multitude of innocent victims, men, women, and children, whom I had fondly indulged the hope of having myself rescued from destruction. . . . My noble friend must allow for my extreme regret, if when at length, after a laborious contention of so many years, I had seemed to myself in some degree in possession of the great object

minister for the colonies, Malouet said, Did we English mean to *bind* all the world? Macaulay should have reparteed. His first words to Macaulay showed he confounded Abolition with Emancipation.''

[27] R. I. and S. Wilberforce, *op. cit.*, IV, 184.

[28] For an excellent account of Castlereagh and the Abolition of the Slave Trade see C. K. Webster, *The Foreign Policy of Castlereagh* (1925), pp. 454-466. *Parliamentary Debates*, XXVIII, 198; Wellington, *Supplementary Despatches*, IX, 130. This treaty contained an additional article which en-gaged the two powers to endeavor to induce the approaching congress of Vienna ''to decree the abolition of the slave trade, so that the said trade shall cease universally, as it shall cease definitely, under any circumstances, on the part of the French Government, in the course of five years; and dur-ing the said period no slave merchant shall import or sell slaves, except in the Colonies of the State of which he is a subject.'' In addition to this, the next day a circular letter was despatched by Castlereagh to Austria, Russia, and Prussia, expressing the hope ''that the Powers of Europe, when re-storing the Peace to Europe, with one common interest, will crown this great work by interposing their benign offices in favor of those Regions of the Globe, which yet continue to be desolated by this unnatural and inhuman traffic.'' *British and Foreign State Papers*, 1815-1816, pp. 890-891. These powers replied favorably. *Parliamentary Debates*, XXVIII, 283.

of my life,—if then, when the cup is at my lips, it is rudely dashed from them, for a term of years at least, if not for ever."[29]

This speech produced such a powerful effect that Lord Liverpool, the British prime minister, and Talleyrand joined hands in trying to persuade Wilberforce that everything possible had been done. The former explained, "That the French took the matter up in a high tone, and resented our dictating to them, believing that all our plea of having abolished ourselves, or urging them to abolish, on grounds of religion, justice, and humanity, were all moonshine—mere hypocrisy."[30] Talleyrand argued that because France had so long been forbidden the trade, she needed five years in which to enable her colonies to adjust themselves, really a short time when Great Britain had had twenty years. To this argument Wilberforce replied with spirit that, "France needed no time to prepare its colonies for the abolition of the Slave Trade, since they had in fact been going on without it for twenty years. Great Britain had a vast capital engaged in it, several thousand tons of shipping, etc. On the contrary, France has not now the poor excuse to plead that Abolition would demand sacrifices which she cannot afford to make. Not a solitary vessel, not a single seaman, not a livre of capital is now employed in the Slave Trade. Further, since the trade in men has been for many years practically discontinued, you cannot plead for it the excuse of established habits or inveterate prejudices; you, in truth, would begin a new Slave Trade."[31]

The peace of Paris was, as a whole, popular. After

[29] *Parliamentary Debates*, XXVIII, 268-297; R. I. and S. Wilberforce, *Life of Wilberforce*, IV, 187-188.
[30] R. I. and S. Wilberforce, *Life of Wilberforce*, IV, 189.
[31] *Ibid.*, IV, 189.

careful consideration, therefore, the English abolitionists decided not to oppose their own government and thus
throw themselves into hopeless opposition, but rather to
accept what had been done and to work earnestly for
greater concessions from other nations at the coming
congress of Vienna.[32] With this aim in mind the plan of
campaign was carefully worked out. Wilberforce had an
interview with Alexander on June 12, 1814, while the
czar was in England, and assured himself of Russia's future support in enforcing abolition as well as securing it
at the congress. The czar managed to shift the blame for
the small gains of the first peace of Paris by saying,
"What could be done, when your own ambassador gave
way?"[33] Castlereagh had been far from idle. He was
honestly in doubt, however, as to how far he should go in
pressing France on this particular question. He wrote:
"My feeling is that on grounds of general policy we
ought not to attempt to tie France too tight on this question. If we do, it will make the abolition odious in France
and we shall be considered as influenced by a secret view
to prevent the revival of her colonial interests."[34]

A campaign was inaugurated to arouse public opinion
to fever heat. "Let the nation loudly and generally,"
wrote Wilberforce, "express its deep disappointment
and regret and most earnestly conjure both Houses, but
especially the House of Commons, to use its utmost efforts in behalf of the unhappy Africans; expressing willingness to make further sacrifices (Mauritius, St. Lucia,
etc.) as the price of the detestable five years' Slave
Trade, and of consenting to an immediate Abolition."[35]

[32] R. I. and S. Wilberforce, *op. cit.*, IV, 190 ff.

[33] *Ibid.*, IV, 191.

[34] *Cambridge History of British Foreign Policy*, I, 451. Castlereagh had
stated the matter in the same way in the debate on the first additional article. *Parliamentary Debates*, XXVIII, 279-281.

[35] R. I. and S. Wilberforce, *Life of Wilberforce*, IV, 192.

The disappointment among the abolitionists was the more acute because on May 3d the Commons had voted an address stating that "they relied with perfect confidence on the assurances received by Parliament in 1806 and 1810, that His Majesty's Government would employ every proper means to obtain a convention of the powers of Europe for the immediate and universal abolition of the African slave trade . . . that the nations of Europe whose independence had been saved by the efforts of the British people, could not but listen with respect to their voice raised in the cause of justice and humanity. Among the great nations till of late their enemies, maritime hostility had abolished the trade, so that there was no financial interest involved in it." Consequently, legal permission to carry it on would be practically its reestablishment with all its horrors.[36]

This address embodied the hopes and expectations of the people of England in regard to the slave trade as an international problem. They were, therefore, deeply disappointed when they learned of the contents of the additional article of the treaty of Paris with France, giving that country five years' time in which to abolish the slave trade. As a result, petitions against the treaty began to pour into parliament. On June 27th, twenty-five[37] were received, of which the one from London was typical. The petitioners regretted that no provision had been made for the immediate abolition of the trade, and that consequently it would revive to an unlimited extent in five years, at the end of which time there would be powerful financial interests to fight against its suppression. Moreover, great and populous colonies, in which, during the last seven years, practically no slave trade had existed,

[36] *House of Commons Journals*, LXIX, 231; *Parliamentary Debates*, XXVII, 640-642.

[37] *House of Commons Journals*, LXIX, 387-388.

were turned over to France without any stipulation for the continuance of that prohibition, but with the declared purpose of renewing the trade.[38] The forts and factories of the African coast were likewise given over to the renewal of slave hunting. The recognition of the injustice of the trade on the part of France should have led to immediate abolition.[39]

The same day a second address respecting this traffic was voted, in which satisfaction was expressed on account of the immediate and unqualified abolition of the slave trade by Holland and Sweden.[40] It was hoped that further advances toward abolition or limitation might be obtained at the approaching congress, and that France would agree to the reduction of the term of five years. Finally, it was urged that no exertion be omitted at the congress of Vienna to secure the ultimate abolition of the slave trade within five years at the very most.[41]

Wilberforce, who moved the resolutions which were embodied in the address of the Commons, expressed his sorrow that the additional article of the treaty with France had not been submitted to the House of Commons before ratification. He maintained that abolition should have been made a condition of the restoration of the colonies and that under the circumstances France could not have refused.[42] The view of the government was given by Castlereagh, who had negotiated the treaty. He was well

---

[38] Lord Liverpool had foreseen the difficulty with the first additional article. In a letter to Castlereagh, May 19, 1814, he pressed for abolition as easier then than later. Wilberforce and Clarkson had written Castlereagh that the French and the English expected abolition in return for colonies. The Earl of Liverpool to Viscount Castlereagh, May 19, 1814, *Supplementary Despatches*, IX, 88.

[39] *House of Commons Journals*, LXIX, 387-388.

[40] *Ibid.*, LXIX. Appendix, no. 13, pp. 848 ff., gives decree June 15, 1814, by the Prince of Orange.

[41] *Ibid.*, LXIX, 389; *Parliamentary Debates*, XXVIII, 277-278.

[42] *Parliamentary Debates*, XXVIII, 277-278.

aware that the nation was willing to make great sacrifices for the cause, but even among the better classes of people in France, the British government did not get full credit for its motives. They were thought to arise not from benevolence, but from a wish to impose fetters on the French colonies, and injure their commerce; if it had been made a question of power, he was convinced that interest would be supposed to have a share in it.[43] If England had preferred to retain the colonies rather than to agree to the first additional article, it would have been said that they had been retained for commercial reasons, and that humanitarianism was only a pretense for keeping up the war and retaining possession of them. He had done his best, and had endeavored to secure abolition in the shortest possible time and to limit to the region south of the equator the area of the African coast on which slaves could be taken. France, however, claimed these things as within her control and subject to her jurisdiction. Moreover, much had been secured by the treaty. The good will of the French government had been gained, and this would be worth much at the coming congress, where the most vital problems would come up for solution. As a result of Napoleon's tyranny, France felt absolutely no sentiment in favor of abolition, and for this reason the surrender of the trade on condition of restoration of the colonies would have been considered disgraceful by the French people. But with the pledge of coöperation at the congress, much good might be accomplished, and France would abolish the trade at the specified time. Even if this trade had been abandoned by France, it would still be carried on by Spain and Portu-

---

[43] This view was substantiated by Wellington in his *Despatches*. Wellington to Wilberforce, Oct. 8, 1814, Wellington, *Despatches*, XII, 142; Wellington to Wilberforce, Oct. 15, 1814, *Ibid.*, XII, 148; Wellington to Wilberforce, Dec. 14, 1814, *ibid.*, XII, 213.

gal. In fact, the situation in France was far more satisfactory than in the latter countries, where vast colonial
interests put the question fairly beyond the control of
their government.[44] "Anxious as they were," continued
Castlereagh, "for the adoption of the principle, contended for by his honourable friend [Wilberforce], they
did not think it right to force it upon nations, at the expense of their honour, and of the tranquility of the world.
Morals were never well taught by the sword; their dis-
semination might sometimes be made a pretext for ambition, but it was to the light of experience, to the promul-
gation of wisdom, and not to the exercise of violence, or
the influence of war, that they could look with any prospect of success, for the abolition of the slave trade."[45]

In this same discussion many expressed the fear that
the trade would not be abolished at the end of five years,
and one member stated his doubts in the following words:
"But the evil is to end in five years. This, Sir, is the
usual way in which vice tries to flatter and deceive itself,
and to stifle the upbraidings of conscience. Another
throw, and the gamester will quit his play—but he per-
sists to his ruin, another winter, and the house-breaker
and highwayman will abstain from acts of violence, and
discontinue their nightly depredations—but they go on in
their guilty career till they meet with the condign punishment which they have merited—and will the course of
the French government be different?"[46]

In the Lords, where the opposition was led by Grenville, the debate and the address were not unlike those in
the Commons. Grenville's speech was an able oratorical
effort; his main point was that the abolition of the slave
trade should have been the condition of restoration of

[44] *Parliamentary Debates*, XXVIII, 280 ff.
[45] *Ibid.*, XXVIII, 284.
[46] *Ibid.*, XXVIII, 293.

the colonies. But he went further, and declared the article in question contrary to the constitution because the slave trade had been abolished in England and made a felony. He, therefore, called on the Lords ''to suspend at once the execution of this unhallowed article.'' ''Withhold the restitution of your conquests,'' he said. ''Persevere in that decision, unseduced by promise, unterrified by menace, until you have irrevocably established the abolition of the slave trade. No contract is binding whose performance is unlawful; no treaty valid which stipulates for crimes.''[47] Grenville's motion calling for the correspondence was rejected by a vote of sixty-two to twenty-seven, whereupon a protest was entered on the journals by the minority.[48]

In the Commons on June 29th, Wilberforce moved an amendment to the address on the treaty of peace, in which confidence was expressed in the government and further expression of opinion was deferred till after the congress.[49] Canning felt that any blame in this matter rested on himself and Wilberforce. They should have demanded the insertion, in the address of May 5th, of a sentiment sufficiently decisive to have forced Castlereagh to insist upon the immediate and general suppression of the slave trade. As the house had declined to speak in decisive language, discretion was left to Lord Castlereagh, which he had doubtless exercised to the best of his judgment.[50]

It is necessary to bear in mind the strength of the anti-slave trade movement in England in order to understand the efforts which were made by the government to secure universal abolition of this traffic during the years 1814-

[47] *Parliamentary Debates*, XXVIII, 299 ff., 330, 331.
[48] *Ibid.*, XXVIII, 356-357; *House of Lords Journals*, XLIX, 1012.
[49] *Parliamentary Debates*, XXVIII, 442.
[50] *Ibid.*, XXVIII, 447.

1815. The country was thoroughly aroused on this question. In thirty-four days, beginning June 27, 1814, petitions to the number of seven hundred and seventy-two were presented to the House of Commons alone, with nearly one million signatures.[51] When one considers that at this time the population of Great Britain was thirteen million, a number far smaller than at present, the meaning of this vast number of signatures becomes apparent.[52] The feeling of the British people was one of the mysteries of the time which they hardly understood themselves, and which was entirely misunderstood in other countries. When parliament adjourned at the end of July, 1814, England was in a mood to fight for the abolition of this traffic,[53] and willing to make almost any sacrifice. Even before the treaty of Paris, Zachary Macaulay had written a letter to Castlereagh which throws much light on the unity of feeling in England: ''In England a very sanguine and general wish, and even an expectation prevail, that the treaty about to be concluded will contain an explicit renunciation of the slave trade on the part of France. And this wish and expectation are by no means confined to those who on general grounds are adverse to the slave trade, but extend to almost every individual connected with our colonial possessions. The former apprehend, from the renewal of the slave trade by France, among a great variety of other evils, the extinction of all their hopes respecting Africa; while the latter anticipate from it the eventual ruin of the British Colonies.''[54] The people felt that they had been engaged

[51] *House of Commons Journals*, LXIX, 450.

[52] In 1816 England and Wales had a population of about 11,000,000; and Scotland of about 2,000,000.

[53] Wellington to Sir Henry Wellesley, July 29, 1814, *Supplementary Despatches*, IX, 165.

[54] Zachary Macaulay to Castlereagh, May 29, 1814, *Castlereagh Correspondence*, X, 47, 48.

in a twenty-five years' war for the freedom of Europe,
and when the war ended and this freedom was to be secured at a congress of the powers, the one interest of
many Englishmen was to secure the universal suppres-
sion of a commerce in human flesh. The nations still openly and legally engaged in the
slave trade were France, Spain, and Portugal. Of these,
France had made stipulations in the treaty of Paris,
which, as we have seen, were very unsatisfactory to the
English abolitionists. Spain and Portugal had taken no
steps for the abolition of the trade. After the additional
article in the treaty of Paris had been agreed upon, but
before the signing of the treaty, Castlereagh pressed
Talleyrand, but without success, to agree to immediate
abolition or, at the very least, to a limitation of the trade
on the African Coast south of Cape Palmas.[55] Talleyrand
would only promise that the king would do all he could
to carry out the wishes of Castlereagh's government in
restricting and discouraging the trade. Marked improvements had been made on the coast of Africa north of the
equator, and especially north of Cape Three Points, lo-
cated on the Gold Coast about 2° 30′ west longitude, and
this fact accounted for the efforts made to limit the trade
south of this territory. The agitation in parliament had
a decisive effect on Castlereagh, and he wrote Talleyrand a personal letter, asking for aid in his embarrass-
ment, and praying for a French order confining the slave
trade south of the equator. He urged this especially, as
the Portuguese were bound by treaty not to resort to this
coast for slaves while other nations abstained from it.[56]
The Duke of Wellington wrote from London that the

[55] Castlereagh to Prince Bénévent, May 26, 1814, *Supplementary Despatches*, IX, 110; Prince Bénévent to Castlereagh, May 5, 26, 1814, IX, 111,
113; Castlereagh to Prince Bénévent, IX, 112.

[56] Castlereagh to Prince Bénévent, July 16, 1814, *ibid.*, IX, 163.

people were ready to go to war for abolition.[57] In order to provide against the reluctance of the powers to agree to the abolition of the slave trade even in a limited time, it was suggested that, acting in concert, they prohibit the importation into their respective dominions of colonial produce grown by such nations as refused to enter the proposed concert. This measure would leave each power in possession of its own market, but would take away any motive for increasing its cultivation to supply other nations.[58] Wellington, who was in France at this time, was instructed on August 6, 1814, to make another effort to secure immediate abolition on account of public feeling, but, failing in this, he was to try to secure a limitation of importation to the number actually needed to supply existing plantations. He was especially urged to press for a decree securing abolition north of the line, at least not further west than Cape Formosa, and vessels to the northward were to be subject to seizure. Secondly, he was to prevail upon France to grant reciprocal right of search within certain latitudes.[59]

At the beginning of September, 1814, Clarkson called the attention of the government to a rumor that France would give up the trade immediately for a colony in the West Indies.[60] Accordingly, the government decided to offer Trinidad or the option of a money compensation for immediate abolition. The question of presenting the proposition at Paris or at Vienna was left to Castlereagh and Wellington.[61] They decided to present it at both

[57] Wellington to Sir Henry Wellesley, July 29, 1814, *ibid.*, IX, 165.

[58] Castlereagh to Wellington, Aug. 6, 1814, *ibid.*, IX, 167.

[59] The mutual right of search was suggested by the Secretary of the African Society to Earl Bathurst June 22, 1814. *Ibid.*, IX, 150. Castlereagh to Wellington, Aug. 6, 1814, *ibid.*, IX, 175.

[60] Wellington to Castlereagh, Sept. 1814, *ibid.*, IX, 211.

[61] Liverpool to Castlereagh, Sept. 7, 1814, *ibid.*, IX, 225; Liverpool to Wellington, Sept. 7, 1814, *ibid.*, IX, 225 ff.

places at about the same time, so that the mind of the
king would be prepared when he received a notice of the
offer from his minister at Vienna. The offer was made
and received unfavorably, but not positively rejected.[62]
The British people, in the meantime, had become very
anxious about the proposed decree to prohibit the traffic
north of the line.[63] In France such popular sentiment as
existed was against prohibition.[64] Consequently, there
was a considerable delay in issuing this promised order,
which did not appear until the first days of November.[65]
The negotiations with Spain and Portugal were largely
of a financial nature. Spain was promised a subsidy of
about £800,000 for limitation south of the equator and
prohibition within five years, and a loan of £10,000,000 in
case of immediate abolition.[66] Very little was done in regard to Portugal before the opening of the congress, as
the Portuguese king and court had fled to Brazil during
the Napoleonic wars.

The practical problem of having the British representatives at the congress not only willing to help but also
well prepared with facts and arguments, received close
attention. The leading slave trade experts were assigned
their respective tasks. On August 3, 1814, Wilberforce
wrote Macaulay: "You will concur with me that it may
be well to furnish Lord Castlereagh with short notes like
a lawyer's brief, of all the main propositions on which
the case of abolition rests, or rather I mean of all the

[62] Wellington to Castlereagh, Oct. 4, 1814, *ibid.*, IX, 316. *Talleyrand's
Briefwechsel mit König Ludwig XVIII während des Wiener. Congresses,*
Feb. 15, 1815, p. 257.
[63] Liverpool to Wellington, Oct. 5, 1814, *Supplementary Despatches,* IX,
321; Liverpool to Castlereagh, Oct. 14, 1814, IX, 343.
[64] King of France to Prince Regent, Sept. 2, 1814, *ibid.*, IX, 217. This
letter was written in reply to a personal letter from the Prince Regent,
Aug. 9, 1814, *ibid.*, IX, 176.
[65] Wilberforce to Wellington, Nov. 16, 1814, *ibid.*, IX, 435.
[66] Wellington to Sir Henry Wellesley, July 29, 1814, *ibid.*, IX, 165, 166.

facts. For having been our opponent, he never, depend on it, admitted into his mind any of those considerations which were so firmly established in ours, as to be a sort of self evident proposition in the last years of our warfare."[67] Copies of this document were to be furnished to the Duke of Wellington and to other Britishers. So well did Macaulay show that the slave trade had almost disappeared from the northwest coast of Africa, except for the Portuguese island of Bissao, that the Duke of Wellington felt that the French ministers could not deny the weight of the evidence collected, remarking, "I do not see how on earth they can."[68] While Macaulay undertook this duty, James Stephen was given by Wilberforce the task of providing a memorandum on Santo Domingo: "Lord Castlereagh must also be provided with such a statement of the present condition of St. Domingo as will enable him to convince Talleyrand that the attempt to recover it by force will end in disgrace. Stephen can best draw up the account I mean. I see nothing else to be said to Lord Castlereagh, except what I mean to press as strongly as I possibly can without offending him—the opposite reception he will have succeeding or failing for us."[69]

Wellington, though aided by Clarkson, could accomplish nothing in Paris before the congress of Vienna opened beyond exerting some influence on public opinion. Slave ships, perhaps aided in part by British capital, were being fitted out in the ports. Talleyrand, learning that the English abolitionists were ready to destroy the traffic at almost any price, hinted for a colony, and Wellington in reply was authorized to offer a sum of money, but nothing was accomplished.[70] The campaign to win

[67] R. I. and S. Wilberforce, *Life of Wilberforce*, IV, 209-210.
[68] *Ibid.*, IV, 211.          [69] *Ibid.*, IV, 210.
[70] *Cambridge History of British Foreign Policy*, I, 495, 496.

French opinion was continued, however. Wilberforce addressed an open letter to Talleyrand; Madame de Staël translated Wilberforce's letter to his Yorkshire constituents; and Wellington and William Humboldt busied themselves in circulating abolition literature. Louis XVIII had been approached while still in England, and so, even if the congress of Vienna took no action, the hope was that France would soon fall into line.[71] Lord Wellesley got the promise that Spain would limit the traffic to Spanish ships, but financial inducements to limit trade to the south of the equator and to abolish it entirely in five years were rejected.

Meanwhile, Castlereagh had gone to the congress of Vienna as the chief British representative. He was instructed to press for three things in regard to the suppression of the slave trade. In the first place, an immediate and universal abolition by the European powers; secondly, a concession of mutual right of search within limited areas; and lastly, the exclusion of colonial produce from those countries which would not agree to this system of abolition.[72] Castlereagh was an able man, but, as has been pointed out, the people of England had no comprehension of the work to be done by the congress; they seemed to be interested in the slave trade to the exclusion of almost everything else. Consequently, they much overrated Castlereagh's ability to move the plenipotentiaries of the congress, intent on other matters more immediately interesting to themselves. The great continental powers, with the exception of France, having no colonial possessions, regarded the slave trade as a remote question with which they had little concern. They were willing, however, to follow England a reasonable

[71] R. I. and S. Wilberforce, *Life of Wilberforce*, IV, 214, 215, 223.
[72] Liverpool to Castlereagh, Dec. 9, 1814, *Supplementary Despatches*, IX, 469, 470.

way because of the assistance which they had received from her during the struggle with Napoleon. This assistance had been largely financial, and besides they were deeply indebted to her for many subsidies, without which their armies could not have been equipped and maintained. Unable to fathom the deep feeling existing in England on this question, they could not understand the earnestness with which Castlereagh pleaded the abolition cause. Accustomed, moreover, to suspect an interested motive in every political change that was strenuously advocated, they settled into the belief that selfish objects were in reality at the bottom of this pretended zeal for the interests of humanity. They imagined that the British, having become aware of the folly of their own action against the slave trade, were now desirous of preventing any other nation from enjoying the advantages of it.[73] With such a feeling existing at the congress, it was not

[73] Castlereagh to Liverpool, Dec. 18, 1814, M. S. Alison, *Lives of Lord Castlereagh and Sir C. Stewart*, II, 583. Castlereagh felt that the pressure of English public opinion was doing more harm than good and wrote home that, ''The more I have occasion to observe the temper of foreign Powers on the question of abolition the more strongly impressed I am with the sense of prejudice that results, not only to the interests of the question itself but of our foreign relations generally, from the display of popular impatience which has been excited and is kept up in England on this subject. It is impossible to persuade foreign nations that this sentiment is unmixed with views of Colonial policy, and their Cabinets, who can better estimate the real and virtuous motives which guide us on this question, see in the very impatience of the nation a powerful instrument through which they expect to force at a convenient moment the British government upon some favorite object of policy.

''I am conscious that we have done an act of indispensable duty, under the circumstances in which we have been placed, in making to the French and Spanish Governments the propositions we have done, but I am still more firmly persuaded that we should be at this moment in fact nearer our object, if the Government had been permitted to pursue this object with its ordinary means of influence and persuasion, instead of being expected to purchase a concession on this point almost at any price.'' *Cambridge History of British Foreign Policy*, I, 496.

strange that Castlereagh should have experienced the greatest difficulty in securing any action. He made every effort to prepare the minds of the plenipotentiaries on this question, and he published some of the best works of the English abolitionists, adding to them such evidence as proved that the suppression of the slave trade was not inconsistent with the best colonial policy.[74] From Spain and Portugal Castlereagh met with determined resistance. They refused to agree to abolish the slave trade within less than eight years. France was unwilling to go farther than she had already gone in the treaty of Paris. A resolute effort to force her to shorten the period of five years might have led her to make common cause with the two peninsular powers. These three colonial powers thought the traffic necessary to their colonies; the other powers alleged that they did not understand the question and were averse to taking positive stand upon it.[75] Castlereagh argued that it would be better for the powers to confine themselves to the slaves they already had than to increase the inequality between the whites and blacks by fresh importations. To this the Spanish and Portuguese plenipotentiaries at the congress replied that this was true in the English colonies, which had been stocked with slaves during the war, whereas no importations had been made into Spanish and Portuguese colonies.[76] Castlereagh offered to indemnify the Portuguese for captured ships in return for im-

[74] Castlereagh to Wilberforce, Nov. 11, 1814, *Castlereagh Correspondence*, X, 199; Castlereagh to Clarkson, Nov. 11, 1814, *Castlereagh Correspondence*, X, 201. The attitude of France is set forth in Wellington to Wilberforce, Dec. 14, 1814, Wellington, *Despatches*, XII, 212, 213. Wellington to Wilberforce, Oct. 15, 1814, Wellington, *Despatches*, XII, 148.

[75] Liverpool to Canning, Dec. 15, 1814, *Supplementary Despatches*, IX, 483; Liverpool to Castlereagh, Jan. 16, 1815, *ibid.*, IX, 529. Liverpool to Canning, Feb. 16, 1815, *ibid.*, IX, 566.

[76] *Talleyrand's Briefwechsel mit Ludwig XVIII*, Feb. 8, 1815, p. 238.

mediate abolition north of the equator, but he was urged by Lord Liverpool, the prime minister, to fight for the adoption of the French rule of five years, as this was the utmost limit permitted by the parliamentary addresses.[77] Numerous conferences on the subject took place, in most of which Castlereagh stood alone. In spite of the parliamentary addresses he had to content himself with a general declaration against the slave trade, branding it as a crime against civilization and humanity. He succeeded, however, in inducing Spain and Portugal to promise rather vaguely that they would abolish the trade in eight years. Portugal also agreed to confine the trade to the south of the line, and received in return £300,000 for captured ships and the balance of a loan of £600,000 made in 1809.[78] Spain was offered £800,000 on similar conditions.[79] France stuck to the agreement made in the treaty of Paris. She received neither a money compensation nor an island, but used the opportunity to draw Great Britain nearer to her on various questions before the congress, especially on the question of Naples.[80] The demands of Castlereagh in regard to the right of search met with decided resistance, as it was well known that this right would be exercised by no power but England, which alone had the means and the desire of putting down the slave trade. The discussion of this point should have been confined to the maritime powers, but, as

[77] Liverpool to Castlereagh, Jan. 6, 1815, *Supplementary Despatches,* IX, 529.

[78] *Parliamentary Debates,* XXXII, 217, 218. Convention between Great Britain and Portugal signed at Vienna, Jan. 21, 1815, *ibid.,* XXXII, 219. Convention between Great Britain and Portugal signed at Vienna, Jan. 22, 1815.

[79] Wellington to Sir Henry Wellesley, July 29, 1814, *Supplementary Despatches,* IX, 166.

[80] *Talleyrand's Briefwechsel mit Ludwig* XVIII, Feb. 8, 1815, p. 238; Feb. 1815, p. 257.

Castlereagh stood alone among them, he improved his position slightly by securing the admission of all the powers, but he had to accept the principle that during peace every nation had a right to regulate its own vessels according to its inclination. The exclusion of colonial produce was held to be premature when the traffic was formally permitted to certain nations by treaty.

Castlereagh, who was instructed to secure something definite to present to parliament, was compelled, as we have seen, to content himself with a general declaration from the congress, condemning the slave trade as a crime against civilization and humanity, and expressing a unanimous wish for its speedy abolition, for which the "public voice in all civilized countries cried aloud."[81] His work at the congress has been well stated: "By obtaining a general Declaration against the Trade in the Treaty, by awakening public opinion among the statesmen by the discussions of the final Conference, and by initiating practical measures to ensure that Abolition, once obtained, should be faithfully carried out, Castlereagh had done an immense amount to bring this odious practice to an end."[82] The abolition leaders had conducted their campaign with rare skill, and there can be no doubt "that, without the sustained and eager insistence of an organized public opinion in this country, the responsible statesmen would have allowed the iniquitous traffic to continue under the pretext that it was impossible to do otherwise."[83] The actual carrying out of this desire was, however, left to negotiation between the individual powers. Castlereagh left the congress in February, shortly after the above-mentioned arrangements

---

[81] *Parliamentary Debates*, XXXII, 200 ff.; Act, no. 15. Declaration of the Powers on the question of the slave trade, Feb. 8, 1815.

[82] *Cambridge History of British Foreign Policy*, I, 499.

[83] *Ibid.*, I. 499.

had been made, in order to be in his place in the House of Commons.

By this time, Napoleon had left Elba and landed in France. On March 29th he issued a decree abolishing the French slave trade. His motive in doing so was very simple. He wanted the good will of the British people, and sought to gain it by this means, as he was well acquainted with public feeling in Great Britain on this question.[84] Castlereagh had been forced to defend himself against the bitter attacks of parliament during the summer of 1814, and he knew that it would not be possible to face English public opinion without having secured the abolition of this traffic by France. Louis XVIII had pledged himself to immediate abolition before the battle of Waterloo was fought, while he was still a fugitive. Therefore, when he was restored to his throne by England, Prussia, Austria, and Russia, these powers, under the inspiration of the British minister, drew up a protocol in which they commanded the French king to maintain the abolition of the slave trade, the act for the abolition of which they held as being still in force.[85] In accordance with this protocol, Castlereagh sent a note to Talleyrand stating that, ''The British conceive that under the operation of the Law of France, as it now stands, it is strictly prohibited to French subjects to carry on a traffic in slaves; and that nothing but a specific ordinance could again revive the commerce, but, whether this be the true construction, or not, of the law in a technical sense, they feel persuaded that his Most Christian Majesty will never lend his authority to revive a system which has

[84] *Parliamentary Debates*, XXXII, 307, no. 19; Despatch from Castlereagh to Liverpool, July 31, 1815, giving letter from Talleyrand to Castlereagh, July 30, 1815, *Cambridge History of British Foreign Policy*, I, 452.

[85] *Parliamentary Debates*, XXXII, 305, 306.

been, de facto, abolished."[86] Castlereagh's note had the desired effect.[87] On July 30, 1815, therefore, Talleyrand informed Castlereagh that the king had abolished the French slave trade, taking occasion, moreover, to claim that the abolition was due, not to the decree of the usurper, Napoleon, but to the king's decree alone.[88] The decree of the French king abolishing the slave trade led to the insertion of an additional article in the new treaty of Paris of November 20, 1815, which engaged Great Britain and France to spare no efforts "to secure through their ministers at London and Paris the most effectual measures for the entire and definitive abolition of a commerce so odious and so strongly condemned by the laws of religion and of nature."[89] A similar article was included in the treaty of peace between Great Britain and the United States at the close of the War of 1812.[90] Both articles were general declarations against the trade and were intended as foundations for further negotiations and pledges of coöperation. The formal suppression of the French slave trade marked the end of another period in the movement which resulted in the emancipation of the slaves in the British colonies. The trade was abolished by all Europe except Spain and Portugal, and those two powers had given promises of abolition in the near future. Thus the part of Africa which had made the greatest advances toward civilization was secured against the slave hunters. Obviously, then, the results of the efforts made in the years 1807-1815 were quite as important as those of the years 1787-

[86] *Parliamentary Debates*, XXXII, 306, no. 17, Despatch from Castlereagh to Liverpool containing the note sent to Talleyrand, July 27, 1815.

[87] *Ibid.*, XXXII, 306, no. 17, Despatch from Castlereagh to Liverpool giving a copy of the note sent to Talleyrand.

[88] *Ibid.*, XXXII, 307, no. 19, Talleyrand to Castlereagh, July 30, 1815.

[89] *Ibid.*, XXXII, 253.

[90] United States, *Treaties and Conventions* (1910 edition), p. 618.

1807. The end of the slave trade as a legalized commerce seemed near at hand.

It is perhaps well to continue at this point the story of the British efforts to secure universal abolition of the slave trade up to the time when that effort met with almost complete legal success. This narration will take us chronologically almost a decade beyond the year 1833, when the emancipation of the slaves was voted by the British parliament. The securing of universal abolition was a first charge upon the British government. Moreover, self-interest, which for so long had been against the abolition of the British slave trade, after 1807 was largely if not wholly on the side of universal abolition.

Soon after 1815 it became apparent that so long as Spain and Portugal could carry on the trade legally, the benefits arising from the abandonment of the trade by the other powers would in a large measure be nugatory, as under their flags all the West Indies could be supplied from the Spanish islands. To induce Spain and Portugal to agree to abolition at the earliest possible time, the proposition of excluding colonial produce was brought forward. To secure the suppression of all illicit trade, efforts were made to obtain at least a limited mutual right of search, the only means by which the clandestine trade could be driven from the seas.

The whole question entered on a new phase when the people of Great Britain learned not only that abolition was not effective, but that the trade was still carried on to an enormous extent. To check any illicit trade into the British colonies, a slave registry bill was proposed in parliament. But more than ever before, it now became clear that slavery itself was as much of an evil as the slave trade. This fact was brought home to the people when they learned of the actual conditions of slavery and how the principles of justice and morality were defeated on every hand. Early in 1823, when they perceived these conditions clearly, the champions of the suppression of the slave trade formed the Anti-Slavery Society. Universal abolition and the suppression of the illicit trade became a major purpose of British foreign policy. Castlereagh constantly called slave trade matters to the attention of the other powers. At first he thought Spain would adhere to the eight year limit,[91] but a little later he said that negotiations with Spain to shorten this period of eight years were in progress. In September, 1816, he addressed a note to the czar in which he called attention to the fact that at the congress of Vienna it was decided by the plenipotentiaries of Russia, Austria, Prussia, and Great Britain that May, 1819, the period then fixed by France for final abolition, was the utmost period which the respective sovereigns could possibly be induced to recognize as justifiable or necessary for the trade to endure; and that they reserved to themselves the right to exclude from their dominions, upon a principle of moral obligation, the colonial produce of states continuing to trade in slaves beyond that period. The question at issue was the formation of an alliance against the Barbary States, and Castlereagh suggested that abolition by Spain and Portugal in May, 1819, be made a condition of their accession to the proposed alliance, as it was extremely illogical for these powers to frown on the actions of the Barbary pirates while they themselves were engaged in an inhuman traffic.[92]

The negotiations with Spain were tedious, however, and the subject was kept quiet till July, 1817, when Lord Grenville complained of the extent to which the slave trade was carried on by the subjects of Spain, and that,

[91] *Parliamentary Debates*, XXXIII, 599, 600.
[92] *Castlereagh Correspondence*, XI, 301 ff.; *Parliamentary Debates*, XXXVI, 136 ff.

too, on the very coast of Africa which had been singled out by Great Britain for civilization. Not only was the trade carried on to a very great extent, but with redoubled horrors, as absolutely no rules or regulations controlled the traders. The vessels employed in it were armed as if intended for war, and were built for speed and not for the comfort of the cargo. These vessels became involved in frequent contests with British cruisers, and this friction threatened to lead to hostilities between the governments.

Wilberforce in the Commons dwelt on the horrors of the "middle passage." He referred to a letter from Sir James Yeo in which it was stated that a vessel of one hundred and twenty tons had conveyed six hundred slaves. In another case where five hundred and forty negroes were embarked three hundred and forty had died. The greater part of the Spanish slaves were sent to Havana, which served as a distributing centre. From a paper obtained from the Cortes, it appeared that there had been imported into Cuba, in eleven years, from 1799 to 1811, about one hundred and ten thousand slaves or about ten thousand a year; and in the last three years, the importation had been much greater, amounting to twenty-five thousand a year. Hence the contention that the Spanish colonies were denuded of slaves was mere pretense. In fact, the Spanish colonies were being well supplied with slaves, so that they threatened to rival the British colonies in prosperity. Consequently, it was necessary to put an end to this traffic, if there was to be any hope of the British colonies selling their produce beyond the confines of the empire. In case of hesitation on the part of Spain and Portugal, Wilberforce advised the exclusion of produce from the colonies of these states.[93] He moved an address in which these ideas found expres-

[93] *Parliamentary Debates*, XXXVI, 1321-1326.

sion and in which His Majesty was urged to push the negotiations with unflinching zeal, and to resort, if need be, to the exclusion of colonial produce. It was hoped, moreover, that some concerted action might be taken for ascertaining and bringing to punishment the offending parties.[94] Castlereagh was in sympathy with the address, and he said that negotiations for that purpose were in progress, and he hoped that they would be completed soon.[95] Brougham was not sanguine about inducing Spain and Portugal to agree to abolition, and even if they agreed, he thought some arrangement among the greater powers of Europe, by which a mutual right of search would be established, was absolutely essential. Otherwise, these peninsular powers would not observe their public declarations.[96] Marryat called attention to the instructions given to naval officers, which were not in accord with the decisions of the High Court of Admiralty. In consequence, the decisions of the vice-admiralty courts had been reversed quite frequently, and restitution made far beyond the original value of the cargo.[97]

In January, 1818, Castlereagh was able to lay before the house a treaty with Spain relative to the slave trade, signed at Madrid, September 23, 1817. This treaty was long and very elaborate. It provided for the mutual right of search, the abolition of the slave trade in all the Spanish dominions after May 30, 1820, and the immediate prohibition of the traffic north of the equator. For these concessions, Spain was to receive £400,000 to cover captured vessels and other losses, which were a necessary conse-

---

[94] *Parliamentary Debates*, XXXVI, 1325-1326; *House of Commons Journals*, LXXII, 470.

[95] *Parliamentary Debates*, XXXVI, 1330.

[96] *Statutes*, 11 and 12, Will. III, c. 7. The accused, in an effort to escape the jurisdiction of the court, declared he was an American citizen. *Parliamentary Debates*, XXXVI, 1332 ff.

[97] *Parliamentary Debates*, XXXVI, 1336.

quence of abolition.[98] The traffic was declared illicit: first, by British ships and under the British flag, or for the account of British subjects by any vessel or under any flag whatsoever; secondly, by Spanish ships north of the line, and by Spanish ships, or for the account of Spanish subjects by any vessel or under any flag; thirdly, under the British and Spanish flags, for the account of the subjects of any other government; and lastly, by Spanish vessels bound for any port not in the dominions of his Catholic Majesty. Spain pledged herself to adopt measures to enforce these provisions. Until 1820 vessels engaged in the traffic were to be furnished with passports by the Spanish government, which pledged itself to make every effort to render the voyage as comfortable as possible for the negroes. Vessels engaging in traffic contrary to these rules might be visited by cruisers of either nation especially designated for this purpose and furnished with instructions. In case slaves were actually found on board, the captain or owner was to be brought to trial before mixed tribunals established for this purpose. These mixed commissions were to have primary and final jurisdiction in all cases. One was to reside on the coast of Africa, and one in the West Indies; one in Spanish, the other in British territory. The form of a passport for Spanish vessels destined for the lawful traffic in slaves was made part of the treaty. This provided that not more than five slaves for every two tons burden should be carried. Another part of the treaty consisted of instructions for the British and Spanish cruisers. These provided, among other things, that the captain and two-thirds of the men were to be Spanish; this provision can be accounted for by the fact that not only a large amount of British capital, but a large number of English-

<hr>

[98] *Cambridge History of British Foreign Policy*, II, 237.

men were engaged in the Spanish trade. The last addition to the treaty was the regulation for the mixed commissions, which described the composition, jurisdiction, and form of procedure of these tribunals.[99]

It has been necessary to describe this treaty in some detail not only because it was drawn up with great care, but also because the treaties concluded between Great Britain on the one side and Portugal and Holland on the other were but little different in their essentials. Castlereagh in discussing the treaty called attention to its importance. All the crowned heads, except Portugal, had either abolished the slave trade or entered into stipulations for its abolition at some future period, at least north of the equator. Consequently, there was a broad line of demarcation between legal and illicit trade. At the congress of Vienna the great powers had made a declaration which stamped the slave trade as disgraceful, and made every state anxious to get out of it as soon as circumstances would admit of doing so. France had been faithful in her efforts to check the illicit trade, but in spite of this fact the trade had greatly increased during the years of peace. It was perhaps carried on to a less extent, but it was carried on with greater cruelty. To check the illicit trade the states of Europe now bound themselves, for the first time in diplomatic history, by a mutual stipulation to exercise the right of visit over their merchantmen.[100]

Castlereagh thought the £400,000 granted quite reasonable for the results obtained, especially in view of the fact that at one time Spain had been offered £800,000 upon the conditions of this treaty, together with a loan of 10,000,000 Spanish dollars for immediate abolition, and at that time no member of parliament had been heard

[99] *Parliamentary Debates*, XXXVII, 67-79.
[100] *Ibid.*, XXXVII, 232 ff.

against it. Sir Gilbert Heathcote called attention to what
£400,000 would buy for the poor. Several members feared
the money would be used by Spain to crush the South
Americans.[101] One member thought Spain was already
under a pledge to abolish the slave trade in eight years,
that is, in 1823, but Castlereagh explained that the Spanish minister had only stated eight years as the period at
the end of which Spain might find it convenient to enter
into arrangements with a view to the abolition of the
slave trade, and that there was no positive engagement
which pledged the Spanish nation to the discontinuance
of the traffic at the expiration of eight years.[102] Charles
Grant called the attention of the house to the fact that if
the Spanish government had been interested merely in
the amount of money it could receive, it would have accepted the offer of the merchants of Havana for the
continuance of a trade which was five times the amount
stipulated in the treaty. The division resulted in a vote
of fifty-six in favor of the treaty with but four against it,
a surprisingly small vote for the Commons.[103] In the
Lords, as in the Commons, some thought the treaty obtained at too high a price, but on the whole it was considered quite satisfactory.[104]

Portugal made no agreement for the abolition of the
slave trade, but the treaty signed with her for establishing the mutual right of search was similar to that with
Spain.[105] The treaty with the Netherlands for establish-

[101] *Parliamentary Debates*, XXXVII, 240 ff.
[102] *Ibid.*, XXXVII, 249.          [103] *Ibid.*, XXXVII, 255, 260.
[104] *Ibid.*, XXXVIII, 856.

[105] *Ibid.*, XXXVIII, 996. Portugal was the first country to concede the
right of search. Moreover, a treaty with her was signed by which a certain
period for the total abolition of this evil was fixed. But this treaty, it
seems, was abortive, as there was no further mention of it, and Portugal
did not abolish the slave trade south of the equator until a number of years
later. *Ibid.*, XXXVII, 234.

ing the right of search also followed closely the provisions of the Spanish treaty except in two particulars. European waters were exempted from its operation, and each country was to have an equal number of cruisers of search, so that Great Britain would have no advantage on account of her superior navy.[106] Regarding France, Wilberforce presented an address in which he complained of the renewed activity of the French slave traders on the northwest coast of Africa, but when Castlereagh assured him that the matter had not escaped the attention of the government, he withdrew his motion.[107]

At the congress of Aix-la-Chapelle, which opened in October, 1818, the slave trade was one of the subjects of discussion. Castlereagh made two propositions: that the five powers join in urging Portugal and Brazil to abolish the traffic in May, 1820; and that the powers adopt the principle of a mutual qualified right of search. Both of these propositions failed, although they were strongly urged by Great Britain.[108]

The next European congress at which the subject was discussed was that of Verona in 1822. In the meantime, the matter had been taken up with the United States. Castlereagh opened the question by suggesting to Minis-

[106] *Parliamentary Debates*, XXXVIII, 1040 ff.

[107] *Ibid.*, XXXVIII, 1317, 1318.

[108] *American State Papers, Foreign Relations*, V, 113-127. In a letter written by James Stephen to Castlereagh before the opening of the convention, the importance of getting France to give up her claim of sovereignty over Santo Domingo was clearly set forth. Stephen held that an effort by France to reconquer the island would lead to the renewal of the slave trade to an unlimited extent, as during the struggle many of the negroes would be killed. To supply these and to bring the island back to its former economic condition would mean an enormous slave trade. This would also result in great economic loss to the British West Indies, which Stephen made clear in his letter by showing what the feeling of the English planters was toward such a revival. James Stephen to Lord Castlereagh, September 8, 1818, *Castlereagh Correspondence*, XII, 3 ff.

ter Rush in June, 1818, a mutual but strictly limited right of search.[109] Rush was instructed to tell him that the United States was anxious to suppress the traffic, but that the proposals asked for were of a character not adaptable to her institutions.[110] The negotiations were then transferred to Washington, and the new British minister, Stratford Canning, approached J. Q. Adams, secretary of state, with full instructions in December, 1820.[111] By this time the people of the United States had come to realize that the suppression of the slave trade was an absolute impossibility without some exercise of a right of search. In 1817, a house committee had urged this concession,[112] and a motion to the same effect was made in the Senate.[113] In 1820 and 1821, two committee reports were made in the house, and the one urging the granting of a right of search was adopted but failed in the Senate.[114] Adams saw constitutional objections to the plan, and he wrote to Canning on December 30, 1820, setting forth his ideas very clearly and forcibly. As a counter-proposition, he suggested coöperation of the fleets on the coast of Africa, and this proposal was promptly accepted.[115]

[109] *Annals of Congress*, 16 cong., 2d sess., p. 1318; *American State Papers, Foreign Relations*, V, 71, 72, 111, 112.

[110] *Annals of Congress*, 16 cong., 2d sess., p. 1320; *American State Papers, Foreign Relations*, V, 112, 113.

[111] *Annals of Congress*, 16 cong., 2d sess., p. 1327; *American State Papers, Foreign Relations*, V, 75, 76.

[112] *House Documents*, 14 cong., 2d sess., II, no. 77.

[113] *Annals of Congress*, 15 cong., 1st sess., pp. 71, 73-78, 94-109. The motion was opposed largely by Southern members, and passed by a vote of 17 to 16.

[114] One was reported, May 9, 1820, by Mercer's committee, and passed May 12, *ibid.*, 16 cong., 1st sess., pp. 697-699. A similar resolution passed the house next session, and a committee reported in favor of the right of search. *Ibid.*, 16 cong., 2d sess., pp. 1064-1071; also pp. 743, 865, 1469.

[115] *Ibid.*, 16 cong., 2d sess., pp. 1328-1330; *American State Papers, Foreign Relations*, V, 76-77.

At the congress of Verona in 1822 the five great European powers were represented. The Duke of Wellington was the leading British delegate. He was fully instructed on this question by George Canning, the new secretary of state for foreign affairs, who had just succeeded Castlereagh.[116] The instructions contained the demands which had been made in previous negotiations—such as the exclusion of colonial produce, the construing of the slave trade as piracy, and the withdrawing of the flags of states from persons not their own citizens. In addition, Canning called for a renewal of the declaration of 1815 and hoped that the peculiar equipment of a ship might be considered as sufficient evidence for condemnation. He also gave an excellent summary of the whole question. He attributed the lowered tone of sentiment abroad on this question to a change in the spirit of the times, and also to the idea inculcated by other colonial powers that Great Britain was now endeavoring to share with her rivals the injury she had inflicted on herself by abolition. He denied that British colonial depression was due to the extinction of this inhuman traffic, although he admitted that the abolition of the slave trade had not been made effective. He dwelt on the extent and horrors of the traffic. "The slave trade," he said, "so far from being diminished in extent by the exact amount of what was in former times the British demand, is upon the whole, perhaps, greater than it was at the period when that demand was highest; and the aggregate of human suffering and the waste of human life, in the transport of slaves from the coast of Africa to the colonies, is increased in a ratio enormously greater than the increase of positive numbers. It seems as if those who continue this abominable traffic had a malicious pleasure in defeating the cal-

116 G. R. Gleig, *Life of Wellington*, IV, 372-377. Gives the instructions of Castlereagh, intended for himself, but given to Wellington.

culations of benevolence, and in visiting upon the innocent victims of their avarice the fruitless endeavors to
rescue those victims from their power.''[117]

When the subject of the slave trade was taken up in
the congress, the British delegate declared that, although
only Portugal and Brazil allowed the trade, the traffic
was at that moment carried on to a greater extent than
ever before. He said that in seven months of the year
1821, no less than twenty-one thousand slaves were ab-
ducted, and three hundred and fifty-two vessels entered
African ports north of the equator.[118] This crime, it was
pointed out, was committed against the laws of every
European power excepting Portugal, as well as those of
America; for that reason it required something more
than the ordinary operation of law to prevent it.

In accordance with the instructions and suggestions of
Canning, the English plenipotentiary recommended three
things: 1. That each country denounce the trade as
piracy, with a view of drawing from the aggregate. of
such separate declarations a general law to be incor-
porated into the law of nations. 2. A prohibition of the
use of the flags of Portugal and Brazil to cover persons
not natives of these two states. 3. A refusal to admit the
produce of the colonies of states allowing the trade, a
measure which would apply to Brazil and Portugal alone.
But little was accomplished by the congress of Verona.
Portugal continued the trade and France was openly
hostile. In France there was no public feeling on the
question, and the anxiety of Great Britain was attributed
to selfish motives. In fact, a ministry which agreed to a
mutual right of search would sign its own immediate
downfall, and it was impossible to secure any effective
laws from the legislature. The French had suggested the

---

[117] Wellington, *Despatches, Correspondence, and Memoranda*, I, 323-324.
[118] Minute upon the slave trade by Wellington, *ibid.*, I, 549.

exchange of the French West African settlement for the Isle of Bourbon, so that England could guard this coast effectively, but Canning pointed out that England would be trading a good island for nothing without aiding the cause in the least, as the French in possession of both the Indian islands would carry on the trade on the east coast of Africa more vigorously than ever before. The best chance of success was in the exclusion of colonial produce.[119] None of the British proposals was accepted. Austria and Russia agreed to the first two only; France refused to denounce the trade as piracy; Prussia was non-committal. The utmost that could be gained was another denunciation of the trade in general terms.[120] Thus at the end of this period, 1823, the trade was carried on as vigorously as ever before, if not more vigorously, and the continental powers and America refused to make the concessions necessary for its suppression.

France had been largely responsible for blocking effective action. The Revolution of 1830, however, effected such political changes in that country that by treaties in 1831 and in 1833, she agreed to the reciprocal right of search with the provision that captured vessels were to be brought before a competent court of the country to which they belonged. Nine years later this was followed by the conclusion of a quintuple treaty by Great Britain with France, Austria, Prussia, and Russia, based on the agreements with France.[121] These agreements left the United

119 Wellington, op. cit., I, 322-328.

120 Wellington to Canning, Oct. 28, 1822, ibid., I, 451-452. Wellington to Canning, Nov. 19, 1822, ibid., I, 547-555. This includes the minute upon the slave trade which the Duke of Wellington drew up before the Emperor of Russia before presenting it to the conference. Besides the three recommendations of general application, France was urged to establish a registry of slaves in her colonies, to pay head money for slaves captured on the seas, and to regard a vessel equipped for the slave trade as evidence that she was a slaver.

121 Cambridge History of British Foreign Policy, II, 238.

States, which still refused to provide for a mutual right of search, standing alone. The feelings aroused by the War of 1812 were so vivid, the disputes with Great Britain were so acute and numerous, and the slave interests of the country were so powerful, that the mutual right of search was not conceded at this time. As W. E. B. Du Bois has pointed out, the result was that "the American Slave-trade finally came to be carried on principally by United States capital, in U. S. ships, officered by U. S. citizens, and under the U. S. Flag."[122]

Legal abolition, however, went on side by side with the actual transportation of slaves. In 1830 Brazil abolished the traffic, followed in the years between 1833 and 1839 by treaties granting the mutual right of search on the part of Haiti, Uruguay, Venezuela, Bolivia, Argentina, Mexico, Texas, Denmark, and the Hansa towns.[123] The notorious traffic was abolished in law but not in fact; cotton, coffee, tobacco, and sugar plantations still demanded their quota of slaves.

[122] W. E. B. Du Bois, *Suppression of the Slave Trade*, p. 162.
[123] *Cambridge History of British Foreign Policy*, II, 244.

# CHAPTER VII

## SLAVE REGISTRATION AND THE BEGINNING OF PARLIAMENTARY INTERFERENCE WITH SLAVERY

In turning back to the time of the abolition of the British slave trade in 1807, we should remember that the struggle for universal abolition, discussed in the last chapter, absorbed but a part of the attention of those interested in the welfare of the negro race, and that during the same period of time the movement for the emancipation of the slaves in the British islands was begun and carried to completion in 1833. Thus two chief objects were pursued simultaneously. The improvements in the West Indies that were to grow out of the cessation of the trade were watched for eagerly. The smuggling in of negroes was greatly feared, as this would keep the masters from attempting to better the lot of their slaves and would introduce a fresh supply of savage Africans, thus making the problem of civilizing the slaves impossible.

James Stephen, whose practical mind early conceived the idea that there would be illicit introduction of slaves, proposed that all the slaves in the West Indies be registered, that the register be kept up to date, and that a copy of it be sent to London. A careful description of each individual slave would make the clandestine slave trade practically impossible because a non-registered slave would be presumed to be a freeman, and no transfer of a negro could be made without the certificate of registration. The biographers of Wilberforce present the significance of the registry question as follows: "the Register

of Negroes was the first move in this new conflict; . . .
For it was in truth the appeal of the slave population
from the narrow-minded island legislatures to the supreme council of the empire; from the corrupted currents of Jamaica and Barbadoes to English sympathy
and moral feeling. It led therefore to every after-effort
for the mitigation of their sufferings; and when all these
had been tried in vain, it led step by step to the great
principle of entire emancipation. But he [Wilberforce]
and others around him saw not as yet to what they should
be led. They had never acted upon the claim of abstract
rights, and they reached emancipation at last only because it was a necessary conclusion of a series of practical improvements.'"[1]

The struggle for registration extended over a period
of eight years. In January, 1812, the government promised to introduce registration into Trinidad by order in
Council as an experiment, but the abolitionists voted to
proceed by means of legislative action also. Opposed by
the ministry, they were forced to delay their measure so
as not to suffer defeat.[2] Denial of the existence of smuggling on the part of the West Indians naturally threw the
burden of proof on the abolitionists, forced them to
gather statistics, and thus focused attention on the condition of the negroes in the islands.[3] The gathering of

---

[1] R. I. and S. Wilberforce, *Life of Wilberforce*, IV, 241-242. It is doubtless true, as the authors say, that the abolitionists did not act upon the
principle of "abstract rights" as the term is usually understood, but they
were firmly moved by religious feelings of the age. When Stephen is tired
of the long periods of defeat and delay he declares himself "beyond all
patience" and then adds, "If it prove otherwise, it is not because either
philanthropy, or a stronger principle with me (hatred of injustice and oppression) excite, but because duty to God will constrain me while I still hope
to do Him service. I sometimes feel like St. Paul, I do this thing not will-
ingly, but of necessity; a dispensation of negroism is committed to me, and
woe is me if I do not work for them." *Ibid.*, IV, 240.

[2] *Ibid.*, IV, 3, 19.            [3] *Ibid.*, IV, 132-133. Date is 1813.

proof, however, required time, and so the question was postponed until 1814, when the defeat of Napoleon occurred and attention was drawn to general abolition.[4] The government was so absorbed with the peace settlements that it ignored the registry problem.[5] This delay caused Wilberforce to write Lord Liverpool a strong remonstrance on March 17, 1815: "For it is not merely this measure of the Registry Bill that is in question. But the same consideration that leads you to decide against its adoption, would still more clearly prompt you to decide against a bill to attach slaves to the soil; indeed against all measures which should be brought forward for mitigating the sufferings and improving the condition of the slaves and free coloured population of the West Indies; . . ."[6]

When the registry bill was finally introduced on July 5, 1815,[7] it met with the strenuous opposition of the West Indians, who denied that slaves were smuggled in. Ma-

[4] R. I. and S. Wilberforce, *op. cit.*, IV, 177, April 19, 1814.

[5] Viscountess Knutsford, *Life and Letters of Zachary Macaulay*, p. 312; Sir George Stephen, *Antislavery Recollections*, pp. 25-27. In 1812 an order in Council provided for the registration in Trinidad. By 1815, registration had been extended to Mauritius and St. Lucia. Stephen, the author of the plan, was so disappointed at the delay of the ministers that he gave up his seat in parliament, which he owed to the prime minister, Perceval. For an illuminating discussion of the constitutional significance of the registry question see Robert Livingston Schuyler, "The Constitutional Claims of the British West Indies" in the *Political Science Quarterly*, March, 1925, XL, no. 1. West India Standing Committee *Minutes*, IV, 358-368.

[6] R. I. and S. Wilberforce, *Life of Wilberforce*, IV, 250. James Stephen on June 12, 1815, stated the arguments in favor of an English registry in a letter to Earl Bathurst saying, "Without a duplicate registry *here*, . . . and without public access to that registry, it would be worse than useless; nor would the desired object be secured unless the English registry were made the test of the validity of titles created or transferred in this country." Historical Manuscripts Commission, *Report on the Manuscripts of Earl Bathurst* (London, 1923), pp. 351-353.

[7] *Parliamentary Debates*, XXXI, 1127 ff., July 5, 1815; *ibid.*, XXXIII, 523 ff.; XXXIV, 719 ff., 908 ff., 1271 ff.; C.O., 137: 143, Jan. 21, 1816.

caulay and Stephen at once prepared to submit their evidence to the public; Wilberforce, too, decided to write a pamphlet. The West Indians on their side were by no means idle and three tracts against registration appeared from the pens of Marryat, Mathison, and Hibbert.[8] When Lord Grenville, in March, 1816, urged a registration of slaves under act of parliament, all the old arguments that had been used against abolition were brought to bear against this measure: it was an unjust interference with the local affairs of the colonies; it would alienate their affection; no slaves were smuggled in; and the discussion of the question would lead the negroes to think they were free and cause them to rebel.

The conflict continued through the years 1816 and 1817. The result was that by 1818 the word emancipation appeared for the first time among Wilberforce's secret memoranda. Indeed, the matter came up on January 31, 1818, in an interview with Castlereagh, who cautioned Wilberforce against working for emancipation at this time.[9] The decision reached by the abolitionists was not to work for emancipation but to call the attention of the British people to the state of the negroes by "contending for various principles, as independence, and non-plantership of governor, and even still more of judge. Also marriage, schools, overseer being incapacitated when cruel, etc."[10]

The British government urged upon the colonial legislatures registration and laws for the improvement of the

[8] R. I. and S. Wilberforce, *Life of Wilberforce*, IV, 282-283. Date is 1816.

[9] *Ibid.*, IV, 368. Castlereagh "also impressed me with a danger of pressing for too entire a change, in short for slaves' emancipation, till abolition by other powers secured—the French, Dutch, and American right of search. Much struck with his remarks and information."

[10] *Ibid.*, IV, 371, Feb. 19, 1818.

condition of the slaves.[11] In accordance with such suggestions, registration bills were passed by the different
colonies. In April, 1818, Wilberforce moved for copies of
all laws passed in or for any British colony since 1812
and for accounts showing the increase and decrease of
the numbers of slaves in the different islands.[12] By passing registration laws the colonies admitted the principle
and necessity of such legislation and made it possible for
the British government to introduce a uniform system
throughout the British dominions, to become effective on
January 1, 1820.[13] The importance of the registration act
can hardly be overstated. The planters were forced to
furnish the statistics showing a decrease in population.
The anti-slavery leaders contended that this decrease was
proof of the brutality of slavery and that emancipation
was the only remedy. Thus the West Indians, themselves,
were made to sign the death warrant of slavery.[14]

The registration of slaves was not the only interference with the institution of slavery shortly after the
abolition of the slave trade. The attention of the humani-

[11] *Parliamentary Debates*, XXXIV, 1277.

[12] *Ibid.*, XXXVIII, 294 ff.

[13] *Ibid.*, XL, 976 ff.; Knutsford, *Zachary Macaulay*, p. 312. Parliament
established a registry of colonial slaves in England and provided that after
January 1, 1820, it should not be lawful for any British subject in the
United Kingdom ''to purchase, or to lend or advance any money, goods, or
effects upon the security of any slave or slaves in any of his Majesty's colonies or foreign possessions unless such slave or slaves shall appear by the
return received therein to have been first duly registered in the said office
of the Registrar of Colonial Slaves.'' 59 Geo. III, c. 120.

[14] Sir George Stephen, *Antislavery Recollections*, pp. 18, 19, called this
''a measure which not only gave the finishing stroke to the Slave Trade
Abolition and Felony Acts, but happily laid a foundation for those awful
statistics of slavery which proved the battle-axe of Mr. Fowell Buxton in
his many fearful contests for its total abolition.'' On the other hand slave
registration was a most direct recognition of the legal rights of the master
to his slave by parliament, thus adding this title to the various statutes encouraging or regulating the slave trade in earlier years. *Antislavery Recollections*, p. 21. *Review of Colonial Slave Registration Acts*, p. 4.

tarian party was attracted to the effects of abolition on the condition of the bondsmen, and this close attention in itself was dangerous to the perpetuation of slavery. The mind long familiar with the horrors of the slave trade was naturally quick to detect the horrors of slavery as well.

In 1809, two years after abolition, Wilberforce gave his opinion to a friend on the situation in the sugar islands: "It has grieved me not a little to hear that the planters in the West Indies are not at all proceeding to make such improvements in their system as their new situation requires. I have often thought it might do much good, if Collins' excellent work on the management of the negroes were generally circulated. It is astonishing how little it is known by the West Indians of education and knowledge of colonial concerns. But the subject to which I wish to draw your attention, is that of an institution for the religious instruction of the children of the slaves. Depend on it, their education would operate powerfully to produce marriage with all of its happy consequences."[15] Very likely the writer of the letter was not aware that in one paragraph he had curtailed the power of the owner of slaves in three aspects: The planters were to be taught better management; the children of the slaves were to be educated; and marriage was to be the consequence of education. Two years later Wilberforce heard that the masters were forbidding the teaching of religion in Trinidad and Demerara, and he protested vigorously to the prime minister that the teaching of religion must be permitted even though the missionaries were not members of the established church but Methodists.

But public interest in slavery in the British colonies was lukewarm. To revive it, Sir Samuel Romilly, a crimi-

15 R. I. and S. Wilberforce, *Life of Wilberforce*, III, 481-482.

nal law reformer, in 1818 asked for information regarding certain occurrences in the islands of Dominica and Nevis which threw much light on the treatment of slaves in the West Indies. Romilly attributed the loss of interest to the circulation of an ill-founded story of cruelty put forth by the African Institution.[16] This society in 1817 published a story which had been given to them of the cruel treatment of a slave in Antigua, and of the grand jury having thrown out a bill of indictment which was preferred against the author of the cruelty.[17] There was no foundation for the story and the printer of the society was prosecuted, convicted, and fined.[18] The West India party represented that all stories of cruelty in the West Indies were of an equally groundless nature,[19] and they began a regular propaganda, publishing numerous pamphlets, by means of which many of the newspapers were won over. It was practically impossible, moreover, to counteract the effect thus produced, because the press could not be used, as the judges of the king's bench, when they passed sentence on Hatchard, the printer of the African Institution, declared it was a libel to say of a West Indian grand jury that they were disposed to refuse justice to an injured individual.[20] Consequently, no one could write in defence of the negroes without exposing himself to a prosecution, for all the severities and cruelties were due to the injustice of the legislatures and tribunals. Therefore, it was only in parliament that facts

---

[16] *Memoirs of Romilly*, III, 337; *Parliamentary Debates*, XXXVIII, 298 ff., 841 ff. The suicide of Romilly occurred during the period of depression after the war. His suicide and that of Castlereagh and Whitbread, Wilberforce attributed to work on Sunday.

[17] This was published in *The Tenth Report of the Directors of the African Institution* and read at the annual meeting, March 27, 1816.

[18] Howell, *State Trials*, XXXII, 673-756.

[19] *Memoirs of Romilly*, III, 338.

[20] Howell, *State Trials*, XXXII, 752.

respecting the courts of justice in the West Indies, however well authenticated, could be brought forth.[21]

Romilly gave certain specific instances of cruelty and injustice. Slaves in Dominica were quite frequently sent to the public chain for private offences of which their masters might think them guilty. Governor Maxwell wished to remit the punishment of some of these slaves, but was told that he had no authority. Whereupon he consulted Glanville, the attorney-general of the island, who gave it as his opinion that, although the governor might by royal prerogative pardon slaves who had been judicially condemned to this punishment, he had no power whatever to release any slave who had been sentenced by the sole will of his master.[22]

A grand jury in Dominica, on February 4, 1817, threw out the bills preferred against masters for cruelty toward their slaves.[23] Upon this the governor determined to try to obtain justice for injured slaves without the intervention of a grand jury. Accordingly, by his direction, the attorney-general of the island filed three informations against persons for making their slaves work in chains and with iron collars round their necks, against the positive terms of an act of the assembly. The facts were clearly proved, but all the defendants were acquitted; and the grand jury again presented, as a matter

[21] *Memoirs of Romilly*, III, 338, 339.

[22] *Ibid.*, III, 340; *Parliamentary Debates*, XXXVIII, 301. The difficulty the governor of a colony had in interceding for a slave was stated by the wife of the governor of Jamaica: ''This case was, that two slaves, one, an old offender, the other a boy of sixteen, robbed a man of his watch, etc. . . . The old man has been condemned to hard labour, and the boy to be hanged. General N[ugent] made every exertion, but in vain, to save the life of the boy, and send him out of the country; but it appears that it could not be done, without exercising the prerogative very far, and giving great offence and alarm to the white population. . . .'' Lady Nugent's *Journal* (edited by Frank Cundall, 1907), pp. 71-72.

[23] *Parliamentary Debates*, XXXVIII, 298-300.

dangerous to the community, the interposition of the executive government between master and slave. The court, however, refused to receive this presentment, and it was withdrawn.[24]

A law was passed which imposed a restriction and a heavy tax on the manumission of slaves, and another law declared that no person of color, who landed in the island, should be considered as free, unless he produced a certificate of his freedom and paid a duty. "A slave," said Romilly, "no sooner sets his foot on the shores of Great Britain than he becomes free; while in Dominica, when a free negro lands upon their coast, he instantly sinks into a slave and it is only by money that he can redeem himself from that degraded condition."[25]

Another instance of cruelty to which Romilly referred was the treatment of a slave at Nevis. The owner, Huggins, had caused one hundred lashes with a cart whip, the usual instrument of punishment, to be inflicted on two very young boys; and he had been barbarous enough to inflict twenty lashes on the sister and a female cousin of the poor youths, because they had shed tears at witnessing the tortures of the boys. The case was clearly proved on trial, no witness was called for the defendant, and yet he was acquitted.[26]

In June, 1818, Romilly brought to the attention of the house another case of a slave in St. Kitts who was killed by punishment. A certain slave named Congo Jack had run away, but was captured and flogged. That night he was chained to another runaway slave, and the following day set to work without food or drink, still chained

24 *Memoirs of Romilly,* III, 339, 340; *Parliamentary Debates,* XXXVIII, 300.
25 *Memoirs of Romilly,* III, 341; *Parliamentary Debates,* XXXVIII, 303.
26 *Memoirs of Romilly,* III, 343. *Parliamentary Debates,* XXXVIII, 304, 841; Sir George Stephen, *Antislavery Recollections,* pp. 13-14.

to his fellow. Exhausted, he sank to the ground, but was flogged so mercilessly by two drivers that he died within a few hours. He was buried without a coroner's inquest, although the law of the island of St. Kitts provided that a coroner should be summoned in case a slave died without medical attention. However, the cruelty created some stir, so that the body was dug up, and it became plainly evident that death had been caused by physical violence. Nevertheless, the coroner's jury found that Congo Jack had died "by the visitation of God." But it proved impossible to dispose of the matter in this way, and one of the drivers was indicted for murder. In the course of the trial, it appeared that the Rev. Henry Rawlins, the owner of the slave, had taken the whip from the drivers and had himself flogged the slave until he sank to the ground. As a result, he was convicted of manslaughter and sentenced to pay a fine of £200 and to submit to three months' imprisonment.[27] Romilly concluded with a motion for copies of the deposition taken before the coroner, which was agreed to. The minutes of evidence had been laid before the house previously and printed. The secretary of state found it extremely difficult to obtain information on this case, as the assembly of St. Kitts was inclined to defend Rawlins, because he and his relative were members of it. These and other cases of cruelty and injustice in the islands, together with the great extent of the slave trade, served to arouse interest in the slavery question again.

The men who began the agitation against the slave trade had in mind two objects. They wanted to suppress this inhuman traffic, and by so doing to ameliorate the condition of the slaves in the British possessions. Up to the year 1823, they had failed in both their objects. The

[27] *Memoirs of Romilly*, III, 348; *Parliamentary Debates*, XXXVIII, 1201, 1202.

slave trade, though outlawed by most countries, was carried on as actively as ever before and with greater cruelty, and the condition of those negroes already in the islands was not improved. As the condition of the slaves in the British possessions was quite unsatisfactory, pressure was brought to bear on the colonies to induce them to pass laws to improve these conditions. But the laws passed by the colonies, as well as the treaties made by Great Britain with other nations, remained a dead letter. The efforts of thirty-five years, then, as far as actual results were concerned, had been unavailing. Indeed, the whole situation was so discouraging that it was decided to attack the problem in an entirely different manner. Instead of concentrating their efforts chiefly against the slave trade, the abolitionists determined to begin a struggle against the obnoxious institution of slavery itself. In this way they hoped to abolish the slave trade by removing the demand for it, for, with the slaves emancipated, there would be no object in bringing in fresh supplies.

# CHAPTER VIII

## THE GOVERNMENT POLICY OF GRADUAL EMANCIPATION

To effect the gradual emancipation of the slaves, the Anti-Slavery Society was organized in 1823. Many of the men who had fought for the abolition of the slave trade were dead; among them were Granville Sharp, John Newton, the younger Pitt, Charles James Fox, and Henry Thornton. On the other hand, William Wilberforce, William Smith, James Stephen, Zachary Macaulay, and Thomas Clarkson were still active. Although Clarkson's health had given way in 1794, he helped in the final struggle against the British slave trade, took part in the anti-slavery movement, and outlived all of his earlier helpers, remaining alert until 1846.

A few men deserve most of the credit for the emancipation of the slaves. Henry Brougham and Thomas Fowell Buxton were the chief parliamentary champions of the negro, Buxton becoming the successor of Wilberforce. James Stephen and Zachary Macaulay were the two main supporters of the cause outside of parliament, and they did the greater part of the hard work. In order to have his hands free for the coming struggle Macaulay, who had amassed a small fortune of about £100,000, early in 1823 gave over the conduct of his firm to his junior partner, his nephew, Babington, who in three years dissipated the property by bad management.

Macaulay was distinguished by his strong nerves, his earnest and monotonous expression of countenance, his overhanging brows, and his athletic, awkward figure. He was loved in his own circle despite the impression of austerity which he conveyed.[1] "Mr. Macaulay's mission," wrote Sir George Stephen, "most undoubtedly was to be the indomitable friend of the negro race. Mr. Wilberforce required his systematic industry; Mr. Stephen needed his affectionate restraint; Mr. Brougham desiderated his practical sobriety of mind; Dr. Lushington his shrewd experience; Mr. William Smith, his sturdy independence of party. And one and all derived firmness and assurance from his encyclian colonial knowledge, and his painfully veracious accuracy."[2]

His devotion to the African race covered a lifetime. "While yet a boy," said Sir James Stephen, "he had watched as the iron entered into the soul of the slaves, whose labours he was sent to superintend in Jamaica: and abandoning with abhorrence a pursuit which had promised him early wealth and distinction, he pondered the question—how shall the earth be delivered from this curse? Turning to Sierra Leone, he braved for many years that deadly climate, that he might aid in the erection and in the defence of what was then the one city of refuge for the Negro race; and as he saw the slave trade crushing to the dust the adjacent tribes of Africa, he again pondered the question—how shall the earth be delivered from this curse?"[3]

Macaulay was blessed with an iron constitution, which enabled him to work longer hours than were ever required from a slave on a West Indian plantation. He rose every morning at four and disposed of his own work for the day before others appeared at theirs. His industry was astonishing: "Blue books and state papers were

---

[1] Sir James Stephen, *Essays in Ecclesiastical Biography*, II, 325-326.
[2] Sir George Stephen, *Antislavery Recollections*, p. 52.
[3] Sir James Stephen, *Essays in Ecclesiastical Biography*, II, 327.

child's play to him, however dull or voluminous; he would attend half a dozen charitable committees in every quarter of the town, during the day, and refresh himself after dinner with a parliamentary folio that would have choked an alderman by the sight of it alone. His memory was so retentive, that, without the trouble of reference, he could collate the papers of one session with those of the three or four preceding years; he analyzed with such rapidity that he could reduce to ten or twenty pages all that was worth extracting from five hundred; his acuteness was so great that no fallacy of argument escaped him, and no sophistry could bewilder him; and more than that he was accuracy and truth itself.''[4]

Macaulay was, in fact, the bulwark of every man who fought in the anti-slavery ranks. He was quickly recognized by the West Indians as the most dangerous enemy of their system, and in consequence no effort was spared to crush his fighting spirit. The editor of *John Bull* attacked him and he, in turn, brought action for libel against the paper.[5] Thus in addition to the loss of his fortune he suffered a journalistic attack and the loss of

[4] Sir George Stephen, *Antislavery Recollections*, pp. 50-51.

[5] Characteristic of *John Bull* is its treatment of Macaulay's part in securing an order in Council to limit the shipment of gunpowder to Africa so that there might be less civil war there. After some introductory remarks *John Bull* continued: ''Now for a 'Touch of the Trader.' While Zachariah, the Saint, was pressing this measure upon the Lords of the Treasury, Mr. Zachary, the merchant, was freighting a vessel with gunpowder, her foretopsail loose, her Blue-Peter flying, and the capstan manned to 'Up anchor and away,' the moment the order in Council should issue, he having previously procured from Zachariah, the Saint, a copy of the said order to send out per said ship—which all came to pass, no other African merchant being in the slightest degree in the secret—so, out went the ship, powder and order and all, up rose the commodity to £20 per barrel on her arrival on the Coast, and Mr. Zachary Macaulay pocketted somewhere about five hundred per cent upon the shipment.

''We need say no more—next week we shall continue to pluck the daw, it is all we wish, all we want, we have no desire but that Mr. Zachary Mahis robust health. Nothing could dismay him; he rose from a sick bed to rally his forces and lead them to victory.

No tribute paid to Zachary Macaulay can detract from the credit due to James Stephen, the brother-in-law of Wilberforce, and his two sons, Sir James and Sir George. James Stephen fought for the abolition of the slave trade; he devised the system of registration; he wrote the leading treatise on slavery.[6] Sir James became the most influential man in the colonial office and drafted the emancipation act. Sir George organized the agency committee of the Anti-Slavery Society and conducted the whirlwind campaign during the two years prior to the emancipation act of 1833. The services of these high-spirited men, all of them lawyers, were invaluable because they held themselves ready at all times to undertake the hardest tasks of grinding research. Actuated by deep religious motives, they were invincible leaders of a large humanitarian following.

caulay should enjoy the fruits of a long and active mercantile life in quiet and comfort, but against Saint Zachariah we wage eternal war.

''When we find this great Mumbo Jumbo exalted as one of the stalking horses, behind which the most debased and depraved anarchists and terrorists, quacks, charlatans, depredators, and disturbers, intend to frighten the people of England out of their senses and their colonies, and bully the West Indian proprietors out of their rights and their property, it is high time that the idol and his fellows should be stripped and served as the stuffed effigies of Guy Fawkes were on Wednesday, exhibited to the populace, at once objects of ridicule and contempt in themselves, but commemorating in their exposure the preservation of the country from a dreadful explosion.'' *John Bull*, November 10, 1823, p. 356. Macaulay was pursued in this manner at every step. He was charged with such gross cruelty as an overseer in Jamaica that he was dismissed by the owner. All the anti-slavery leaders were charged with having a lust for holding lucrative positions and the like. *John Bull*, June 15, 1823, p. 188.

[6] James Stephen, *The Slavery of the British West India Colonies Delineated, as it exists, Both in Law and in Practise, and Compared with the Slavery of other Countries, Antient and Modern* (2 vols. London, 1824, 1830). Cited hereafter as *Slavery Delineated*.

The West Indians attributed various interested motives to James Stephen and hinted that there were mysterious reasons for his opposition to slavery.[7] This led him in his old age to publish in volume two of *Slavery Delineated* a statement of the reasons why he had never owned a slave and had devoted his life to the negro race.[8] The shocking procedure of a West Indian trial of four negroes at which he was present in 1783 made an indelible impression on him and caused him to vow eternal hatred to the slave system. "The court, consisting of a bench of justices of the peace, five, I think, in number, without a jury," he wrote in 1830, "was no sooner constituted than the four black prisoners were placed at the bar; and as they were the first common field negroes I had seen, their filthy and scanty garb would have moved my pity if I had not been more strongly excited by the pain they were visibly suffering from the tight ligatures of cord round their crossed wrists, which supplied the place of handcuffs. I noticed it to my companion and said, 'surely they will be put at bodily ease during their trial,' but he replied that it was not customary.'"[9]

The justices were bent on the conviction of the pris-

[7] *John Bull* constantly referred to interested motives on the part of Macaulay and Stephen: "Macaulay (who is the most active of the *set*) having made a fortune by trade in Sierra Leone, has established himself as an East India merchant, and is deeply interested in the success of the *East India* sugar trade, that Stephen (another of them) sold when he could get the highest price for them, all his slaves and property in St. Kitts." *John Bull*, Oct. 19, 1823, p. 332.

[8] Sir George Stephen described his father as having a noble countenance "marked by frankness, intelligence, and ardour. He was somewhat above the middle heighth, and his features were open and regular . . . his deep-seated eye gleamed like a star when he was excited." On one occasion when disappointed with the government, even Macaulay, to whom he generally deferred more than to any other man, could not soothe him. "When we left the room, Mr. Macaulay turned to me and said, 'In anger, your father is terrific.'" Sir George Stephen, *Antislavery Recollections*, pp. 32-33.

[9] James Stephen, *Slavery Delineated*, II, xix.

oners and frightened the only material witness, a young
crippled negro girl, by dire threats if she refused to tell
the truth. All four were convicted, but the owner of two of
the slaves, on learning the nature of the evidence, readily
established an alibi for his negroes; the other negroes,
however, convicted on the same evidence, were burned
alive with the approval of the royal governor. ''Such was
the case,'' Stephen continued, ''which gave me my first
right views of negro slavery in the sugar colonies, almost
as soon as I reached their shores. . . . If I have contributed in any degree to the abolition of the slave trade, or
shall ever have the happiness to promote the deliverance
of its much injured victims in our colonies, the blood that
was cruelly shed at Bridgetown, forty-seven years ago,
was not shed in vain.''[10]

When the weight of years and the feebleness of health
had diminished Wilberforce's capacity for work, and it
was necessary, therefore, to find a new parliamentary
leader, Wilberforce naturally looked for his successor
among the members of his own religious sect. Nearly all
of the conspicuous abolitionists, Granville Sharp, James
Stephen, Zachary Macaulay, Newton, and Thornton, were
numbered among the band of low churchmen, whom it was
customary to deride as ''the saints.''[11] Among them also
was Thomas Fowell Buxton, who had entered parliament
in 1818 and who had already taken a prominent part in
reform measures, notably the reform of the criminal law.
Now, at the invitation of Wilberforce, he undertook the
task of pleading the cause of the slaves, and became their
militant champion both in and out of parliament.

Buxton had the misfortune to lose his father at an early
age. His mother, a Quakeress and a woman of talent and

---

[10] James Stephen, *Slavery Delineated*, II, xxvii-xxix.
[11] Sir James Stephen, *Essays in Ecclesiastical Biography*, II, 287-383;
*Parliamentary Debates*, second series, IX, 255 ff.

energy, exerted a marked influence on the character of each of her children. An acquaintance, formed at a very early period of his life, with the Gurneys of Earlham increased the impression which his mother's precepts had made on him. Gurney was a Quaker. His fifth daughter, Hannah Gurney, gained the affections of young Buxton, was engaged to him before he was out of his teens, and was married to him when he had only just completed his twenty-first year.

Buxton's early marriage had an immediate influence on his future career. He had recently graduated at Dublin, and the distinction which he had gained in his academic work had brought him an offer to stand for the university. He hesitated, however, to incur at the same time the expense of married life and that of a parliamentary contest. He accordingly refused to stand for parliament at this time and accepted a situation in Truman's brewery; he did not enter the Commons till about ten years later, in 1818. Constantly engaged in the east end of London, he set himself to alleviate the terrible distress which was hardly ever absent from Spitalfields, and devoted almost the whole of his leisure to works of charity. He soon joined the ranks of the reformers and became a member of the African Institution—the society which proposed to watch over the law abolishing the slave trade. The society, however, slumbered over its victory and was only reawakened in January, 1821, by Buxton's 'vehement reprobation.'[12]

Described by Sir George Stephen as a "tower of strength," and by Wilberforce as like one of his own dray horses, powerful, sleek, and slow, Buxton was known to be a man of immense energy, determination, and inflexibility, once he had chosen his course of action. He was

[12] Buxton, *Memoirs*, pp. 104-105.

fond of elaborate statistics and was not an exciting speaker, but his speeches were certain to be fully reported. He was upheld by thousands and tens of thousands of loyal followers outside of the house. He was a man "who when he had resolved that anything should be done, *would do it* . . . he might be coughed down or counted out fifty times; all would prove of no avail; session after session the motion would be renewed and the debate revived; . . ."[13] He was deliberate, even timid, in studying the bearings of every course that he took. He had a good judgment of men, but was charitable and large in heart as he was in every other way. Even his height was gigantic.

Besides his "all-powerful out of doors" following, he was supported by his household and a devoted group of friends. The Gurneys were all identified with him, and Samuel Gurney was always ready with advice and assistance, as was Samuel Hoare, whose wife belonged to a family "as celebrated on the female side, for its beauty, as for its insatiable benevolence on both sides." These men carried with them many supporters. "They held up his arms in battle and prayed with him in the closet; they buckled on his armour in the morning, and they unclasped it in the evening, and prepared it for the morrow, while they cheered his depressed spirits and rallied his exhausted strength."[14]

In the language of the abolition oratory, his home was described as a conservatory in which the exotic of negro freedom was nurtured until strong enough to bear transplanting for future generations to see the extension of its foliage over America and Africa itself.[15] The great inter-

---

[13] Sir George Stephen, *Antislavery Recollections*, p. 224, 231.

[14] *Ibid.*, pp. 236-237.

[15] The charges brought against the character of Buxton were very similar to those directed against Stephen and Macaulay. Writing in 1832, he dis-

est of his life Buxton showed even in his playfulness in his home. For his daughter, Priscilla, he bought a horse, naming it Stephen in honor of George Stephen. He refused to sell one of his horses to the prince regent, saying "Yes it was a likely thing truly, that I should degrade John Bull to serve for his royal seat."[16]

Before beginning the story of the final movement, which gave freedom to the slaves, a definition of slavery is necessary in order to make clear the steps taken by the English government to bring about the desired result. Nieboer has a satisfactory definition: "We may define a slave in the ordinary sense of the word as a man who is the property of another, politically and socially at a lower level than the mass of the people, and performing compulsory labor."[17] By a process of reasoning, he reduced his definition to the following: "Slavery is the fact that one man is the property or possession of another."[18] According to James Stephen, "By the law of the colonies, slavery is a constrained servitude during the life of the slave; it is service without wages; the master is the

cussed the five accusations brought against him in 1824. "The fifth charge is simply, that 'I am Judas Iscariot,' an enemy to slavery, though every shilling I possess was wrung from the bones and sinews of slaves. *I repeat I never was the master of a slave—I never bought one, or sold one, or hired one. I never owned a hogshead of sugar or an acre of land in the West Indies.*

"I may as well here state what foundation there is for this widely circulated report. 'Some truth there is—though brewed and dashed with lies.' There was a Mrs. Barnard. She was my grandfather's sister. She embarked a sum of money in a West India House, the greater part of which she lost. The remnant descended to some of my near relations. So far is true. But it is also true that in that property I never happened to be a partaker. I am not, and, to the best of my knowledge, *never have been, the owner of a shilling derived from Slaves.*" Anti-Slavery Reporter, V, 306, Nov. 15, 1832.

[16] Sir George Stephen, *Antislavery Recollections*, pp. 226-228.

[17] H. J. Nieboer, *Slavery as an Industrial System* (The Hague, 1910), p. 5.

[18] *Ibid.*, pp. 7-8.

sole arbiter of the kind, and degree, and time of labor, to which the slave shall be subjected; and of the subsistence, which shall be given in return.'"[19] He, likewise, contracted his definition as follows: "The main object of slavery in the sugar colonies is the obtaining, by compulsion, the labor of negroes in the cultivation of the land.'"[20]

The object of the anti-slavery men was to destroy the "possession" of negroes, to do away with compulsion, and to substitute for it some other inducement to work. They thought that negroes would work for the same reasons as white men if but given the chance. They wished to substitute wages for the whip. To this the West Indians replied that they had no abstract love for slavery and would gladly adopt any other satisfactory system; but that negroes would not do a very satisfactory amount of work except under compulsion. As their wants were few and easily satisfied in the rich islands, they were naturally lazy, so that, without compulsion, they would work but little. The result, they thought, would be that all West India property would be ruined, as its value was entirely dependent on negro labor. Cases of cruelty, they said, were but incidental to slavery and not its aim, as the anti-slavery people seemed to think. Moreover, slave property was sanctioned by the laws of England, by acts of parliament, and by decisions of courts; through the encouragement of the slave trade given by the mother country, Englishmen had been induced to invest money in the West Indies.

In the destruction of the master's power over his slave, every act of whatever nature which interfered with the master's possession was a step toward emancipation. This fact must be kept in mind in order to understand the history of the movement during the next ten years. It ex-

[19] James Stephen, *Slavery Delineated*, I, 33.
[20] *Ibid.*, II, 44.

plains the policy of the two contending parties in the struggle and also the policy of the government.

The anti-slavery champions had to undertake a new campaign of education against a long established system, in order to arouse the people of Great Britain. As in the past, they published books and pamphlets, wrote reviews for the magazines and articles for the newspapers, delivered lectures, and circulated petitions. In all these ways they acquainted the people with the horrors of slavery. They were joined by men of ulterior motives; representatives of the East India interests, who wished to secure the market of Great Britain on the same terms as the West Indies; men who were chiefly interested in other reforms which they hoped to further by this campaign; men who were desirous of bringing themselves before the public. In other words, this movement, like many other humanitarian movements, enlisted the support of all kinds of people.

The public campaign, begun in 1823, was conducted energetically. Wilberforce published an address to the people of Great Britain;[21] his friends prepared for the parliamentary contest by correspondence and conferences;[22] James Stephen was induced to resume his treatise on slavery;[23] Zachary Macaulay busied himself in collecting evidence, wrote a tract on *Negro Slavery* and later edited *The Anti-Slavery Reporter*. Buxton agreed to lead the cause in parliament, while Brougham pledged his assistance there and in the public press. The West Indians were ready to refute every fact and any argu-

[21] William Wilberforce, *An appeal to the Religion, Justice, and Humanity of the Inhabitants of the British Empire in behalf of Slaves in the West Indies.*

[22] R. I. and S. Wilberforce, *Life of Wilberforce*, II, 157-160, 162-163, 164-171; Viscountess Knutsford, *Life and Letters of Zachary Macaulay*, pp. 379 ff., 383-388.

[23] James Stephen, *Slavery Delineated*, I, i-iii.

ment, and could rely upon the support of the many people whose interests were involved.[24] To bring about the change from slavery to freedom was one of the most difficult tasks ever undertaken. The great mass of evidence and the complexity of the subject called for patience, skill, and courage.

It was Wilberforce, again, who in March, 1823, started the struggle against slavery by presenting in parliament a Quaker petition. The petitioners asserted that it was the duty of parliament to put an end to slavery in the British dominions, and to restore those unhappy persons who were suffering under its yoke to the moral dignity of the enjoyment of liberty.[25] This appeal was considered the first shot in the campaign. Wilberforce felt that emancipation was enjoined on Great Britain by the highest motives which could actuate human beings, and which also seemed expedient from every point of true policy and of the best interests of the West India proprietors themselves. The difficulty with him and the other anti-slavery leaders was that they did not know negroes, and their policy was grounded on a too optimistic belief in the black man's capacity for rapid improvement.[26] They

[24] Sir George Stephen wrote of the strength of the West India interest in his *Antislavery Recollections*, p. 113. ''The colonial interest did not reside in the colonies, the colonies were to legislate, it is true, but the wires were pulled by the West India body at home. The consignees and mortgagees of West India property resided in London, Liverpool and Glasgow. Bristol too was a favoured spot, and the slaves were scarcely more the property of the planters, than the planters themselves were the property of their consignees and creditors on this side of the Atlantic.'' Many of the peers, too, were interested in slave plantations and the bishops held negro property as trustees of the Society for the Propagation of the Gospel, which had an estate in Barbadoes.

[25] *Parliamentary Debates*, second series, VIII, 624-630.

[26] Wilberforce stated his view by declaring that the negroes were ''men, who, when transplanted to a more genial soil, and blessed with the benefits of education, had shown, by the very rapid progress which they made in

believed that the negro was a white man enslaved, and based their crusade on this assumption. They were not opposed to compensation for the slave owner if injury were done him, but thought a free negro would outwork a slave, and consequently they did not believe that compensation would be necessary. In any case they were determined to persevere until they succeeded, even as they had done in the cause of abolition.

At the end of Wilberforce's speech, Buxton gave notice of his intention to bring in a motion on slavery.[27] Well acquainted with his subject and with plans carefully matured, Buxton, in May, 1823, brought the question of slavery before the House of Commons. In the debate which ensued the three factions or parties to the struggle appeared as they always did whenever the subject was under discussion, each regarding the question from an entirely different point of view. The anti-slavery party idealized the negro and emphasized the humanitarian side of the question; the West Indians had their property at stake and consequently were prejudiced by self-interest; the government, on which the responsibility finally rested, looked at the matter from the standpoint of the interests of the empire, and their own voting strength in the House of Commons.

Buxton began his speech for emancipation by denying that the dangers of agitating the question were very great. The West Indians had constantly predicted insurrections during the agitation against the slave trade, but events had proved the incorrectness of their prognostications.[28] The peril of the West Indies lay in slavery, not in freedom. The ruler of Haiti might conquer them, pro-

---

humanity, religion, and civilization, that they were not inferior to any other nation in capability of improvement.'' *Ibid.*, 628-629.

[27] *Parliamentary Debates,* second series, VIII, 630.

[28] *Ibid.*, IX, 259 ff.

claiming freedom to the slaves, and Buxton quoted Pitt who said that "it was impossible to increase the happiness or enlarge the freedom of the negro without in an equal degree adding to the security of the colonies, and of their inhabitants."[29]

Buxton, therefore, moved the following resolution as the basis of his policy: "That the state of slavery is repugnant to the principles of the British constitution, and of the Christian religion, and that it ought to be abolished gradually throughout the British colonies, with as much expedition as may be found consistent with a due regard to the well-being of the parties concerned."[30] His plan consisted of two parts: first, all children born after a certain date were to be free; and secondly, the negroes who were slaves were to have the benefit of measures of amelioration.[31] The first part of his plan meant the extinction of slavery. "The operation of this one principle would be," he said, "that slavery would burn itself down into its socket and go out."[32] Every child born would increase the body of the free; every slave dying would decrease the number of those in bondage. This course was defended as practicable. It had been adopted in New York, Ceylon, Bencoolen, Saint Helena, and Colombia, and had been successful wherever tried. It meant the certain extinction of slavery, and Buxton warned the government that he considered it the main part of his plan. He would call on the public loudly to express their opinions, till justice had so far prevailed that every child was entitled to liberty.

As for the second part of his plan, he admitted that he could not call for the immediate emancipation of the ex-

[29] *Parliamentary Debates*, second series, IX, 263-264.
[30] *Ibid.*, IX, 274-275.
[31] *Ibid.*, IX, 265 ff.
[32] *Ibid.*, IX, 265 ff.

isting slaves, because they were not ready for deliverance. Were they ready, he should not hesitate on the ground that the master had the least shadow of a title to them. What he did ask for were certain improvements which had been communicated to the government. They were: that the slaves should be attached to the island and, under modifications, to the soil; that they should cease to be chattels in the eye of the law; that their testimony should be received, *quantum valet;* that when anyone claimed the service of a negro, the *onus probandi* should rest on the claimant; that all obstructions to manumission should be removed; that the provisions of the Spanish law (fixing by competent authority the value of the slave and allowing him to purchase his freedom a day at a time)[33] should be introduced; that no governor, judge, or attorney-general should be a slave owner; that an effectual provision should be made for the religious instruction of the slaves; that marriage should be sanctioned and enforced; that Sunday should be devoted by the slave to repose and religious instruction; that other time should be allotted for the cultivation of his provision grounds; that some measures (but what, he could not say) should be taken to restrain the authority of the master in punishing his untrained slave; and that some substitute should be found for the driving system.[34]

Such were the principal points of his plan. In the first place, by freeing children thereafter to be born, it changed the master's property from one of perpetual possession to one of life tenure. In the second place, it meant that the "possession" of the master was limited, that his authority was circumscribed by certain fixed

[33] A slave was to be permitted to buy his freedom in installments, purchasing first one day's freedom per week, then two day's and so on until he had purchased total emancipation.

[34] *Parliamentary Debates*, second series, IX, 273.

regulations, and that the negro was to be given certain personal rights which he had not before enjoyed. This measure was to be merely preparatory, for with the negro's advance in moral and religious training, his personal rights would doubtless be increased, and he might even be accorded political rights. Indeed, the present slave was not doomed to slavery for life, as some provision was to be made for his manumission.

Buxton's speech, like so many others on the same topic, combined abundant declamation against slavery and logical and Scriptural demonstrations of its unreasonableness with pictures of the cruelties with which it was, had been, and might be connected.[35] It was in many ways a "higher law" speech. The slave had been made a captive by robbery, and so had a better right to his body than the master, though the latter had paid a price for him. Children were the greatest victims of this cruel system, as they were born to a state from which there was no escape. To make a slave of a full-grown negro had been declared piracy, but the law made slaves of the children by the fact of their birth. These children, Buxton proposed, should be stripped of every vestige of servitude; "and by taking upon ourselves for a season the whole burthen of their maintenance, education, and religious instruction, we may raise them into a happy, contented, enlightened, free peasantry."[36]

Secretary Canning spoke for the government.[37] After deprecating the introduction of declamatory topics, and particularly of the delineation of cruelties that had long ceased, he contended that the proposed resolutions proceeded from a principle which, though true in one sense, was not true in the sense in which it was used. The Brit-

35 *Parliamentary Debates,* second series, IX, 257-275, *passim.*
36 *Ibid.,* IX, 274.
37 *Ibid.,* IX, 275 ff.

ish constitution and the Christian religion were in their spirit unfavorable to slavery, and naturally hostile to it; but neither that constitution nor that religion prohibited slavery. The name of Christianity, he thought, ought not thus to be used, unless parliament was prepared to act in a much more summary manner than Buxton proposed, and in such a case, it was impossible to divide slaves into two classes, one of which was to be freed immediately, the other only to have their condition ameliorated. Canning protested against the literal sense and the too positive language of Buxton's resolution, but sympathized with its intention and was ready to favor all reasonable and practicable measures for the purpose in view.[38] His criticism of the plan to give freedom to children born after a certain date[39] was that this did not appear to him to be the kind of measure just mentioned, for it would not work well. At the same time, he abjured the principle of perpetual slavery, and thought the progeny of slaves should not be slaves eternally, though he had no plan to propose. In other words, he evaded the first part of Buxton's plan.

Concerning measures for the mitigation of slavery, there was more agreement. Canning opposed the flogging of females, either as a stimulant to labor in the field or as an instrument of punishment. He regarded the time allowed the negro for religious and moral instruction as insufficient.[40] He was strongly inclined to agree that property commonly considered the slave's should be secured to him by law; that it would be beneficial if the liberty of bequest were assured to him (perhaps conditional on marriage); that it might possibly be desirable to do something with regard to admitting the evidence of ne-

---

[38] *Parliamentary Debates*, second series, IX, 281.
[39] *Ibid.*, IX, 285 ff.
[40] *Ibid.*, IX, 282 ff.

groes; and that the process of the writ of *venditioni exponas*, by which slaves were sold separately from the
estates, ought, if possible, to be abolished.[41] He wished
the adoption of such a policy as should not only embody
the hopes held out for the future, but also express the
doubts, delays, and difficulties to be surmounted before
those hopes could possibly be realized. With these things
in mind, he had prepared and submitted the following
resolutions:

"1. That it is expedient to adopt effectual and decisive
measures for ameliorating the condition of the slave
population of his Majesty's colonies.

"2. That through a determined and vigorous, but at
the same time judicious and temperate, enforcement of
such measures, this House looks forward to a progressive
improvement in the character of the slave population,
such as may prepare them for a participation in those
civil rights and privileges which are enjoyed by other
classes of his Majesty's subjects.

"3. That this House is anxious for the accomplishment
of these purposes at the earliest period that may be, consistently with the welfare of the slaves themselves, the
well-being of the colonies, and a fair and equitable consideration of the state of property therein."[42]

Canning summarized the whole problem from the government point of view in a single sentence: "The question to be decided is, how civil rights, moral improvement and general happiness are to be communicated to
this overpowering multitude of slaves, with safety to the
lives and security to the interests of the white population,
our fellow-subjects and fellow-citizens."[43] The carrying
out of measures was to be left in the hands of the execu-

41 *Parliamentary Debates*, second series, IX, 283, 284.
42 *Ibid.*, IX, 285-286.
43 *Ibid.*, IX, 277.

tive, and the West Indians were assured that their interests would not be sacrificed in righting a national wrong.[44] Canning's plan placed the emphasis on the mitigation of slavery, and, if the second resolution meant anything, it meant preparations for ultimate emancipation. No provision was made for compensation, as the government felt that the proposed measures of interference would not lessen the value of the slave to his master. The plan was, however, far less radical than that of the emancipationists, as everything was left vague and indefinite. Canning said, "I am disposed to go gradually to work, in order to diminish both the danger to be risked and the burden to be incurred."[45]

The best presentation of the planters' side of the case was made by Charles Ellis, who remained throughout the struggle their ablest champion, first in the House of Commons and later, as Lord Seaford, in the Lords. Slave owners had obtained their property under the guarantee of parliament.[46] They had been encouraged by the colonial system, and that system was not established for the sake of the colonies, but for the encouragement of British commerce and manufactures; for the purpose, to use the words of the navigation act, "of rendering His Majesty's plantations beyond seas beneficial and advantageous to this kingdom in the employment of English ships and Englishmen."[47] Parliament had made efforts to secure to British subjects the exclusive profits of this traffic, and to render it, under the navigation laws, one of the means of maritime strength; therefore, the responsibility for West Indian conditions could not be thrown on the planters. Immediate emancipation would probably lead

[44] *Parliamentary Debates*, second series, IX, 287.
[45] *Ibid.*, IX, 282.
[46] *Ibid.*, IX, 295-296.
[47] *Ibid.*, IX, 297.

the slaves to desert their work and retire to the mountains to live by robbery and plunder. Ellis expressed his ideas as to the course to be pursued in regard to slaves by saying that it was "Our duty so to prepare them by religious instruction, by the gradual acquisition of civil rights, and by the habits of civilized life, that the influence of these habits may be substituted for the authority of the master whenever that authority shall be withdrawn; that they may become honest, peaceable, moral, and industrious members of a free society, and that the transition may take place without a convulsion."[48] But parliamentary interference, he contended, would only lead to disaster; the work should be left to the executive and the colonial legislatures. The difficulty of the question was much increased by race prejudices, by the overpowering numbers and physical force of the slave population as compared with those of the whites in the colonies, and by the great political power which would of necessity be conveyed by an equal participation in all the civil rights.[49]

These considerations, complicated by fears on one side and claims on the other, made the question one of the most difficult ever presented to the legislature of any country. Buxton, Wilberforce, and William Smith argued that no reliance could be placed on the colonial legislatures,[50] as they had made few laws in the negro's behalf, and these few were not enforced, having been passed only for effect. Ellis thought that the difficulties ought to be taken into consideration before the assemblies were condemned. Jamaica was cited to show how much the colonies had done to improve the condition of the slaves.[51]

48 *Parliamentary Debates*, second series, IX, 299.
49 *Ibid.*, IX, 300.
50 *Ibid.*, IX, 290-293, 308.
51 *Ibid.*, IX, 301 ff.

Curates had been induced to settle on the island, and the consolidated slave law of 1787 had been revised in 1801, 1807, 1809, and 1816. The last revision made easier regulations for manumission by will and for the alleged freemen; purchase of slaves by middlemen was then prohibited, and the powers of vestries, as a council for protection, were enlarged. An effort was made to prohibit the sales of slaves under the writ of *venditioni exponas,* but the legal difficulties were found insurmountable. In 1811 a law was passed compelling the overseer or manager of an estate to give information to the coroner of the unnatural death of any slave. The laws were not a dead letter, Ellis argued, because there had been improvements in the habits and behavior of the negroes. The cart whip, he declared, was a mere badge of authority. In short, the West Indians were ready to accept every fair and reasonable proposal. There had been many marriages and baptisms, but the bad morals and licentiousness of the clergy were due to the fact that the superintendence and patronage of the Church establishment were retained by the mother country.[52]

Representatives of the West India interest called attention to the difference between slavery in the West Indies and that in New York and the other places Buxton had mentioned, where white men were in the great majority, and the loss incurred by freeing children was insisted on. It was said that in London the fashionable way

[52] *Parliamentary Debates,* second series, IX, 303-308. It is perhaps well to notice at once one of the great sources of dispute between the anti-slavery party and the West Indians. The former always charged the latter with defying the suggestions and exhortations made by the government to the colonial assemblies for the sake of improving their laws. Laws passed were either not enforced or were defective chiefly because they lacked power of execution and had no penalty attached. The West Indians denied this, and cited many acts in their support, but without convincing the anti-slavery party. The fact is, as can be seen if we look ahead, the anti-slavery party was nearly right in its contention.

to quiet one's conscience was by subscribing to a missionary society or signing a petition against slavery.[53] Brougham pointed out that one of the chief causes of cruelty to
slaves lay in absenteeism. Property in the West Indies
was held by men living in England, and ownership par-
took of the nature of a hazardous commercial speculation;
therefore, the landlord was anxious to secure the largest
returns in the shortest time, while the estate was in his
possession, having no regard for the interests of his
slaves.[54] At the end of the long debate, which lasted far
into the morning, Buxton withdrew his resolutions, and
those of Canning were agreed to unanimously.[55]

At the very time that the anti-slavery leaders were beginning their attack on the institution of slavery, the
merchants of London engaged in the East India trade
were asking for the same rates of duty on their sugar as
those levied on the West India product. An economic conflict existed between the two Indies. The question arises
as to what influence that fact had on the struggle against
slavery? Was there, indeed, an alliance between the East
Indians and the anti-slavery party? There certainly was
coöperation. The anti-slavery men wrote and spoke in
favor of the East Indies, both in and out of parliament,
while the East Indians eagerly supported the negro
cause.[56] A short discussion of the sugar duties levied on

[53] *Parliamentary Debates*, second series, IX, 342-349.

[54] *Ibid.*, IX, 334-335.

[55] *Ibid.*, IX, 359-360.

[56] *Ibid.*, IX, 467; R. I. and S. Wilberforce, *Life of Wilberforce*, V, 180.
"W. Whitemore's motion about sugar duty. None interested for the question but the East Indians and a few of us anti-slavers, and the West
Indians and government against us; so that 161 a less majority over 34
than might have been expected." The sugar duties were discussed by several
anti-slavery leaders: Zachary Macaulay, *East and West India sugar; or a
refutation of the claims of the West India colonists to a protecting duty
on East India sugar* (London, Relfe, 1823, viii, 128 pp.); James Cropper, *
*Letters to Mr. Wilberforce, M.P.*, recommending the encouragement of the

the two Indies and of the economic condition of the American Indies may make it possible to understand better the anti-slavery movement.

Sugar imported from the East Indies was subject to a duty, in one instance of ten shillings per cwt., and in another, of fifteen shillings higher than that payable upon sugars brought from the West Indies. This discrimination was obnoxious to the East Indians, so that repeated efforts were made by them to obtain its removal. For this purpose, a petition was presented in March, 1823, by the body of merchants, agents, and shipowners interested in the East Indian trade who lived in London,[57] praying for a just classification of East Indian sugars according to their quality, and the imposition of the same duties on them as were imposed on West Indian sugars. The petitioners defended their demands by pointing out that the colonial system of the country had been changed so that the West Indians were no longer confined, in their trade, to the mother country, but by the acts 3 Geo. IV, cap. 44 and 45, their freedom of trade had been extended, so that they might trade with the United States of America, with Spanish America, and with the continent of Europe.[58] Therefore the East Indian trade and the people of Great Britain ought to be relieved from the burden of the protective duty and from the virtual monopoly of the home market to the West Indians. The fact that their sugars were allowed to enter into direct competition with East Indian sugars in foreign markets conferred an undue advantage on the West Indians over the East Indians. Be-

cultivation of sugar in the East Indies, as the certain and natural means of effecting the total abolition of the slave trade (1822); James Cropper, *Relief for West Indian distress* showing the inefficiency of protecting duties on East Indian sugar, and pointing out other remedies of certain relief (London, Hatchard, 1823, 2, 33 pp.).

[57] *Parliamentary Debates,* second series, VIII, 337 ff.

[58] 3 Geo. IV, cc. 44, 45, June 24, 1822.

sides this, it was alleged, the duty raised the price to the consumer, decreased consumption, and hence reduced the revenue. Finally, the duty was highly injurious to the merchants, manufacturers, and shipowners engaged in the trade between Great Britain and India, because sugar as ballast in ships returning from India was necessary to the existence of the trade with that country. The population of India was large, and commerce with Great Britain was capable of unlimited expansion. The people of India, as British subjects, were entitled to a fair participation in the home market, especially since their own industries had been destroyed by British policy.[59] These demands were strongly resisted by the West Indians, who regarded the proposed equalization of duties as the climax of their troubles. They were suffering great distress and receiving small, if any, returns on their investments. Why then at such a crisis, they asked, was a change of policy proposed, a change which could only increase their difficulties?[60]

On May 22, 1823, that is, after the resolutions on slavery of May 15 had been adopted, the East Indian aspect of the question was brought up for discussion by a motion for the appointment of a select committee to enquire into the duties payable on East and West Indian sugar.[61] Whitmore, who made the motion, said there had been a rapid increase in the sale of manufactured goods to India, especially woolen and cotton. Raw cotton was imported into Great Britain from India and exported to it as a finished product. However great the desire of the natives might be for English goods, they could not buy them if they had nothing to offer in exchange. They produced no bullion, and their country might be totally

59 *Parliamentary Debates*, second series, VIII, 337 ff.
60 *Ibid.*, IX, 451 ff.
61 *Ibid.*, IX, 444-467.

drained of specic. Whitmore then considered the question from the standpoint of the West Indies. It had been said that it was a grievance to bring his motion forward at a crisis in West Indian history; he lamented the distress, but declared the suffering was caused not by the competition of East Indian sugar, but by the system of slavery. As long as slavery existed, as long as the poor lands were made to produce sugar, and as long as freights continued. so high, so long would the West Indies be distressed.[62] He said the West Indians seemed to assert that they had a charter right to these protecting duties, whereas, in fact, the duties had at times been lower on East India sugar than on West Indian; for previously to 1803 the duties on the Eastern sugar were *ad valorem* duties, and though generally higher yet, whenever the price of sugar was considerably depressed, they were lower than the duties on West Indian sugar. He ended by contending that although the West Indians had had some claim to special protection when the colonial system was in full force, they had none now.[63]

Whitmore's motion was resisted by Charles Ellis, James Marryat, and other representatives of the West Indian interest, who argued that the West Indian colonies, though free from some restrictions, were still fettered by many regulations imposed with a view to the benefit of Great Britain, and that therefore they had a right to some protection in the home market. They remained subject to all the restrictions regarding the supply of British manufactures. The changes made in the British commercial policy were of little material gain to the West Indies, for the protection to the farmers and provision merchants of Ireland was the same as formerly, that of the British fisheries remained untouched, and the

[62] *Parliamentary Debates,* second series, IX, 450.
[63] *Ibid.,* IX, 450.

British shipowners were still allowed the exclusive carrying trade—restrictions which were extremely burdensome to the West Indian planter and for which he was entitled to compensation. The result of an equalization of duties would be a great fall in the price of sugar, and the ruin of the colonies and of all the population dependent on them.[64] David Ricardo, a free trader and political economist, contended that the effect of the proposed alteration would make little difference in the price of sugar in England as long as an amount exceeding consumption was imported by England, as the price was regulated by the world market, but that the change would prevent prices from rising above their value.[65] Huskis-

[64] *Parliamentary Debates*, second series, IX, 451 ff. Joseph Marryat stated the claims of the West Indians in a pamphlet, *A reply to the Argument Contained in Various Publications Recommending an Equalization of the Duties on East and West Indian Sugar* (1823). They were entitled, he wrote, to "the continuance of the protecting duty, because they pay a valuable consideration for it, in the restriction to which they are subjected. They further consider, that although the preference they have in the home market is of little benefit to them while the growth of their sugar so much exceeds the home consumption of the mother country, as to render them dependent on the European market; yet it may be valuable hereafter, when their cultivation is reduced, as must soon be the case if the present low price of sugar continues, for the planter must raise more provisions and less sugar." P. 88. On page 111, he continued: "the popular cry of free trade is set up by those, whose real object is to obtain a share in an existing monoply: the interests of the British manufacturers and consumers are made the pretense for promoting those of the East Indian traders; philanthropy is used as a plea for involving the population both of the East and West Indies in misery and distress; and the adoption of which would lay the axe to the root of that navigation system, which is the basis of the naval supremacy of Great Britain."

Alexander Macdonnell in his book on *Colonial Commerce* (1828), pp. 111-125, made similar statements to the effect that the changes in the British commercial code were of no more than paper value to the West Indians. "The innovations in our commercial policy were unsolicited, unsought, and at best acquiesced impassively by the West Indians." P. 119. The *Minutes* of the West India Literary Committee record its vigorous pamphlet and newspaper warfare on the questions of slavery and the sugar duties. The distribution of pamphlets proved difficult.

[65] *Parliamentary Debates*, IX, 458.

son, president of the Board of Trade, who spoke for the government, opposed the motion, although agreeing in theory with Ricardo. The East Indies might now send their sugar to the continent of Europe and the United States, and the largest export from the East Indies to all parts of the world (exclusive of England) in any one year was about four thousand tons. Why, he asked, were not those countries of Europe which had no colonies of their own supplied before now with this cheap East Indian sugar? It was because the supply from the East Indies could not come more cheaply into the European market. He admitted that, considering the question abstractly and without reference to the state of things which had grown out of the colonial policy of the country for the last century, the only point to be taken into account was this—where could Englishmen, as consumers, get sugars at the cheapest rate? The question, however, was to be looked at with reference to a number of complicated circumstances; and he could not agree that the house might press hard upon a West Indian because that West Indian happened to be a slave owner. That the West Indian was an owner of slaves was not his fault but his misfortune, and if it was true that production by slaves was more costly than that by free labor, that would be an additional reason for not depriving the West Indian of the advantage of the protective duty. Huskisson denied that the East Indian inhabitants would derive any benefit from the change even if it were made, for the caste system would prevent their changing from manufacturers to sugar growers. At all events, the British consumer would benefit little. The produce of sugar in the old colonies—those held by England before the year 1763 —had been 90,000 tons in 1789; and the home consumption in the same year had been 70,000 tons. The present production of those same colonies was 140,000 tons a year, and the consumption in England now 140,000 tons a year. India was not a great sugar producing colony and really imported more sugar than it exported.[66] The motion was rejected by a vote of one hundred and sixty-one to thirty-four.[67]

The East Indians, however, continued their efforts to have the British markets thrown open to them on the same terms as those given to the West Indians.[68] They were not successful in securing a competitive rate, but about two years later the sugars of Mauritius were placed under the same duty as West Indian sugar.[69] The result was a tremendous increase in the production of sugar in that island, of which both the West Indians and anti-slavery people complained bitterly.[70]

The West Indians were anxious to secure an increased market at home by stimulating consumption, hoping in this way to get some benefit from their monopoly, which, as the debate just described shows, had been of no very great advantage to them. They demanded a decrease in duties on their products year after year, and some concessions were made to them, although none of great consequence.[71] They insisted that lower duties would increase consumption, and so the revenue would not be diminished, but when the duties on sugar were lowered from twenty-seven shillings to twenty-four shillings, the increase in

[66] *Parliamentary Debates*, second series, IX, 463-467. Huskisson declared himself willing to take off the 5s. duty on a special kind of sugar, as it could not be identified.

[67] *Ibid.*, IX, 467. List of minority given.

[68] *Ibid.*, XI, p. 730 ff.; XII, 1081 ff.; XIX, 1209 ff.; XXI, 1565 ff.

[69] *Ibid.*, XIII, 1039 ff.; 6 Geo. IV, c. 76, June 27, 1825. Done, it was said, according to the terms of the treaty of cession.

[70] Imported in Great Britain in 1825, 244,070 cwt.; in 1830, 779,479 cwt. ''Tables of the revenue, population, commerce . . . of United Kingdom,'' pt. III, *Parliamentary Papers*, 1835, XLIX, 1, p. 152.

[71] *Parliamentary Debates*, second series, X, 782 ff.; XVIII, 1422; XIX, 1206 ff., 1373 ff.; XXI, 1565 ff.; XXII, 848 ff.; XXIII, 622 ff., 1053 ff.; XXV, 307, 952 ff., 314, 525, 828, 858; third series, II, 784; III, 373.

consumption was not as great as had been expected.[72] West Indian distress continued, and this state of affairs was attributed by Huskisson to the changed conditions in the world which were beyond the power of legislative control, such as increased production in the non-British islands, especially Cuba, and in Brazil. The fact was that the West Indies had been raised to a fictitious state of prosperity by the Napoleonic wars. They were given over entirely to the raising of staple products, and did not, therefore, have either the labor or other conditions necessary to diversified agriculture or industrial life. An exhausted soil, due to the raising of staples cultivated by unskilled labor, meant distress, while increased production of beet sugar in Europe tended to lower the price of continental sugar.[73] West Indian distress[74] was admitted on all sides, and must constantly be borne in mind. Investments in the colonies were yielding but a small profit, credit could be secured with difficulty, and it was proposed to organize a large West India company in order that money might be borrowed on more advantageous terms.[75] A large number of the people of England from the lowest to the highest were financially interested in the colonies. Many of the large landholders in England also had property in the islands.

These facts explain the power of the party that resisted emancipation. The distress explains in part the reception given to the orders in Council issued by the government. The colonists looked upon any interference between master and slave in their present condition as insult added to

[72] 11 Geo. IV and 1 Will. IV., c. 50, July 16, 1830.

[73] G. N. Surface, in *The Story of Sugar* (New York, 1910), pp. 26-28, 110 ff., shows that beet sugar competition was not serious at this time.

[74] *Parliamentary Debates*, third series, II, 784 ff.

[75] *Ibid.*, second series, XII, 1278 ff.; XIII, 605 ff. This plan was opposed by the anti-slavery leaders because they thought that the many stockholders it was proposed to have would only be so many champions of slavery.

injury. Canning said repeatedly that the slavery question
was one of the greatest difficulty, but neither he nor the
other members of the government anticipated the resistance and the related problems they were to meet.
The resolutions of May 15, 1823, providing for the
amelioration and gradual abolition of slavery, formed
the basis of the government's policy[76] almost up to the
time of the emancipation act in 1833. Upon them were
founded various orders in Council which gradually became more minute and specific. The main object of the
government was the amelioration of the condition of the
slaves, or, as often expressed, mitigation and gradual
abolition. Thus a central aim throughout the period uni-
fied the forces at work and made it impossible for men to
lose themselves in mere details. The sequence of events
was something like this: an order in Council; resistance
by West Indians, generally including some form of violence; and a stir among the anti-slavery party, having for
its object more radical measures on the part of the government.

The West Indian legislatures had adopted slave codes
of their own in the early days of slavery and these were
revised and enlarged from time to time. The purpose of
the orders in Council was to modify these codes in essential particulars; as time went on the orders became so
minute that they were in themselves slave codes sent out
from the mother country. The first volume of James
Stephen's *Slavery Delineated*, published in 1824, was
largely an elaborate analysis of the slave codes of the
colonies, attempting to prove from these that the state
of slavery was intolerable. The almost constant criticism
made by him and also by the British government was that
the slave laws of the sugar islands lacked the machinery

[76] The adoption of the Canning resolutions meant that the policy of
mitigation would have to be given a thorough trial.

of enforcement; that a law might in itself be quite good but that unbiased and independent officers were lacking to secure its due execution.

The West Indians resisted the orders in Council because they were an interference with the absolute power of the master over his slave, and so were a first step of emancipation. The British government, in fact, asked the slave owner to prepare his slave for freedom, and the more quickly the slave was so prepared the sooner would the master lose his services. Many men had held that the best slavery was that which was most absolute, and in which the power of the master was most unrestrained. Then the owner would act according to his best instincts, whereas constant criticism of the master, even though slight, aggravated the lot of both master and slave. The British government, however, stood committed to a policy of interference in the hope that the slaves could be prepared for freedom while still in slavery and would gradually and almost imperceptibly change from one condition into the other.

No one appreciated the difficulties of preparing the slaves for freedom more truly than did Macaulay, and he wished to avoid all direct interference between master and slave as long as possible. He was greatly alarmed to learn that the government had decided to abolish the whip in the field, and, when he heard of the insurrection in Demerara, he wrote Buxton denouncing this measure as an act of ''the most direct interference between master and slave, . . . an act of the utmost delicacy and difficulty. The whip, be it remembered, is the grand badge of slavery in the West Indies. Its use is identified with the servile state. Can we wonder that the poor slaves should confound this ever present symbol of slavery with slavery itself, and that they should regard its abolition as but another name for emancipation?

"You may also recollect what was *our* plan had we been allowed to proceed in our own way by Parliamentary enactment. It was not to interfere with a rash hand and in the first instance with the plantation discipline, or with the direct authority of the master, but to adopt measures which would have a powerful influence on the condition and character of the slave, without disturbing for the present the settled relations of plantation economy. Our plan was: (1) To remove all fiscal obstructions to manumissions; (2) To oblige the master to manumit whenever the value of the slave as appraised should be offered to him; (3) To abolish compulsory labor and markets on the Sunday; (4) To promote religious instruction; (5) To legalize and protect marriage; (6) To make the evidence of slaves admissable *pro tanto;* (7) To cause them to cease from being treated as chattels; (8) To secure them in the possession and transmission of property. These various measures would have interfered little, at least visibly, with the exercise of the master's authority. They would be either measures of remission, not leading at all to relax the bonds of discipline, or measures of silent and progressive improvement, producing no sudden change of state, but preparing the slaves gradually, and in no long time, for the grand change of substituting a moral impulse to labour for that of the whip, and of making the slaves amenable to law and not to individual caprice."[77]

Lord Bathurst, secretary of state for the colonies, was not slow in following up the resolutions adopted by the House of Commons on May 15, 1823, and sent two despatches to the West India colonies, dated May 28 and July 9. The first of these, sent to all the colonies but designed to be enforced only in the crown colonies, commanded that the use of the whip in the field and the prac-

[77] Viscountess Knutsford, *Zachary Macaulay,* p. 394.

tise of punishing females by flogging be given up. Canning's speech, which was enclosed, was intended to prepare the minds of the planters for the further measures they might expect as soon as the government could give its attention to the matter. In the second despatch, sent to the legislative colonies, it was recommended that provision be made: (a) for religious instruction; (b) the consequent abolition of Sunday market; (c) the discontinuance of the flogging of female slaves; (d) the regulation of the punishment of male slaves; (e) the prevention, in the sale of slaves, of the separation of husband and wife, and of infant children from the mother; (f) the giving of security to the property of slaves by the establishment of banks of deposit; (g) the establishment of facilities for the manumission of slaves; (h) and finally, the allowing of the evidence of slaves, under certain regulations, in courts of justice.[78]

The extent to which the British government seemed disposed to interfere directly between the slave and his master, was in itself objectionable to the planters, though the plan of government received the approval of West Indian residents in England. The prospect of unceasing future interference, ending in ultimate emancipation, was still more unpleasant to them. These grounds of dissatisfaction were further increased by their apprehensions of insubordination and insurrection which might be excited among the negroes; and these were not lessened by the inevitable misrepresentation of the views and plans of parliament.[79]

The opposition was most marked in Jamaica, where it

[78] Papers in explanation of measures adopted by His Majesty for amelioration of the slave population in the West Indies. *Parliamentary Papers*, 1824, XXIV, 427, schedule 1, pp. 3, 8-13; *Parliamentary Debates*, second series, X, 1047.

[79] *Ibid.*, X, 1047.

was hinted that the West India islands would assert their independence, if Great Britain persisted in parliamentary legislation interfering with their domestic concerns.[80] One of the assemblymen recommended an address to His Majesty asking for the removal of Lord Bathurst, alleging that he was under the influence of the anti-slavery party. Another member angrily moved for the repeal of the Jamaica Registry Act, for it had been previously understood that after this Act was passed, parliament would interfere no more with the internal affairs of the colonist.[81] The assembly appointed a committee to enquire what steps were necessary to be taken on the subject of slavery, in consequence of the proceedings of the House of Commons. The report of this committee, after mentioning the resolutions proposed by Canning, states, "That his majesty's ministers had, by those resolutions, sanctioned the principles laid down by the enemies of the colonies in the mother country, and pledged themselves to enforce such measures as should tend ultimately to the final extinction of slavery in the British colonies; that the ministers, in their conference with the agent of the island, had refused to acknowledge any claim to compensation for the injuries the colonies would sustain in the mere endeavor to carry the scheme of emancipation into effect; that by this refusal the ministers showed an inclination, not only to dispose of the property of the colonists without their consent, but even to violate the common rules of honesty; and that the House ought to adopt the most firm, strong, and constitutional measures, to preserve to the inhabitants of the island those rights which had been transmitted to them from their ancestors.'"[82] Upon this report in December, immediately before the close of its session,

---

[80] *Parliamentary Papers*, 1824, XXIV, 427, schedule 2, Jamaica pp. 1-7.
[81] *Annual Register*, LXV, 131.
[82] *Parliamentary Papers*, 1824, XXIV, 427, schedule 2, p. 6.

the assembly voted unanimously a series of resolutions[83] expressing general dissatisfaction with the high taxation to which they were subjected and astonishment at the new government policy regarding slavery, which they were ready to resist at all hazards. On the other hand, they

[83] "That the patient endurance with which the people of this island have for years past struggled against pecuniary difficulties, proves how much they are disposed to submit to, where the evil arises from inevitable causes, or from circumstances affecting the general interests of the empire. But this House would be unmindful of their duty, were they not to protest most solemnly against the continuance of heavy and ruinous taxation on the produce of their soil, at a time when the demands of a state of warfare can no longer be urged in its defence, and the blessings of restored tranquility have been extended to their fellow-subjects in the mother country.

"That this House cannot contemplate without sensations of astonishment, and the most serious apprehension, the measures which have been adopted by the Commons, House of Parliament in their unanimous vote of the 15th of May last; as if the machinations of a powerful and interested party were not sufficiently active for the work of destruction, the sanction of ministerial authority has been made subservient to their views, and a decree has gone forth, whereby the inhabitants of this once valuable colony (hitherto esteemed the brightest jewel in the British crown) are destined to be offered a propitiatory sacrifice at the altar of fanaticism.

"That this House, composed of the representatives of the people, are bound to guard the rights of their constituents against every endeavor that may be made to infringe upon them: they pause, in awful expectations of the consequences which must result from the threatened innovation, and whilst they wait the event, they are prepared to meet it; the blood which flows in their veins is British blood, and their hearts are animated with the same fearless determination, which enabled their ancestors to resist, with success, every encroachment of despotic power.

"That the enactment of laws for the internal regulations of the island is exclusively the province of the local legislature, subject to the sanction and approval of his Majesty's; this House, however, will at all times receive, with attention and respect, any suggestions of his Majesty's ministers, relating to legislation, when offered in a consistent and becoming manner, and will be ready to adopt such regulation as can be introduced without hazard, and may appear likely to promote the welfare of the island; but this House cannot yield to any measure proposed for their consideration, when the unqualified right of rejection is denied, however specious the object may be, or however high the authority from which it emanates.

"That this House, impressed with a due sense of their own dignity, and the integrity of the colonial character, set at nought the malicious and undeclared themselves willing to make any[84] necessary changes by their own legislature. In an address to the governor, the Duke of Manchester, however, they went on to declare the slave code as satisfactory as it could be and the slave population happy and comfortable.

In Grenada,[85] St. Vincent,[86] and St. Christopher,[87] His Majesty's suggestions were rather favorably received and the assemblies were disposed to carry into effect the greater part of the propositions. In St. Vincent the answer returned by the assembly amounted to this—that they had already amended the act which they passed two years before for the amelioration of the condition of the

founded aspersions which have been cast upon the inhabitants of Jamaica: proud of their attachment to his Majesty, his family and government, devoted to the interests of those they represent, and alive to the impulses of humanity, the House need no pharisaical dictation to promote them to discharge their duty; but, if left to their own guidance, steadily pursue that line of conduct which comports with the loyalty of their feelings, their regard to the safety, honour, and welfare of the island, and the peace and happiness of their fellow-subjects and dependents.'' *Parliamentary Papers*, 1824, XXIV, 427, schedule 2, Jamaica, p. 7.

84 ''The House in compliance with their answer to the speech your Grace was pleased to make at the opening of the present session, have proceeded to a deliberate and careful revision of the consolidated slave law, and find it as complete in all its enactments as the nature of the circumstances will admit to render the slave population as happy and comfortable in every respect as the labouring class of any part of the world. This House also most solemnly assures your Grace, that they will at all times be ready (if left to themselves) to watch and take advantage of every opportunity of promoting the religious and moral improvement of the slaves, and to make such ameliorating enactments as may be consistent with their happiness and the general safety of the colony; but, under the critical circumstances in which the colony is now placed, by reason of the late proceedings in the British Parliament, the House think the present movement peculiarly unfavorable for the discussion, which may have a tendency to unsettle the minds of the negro population which, the House have the greatest reason to believe, is at present perfectly quiet and contented.'' *Parliamentary Papers*, 1824, XXIV, 427, schedule 2, p. 6.

85 *Ibid.*, pp. 60-61.

86 *Ibid.*, pp. 73-92.

87 *Ibid.*, pp. 69-73. *Parliamentary Debates*, second series, X, 1048.

slaves and were of the opinion that all measures recommended in the two despatches were to be found therein.[88] In the council and assembly of Barbadoes, the measures of the government met with an opposition no less firm than that in Jamaica, though more mild and conciliatory in tone.[89] The general temper of the white inhabitants of the colony was well shown in the treatment of a missionary who was believed to be connected with the supposed enemies of the colonies at home. This man, named Shrewsbury, was suspected of having sent home to the society by which he was employed, statements highly injurious to the moral character of the lower classes of the white population in Barbadoes. At first an effort was made to compel him to give up his work by interrupting the services. When this attempt failed, his meetinghouse was completely demolished and he was forced to flee from the island.[90]

That the apprehensions of danger entertained by the planters were not entirely unfounded was proved by events in Demerara. The negro population there knew that something was to be done for them. The proprietors were so alarmed by the general unrest among the negroes that, in many instances, they went to the capital to learn what course the assembly would pursue. Several meetings of that body were held, but without any resulting measure, as the large and small proprietors disagreed. The latter were opposed to any concessions. The excitement among the proprietors and members of the assembly had by this time caused the negroes to believe that they had

[88] *Parliamentary Debates,* second series, X, 1049. Bathurst said that the suggested changes were not in the amended act.

[89] *Parliamentary Papers,* 1824, XXIV, 427, schedule 2, Barbadoes.

[90] *Parliamentary Papers,* 1825 (113, 127), XXV, 169, 177. He had represented the lower classes as bred in ignorance of Christianity, and incapable, from their depraved habits, of acquiring any knowledge of its doctrines.

been freed by the king and that their freedom was withheld by the local authorities. They, therefore, resolved to obtain liberty by force and began an insurrection on the eastern coast, news of which arrived at the capital on August 18, 1823. The revolt spread from the estate on which resided a certain John Smith, a missionary of the London Society. He was successful in rescuing the manager from the negroes, and continued his exertions in an effort to induce them to return to their work. The governor, likewise, attempted to dissuade the negroes from their course, but found it necessary to crush the revolt by force. A considerable loss of the black population resulted, and the ringleaders were tried and condemned by courts-martial.[91] The vengeance obtained by the execution of slaves did not satisfy the planters, and Smith was brought up for trial on the charge of being in the conspiracy. All his papers were seized, and he was kept in strict confinement. The trial before a court-martial began October 13, 1823, and was continued by adjournment to November 24, when the accused was found guilty of a capital offence. But the men who had courage to condemn were afraid to carry their sentence into execution, and proceedings were suspended till His Majesty's determination on the case could be known. In the meantime, Smith was subjected to the closest confinement, and a disease from which he suffered caused his death before the news arrived that the king had rescinded the sentence of the court-martial.[92] Information concerning his trial and death reached England later than that of the reception given in the West Indies to Lord Bathurst's circular letters.

91 *Parliamentary Papers*, 1824, XXIV, 427, schedule 2, Demerara, pp. 115-117.

92 Information taken from *Parliamentary Papers*, 1824 (158, 333, 338), XXIII, 373, 465, 565, *passim*.

So strong was the feeling of revulsion against the anti-slavery party that the hopes of emancipation seemed shattered, until Brougham by his masterly handling of the case of the missionary, Smith,[93] revived the cause and dealt British slavery a blow from which it never recovered. Probably it is not too much to say that the case of this missionary produced the same effect in Britain that John Brown's execution did on Northern opinion in the United States. Smith's absolute innocence was clearly established, whereas Brown had attacked a national fortress.

Brougham was terrific in his indictment of the legal proceedings. He reviewed the whole case in a speech on June 1, 1824, and replied to his opponents on June 11: "I have no hesitation in saying that from the beginning of

[93] Papers relating to the proceedings of a court-martial on the trial of John Smith, a missionary, and to the insurrection of slaves in Demerara, and the trials thereon, *Parliamentary Papers*, 1824 (158, 333, 338), XXIII, 373, 465, 565. Facts on which the debate was based are found in *Report of the Proceedings against the late Rev. J. Smith, of Demerara . . . with an appendix.* Published by London Missionary Society, London: 1824.

Smith was given nothing corresponding to a trial. He was convicted because his accusers suspected and later learned from his private journal that he resented the treatment the negroes received. He was convicted for having the wrong mental attitude toward slavery. The reasons for West Indian objection to Dissenting ministers are given as follows: Roman Catholics and Jews "preach no war of extermination against slave holders but the Protestant Dissenters do. The Wesleyan Methodists have stated again and again their implacable hostility and determined perseverance in the effort to abolish slavery. They may be right, but the Planters are not wrong in looking on their Missionaries with suspicion. Dr. Johnson might have been perfectly justified in drinking to the success of a general insurrection among the negroes; but it would be ridiculous to accuse the Planters of making an 'invidious' distinction, were they to prohibit his being toast-master at a Negro feast, while they allowed the privilege to Las Casas. Self-preservation is the first law of society." The Jamaica people said, "we are convinced, from our own experience, as well as from the testimony of the sectarian ministers themselves, that the restrictions contained in our Slave Law with respect to Dissenters are indispensable." *The West Indian Reporter*, XII, 217, 222.

those proceedings to their fatal termination, there has
been committed more of illegality, more of the violation
of justice—violation of justice in substance as well as
form—than, in the whole history of modern times, I ven-
ture to assert, was ever before witnessed in any inquiry
that could be called a judicial proceeding.'"[94] His speeches
consisted of a close legal examination of the whole case,[95]
with occasional flights of eloquence calculated to impress
the British public. "The calumniated minister," he said,
"had so far humanized his poor flock—his dangerous
preaching had so enlightened them—the lessons of himself and his hated brethren had sunk so deep in their

[94] *Parliamentary Debates*, second series, XI, 963; Brougham, *Speeches*,
II, 54.

[95] Brougham made a motion to secure a better administration of law in
that colony so as to protect the negroes and their instructors from oppression. *Parliamentary Debates*, second series, XI, 999. In support of his motion he argued that Smith could not legally be tried by a court-martial.
*Ibid.*, XI, 968 ff. That the court-martial, even supposing it possessed any
jurisdiction, had exceeded its authority; that every rule of evidence had
been most flagrantly violated; that upon the evidence, as it stood, there was
clear proof not of Smith's guilt but of his innocence; and that even if it
were allowed that he had been guilty of misprision of treason, he could not
be condemned capitally for that offence. Brougham held that there was only
one charge entitled to consideration, that of communicating with Quamina
(one of the rebels) about the revolt. Three things had to be established before the guilt could be maintained on that charge: firstly, that Quamina
was a revolter; secondly, that Smith encouraged him to be so; and thirdly,
that he had advised and encouraged him in the revolt. The evidence con-
tradicted all those suppositions: Smith did not know of the revolt; he told
all he knew to the proper authorities. In short, the court had no jurisdiction,
tried him for things which were wholly beyond their commission; and of
those things no evidence was produced upon which any man could suspect
his guilt. *Ibid.*, XI, 990 ff. Wilmot Horton, Nicholas Tindal, and Canning
defended the government. *Ibid.*, XI, 1032 ff. The last named proposed the
previous question, as the discussion had been quite sufficient to convince the
West Indians that it was firmly believed by the people of England that
religion was the chief means by which the condition of the slaves could be
improved. *Ibid.*, XI, 1288 ff. Brougham restated his position, and the vote
stood 146 ayes and 193 noes, a defeat of Brougham's motion by 47 votes.
*Ibid.*, XI, 1295-1313. List of minority given on pp. 1313-1315.

minds, that, by the testimony of the clergyman, and even of the overseers, the maxims of the Gospels of peace were upon their lips in the midst of rebellion, and restrained their hands when no other force was present to resist them. 'We will take no life,' said they; 'for our Pastors have taught us not to take that which we cannot give:' a memorable peculiarity, to be found in no other passage of negro warfare within the West-Indian seas, and which drew from the truly pious minister of the Established Church the exclamation, that 'He shuddered to write that they were seeking the life of the man whose teaching had saved theirs!' "[96]

The anti-slavery champion ended his presentation of the matter by warning the West Indians that they were "blind alike to the duties, the interests, and the perils of their situation, they rush headlong through infamy to destruction; breaking promise after promise to delude us; leaving pledge after pledge unredeemed, extorted by the pressure of the passing occasion; or only, by laws passed to be a dead letter, forever giving such an elusory performance as adds mockery to breach of faith; yet a little delay; yet a little longer of this unbearable trifling with the commands of the parent state, and she will stretch out her arm, in mercy, not in anger, to those deluded men themselves; exert at last her undeniable authority; vindicate the just rights, and restore the tarnished honour of the English name!"[97]

[96] *Parliamentary Debates,* second series, XI, 995; Brougham, *Speeches,* II, 94-95.

[97] Brougham was ably seconded by Mackintosh, Lushington, Williams, and Denman, all men of great ability, who spoke so as to convince the people that parliament was the only body capable of grappling with the difficult problem of slavery. The religious public of England in particular was turned against the slave system by the Smith case. The tremendous effect produced upon public opinion by this case can be readily traced in the literature of both sides. Before Brougham's speeches, on May 2, 1824, p. 149, *John Bull* stated that the trial has "excited our disgust at the con-

Some months before the great debate on the Smith
case, the events in the West Indies were alluded to in the
address from the throne, with the advice that it was best
to go slowly and cautiously in the solution of such a difficult problem.[98] Canning had decided not to press the
question on the colonial legislatures, but rather to make
the experiment of sending to Trinidad, a crown colony,
an order in Council which should embody the views of
the government, and serve as a model for the legislative
colonies.[99] Lord Bathurst admitted that this change of

temptible hypocrisy of the Sectarists, and . . . awakened in our mind the
most powerful sensation of surprise—not that Smith should have been sentenced to death, but that the Court could possibly have found one qualifying circumstance in his case to induce it to recommend him to mercy.'' On
June 13, 1824, p. 196, the tone has changed to one of seriousness. ''The
fact seems to us to be, that advantage is taken of Smith's death, to effect
a purpose which could not have been accomplished had he lived. That purpose is, I believe, to intimidate the governors and governments of other
colonies from the discharge of their duty in perilous cases and times, to
prostrate them at the feet of every agitator who may call himself a Missionary, and by the terror of a thousand petitions, and the consequent proceedings in Parliament, to give an ascendancy to a class of persons, who,
whether intentionally or not, are, we are perfectly convinced, most dangerous to the very existence of our colonial system.'' John Bull recurs to the
case for many subsequent issues.

Wilberforce made his last public speech in parliament on Smith's case.
His comment was, ''The case proved against him is greatly short of what I
thought it might have been. I myself once saw a missionary's journal, and
its contents would have been capable of being perverted into a much stronger
charge of promoting discontent amongst the slaves. Had I happened for instance to correspond with Smith, that alone would have hanged him.'' R. I.
and S. Wilberforce, Life of Wilberforce, V, 222.

[98] Parliamentary Debates, second series, X, 4. The members of the government discussed their policy carefully. ''Are we prepared,'' Lord Liverpool asked Canning, ''to enforce our new system and regulations by law and
if necessary ultimately by force in these colonies to which we have granted
constitutions?'' Liverpool to Canning, January 9, 1824, Historical Manuscripts Commission, Report on the Manuscripts of Earl Bathurst (London,
1923), p. 560.

[99] Appendix, Parliamentary Papers, 1824, XXIV, 427, schedule 3, pp.
141-158; Parliamentary Debates, second series, X, 1051. The effect of the

policy was made necessary by recent events in the sugar islands.[100] He defended the proposed plan as strictly in accordance with the resolutions of 1823, and also as the best mode of procedure in such a difficult situation.[101] The intention of those resolutions was that ministers should consider not only what might be right in theory, but what would be wise in practice; not how to do the greatest possible good, but how to do it with the least possible mischief.[102] With that understanding the order in Council had been drafted in coöperation with the West India interest.

This order,[103] dated March 10, 1824, marks another important step in the development of the government's policy. It is, in effect, the carrying out of the points expressed in Canning's speech in 1823, and as such deserves careful study. Its provisions were: the Procurador Syndic of the Cabildo of the town of the Port of Spain was confirmed in his ancient office of protector and guardian of slaves, with new honors, but was placed under new regulations; the commandants of the several quarters of the island were declared assistant protectors and guardians of slaves, and notice of all suits and actions against slaves was required to be given to the guardian, who was obliged to attend the trial of the case. All markets were to be discontinued on Sunday, and the employment of any slave in labor between sunset on Saturday and sunrise on Monday was strictly prohibited. The whip was no longer to be carried as an emblem of authority; the male slave could not be punished for any offence until twenty-four hours after its commission, and

debate on the missionary, Smith, was that the government decided to extend the Trinidad order in Council to St. Lucia and Demerara.

100 *Parliamentary Debates*, second series, X, 1061.
101 *Ibid.*, X, 1052-1092.
102 *Ibid.*, X, 1093, 1051 ff.
103 *Parliamentary Papers*, 1824, XXIV, 427, schedule 3, pp. 141-158.

in no instance should more than twenty-five lashes be given in one day, nor should a second punishment take place until the person of the slave was free from any lacerations which might have been occasioned by a previous flogging; no punishment should be given unless one free person was present as a witness; a record of all punishments was to be kept, particularizing the number of lashes,[104] and was to be transmitted to the commandant of the quarter; the practice of flogging females was to be abolished, and other forms of punishment were to be used. Marriages of slaves were encouraged by giving the guardian power to overrule the will of masters; married slaves and their children, moreover, were not to be separated, but were to be sold in one lot. The property of slaves was to be secured to them by a positive law, and they were to be enabled to dispose of it by bequest, to sue in their own names, to put out their funds at interest, and to dispose of all their goods by bequest; to enable the slaves to put aside their money, savings banks were to be provided. Facilities were provided for the manumission of slaves, according to which the registration of manumitted slaves should be paid by the state. The slave was to have the right to purchase not only his own freedom, but that of his wife, his sister, or his brother. Any difficulty respecting the price of the person was referred to the guardian or protector, who would arbitrate between the parties. A slave was to be received as a witness, and allowed to give his evidence on oath, on condition that he could procure a certificate from any clergyman that he was so far instructed in religious knowledge as to be sensible of the obligation of an oath. Subject to this regulation, the testimony of slaves was to be received in all civil cases, except where the interests of the master were

104 The records of the protectors of slaves furnished excellent ammunition to the anti-slavery party.

concerned; and in all criminal cases, except where the life
of white persons was at stake. The order in Council with
necessary modifications was to apply also to St. Lucia
and to Demerara.[105]

One question brought forward by Canning was not disposed of by the order in Council, namely, the religious instruction of the blacks. The ecclesiastical establishment in
the West Indies had been founded exclusively for the
benefit of the white population, and provision was yet to
be made for instructing the blacks.[106] It was proposed
that this establishment should be founded on the principles of the Anglican Church, but should not exclude other
denominations of Christians. The authority and discipline of the Anglican Church were to be lodged in bishops
resident in the colonies.

The perplexing question in the minds of the members
of parliament was how to deal with the stubborn assemblies. Canning explained the government policy by saying: "There are three possible modes in which parliament
might deal with the people of Jamaica; first, as I have
said, it might crush them by the application of direct
force; secondly, it might harass them by fiscal regulations and enactments restraining their navigation; and
thirdly, it might pursue the slow and silent course of temperate, but authoritative admonition. Now, Mr. Speaker,
if I am asked which course I would advise, I am for first
trying that which I have last mentioned; I trust we shall
never be driven to the second, and with respect to the
first, I will only now say that no feeling of wounded
pride, no motive of questionable expediency, nothing
short of real and demonstrable necessity, shall induce me
to moot the awful question of the transcendental power of

[105] Appendix, *Parliamentary Papers*, 1824, XXIV, 427, schedule 3, pp.
141-158.
[106] *Parliamentary Debates*, second series, X, 1098.

Parliament over every dependency of the British Crown. That transcendental power is an arcanum of empire, which ought to be kept back within the penetralia of the constitution. It exists, but it should be veiled. It should not be produced upon trifling occasions, or in cases of petty refractoriness and temporary misconduct. It should be brought forward only in the utmost extremity of the state, where other remedies have failed to stay the raging of some moral or political pestilence.'"[107]

The two contending parties were almost equally dissatisfied with the governmental policy. On the one hand the power given slaves to purchase their own freedom did not receive the cordial assent of the West India party[108] and, on the other hand, it was far from what the anti-slavery party had asked for when they requested that all children be free at birth. The anti-slavery leaders were roundly abused for stirring up this trouble, and Buxton found himself the most unpopular man in England.[109] He and his followers, however, determined to persevere in their course; they attacked the government on the ground that it had not carried out the policy agreed to the year before, as the proposed measures were limited to a few colonies, whereas the resolutions of the previous year had made no distinction between crown colonies and legislative colonies.[110] Canning in defence of the governmental policy held that freedom to be safely enjoyed must be gradually and diligently earned. In oft quoted words, he said: "In dealing with the negro, we must remember that we are dealing with a being possessing the form and strength of a man, but the intellect only of a child. To turn him loose in the manhood of his physical strength, in

---

[107] *Parliamentary Debates*, second series, X, 1105-1106.
[108] *Ibid.*, X, 1101.
[109] Buxton, *Memoirs*, 142 ff.
[110] *Parliamentary Debates*, second series, X, 1113 ff.

the maturity of his physical passions, but in the infancy of his uninstructed reason, would be to raise up a creature resembling the splendid fiction of a recent romance; the hero of which constructs a human form with all the corporeal capabilities of man, and with the thews and sinews of a giant, but being unable to impart to the work of his hands a perception of right and wrong, he finds too late that he has only created a more than mortal power of doing mischief, and himself recoils from the monster which he has made.'"[111] Such, he thought, would be the effect of sudden emancipation, before the negro was prepared for the enjoyment of well-regulated liberty. The anti-slavery people were mollified by the promise of an act making the slave trade piracy,[112] but they could secure nothing more, as the sympathy of the country was still largely with the West Indians.

The religious and moral instruction of the slaves, preparatory to final emancipation, formed such an important part of the program, both of the anti-slavery leaders and the government, that attacks on the missionaries in the sugar islands were viewed with the utmost concern in England. The Smith case was still fresh in mind when the very next year, in 1825, the attention of the country and of parliament was directed to the case of another missionary, named Shrewsbury.[113] He was for some time a Methodist minister in England. In 1816 he was sent as a missionary to Tortola; in 1818, in the same capacity, to Grenada; and in 1820 to Barbadoes. His conduct was such that he received the approbation of governors and

[111] *Parliamentary Debates*, second series, X, 1103.

[112] *Ibid.*, X, 1198; 5 Geo. IV, cc. 17, 113.

[113] *Parliamentary Debates*, second series, XIII, 1285-1347; demolition of the Methodist chapel in Barbadoes and expulsion of Mr. Shrewsbury, the Methodist missionary, *Parliamentary Papers*, 1825 (113, 127), XXV, 169, 177.

planters.[114] At Barbadoes, he was charged with being an emissary of the African Institution, and was criticized for a report he had sent to his missionary society concerning the state of his congregation. This report contained some criticisms of the planters.[115] A fairly large number of poor whites in Barbadoes[116] felt bitterly against the slaves, and this probably accounts in part for what happened. At first an effort was made to break up the meetings of the congregation by disturbance. The magistrates would give no protection, and finally the chapel was destroyed. The governor's offer of a reward for the detection of the rioters brought in response a declaration of intimidation, and Shrewsbury was forced to go to St. Vincent, where, after investigation of his record and work, he was permitted to continue his labors. The rioters in Barbadoes sent a committee to the various islands to protest against all Methodists, but they were, for the most part, coolly received. When the matter came before the House of Commons, the following address was agreed upon after long debate: ''That the House deem it their duty to declare that they view with the utmost indignation that scandalous and daring violation of the Law; and having seen with great satisfaction the instructions which have been sent out by His Majesty's secretary of state to the governor of Barbadoes, to prevent a recurrence of similar outrages, they humbly assure His Majesty of their readiness to concur in every measure which His Majesty may deem necessary, for securing ample protection, and religious toleration, to all His Majesty's subjects in that part of His Majesty's domin-

114 *Parliamentary Debates*, second series, XIII, 1285-1287.

115 *Ibid.*, XIII, 1311-1318.

116 *Parliamentary Papers*, 1835, XLIX, 693. ''Tables of the revenue, population, commerce . . . of United Kingdom and its dependencies, supplement to part III.''

ions.''[117] Brougham on June 23, 1825, in his speech on the expulsion of Shrewsbury, gave notice that if before the next session of parliament he did not find the colonial legislatures acting in good faith, he would present a bill embodying the following objects: ''First, to make negro evidence admissible in all cases, in all courts, leaving, of course, its credit to the consideration of the court and jury; secondly, to prevent the use of the whip, as applied to women, entirely, and as a stimulus to labor, whether for men or women; thirdly, to attach all slaves to the soil, rendering them inseparable from it under any circumstances; fourthly, to prohibit persons holding West India property, or any mortgage upon such property, filling any office, civil or military (except regimental), in the West Indies; and lastly, to secure by such means as may be safe at once to the owner and the slaves, the gradual, but ultimately, the complete admission of that injured class of men, to the blessings of personal liberty.''[118]

The question of the administration of justice to negroes was brought to the attention of parliament by Denman, at the next session;[119] he based a motion on events which had taken place in Jamaica at the end of the year 1823, and the beginning of 1824. A plan for an insurrection among the slaves was discovered, and eight negroes were executed as conspirators.[120] Denman brought the legality and justice of the proceedings under discussion by moving a resolution expressing sorrow and regret at the violation of law which took place at the said trials,

[117] *Parliamentary Debates*, second series, XIII, 1346-1347.
[118] *Ibid.*, XIII, 1337-1338.
[119] *Ibid.*, XIV, 1007-1075, March 1, 1826.
[120] Manumission, population, and government of slaves, *Parliamentary Papers*, 1825 (66) XXV, 37-132. Copy of all judicial proceedings relative to the punishment of rebels, or alleged rebels, in the island of Jamaica, since 1st of January, 1823; with the previous informations, minutes of evidence, and final fate of prisoners.

and lamenting the precipitate manner in which the sentence of death was passed and executed; and recommended some attention to the mode of administering criminal justice as it affected the slaves in that colony.[121] The motion was prefaced by a speech, analysing the evidence upon which the accused had been convicted, demonstrating its contradictions, its insufficiency, and its absurdity, and arriving at the conclusion that such atrocities, perpetrated under the mask of justice and the law of evidence which permitted them, required the abolition of a system which placed a negro on trial before interested masters for his judges and jury; in granting the negro an appeal to the council, the law merely gave him an appeal to another body of masters equally prejudiced. Denman gave a brief account of the occurrences which led up to the trials and of the trials themselves. The trials arose from a conversation between a master and his boy slave in which the boy said that a conspiracy had been plotted[122] to murder the whites. He repeated the story before a magistrate, whereupon the eight accused negroes were thrown into prison without examination. At the trial but one witness besides the boy was called, and he was not put on oath, though others might have been examined. The boy was forced to testify against his own father, one of the victims, who merely had a weapon in his possession. Throughout the whole of the depositions there were repeated and barefaced contradictions.[123] Enough had been disclosed to excite the gravest doubts whether the entire proceedings, besides being founded on unreliable evidence, had not been hurried on from accusation to accusation with a degree of haste which only the alarms of the planters could have occasioned. But the question was,

121 *Parliamentary Debates*, second series, XIV, 1021-1022.

122 *Parliamentary Papers*, 1825, XXV, 38 ff.

123 *Ibid.*, p. 40 ff.; *Parliamentary Debates*, second series, XIV, 1011 ff.

had the proceedings been carried on according to the forms of law? Wilmot Horton, under-secretary for the colonies,[124] in opposing the motion, did not attempt to justify every part of these trials, but maintained that the courts had applied only the law which they were bound to apply, and under circumstances which fairly called for the interference of the legal authorites. The public authorities were convinced that rebellious designs existed among the negroes, who, in turn, were influenced by the idea that the intentions of the government in their favor were disobeyed by the planters. The governor demanded additional troops and prepared to meet the danger.[125] The courts and juries had but carried the law into effect and could not be censured, for the forty-sixth section of the existing statute provided that, if slaves should be convicted of rebellion, murder, robbery, or of compassing or imagining the death of white persons, they should suffer death, and further, that if slaves should be found in possession of firearms, swords, cutlasses, slugs, or balls, without the knowledge of their masters, they were to suffer death.[126] The law might be censured, but not the officers who administered it, and Horton moved the following amendment: "That this House sees in the proceedings which have been brought under its consideration, with respect to the late Trials of Slaves in Jamaica, further proof of the evils inseparably attendant upon a state of Slavery, and derives therefrom increased conviction of the propriety of the Resolutions passed by this House on 15 May, 1823. But that however desirable it is that the law, under which the late Trials took place, should be amended, it does not appear to this House to be expedient or safe to impeach sentences passed by a com-

[124] *Parliamentary Debates*, second series, XIV, 1022-1032.
[125] *Parliamentary Papers*, 1825, XXV, 39 ff.
[126] *Parliamentary Debates*, second series, XIV, 1023-1024.

petent tribunal upon persons brought to trial according to law, and convicted by a Jury duly impanelled, and sworn to give a verdict according to the evidence laid before them.''[127] The attorney-general and the solicitor-general used the same arguments as Wilmot Horton, and supported his amendment. They denounced the law in the most unmeasured terms and suggested a number of changes in it.[128] Brougham, however, insisted that the law as it stood had been violated, and he forced Horton to change his amendment by omitting the part which declared it unwise and inexpedient to censure the conduct of the court and the jurors; whereupon the house divided and the amendment was carried by a vote of one hundred and three to sixty-three.[129]

The anti-slavery party had made thorough preparation to secure the gradual abolition of slavery throughout the British empire, hoping to bring about that result by declaring all children free at birth. They also looked forward to measures of mitigation of the lot of the slaves. But their plans were opposed by the government under the leadership of Canning, who brought in the resolutions of 1823 and had them sanctioned by the House of Commons. The policy of the government did not contemplate a direct interference in the internal affairs of the legislative colonies, and the question was taken out of parliament and left entirely to the executive government. Two circular letters to the West Indies embodied the first measures of the government. The points mentioned for adoption were mostly for the mitigation of the condition of the slaves, but at the same time involved a considerable degree of interference between the master and the slave. The reception of these letters and the news of the

---

127 *Parliamentary Debates*, second series, XIV, 1031-1032.
128 *Ibid.*, XIV, 1039 ff.
129 *Ibid.*, XIV, 1074-1075. List of minority given.

proceedings in parliament caused great excitement in the islands, where, in all of the legislative colonies, the measures of government were rejected.

The news of the events in the West Indies induced the government not to press their measures, but to draw up an order in Council for Trinidad as an experiment for the other colonies to watch. The anti-slavery people were in great disrepute on account of the happenings in the West Indies, and therefore the change in government policy encountered little resistance. The misbehavior of the assemblies was passed over as unworthy of notice, except that these bodies were to be constantly but quietly urged to follow the example of Trinidad. In actual results, the first three years of agitation were almost fruitless, for the legislative colonies did little, if anything, and the order in Council was accepted very reluctantly in three crown colonies. The trial and death of Smith, in Demerara, the expulsion of Shrewsbury from Barbadoes, and the trials of slaves in Jamaica filled the country with horror at the violation of justice in the slave colonies, and brought vividly before the minds of the people the worst features of a system of compulsory slave labor.

# CHAPTER IX

## DISSATISFACTION WITH THE GOVERNMENT POLICY OF GRADUAL EMANCIPATION

The first three years of government policy had ended in failure; the anti-slavery party was disappointed with the progress which had been made and was determined to renew the discussion of the question in parliament.[1] The West Indians, on the other hand, felt that it was only by resistance that their property and, perhaps, even their lives could be saved. They believed that the cultivation of sugar was impossible without slavery. They were convinced that, while the negroes as freemen would work enough to support themselves in a rather primitive way, they would not work enough to produce a great sugar surplus for export. Already heavily in debt and depressed by low sugar prices, the West Indians were unwilling to coöperate in the establishment of a system of ameliorated slavery.

During the period from 1826 to 1832 a bitter controversy raged in Great Britain on old and new questions, such as, the value of free labor, the condition of the slaves, the Mauritius slave trade, and the sugar duties. The battle between the two contending parties was fought for the purpose of winning public opinion in order to coerce the government. But before 1832 neither the anti-slavery nor the pro-slavery men were able to shake the government from its policy of gradual emancipation. Other questions of major importance, overshadowing West Indian issues, were before the country. Roman

[1] *Anti-Slavery Reporter*, I, 71.

Catholic emancipation and the reform of parliament were but two of many such pressing problems. By 1830, however, the younger anti-slavery men lost patience and forced the Anti-Slavery Society to declare for immediate emancipation.[2] This decision made it possible for George Stephen to organize the agency committee of the Anti-Slavery Society in June, 1831, and thereby to inaugurate the intensive campaign which led to victory two years later.[3]

Throughout the six years from 1826 to 1832 the anti-slavery leaders pressed their cause in and out of parliament.[4] Their method of work was well shown in a statement by Buxton: "We are determined to bring forward, without delay, two or three enormities as a prelude to a Bill for coercing the Colonial assemblies." One item selected in 1826 was the incident of the insurrection in Jamaica, in which eight negroes were executed on the evidence of a constable. "He was asked," Buxton said, in

[2] *Anti-Slavery Reporter*, III, 256 ff. Sir George Stephen, *Antislavery Recollections*, pp. 120-123. Meeting was on May 15, 1830.

[3] Report of the Agency Committee of the Anti-Slavery Society, London, 1832. Sir George Stephen, *Antislavery Recollections*, p. 126 ff.

[4] Macaulay wrote the plans for a session to Babington. Brougham was to get the Trinidad order in Council extended to all the colonies; Lushington was to prevent the deportation of the free people of color from the islands; Mackintosh to defend Haiti; Denman, the trial of slaves in Jamaica and Demerara; Sykes, the case of apprentices liberated from slave ships; Buxton to present a new plan of emancipation and to expose the slave trade and slavery in Mauritius. Nothing was left to chance. In the same letter Macaulay explained the public campaign agreed upon: "We are to prepare forthwith a pithy address ready to be printed in every newspaper in the kingdom the moment the Dissolution is announced, rousing electors to require pledges. We are forthwith to prepare our correspondents everywhere for petitioning on the meeting of Parliament, and a Meeting will be held in London about a month before to give the tone and the example. The Speeches will furnish argument to the Country; the Resolutions models. Wherever it may be prudent to do so, public Meetings will be held in the large towns, and reports of the speeches put in the provincial papers." Viscountess Knutsford, *Zachary Macaulay*, p. 431. Sept. 1825.

debate, "whether he had not found guns among the insurgents? His answer was, that he had not; but he was shown a place where he was told guns had been. Then he was asked, if he had not found large quantities of ammunition? And he answered that he had not. Had he not found a number of bayonets? 'No,' said the constable, 'but I was shown a basket in which I was told a great number of bayonets had been.' " The effect of this debate was that the House of Commons declared "that further proof had been afforded them of the evils inseparably attendant upon a state of slavery."[5]

Canning[6] admitted that the legislatures had not done as much as had been expected of them, and consequently the ministers had determined to exercise a privilege which the law allowed, by directing their own officers to introduce into each of the colonial legislatures a bill embracing all the instructions of the order in Council, so that the legislatures would be forced to accept or reject its provisions during the next colonial session. For the present, he said, he should resist all attempt to legislate for the colonies on the subject of slavery, but in order to give more weight to future recommendations, he moved that a copy of the resolutions of 1823 be transmitted to the House of Lords for its approval. This action was taken a few days later by Lord Bathurst.[7] He repeated what had been said

[5] *Parliamentary Debates*, second series, XIV, 1037; Buxton, *Memoirs*, p. 160; Sir George Stephen, *Antislavery Recollections*, p. 93. The effect of calling for petitions was seen during the session of 1826 when 674 were presented to the Commons and a like number to the Lords. The petition from London contained 72,000 signatures; that from Manchester, 41,000; from Glasgow, 38,000; from Edinburgh, 17,000; that from the county of Norfolk, 38,000. *Anti-Slavery Reporter*, I, 197. Anti-slavery dissatisfaction was shown in *Anti-Slavery Reporter*, I, nos. V to XI; no. XL, "Progress of Colonial Reform"; *Edinburgh Review*, XLII, 493 ff.; *Parliamentary Debates*, second series, XIV, 968-1000, *passim*.

[6] *Parliamentary Debates*, second series, XIV, 973 ff.

[7] *Ibid.*, XIV, 1139 ff.

in the Commons concerning the resistance of the colonial legislatures to the recommendations of the government. He thought that Grenada, St. Vincent, and Dominica had done more than other colonies to carry into effect the wishes of the government. For example, by one of the acts passed by those colonies, in the event of any dispute with respect to the right of property, if an alleged slave should assert his freedom, the *onus probandi* was thrown on the master; by another act, the slave, when tried for any offence, was placed in every way on the footing of a white person. In Jamaica, an act had been passed protecting the person of the slave from arrest when going to market. This and another measure of less value were the only proposals of that nature which were favorably received by the Jamaica House of Assembly. A measure had been proposed admitting the evidence of slaves in courts of justice, but the proposition was supported by no one except the individual who had introduced it. The following year a similar measure had met with a more favorable reception, but had been rejected by a vote of twenty-three to thirteen.[8]

Other aspects of the slave problem also engaged the attention of the ministers during the year 1826. The administration of justice in the sugar colonies had been severely criticized, and motions were made to prohibit persons in official stations from being proprietors of slaves. On April 17th, Lord Suffield[9] introduced such a resolution in the Lords, calling attention to the fact that the officers appointed to protect the slaves were their

---

[8] *Parliamentary Debates*, second series, XIV, 1141. Bathurst, the colonial secretary, proposed that the order in Council be divided and classified under distinct heads and that these be sent to the islands, first to be shaped in accordance with the laws of the different colonies and then introduced as bills into the assemblies. If this effort proved unsuccessful, the question would be brought before parliament. After a long discussion, his resolutions were adopted. *Ibid.*, XIV, 1175.

[9] *Ibid.*, XV, 248-264.

masters, and as such were not impartial judges of offences. Lord Bathurst saw no reason why the motion should not apply to the governors and chief justices, but could not consent to its being applied to other functionaries who were compelled to live, in part, on the produce of slave labor.

A last and more formal attempt at this session of parliament to induce the government to abandon its own moderate and cautious plan, and to speak to the colonial legislature in the voice of unbending authority, was made just before the close of the session by Brougham.[10] He moved the following resolution: "That this House has observed with deep regret that nothing effectual has been done by the legislatures of his majesty's colonies in the West Indies, in compliance with the declared wishes of his majesty's government, and the Resolutions of this House of the 15th of May, 1823, touching the condition of the slaves; and this House will, therefore, early in the next session of parliament take into its most serious consideration such measures as may appear to be necessary for giving effect to the said resolutions.'"[11] Brougham approved of the Trinidad order in Council as well fitted to accomplish the desired objects, provided it were adopted and enforced, but the colonies having legislatures of their own had done little or nothing.

On the other side, Wilmot Horton[12] and Charles Ellis[13] maintained: that it was unjust and absurd to consider the

---

[10] *Parliamentary Debates*, second series, XV, 1284-1366.

[11] *Ibid.*, XV, 1308-1309. The particular object of these resolutions was to attract the attention of the country as a general election was impending. For the same purpose, James Stephen issued an address to the electors of England: *England enslaved by her own slave colonies* (second edition, London, 1826), Yale Slavery Pamphlets, vol. VIII. I do not find that the slavery question had any marked influence on the election.

[12] *Parliamentary Debates*, second series, XV, 1309 ff.

[13] *Ibid.*, XV, 1341 ff.

planters as having any love of slavery for its own sake, or resisting its mitigation as the removal of an abstract blessing; but that their reluctance to concur in measures proposed at home arose mainly from a belief that those measures tended to depreciate their property, if not to destroy it; that, as information extended and gradual steps continually added to experience, the planters would take a more accurate view of their own interests, and discern that the gradual amelioration intended was neither objectionable in principle nor dangerous in practice; that the course which had been recommended by parliament and begun by government was the only course properly fitted to gain these ends; and that to comply with the present motion would be an abrupt and total departure from that course.

Canning[14] agreed with Horton and Ellis that the question was decided and that further discussion could be of no service. Parliament had asserted that it would not declare the emancipation of slaves in the West Indies; that this result was to be brought about only through a sober and gradual course of measures; that parliament would not be diverted from that course, except by a degree of resistance amounting to contumacy on the part of the sugar islands—a situation not then to be apprehended. Of the Trinidad order in Council, he said that the clause for compulsory manumission of slaves was undoubtedly the main clause of the whole. It was the only one that was directly operative. All the rest were to mitigate, to improve, to regulate the system of slavery, to render it more tolerable in its existence, and to prepare for its gradual decay without convulsion.[15] Compensation, he argued, could not be admitted into a system of measures of amelioration which regarded the moral improvement

14 *Parliamentary Debates*, second series, XV, 1356 ff.
15 *Ibid.*, XV, 1364.

of the slaves as beneficial to the interests of the master by increasing the value of the slave. At the same time he believed that the principle of compensation properly found its place in the part of the scheme relating to compulsory manumission, where provision was made that the price required for manumission was a just and fair compensation. Brougham's resolution was lost by a vote of one hundred to thirty-eight. This was the last of a series of notable defeats for the anti-slavery party during that session. The time of more decisive measures had not yet come. It was clear to all parties that the government policy was to prevail, and Canning had virtually promised the colonial legislatures at least one year of grace.[16]

During the years that the government left the question of modifying the lot of the slaves to the colonial legislatures, public interest shifted to the region of the Indian Ocean where a vigorous slave trade was carried on against all law.[17] Both the local authorities in the island and the home authorities vigorously denied the existence of such a traffic. This threw the burden of proof on the anti-slavery men and ultimately helped emancipation. Had the matter been immediately acknowledged and remedies instantly applied, no great gain for the opponents of slavery would have resulted.[18] George Stephen,

[16] *Parliamentary Debates*, second series, XV, 1365.

[17] This slave trade was caused by the rapid increase of sugar production in the island, which rose from 6,000 tons in 1814 to 30,000 tons in 1830. *Parliamentary Papers*, 1835, XLIX, 1, pp. 152, 231.

[18] Buxton brought the matter up on May 9, 1826, and obtained a select committee to investigate the existence of the traffic. *Parliamentary Debates*, second series, XV, 1030. Early in 1827, Buxton moved for the renewal of the committee which had been dissolved with the dissolution of parliament. But before anything was done he broke down. Buxton, *Memoirs*, pp. 190-193; *Parliamentary Debates*, second series, XVI, 605-606; *House of Commons Journals*, LXXXII, 209. Wilmot Horton warned Bathurst that the charges were probably justifiable. R. W. Horton to Earl Bathurst, August 16, 1826, Historical Manuscript Commission, *Report on the Manuscripts of Earl Bathurst* (London, 1923), p. 609 ff.

who played a prominent part in collecting the evidence that finally forced the government to admit the truth of all the charges, doubtless exaggerated the significance of the Mauritius question somewhat when he said: "Of all the cases that the indefatigable industry of Mr. Macaulay brought to light . . . this was by far the worst; . . . all the books and all the 'Reporters' that ever were published, . . . all the speeches that ever were made, all the sermons that ever were preached, and all the lectures that ever were delivered on the subject of slavery failed to produce a tenth part of the excitement and indignation provoked by the result of this inquiry. The anti-slavery public, in any true sense of the term, was created by the Mauritius case."[19] The anti-slavery public had been growing for fifty years, but it is nevertheless true that this exposure, following hard on the heels of the persecutions of the missionaries in the West Indies, did much to wipe out slavery.[20]

Buxton was reluctant to bring up the Mauritius controversy and did not enter upon it in parliament until May 9, 1826. A year later, before much had been done, he suffered a stroke of apoplexy and was temporarily forced

[19] Sir George Stephen, *Antislavery Recollections*, p. 84.

[20] George Stephen, however, by travelling all over England and obtaining the testimony of returned soldiers, secured 320 witnesses, of good character, who all spoke of the fact of a trade in slaves. He declared that between 1811 and 1829 the whole slave population of 60,000 was replaced more than once by importation. His statement of the situation in the island is almost beyond belief: "slaves were murdered piecemeal, roasted alive in ovens; flogged, starved, dismembered, tortured, and slaughtered." *Antislavery Recollections*, pp. 105-107. A certain George Bennet, who had visited many missionary stations in the Middle and Far East, reported that "*in the Mauritius it* [slavery] *wore its most horrid and disgusting form.*" *Anti-Slavery Reporter*, III, 298. On the other hand, *John Bull*, XI, 125, April 17, 1831, explained that the cholera was responsible for the great losses in the Mauritius and that the anti-slavery men always found objections: "When the slaves die, they are murdered—when they increase it is the slave trade—this is passing fair."

out of public life. He was back at his post the next year, but the question was kept open until April, 1830, when the government, convinced partly by Buxton's evidence and partly by the report of a commission it had sent out, admitted that the slave trade had been carried on to a vast extent and that all charges to that effect had been true. It promised that all illegally imported slaves would be freed and that the men who had been persecuted and had suffered as a result of the inquiry should receive justice.[21] So intense, however, was the feeling in that island in favor of the slave system that a man named Jeremie, who had served as chief justice of St. Lucia, was driven out and was unable to carry out the task the government had assigned to him.[22]

During the time that Buxton and George Stephen were investigating the Mauritius slave trade, Brougham and Lushington were endeavoring to help along the cause of the free colored people in the West Indies, and in the session of 1828 their efforts were crowned with a promise of an order in Council. This order was issued on March 13, 1829, for Trinidad and later for Berbice. By it the free negroes there were at once placed on the same footing as their white fellow citizens. This measure was of great consequence in the future history of the British West Indies, as it foreshadowed the legal equalization of black and white.[23]

21 Buxton, *Memoirs*, pp. 228-229. "After repeated disappointments, Lushington, Spring Rice, and I saw Sir Geo. Murray today. *He admitted, in the most unequivocal terms*, that slave trading to a *vast extent had* prevailed at the Mauritius, and that *all our statements had been well founded.* I urged a committee for the purpose of putting our evidence on record. He maintained that it was unnecessary *as the Government admitted, and no one denied, all I wished to prove.*"

22 Buxton, *Memoirs*, pp. 230-231.

23 *Anti-Slavery Reporter*, III, 16; *Parliamentary Papers*, 1830, (676) XXI, 413. The government, despite comparative failure, determined to persist in its policy, and, in 1828, Sir George Murray again urged the colonial

Meanwhile, in 1828, Buxton, who had turned his attention to the Hottentots, gave notice of a motion for an address to the king in behalf of these South African slaves. The government promised to agree to his motion provided he abstained from making a speech, and Sir George Murray, the colonial secretary, expressed the concurrence of the government, by which the Hottentots would become free as soon as an order in Council could be issued to that effect.[24] The other results of this session of parliament were of minor importance. The executive government was weakened in its colonial policy by the frequent changes in the colonial office; Huskisson succeeded Bathurst, and was soon followed by Sir George Murray. These changes made any continuous and aggressive policy on the part of the government very difficult.[25] The

assemblies to adopt the proposed reforms. Buxton, *Memoirs*, p. 205; *Anti-Slavery Reporter*, I, no. 21. Recent transactions in the slave colonies, pp. 297-308. Papers in explanation of the measures adopted by His Majesty's Government for amelioration of slave population, etc. *Parliamentary Papers*, 1829, (333) XXV, 153. Wilmot Horton in behalf of the West Indians attempted to recall the Demerara and Berbice manumission order in Council. Buxton, *Memoirs*, pp. 201-202; *Parliamentary Debates*, second series, XVIII, 1023-1048. ''Minutes of Evidence taken before His Majesty's Privy Council, in the matter of the Berbice and Demerara manumission order in Council,'' *Parliamentary Papers*, 1827, (26) XXV, 433.

24 Buxton, *Memoirs*, pp. 208-211.

25 Many West Indians said that it made no difference who the colonial secretary was as long as the dominating personality of James Stephen, the son of James Stephen, was connected with the colonial office. He was one of the first permanent officials in the British service to exert a decisive influence on affairs. He was called ''Mr. Mother Country'' by his enemies because, quite regardless of who the colonial secretary was, the real power of the homeland was exercised by him. He drew up the detailed orders and bills such as the Emancipation Act of 1833. *John Bull* states, ''The West Indian colonists find no fault with the Colonial Secretary—Sir George Murray . . . it is not the individual at the head of the department of whom they complain—or, if they do complain, it is for the negative crime of saving himself all care or consideration upon the subject of their rights, their wrongs, their wants, or their wishes, by delegating the whole management of colonial matters to an individual avowedly prejudiced against the

session of 1829 was chiefly occupied with the question of Roman Catholic emancipation, which left little time for the consideration of the negro question.[26] The comparative failure of the anti-slavery leaders to accomplish anything in parliament was offset, however, by the continuous progress of their cause in the country during the years just considered. The question was constantly kept before the people through the efforts of various anti-slavery societies in the kingdom, whose number and membership increased rapidly. The most important of these societies was, of course, the London Anti-Slavery Society, whose committee directed the propaganda. This organization published books, pamphlets, tracts, and reports touching every phase of the question. Its contributions were voluntary and it kept an agent in the field collecting money. It believed in publicity of campaign contributions, and sent out a list annually, or oftener, of the names of members and the amounts given.[27] Associations similar to that of London were formed in Aberdeen, Birmingham, Bath, Bristol, Edinburgh, Liverpool, Dublin, Cork, and other towns.

The common organ of all these societies was the *Anti-Slavery Monthly Reporter*,[28] published under the direction of the London Society. Zachary Macaulay was editor, assisted by Thomas Pringle, George Stephen, and many others. The *Reporter* gave an account of the meet-

planters and merchants, whose interests, whose fate, whose very existence, are thus put at his mercy, and under his control . . . and how can it be otherwise, so long as one of the saintly fraternity of the *amis des noirs* is retained in the department of Government whence emanates everything vitally connected with the interests of their masters?'' *John Bull*, X, 284, Sept. 5, 1830.

[26] Buxton, *Memoirs*, pp. 220, 224.

[27] For list of anti-slavery writings see *Anti-Slavery Reporter*, II, 175-176. Donations were published about once a quarter, but annual lists were also issued. The former are found in the *Reporter*.

[28] First issue, June, 1825.

ings of the association, discussed the policy of the government, and related the events in the West Indies. It naturally took account of the literature published by the two contending parties, and kept its readers informed of every stage of the question. The cause was aided by men who were not so strictly associated with these groups,[29] and by such publications as the *Edinburgh Review* and the *Christian Observer*. Opposed to the anti-slavery party was the West India party, which was similarly organized with the largest body in London, whose committee issued various publications, among them the *West Indian Reporter*.[30] Its contributions were raised largely by voluntary methods from among those interested in the prosperity of the islands and were said to amount to large sums annually.[31] The journals actively supporting the West Indians were the *Quarterly Review, Blackwoods,*

[29] Such writers as Bickell, Cooper, Tusher, E. Heyrich, Koster, H. More, Riland, E. Schimmelfenning, Sturge, L. Townsend, Watson, and Winn.

[30] Leaders among the West Indian writers were such men as James Macqueen, Alexander Barclay, Alexander McDonnell. *The West Indian Reporter* appeared in forty-one issues somewhat irregularly, beginning in January, 1827, and continuing to 1831. It appeared later, suspended publication earlier, and was smaller than *The Anti-Slavery Reporter*, which it was designed to refute by giving accurate information to the people of England on West Indian affairs. The charge was that ''the characters of the West Indian Planters are vilified, their actions traduced, their proceedings garbled and distorted, till the nation has been almost persuaded to believe that the destruction of the West Indian Colonies is essential to her own prosperity; and that the West Indians must be ruined before the extinction of Slavery can be accomplished.'' *The West Indian Reporter*, I, 1, 2.

[31] Charges of corruption passed back and forth, especially regarding bribery of the press. No definite statement of the receipts and expenditures of the West India committee seems to have been submitted at the time. See the testimony of William Burge in the *House of Lords Journals*, LXIV, appendix no. 2, p. 667. Buxton, however, submitted a detailed account of the receipts and disbursements of the Anti-Slavery Society from 1823 to 1831, see *ibid.*, pp. 646-650. Funds for the West India committee were raised by levies on West India produce imported into England. References in the *Minutes* show substantial sums spent for ''Literary Purposes.''

*John Bull,* and most of the large newspapers. Many publications avoided the issue entirely as long as that was possible.

Such were the means and methods of the two contending parties, but time worked in favor of the friends of the negro, whose efforts were making many converts, during the very years when the struggle in parliament was fruitless. The West Indians were aiding their opponents, by constantly resisting the efforts of the government and by persecuting the missionaries.[32] The Dissenters turned against the West Indians at the news of the death of the missionary, Smith, the flight of Shrewsbury, and similar persecutions. In other words, bodies already organized became their enemies and contributed to their downfall, so that by the end of the year 1829 a new feeling of hope was raised in the ranks of the abolitionists.

Other things, also, tended to encourage the abolitionists after their long period of despondency. For one thing the West Indians were losing some of their most valuable periodical support. The *Quarterly Review* gave up the struggle in their behalf and the *Westminster Review* joined the agitation against slavery.[33] In the second place, the agitation for the emancipation of the slaves was made a part of a general struggle against restrictions and monopolies. The men who fought for the negro insisted that absolute and universal freedom of trade would prove the death of slavery, and that protective duties and bounties kept alive this system of labor, which was really paid for out of the pockets of the people of England. Consequently the abolition of the protective duties on sugar became part of the program. Those who would profit by the removal of these restrictions, no-

32 Buxton, *Memoirs,* pp. 242-244. Resolutions of the Wesleyan Methodist Conference, July 30, 1830, on slavery in *Anti-Slavery Reporter,* III, 349-351.
33 *Anti-Slavery Reporter,* III, 101-103.

tably the East Indians, joined in this attack.[34] Moreover, as the nation as a whole seemed ready to bring about a material alteration or even the abolition of protective duties, the anti-slavery people were receiving much assistance in all their efforts.[35]

In the third place, numbers of the anti-slavery leaders had fought for Roman Catholic emancipation, for which

[34] In estimating the effects of bounties and protecting duties the anti-slavery leaders and West Indians were far apart. Whitmore stated that the benefit conferred was £2,000,000, of which £1,600,000 arose from the protecting duty and the remainder from the bounty. The West Indian reply was that the protecting duty had conferred no benefit and that the bounty amounted to £844,444. *The West Indian Reporter*, II, 2-28.

*Anti-Slavery Reporter*, I, 72. Resolutions of General Meeting of Anti-Slavery Society Dec. 21, 1825. "... this unjust and immoral system, as it exists in the British Colonies, derives great support from those commercial regulations, which, by conferring bounties, and protecting duties on the produce of slave labor, not only materially enhance its price to the British consumers, but increase the miseries of the slaves, and render their liberation more difficult. That if called upon by parliament to contribute to the same, or even to a much larger extent, for the purpose of extinguishing slavery, than they now pay for its support, this meeting would cheerfully obey the call; but that to the existing regulations of the colonial trade they entertain insuperable objections; because while these regulations violate the recognized principles of sound commercial policy, and impose on the nation a heavy pecuniary burden for the maintenance of slavery, they tend to counteract the hope of its reformation, they serve to aggravate and perpetuate its evils; and they involve the people of this country still more deeply in the guilt of upholding it." Additional evidence concerning the opponents of slavery will not be out of place. They are frequently described as "saint and radical." *Anti-Slavery Reporter*, I, 210. Also letter from Macqueen, the editor of the Glasgow *Courier*, to the editor of the *Royal Gazette* of Jamaica published in letter of May 27, 1826. "All the dissenters, and what is called the evangelical party of the clergymen of the Established Church are enlisted, and embarked in the course against you. Their exertions and influence are very great, and the whole of this has been brought about by the activity of your enemies, and the inactivity and apathy of your friends." *Anti-Slavery Reporter*, I, 213. Also called "saints and East Indians." "Saints, Liberals, and the Methodists" in a letter of April 2, 1829, from West India Proprietor in London to the Jamaica *Royal Gazette. Anti-Slavery Reporter*, III, 34.

[35] Change made in sugar duties July 5, 1830, £1.7s. to £1.4s. for West India produce and £1.17s to £1.12s East India.

the Irish members were grateful and were now ready to join in the anti-slavery movement, thus greatly increasing the parliamentary strength of the abolitionists. No account of negro emancipation would be complete without a statement regarding Daniel O'Connell. He took an active part in slavery meetings in England and in Ireland. He was a leader in the debates in parliament. He was ever ready as a counsellor. George Stephen wrote of him: "Mr. O'Connell did what no other man could do. He lent the whole of his powerful influence to keep the Irish public, as well as the Irish members, steady to the cause; he brought all his political weight to bear upon it. Ireland needed no agitation on abolition; from Cape Clear to the Giant's Causeway, Ireland was an abolitionist in heart and in action, irrespective of party feeling, whether in politics or religion; and much, nay most of this was due to Mr. O'Connell. He did it disinterestedly; he made no bargain for reciprocal support; he was content to fight his own battles with his own forces."[36]

Finally the resistance of the colonists to the measures of amelioration suggested by the government, not only helped to swell the ranks of the anti-slavery party but induced it also to adopt a new policy looking toward immediate emancipation. At first the object of the government had been the mitigation of slavery, preparatory to emancipation, as was clearly expressed by Buxton in 1823: "The object at which we aim is the extinction of slavery, not however, the rapid termination of that state —not the sudden emancipation of the negro, but such preparatory steps, such precautionary measures, as by slow degrees, and in the course of years first fitting and qualifying the slave for the enjoyment of freedom, shall gently conduct us to the annihilation of slavery."[37] The

---

[36] Sir George Stephen, *Antislavery Recollections*, p. 221.
[37] *Parliamentary Debates*, second series, IX, 265.

theory that "no people ought to be free till they are fit to use their freedom," seemed so plausible for a long time all parties adhered to it. Macaulay in his essay on Milton compares this maxim to the "fool in the old story, who resolved not to go into water till he had learnt to swim. If men are to wait for liberty till they become wise and good in slavery, they may indeed wait forever."[38]

But since the year 1823 many people had become convinced by the conduct of the colonies that there was no hope of the negroes being prepared for the enjoyment of liberty while they were still slaves. This preparation could not be made without the hearty coöperation of the planters, and such coöperation was not to be had. It seemed, therefore, that there must be either compulsion or a wage system, just as Buxton said: "Under the most mitigated system, slavery is still labor obtained by force; and, if by force, I know not how it is possible to stop short of that degree of force which is necessary to extort involuntary exertion. A motive there must be, and it comes at last to this; inducement or compulsion; wages or the whip."[39] The conviction, then, that slavery could not be modified slowly, with a view to its ultimate extinction, but must be rooted out and that speedily, wrought a thorough change of policy in the anti-slavery leaders. This feeling found expression at a meeting held in London in May, 1830. The first resolution moved by Buxton declared "that no proper or practicable means should be left unattempted for effecting at the earliest period the entire abolition of slavery throughout the British dominions."[40] Speeches and resolutions of the same tenor followed, until a young aggressive leader, Pownall, rose to

38 Macaulay, "Essay on Milton," *Critical, Historical, and Miscellaneous Essays* (6 vols., New York and Boston), I, 245-246.

39 *Parliamentary Debates*, third series, XIII, 44.

40 *Anti-Slavery Reporter*, III, 240-241; Buxton, *Memoirs*, p. 247.

declare that temporizing measures ought at once to be abandoned. "The time is come," he said, "when we should speak out and speak boldly, our determination that slavery shall exist no longer."[41]

Sir George Stephen gave an excellent description of the flood of pent-up feeling released by Pownall, when he moved his amendment in the packed meeting. "It was a spark to the mine! The shouts, the tumult of applause were such as I never heard before and never shall hear again. Cheers innumerable thundered from every bench, hats and handkerchiefs were waved in every hand. Buxton deprecated, Brougham interposed, Wilberforce waved his hand for silence, but all was pantomime and dumb show. I did my best in a little knot of some half dozen young men to resist all attempts at suppression. We would allow no silence and no appeals. At the first subsidence of the tempest we began again, reserving our lungs till others were tired. We soon became the fuglemen of the mighty host, nor did we rest, or allow others to rest, till Wilberforce rose to put the amendment, which was carried with a burst of exulting triumph that would have made the Falls of Niagara inaudible at equal distance."[42] These words expressed the conviction which was already common in the anti-slavery party, and from this time immediate emancipation became its avowed object.[43]

[41] *Anti-Slavery Reporter*, III, 256.

[42] Sir George Stephen, *Antislavery Recollections*, pp. 120-122. Pownall's resolution was, "That from and after the first of January, 1830, every slave born within the King's dominions shall be free."

[43] Buxton, *Memoirs*, p. 247. A meeting held in Edinburgh, in the course of the same year, gave a further impulse to public feeling. After an address by Jeffrey, urging the meeting to aim at nothing short of abolishing slavery, at the earliest practicable period, Andrew Thompson made a vehement protest against any further pretexts for delay, declaring, "We ought to tell the legislature plainly and strongly, that no man has a right to property in man,—that there are 800,000 individuals sighing in bondage, under the in-

While the anti-slavery party was thus becoming more radical, the government was adhering to its old policy of effecting reform through the colonial assemblies, and on February 2, 1830, issued a new order in Council[44] for this purpose. This order was laid before parliament six days later. A comparison between it and the one promulgated in 1824 will throw some light on the progress made by the government in the direction of a more decisive interference with the institution of slavery. By the former order, a protector was debarred from possessing or being interested in plantations cultivated by slaves, in the particular colony to which he was appointed, but he might there possess any number of slaves not attached to plantations, and might also possess in any other colony plantations worked by slaves. He was prohibited by the present order from holding a slave himself or being in any way interested in slaves as property, and could not hire them as domestics unless driven by necessity to do so.[45] Sunday markets and Sunday labor were wholly and absolutely prohibited, and on the market day to be substituted for Sunday, slaves were protected from arrest on account of their masters' debts. But no day was appointed for the slaves to go to market, and no day was set aside for the slaves to raise their own provisions, which they were ac-

tolerable evils of West Indian slavery, who have as good a right to be free as we ourselves have,—that they ought to be free, and that they must be made free.'' Buxton, *Memoirs*, p. 248. This radical expression broke up the meeting, which reassembled, however, a few days later and adopted a petition for immediate emancipation, and this was soon signed by 22,000 persons. *Anti-Slavery Reporter*, IV, 25-33.

[44] Abstract is given as Appendix C in this volume. The following footnotes refer to this appendix. The order may be found in full in *Parliamentary Debates*, second series, XXII, 179-210.

[45] This provision, intended to make those who administered the laws for the protection of the slaves disinterested men, was not applied to the assistant protectors, who could own plantations, slaves, etc. Appendix C, sections 2-11.

customed to do on Sunday.[46] The use of the driving whip
in the field was again prohibited,[47] as well as the flogging
of females and too severe punishment of males, but the
time of twenty-four hours between offence and punishment was dropped[48] All punishments were to be recorded, whereas the former order omitted those consisting of less than four stripes.[49] Marriage of slaves was to
be permitted as before,[50] and the slaves were given the
right to acquire every kind of property, both real and
personal, though there may have been colonial laws which
interfered with this provision, such as the prohibiting of
slaves from raising staples on their land.[51] The clauses
bearing on the non-separation of families were improved by being made to apply to sales of all kinds, and
not to judicial sales only.[52] No important changes were
made regarding manumission, though no man could make
a donation for the slave's benefit, and a slave who had
committed theft or robbery within five years was by just
so much delayed in securing his freedom.[53] The most decided improvement was made in the admission of slave
evidence, placing slaves on the same footing with white
men, though the judge and jury were to value the evidence for what it was worth. Another clause prohibited
the punishing of a slave merely for failing to establish by
evidence the truth of any complaint he might bring
against his master or manager.[54] This order in Council
was carefully drawn up, so that its provisions might be
clear, and was to be made effective by men designated for
that purpose, who, failing in the performance of their

[46] These defects were like those in Trinidad order, which prohibited
Sunday labor but made no provision for going to market or cultivating provision grounds on another day. Appendix C, sections 12-20.

[47] Appendix C, section 21.                    [48] Appendix C, sections 22-24.
[49] Appendix C, sections 26-36.             [50] Appendix C, sections 37-41.
[51] Appendix C, sections 42-44.             [52] Appendix C, sections 45-51.
[53] Appendix C, sections 52-69.             [54] Appendix C, section 72.

duties, were to suffer penalties, while those who violated any of its provisions were to be heavily fined.

In parliament little of moment was accomplished except that on July 13, 1830, Brougham, in what was really a campaign speech in the parliamentary election, obtained a fair minority vote in favor of a more aggressive policy than the government was pursuing.[55] The argument against slavery was strengthened by the fact that the defenders of the slave trade had at one time declared it a relatively innocent traffic which the negroes enjoyed. Now that the trade had been made piracy and efforts for its universal abolition were made ceaselessly, the whole argument regarding the happy lot of the slaves became suspect by this analogy. Brougham quoted Admiral Evans as saying that "The arrival of a Guineaman is known in the West Indies by the dancing and singing of the negroes on board."[56] This speech stressed the higher law argument, which was often used in the United States later. "Tell me not of rights," he exclaimed, "not of the property of the Planter in his Slaves. I deny the right—I acknowledge not the property. . . . In vain you tell me of laws that sanction such a claim? There is a law above all the enactments of human codes—the same throughout the world, the same in all times—such as it was before the daring genius of Columbus pierced the night of ages, and opened to one world the sources of power, wealth and knowledge; to another, all unutterable woes; . . . it is the law written by the finger of God on the heart of man; and by that law, unchangeable and eternal, while men despise fraud, and loathe rapine, and abhor blood, they will reject with indignation the wild and guilty phantasy, that man can hold property in man! In vain you appeal

[55] *Parliamentary Debates,* second series, XXV, 1214. Vote was 56 to 27.
[56] *Ibid.,* XXV, 1181; Brougham, *Speeches,* II, 137.

to treaties, to covenants between nations: the covenants of the Almighty, whether the Old covenant or the New, denounce such unholy pretensions.''[57]

A few days later, Buxton, in his place in the house, made an appeal to the electors of the kingdom in behalf of the slaves, pointing out that the abuses incident to their condition still existed.[58] For this there was ample evidence in the ''Protectors Reports'' made in accordance with the orders in Council, which required that a record be kept of all punishments. In four crown colonies, there were registered for two years, 1828-29, punishments to the number of 68,921, of which 25,094 were inflicted on females.[59]

In July, 1830, parliament was dissolved, and an election held under the influence of the French Revolution of that year. The slavery question was discussed from the hustings and was of considerable importance in a number of places. In Bristol the anti-slavery candidate was defeated by a comparatively small vote in a large poll, while in Yorkshire, Wilberforce's old constituency, Brougham made slavery one of the main topics, and was greeted with great enthusiasm. The abolitionists suffered some losses also, as William Smith retired from political life and Dr. Lushington was defeated. But in spite of these losses the cause gained parliamentary strength by the election, as many members were returned pledged to work for the early abolition of slavery.[60]

In the election Wellington's administration lost about fifty seats and the duke's celebrated declaration against

[57] *Parliamentary Debates*, second series, XXV, 1191; Brougham, *Speeches*, II, 155-156.

[58] *Parliamentary Debates*, second series, XXV, 1294-1295.

[59] ''Reports received from the protectors in the colonies of Demerara, Berbice, Trinidad, St. Lucia. . . .'' *Parliamentary Papers*, 1829, (335) XXV, 255; 1830-1831, (262) XV, 1, 205, 329, 417, 459, 485.

[60] *Anti-Slavery Reporter*, III, 361-368.

parliamentary reform, toward the end of the year, caused the downfall of his ministry, which was succeeded by that of Earl Grey. The new ministry was naturally more in sympathy with the objects of the anti-slavery party, for in the cabinet were Brougham, as lord chancellor, and Althorp, as chancellor of the exchequer. Parliamentary reform, however, was the question of the hour. Buxton was anxious to have the government take up the slavery question, and so, on the 25th of March, 1831, in stating his intention to move a resolution for the complete abolition of slavery, he declared that he would ''most readily leave the matter in the hands of the Government, if Government would take it up''; no reply was made to this offer.[61] The government tried to keep him from bringing forward his motion by offering to bring in ameliorating measures, but he declared in a letter to Lord Althorp that he could not concur in any resolutions which did not assert the extinction of slavery to be their object.[62]

For several months Buxton had prepared himself by gathering statistics and he presented the results of his work to the Commons in a speech on April 15, 1831. He contended that there was one real test of the cruelty of the system of enforced labor, namely the decrease of the blacks in the West Indies, when under all normal circumstances they should increase according to the law of nature.[63] Exclusive of manumissions, the slave population in the ten years preceding had diminished by the number of 45,800,[64] while in the same islands the number of free blacks was multiplying. The free negroes of Haiti, so he said, had increased by about 500,000 in

61 *Parliamentary Debates*, third series, III, 939.
62 Buxton, *Memoirs*, p. 256. April, 1831.
63 *Parliamentary Debates*, third series, III, 1410.
64 *Ibid.*, III, 1410.

twenty years, that is, their numbers had more than doubled.[65] He contended that it was not war, not climate, not the soil, but the forced labor which caused the decline of population among the slaves, while the free blacks were increasing rapidly.[66] The former were subjected to severe physical exertion from sixteen to eighteen hours a day, an amount which weakened the body and made it an easy victim to mortal diseases. He was opposed to temporizing measures and had little regard for the sacredness of property in man. He embodied his convictions in the following resolution: "That in the resolutions of the 15th of May, 1823, the House distinctly recognized it to be their solemn duty to take measures for the abolition of slavery in the British colonies; that in the eight years which have since elapsed, the colonial assemblies have not taken measures to carry the resolutions of the House into effect; that deeply impressed with a sense of the impropriety, inhumanity, and injustice of colonial slavery this House will proceed to consider and adopt the best measures of effecting its abolition throughout the British dominions."[67]

A long debate followed this motion, in which, however, few new arguments were advanced. The West Indians denied the accuracy of Buxton's figures, dwelt on the value of the West Indies to the mother country, and asked that a committee investigate the whole question.[68] Lord Althorp considered the resolutions as too vague, and declared that the slaves were unready for emancipation; he admitted, however, that during the eight years past the colonial legislatures had not adopted the recommendations of the government, and that the time had, therefore, arrived when it was necessary "to adopt other

[65] Parliamentary Debates, third series, III, 1413-1414.
[66] Ibid., III, 1415.          [67] Ibid., III, 1418.
[68] Ibid., III, 1421-1423, 1428-1438.

measures with the colonists than those of mere recommendations."[69] He suggested two ways of interference, one by direct legislation, the other by means of discriminating duties. He proposed to adopt the latter method and moved two resolutions, one declaring dissatisfaction because no laws had been adopted in the legislative colonies and another promising lower duties to those colonies which would comply with the wishes of the government.[70] He felt that the evils of slavery were recognized, and the actions of the legislative assemblies so well known that no committee of inquiry was necessary. Lord Howick, Earl Grey's son, under-secretary for the colonies, said there was an amended order in Council in course of preparation, the adoption of which word for word was to be made imperative upon every colony which sought the promised fiscal privileges. It would include the measures successfully carried out in various crown colonies, such as the abolition of flogging for women, the discontinuance of separation of families, and the granting of the right to slaves to buy freedom for themselves and their children a day at a time, as well as regulations concerning Sunday and for the better feeding and clothing of slaves.[71] Sir Robert Peel criticized the resolutions and the proposed order in Council as going too far, while discriminating duties would be unjust and probably ineffective.[72] The debate was adjourned and, owing to the dissolution of parliament, was not resumed. But the argument of the cruelty of slavery on account of excessive labor had a marked effect on the country, though for the time being the nation plunged into the reform agitation, and the slavery question was again pushed into the background.[73]

[69] *Parliamentary Debates*, third series, III, 1424-1425.
[70] *Ibid.*, III, 1425-1426.          [71] *Ibid.*, III, 1444-1445.
[72] *Ibid.*, III, 1457-1461.
[73] The anti-slavery people issued an address to the people of Great

The Whigs were successful in a new election, and the government continued its work on the new slave code, which was finally issued by the king in Council, November 2, 1831,[74] for the crown colonies of British Guiana, Trinidad, St. Lucia, Mauritius, and the Cape of Good Hope. On November 5, 1831, a circular despatch[75] was sent to the governors of the above mentioned colonies giving the purpose of the government in drawing it up. This was followed December 10, 1831, by a circular despatch to the governors of colonies having legislative assemblies, insisting that in the colonies the aforesaid order in Council be enacted word for word as the law. If accepted, it would be accompanied by a measure of substantial relief to them.[76] The new slave code followed the outlines of the older one, though it was even more detailed, and some new topics were introduced. The first twenty-six clauses were occupied in regulating and prescribing the duties of protectors and assistant protectors and arming them with authority for executing their various functions. They were prohibited from owning any slave property and were given the right to enter any slave's dwelling for consultation, and they represented their wards in ques-

Britain and Ireland, answered by a West India manifesto. *Anti-Slavery Reporter*, IV, 280, 289-290; W. I. Committee, *Minutes*, April 26, 1831.

[74] ''Papers in explanation of the measures adopted for the amelioration of slave population in the colonies,'' *Parliamentary Papers*, 1831-1832, XLVI, 1, p. 93 ff.

[75] *Ibid.*, p. 59 ff.; *Anti-Slavery Reporter*, IV, 37-50.

[76] ''Papers in explanation of the measures adopted for the amelioration of the slave population in the colonies,'' *Parliamentary Papers*, 1831-1832, (279) XLVI, 191. ''Minutes of evidence taken before the select committee of the House of Lords appointed to inquire into the laws and usages of the several West India colonies in relation to the slave population,'' *Parliamentary Papers*, 1832, (127) part II, appendix B, 5, pp. 1249-1251. Also in *House of Lords Journals*, LXIV, appendix no. 2.

tions requiring skill and intelligence.[77] Sunday markets and Sunday labor were again prohibited, but this time a weekly market day was appointed, though there was no provision requiring the master to excuse his slaves on that day.[78] The use of the driving whip to impel labor was absolutely prohibited,[79] and the regulations concerning arbitrary punishments were made very strict,[80] the number of lashes per day being reduced. Persons guilty of cruel and illegal punishments of their negroes were to forfeit them to the crown.[81] False complaints of slaves were not to be punished without any evidence, except in cases where the slave was willfully at fault.[82] Records of arbitrary punishments were to be kept as had been required in the preceding order.[83] The sections concerning marriages and rights of property[84] were not materially changed, but an important improvement was effected by prohibiting the separation of families.[85] Changes were also made in the manumission clauses, according to which a slave was permitted to receive donations with which to buy his freedom, and all fees on voluntary manumissions were abolished.[86] A number of rules were drafted to guide persons in determining whether or not a negro was free,[87] and slave evidence was placed on an equality with that of free persons.[88] Clauses regulating the food and maintenance of slaves were introduced for the first time[89] and the duration of field labor, heretofore unregulated, was limited to nine hours.[90] The clothing and bedding of

[77] *Parliamentary Papers*, 1831-1832, XLVI, 1, p. 93 ff., sections 1-26.

[78] *Ibid.*, sections 27-35.      [79] *Ibid.*, section 36.

[80] *Ibid.*, sections 37-40.      [81] *Ibid.*, section 41.

[82] *Ibid.*, section 42.      [83] *Ibid.*, sections 43-53.

[84] *Ibid.*, sections 54-63.      [85] *Ibid.*, sections 64-69.

[86] *Ibid.*, sections 70-75.      [87] *Ibid.*, sections 75-86.

[88] *Ibid.*, section 87.      [89] *Ibid.*, sections 88-89.

[90] *Ibid.*, sections 90-96.

slaves as well as attendance on divine worship were provided for[91] and a medical attendant was to examine the negroes fortnightly and to keep a journal of the health of each gang.[92] This order in Council of 1831 was the last important measure issued by the government under the resolutions of 1823.

In December, 1831, before this new slave code reached the colonies, an insurrection broke out among the negroes in Jamaica, during which they marched over the country spreading devastation. At the end of the month martial law was proclaimed, the troops quelled the rebellion, and the ringleaders were tried by court-martial and shot. The rebellion was not put down, however, until a great amount of property had been destroyed. The white inhabitants ascribed the insurrection partly to the vague notions excited among the negroes by the orders in Council, and partly to imprudent acts of sectarian missionaries, who, it was said, had encouraged the slaves in the belief that their liberty had been granted to them by the king. The feeling against the missionaries was so strong that Baptist chapels were razed to the ground and both Baptist and Moravian ministers were tried by court-martial but acquitted.[93] Lord Goderich, the secretary of state for the colonies, contended that the disturbance among the slaves in the islands was due rather to the excite-

---

[91] *Parliamentary Papers*, 1831-1832, sections 97-103.

[92] *Ibid.*, sections 104-105. The last sections 106-121, related to miscellaneous regulations, such as providing fines and the like.

[93] *Anti-Slavery Reporter*, V, 107 ff., 134-145. "Missionaries arrested; charges; information as to demolition of chapels," *Parliamentary Papers*, 1831-1832, (482) XLVII, 227. "Report of the House of Assembly of Jamaica on the late Rebellion; with Protests of the Baptist and Wesleyan Methodist Missionaries," *Anti-Slavery Reporter*, V, 233-237. The first charge was made against the British government and the Anti-Slavery Society. The second dealt with the idea that freedom was being withheld from the slaves and that they "must be prepared to fight for it." The third and

ment of the planters than to the discussions at home, for the ferment of the masters caused the slaves to think that they had been declared free.[94] Moreover, every precaution had been taken to prevent such an occurrence by sending circular despatches to the governors of the colonies warning them, whenever it was necessary to issue proclamations explaining the intentions of the government.[95] But the planters had kept the governor of

fourth charges state the objections to the missionaries and are here given in full.

"Thirdly, from a mischievous abuse existing in the system adopted by different religious sects in this Island, termed Baptists, Wesleyan Methodists and Moravians, by their recognizing gradations of rank among such of our slaves as had become converts to their doctrines, whereby the less ambitious and more peaceable among them were made the dupes of the artful and intelligent who had been selected the preachers of those particular sects to fill the higher offices in their chapels, under the denomination of rulers, elders, leaders, and helpers." "And lastly, the public discussions of the free inhabitants here, consequent upon the continued suggestions made by the King's Ministers regarding further measures of amelioration to be introduced into the Slave Code in this island, and the preaching and teaching of the religious sects called Baptists, Wesleyan Methodists, and Moravians (but more particularly the sect termed Baptists), which had the effect of producing in the minds of the slaves a belief that they could not serve both a spiritual and a temporal master; thereby occasioning them to resist the lawful authority of their temporal, under the delusion of rendering themselves more acceptable to a spiritual master." *John Bull*, XII, 222, July 8, 1832. *Parliamentary Papers*, 1831-1832, (561) XLVII, 181.

[94] *Parliamentary Papers*, 1831-1832, (285) XLVII, 259. "Report from the select committee of the House of Lords on the laws and usages of the several West India Colonies in relation to the slave population," *Parliamentary Papers*, (127) part II, appendix E, pp. 1313-1321. Also in *House of Lords Journals*, LXIV, appendix no. 2.

[95] *Parliamentary Debates*, third series, X, 724; "Report from the select committee of the House of Lords on the laws and usages of the several West India Colonies in relation to the slave population," *Parliamentary Papers*, (127) part II, appendix E, 1, p. 1285 ff. *Parliamentary Papers*, 1831-1832, (285) XLVII, 259, pp. 3, 4, 6. Despatches sent June 3, 1831; Sept. 7, 1831. These letters are very clear and it is difficult to see how it would have been possible for Goderich to have done more than he did to prevent the rebellion.

Jamaica in ignorance concerning the feeling among the slaves until too late to prevent the disturbance.

Great excitement continued in the West India Islands throughout the year 1831, for the colonists regarded the measures of government not only as tending to incite insurrection but also as an unnecessary interference with their rights of property and their liberty. Everywhere the government at home was viewed with discontent and irritation, which found expression in Jamaica in parish meetings, where the most violent resolutions were adopted.[96] In the assembly in answer to the speech with which the governor opened the session, the statement was made, "That all measures for the further amelioration of the slave population must emanate from ourselves." The members likewise refused to consider the complaint of Lord Goderich concerning the slave registry returns, avowing that it was a waste of public money to transmit the returns to England. One member, however, made a motion in favor of the abolition of the flogging of women, and of enabling the slaves to purchase their own freedom. These proposals caused the greatest excitement in the island.[97]

In Trinidad, a crown colony, a meeting of the planters was held to oppose the commands of the crown respecting the treatment of the slave population, as contained in the order in Council of November, 1831. At this meeting the parties agreed to protest against the order. Petitions to the king, to the House of Commons, and to the House of Lords were drawn up urging its repeal, and the governor was ordered to transmit their representations to

---

[96] *Parliamentary Papers*, 1831-1832, (285) XLVII 259, p. 7 ff. "Report from the select committee of the House of Lords on the laws and usages of the several West India Colonies in relation to the slave population," *Parliamentary Papers*, (127) part II, appendix E, pp. 1288-1293.

[97] *Anti-Slavery Reporter*, V, 95 ff.

the home government. Violent resolutions were proposed, and a standing committee was appointed to meet every three months. Similar action was taken by the other colonies.[98]

This state of affairs in the sugar islands roused the proprietors at home, who on April 6, 1832, presented a protest to the colonial secretary against the order in Council, which they denounced as unjust and oppressive, inconsistent with the resolutions of 1823, and destructive of the rights of property, as no provision had been made by parliament for compensation for the loss of property sanctioned under parliamentary laws.[99] This protest was followed by a public meeting of persons interested in the colonies, at which it was resolved to petition the House of Lords, "that a full and impartial parliamentary inquiry should be instituted for the purposes of ascertaining the laws and usages of the colonies, the condition of the slaves, the improvements that have been made in that condition, and what further steps could be taken for the amelioration of that condition consistently with the best interest of the slaves themselves, and with the rights of private property."[100] This petition, presented to the Lords on April 17, 1832, was followed by a long debate on the question of slavery, in which Lord Suffield spoke for the abolitionists, Lord Goderich for the government, Lord Seaford for the planters, and the Duke of Wellington for the opposition.[101] The ministers agreed to grant the request for a committee, which was appointed on the

[98] *Annual Register*, LXXIV, 272 ff. "Papers in explanation of the measures adopted by government for the amelioration of the condition of the slave population in His Majesty's possession," *Parliamentary Papers*, 1831-1832, (279, 649, 733) XLVI, 1, 191, 287, 297.

[99] London *Times*, April 6, 1832, gives proceedings of West India meeting on April 5, covering about a page.

[100] *House of Lords Journals*, LXIV, 179.

[101] *Parliamentary Debates*, third series, XII, 596-631.

same day.[102] Thus the policy of the government was thwarted in the colonies and the West India interest succeeded in obtaining a committee to investigate the whole question. In the meantime, it was decided not to press on the legislative colonies the order in Council, which was law in the crown colonies.[103]

The appointment of this committee was regarded by the anti-slavery party as a mere scheme for delay,[104] and its leaders prepared to bring the subject before the Commons. Unfortunately, the anti-slavery leaders were by no means always united on methods of procedure. Buxton recorded that on March 25 twenty of his leading anti-slavery friends dined with him to discuss the question of slavery and to devise means for its extinction, "but," he said, "this select band of our special friends and faithful supporters differed upon every practical point, and opinions wavered all the way from the instant abolition of slavery without any compensation, to the gradual extinction through the agency, and with the cordial concurrence of the planters."[105] More unity of feeling as to the best policy to pursue was expressed at a large public meeting held on May 12, at which James Stephen presided.[106] Resolutions were adopted urging the speedy termination of slavery by an act of the British parliament.[107]

The position in which the government, the West Indians, and the abolitionists in the House of Commons stood to each other in 1832 was nearly that of equilibrium,[108] for, as stated above, the abolitionists had re-

102 Membership is given in *House of Lords Journals*, LXIV, 179.

103 Buxton, *Memoirs*, p. 280. Buxton's speech at general anti-slavery meeting, May, 1832, *Anti-Slavery Reporter*, V, 143 ff.

104 *Parliamentary Debates*, third series, XIII, 387-388.

105 Buxton, *Memoirs*, p. 279.

106 *Anti-Slavery Reporter*, V, 137-176, 143-150.

107 *Ibid.*, 137-176; Buxton, *Memoirs*, p. 282.

108 Division list is in *Parliamentary Debates*, third series, XIII, 97.

ceived a considerable accession of parliamentary strength in the last general election, when many candidates had pledged themselves to vote against slavery. Buxton determined to use this strength by bringing forward the resolutions, moved in the preceding year, aiming at an abolition of slavery at once speedy and safe. But to this idea of rapid emancipation the ministers were by no means to yield, though they fully admitted the principle that slavery should be finally abolished. The question was one of such difficulty that men in positions of responsibility wished to avoid it, and, too, the West Indians were represented by such strength in parliament that the government was more or less dependent on their support. Many of the great English landlords, moreover, had property in the colonies and, though perhaps not opposed to ultimate emancipation, would not support what seemed to them a reckless policy. Nor was the situation in the West Indies one which would induce ministers to intervene in any way that might increase the great distress of the planters, who were constantly clamoring for relief in the shape of lower duties on their produce and of a change of British commercial policy in their favor, and were bitterly opposed to any experimentation with their depreciated property.[109]

The abolitionists, on the other hand, thought that the dangers of rapid emancipation were not nearly so great as they were held to be; that a good police and kind treatment would suffice to prevent those "frightful calamities" which Sir Robert Peel "shuddered to contemplate";[110] that it was hopeless to expect any important reforms from the colonists; and that it was a useless task for parliament to continue to do what Lord Althorp

109 Buxton, *Memoirs*, p. 283. West Indies Merchants Committee, *Minutes*, July 11, 1831.
110 *Parliamentary Debates*, third series, XIII, 65.

called "employing itself most usefully in bringing the slaves to such a state of moral feeling as would be suitable to the proposed alteration in their condition."[111]

The crucial question came up for discussion on May 24, 1832,[112] when a petition was presented to the Commons by the West India interest praying for relief from the distress which was said to be caused by heavy taxation of produce and by the slavery agitation. Buxton then moved his resolution, "that a select committee be appointed to consider and report upon measures which it may be expedient to adopt for the purpose of effecting the extinction of slavery throughout the British dominions at the earliest period compatible with the safety of all classes in the colonies."[113] The government first strove to prevent him from bringing his motion forward and, failing in this, moved to add to the resolution which he proposed, the words, "conformably to the resolutions of 1823."

In the debate Buxton insisted that West India distress had existed for years; that the planters had done little to improve the condition of their slaves and were opposed to religious instruction; that the evils and cruelties of slavery were seen in the decrease of population; and that the great number of punishments went to show that the moral devastation of slavery was the great reason why it should be abolished, even though the West Indian contended that the debased condition of the negro was sufficient reason for his continuance in slavery. Civil war in the islands would follow, he said, if slavery were not abolished, in which war the people of England would take the side of the negroes and Heaven would favor the slaves.[114] He quoted Jefferson with approval: " 'I do, in-

[111] *Parliamentary Debates,* third series, XIII, 60.
[112] *Ibid.,* 34-98.    [113] *Ibid.,* XIII, 38.
[114] *Ibid.,* XIII, 48-49.

deed, tremble for my country, when I remember that God is just, and that His justice may not sleep forever. A revolution is among possible events; the Almighty has no attribute which would side with us in such a struggle.' ''[115]

The opponents of immediate emancipation argued that the slaves were not ready for freedom. This side was represented by William Burge, a former attorney-general of Jamaica, who disputed all of Buxton's facts and deductions, attributing the decrease of population to the disproportion of the sexes, infant mortality, plagues, inaccuracy of earlier returns, manumissions, and fugitives. Moreover, the free people of color had been placed on an equality with the whites, an act which he considered a decided improvement. Burge declared that the planters were ready to provide religious instruction for their slaves, who would not work if free.[116] Peel was opposed to a declaration of immediate emancipation without a plan to carry that declaration into effect, and held up Santo Domingo as a warning to all, for it "demonstrated the fatal consequences of prolonged resistance on the part of the planters; the fatal effects of injudicious haste of immediate abolitionists; and lastly, the fatal crimes into which sudden emancipation was liable to lead the slave population,—so that the most fertile island of all the Antilles was now reduced to import sugar for its own consumption.' '[117]

Buxton persisted in dividing the house in spite of entreaties from friends and fellow workers. On the division the government amendment was carried by a vote of one hundred and sixty-three to ninety.[118] The importance of

[115] Parliamentary Debates, third series, XIII, 49.
[116] Ibid., XIII, 81-93.
[117] Ibid., XIII, 74 ff.
[118] Ibid., XIII, 97, 296.

the debate and especially of the division was shown in Lord Althorp's statement to Thomas Babington Macaulay. "That division of Buxton's has settled the slavery question. If he can get ninety to vote with him when he is wrong, and when most of those really interested in the subject vote against him, he can command a majority when he is right. The question is settled: the government see it, and they will take it up.'"[119]

[119] Buxton, *Memoirs*, p. 296. Before the debate in parliament Lord Althorp and Lord Howick used every argument to dissuade Buxton and succeeded so far that on the morning of the 24th he declared he could not divide and did not become firm in his decision till in the afternoon. Buxton, *Memoirs*, p. 289. His daughter heard the debate and described the pressure brought to bear on her father: "Lord Althorp proposed the amendment of adding 'conformably to the resolutions of 1823.' Then came the trial: they (privately) besought my father to give way, and not to press them to a division. 'They hated,' they said, 'dividing against him when their hearts were all for him; it was merely a nominal difference, why should he split hairs? He was sure to be beaten, where was the use of bringing them all into difficulty and making them vote against him?' He told us that he thought he had a hundred applications of this kind in the evening; in short, nearly every friend he had in the House came to him, and by all considerations of reason and friendship besought him to give way. Mr. Evans was almost the only person who took the other side. I watched my father with indescribable anxiety, seeing the members one after the other come and sit down by him, and judging but too well from their gestures what their errand was. One of them went to him four times, and at last sent up a note to him, with these words, 'immovable as ever?' To my uncle Hoare, who was under the gallery, they went repeatedly, but with no success, for he would only send him a message to persevere. My uncle described to me one gentleman, not a member, who was near him under the gallery, as having been in a high agitation all the evening, exclaiming, 'Oh he won't stand! Oh, he'll yield! I'd give a hundred pounds, I'd give a thousand pounds, to have him divide! Noble! Noble! What a noble fellow he is!' according to the various changes in the aspect of things. Among others, Mr. H— came across to try his eloquence: 'No don't be so obstinate; just put in this one word "interest," it makes no real difference, and then all will be easy. You will only alienate the Government.' 'Now,' said he, 'I'll just tell Lord Althorp you have consented!' My father replied, 'I don't think I exaggerate when I say, I would rather your head were off, and mine, too; I am sure I had rather yours were!' What a trial it was! He said afterwards, that he could compare it to nothing but a continual tooth-drawing the whole evening. At length he rose

Persuant to the amended resolution, a committee was named, of which Sir James Graham was chairman. It prosecuted its investigations from June 1 to August 11. This period of time, however, was far too short for it to receive half the evidence which each side was eager to present, and the committee broke up without coming to a definite conclusion; but stating that the condition of the affairs disclosed by its inquiries demanded the earliest and most serious attention of the legislature.[120] The findings of the committee of the House of Lords were published at the same time, but that report gave no direct answer to any question, merely stating that the committee had collected evidence on certain points.[121] Many men felt that the committees had established two points; first, that slavery was an evil for which there was no remedy but extinction; and secondly, that its extinction would be safe.[122]

to reply, and very touchingly alluded to the effort he had to make, but said he was bound in conscience to do it, and that he would divide the House. Accordingly the question was put. The Speaker said, 'I think the noes have it!' Never shall I forget the tone in which his solitary voice replied, 'no, sir!' 'The noes must go forth,' said the Speaker, and all the House appeared to troop out. Those within were counted, and amounted to ninety. This was a minority beyond our expectations.'' Buxton, *Memoirs*, pp. 289-291. Sir George Stephen said, ''I was under the gallery, and witnessed the reiteration of all this terrible assault upon him in the house itself. I verily believe that Mr. Buxton was the only man in England who could have withstood it all.'' *Antislavery Recollections*, p. 177.

120 See ''Report from the select committee on the extinction of slavery throughout the British Dominions, with the minutes of evidence, appendix and index,'' *Parliamentary Papers*, 1831-1832, (721) XX, 1.

121 ''Report from the select committee on the commercial state of the West India colonies together with the minutes of evidence, an index and appendix,'' *Parliamentary Papers*, 1831-1832, (381) XX, 657. ''Minutes of evidence taken before the select committee of the House of Lords appointed to inquire into the laws and usages of the several West India colonies in relation to the slave population,'' *House of Lords Journals*, LXIV, appendix no. 2.

122 Buxton, *Memoirs*, p. 295.

The work of Lord Suffield in the Lords was described by George Stephen, who was his chief helper. Suffield was denied the aid of counsel, and so Stephen had to help him by calling at his house twice each day to prepare for the examination of witnesses and the like. This work together with daily sessions of the committee injured Suffield's health permanently. Both men were encouraged by Buxton, who remarked to all anti-slavery men, "Never mind; you must kill yourself if need be, but the slave must be emancipated."[123]

Some measures of relief were thought necessary to the sufferers from the insurrection of Jamaica and from the hurricanes in Barbadoes, St. Vincent, and St. Lucia. £100,000 was voted outright and a loan of £1,000,000 was extended to the sufferers. The loss of buildings alone in Jamaica was estimated by the chancellor of the exchequer at £30,000, and the money was granted to enable these premises to be rebuilt, but only on due security for its repayment.[124] A further sum of £58,000 was granted to be applied in giving aid for defraying the internal expenses of the crown colonies in the West Indies, which had adopted the order in Council of November, 1831.[125]

The appointment and reports of the committees of both houses marked the end of the second period of attempted mitigation of slavery by the government in accordance

[123] Sir George Stephen, *Antislavery Recollections*, pp. 179-181. Stephen was severe in his criticisms of the higher clergy, saying that "though their hearts were with us they dare not support a principle that trenched upon the rights of property; if the slaves went tithes must soon follow them! Shortsighted politicians! the same men that emancipated the slave placed tithe property on a surer basis than it had ever enjoyed before! but I believe that their right reverent lordships have long been convinced, and had their opposition, or even their passive resistance, been fatal to emancipation, tithes, bishops, archbishops and all, would long ere this have been reckoned among things that are past."

[124] *Parliamentary Debates*, third series, XIII, 1173-1174.

[125] *Ibid.*, XIV, 1127-1128.

with the resolutions of 1823, for the committees had been appointed on account of the dissatisfaction with the government measures expressed by the contending parties. The West Indians thought the government was going too far in its interference with slavery, and secured the appointment of the Lords committee to investigate the whole West Indian question; the anti-slavery leaders were absolutely dissatisfied with what had been accomplished in behalf of the negro in the sugar islands, and so moved for a committee of the Commons to provide for the extinction of slavery by act of parliament. The government was disappointed with the reception given its measures, and felt that it had exhausted almost every means at its command short of doing what the anti-slavery party asked. The question of the reform of parliament was occupying its attention, however, and the difficulties and dangers of the negro question caused men in positions of responsibility to hesitate before making the abolition of slavery a government measure. Such was the state of the question at the end of the year 1832.

## CHAPTER X

## EMANCIPATION

The dawn of the year 1833 found the two contesting parties prepared for the final battle. Practically nothing in the field of modern propaganda was overlooked. Women threw themselves into the campaign in large numbers. Representatives of both sides toured the country as in a modern political contest, giving series of lectures on slavery, winning over the provincial newspapers, and obtaining the support of the leading men and women in each community.[1] Sometimes one party and then the other hit upon a new method of winning supporters. The idea of placarding London seems to have been conceived by the West Indians, but was most effectively used by George Stephen. "The history of the placards," he wrote, "was simply this: the West Indian body began the strife by defacing the walls of London with pro-slavery matter, and I own, with shame, that this aid in agitation had quite escaped me. I at once saw the advantage of it, as groups were collected around them, spelling them out, though they were a class that probably never opened a book once in a year. I started off to Bagster's the printer's, wrote two or three in the shop, and

[1] One petition carrying 187,000 names was largely gotten up by two women, Anne Knight and Marie Tothill. Sir George Stephen, *Antislavery Recollections*, pp. 196-197. Miss Buxton was her father's helper. She was "like a guardian angel to him," wrote George Stephen. "She acted as his secretary, his librarian, his comforter, and often as his adviser and guide; often have I witnessed, with surprise and admiration, the promptitude of perception with which she comprehended a perplexity, and suggested a solution." *Ibid.*, p. 197.

directed him to have them posted, the same evening, over every West Indian placard that was visible; this, as I anticipated, led to retaliation, and I kept a regular supply in hand, and a little army of bill-stickers, who entered heartily into the fun of the thing, and contrived to follow the West Indian bill-stickers unperceived and veil over their bills before morning. I had only two allies: Mr. Crisp, and a most staunch Anti-slavery man, then Mr. Bagster's reader, but long since established as a publisher himself, Mr. Pardon.'"[2]

Lord Grey and Buxton disapproved of the placards. The latter denounced Stephen at an anti-slavery meeting. Stephen in turn denounced the placards and authors too, " 'I go much farther than my honorable friend; I denounce not only the placards but the author too. I wish I could discover him. I would hold him up to your abhorrence; but he dare not intrude here; he dare not exhibit his incendiary features in such a peaceful right principled assembly as this! he dare not face the withering indignation of my honorable friend,' and here I turned towards Buxton, and looked him full in the face. It was too much even for Buxton's gravity: he burst into fits of laughter, and the meeting, consisting chiefly of young Friends, had been laughing heartily at every pause, and adding loud applause to their laughter.'"[3] So opposed to the use of placards were the Quakers that they refused to pay a bill of £500, but gave Stephen the money on condition that there should be no accounting of it.[4]

The placarding of London was but one form of the great publicity campaign carried on by the agency committee of the Anti-Slavery Society. At the time of the founding of this committee in June, 1831, much doubt ex-

[2] Sir George Stephen, *Antislavery Recollections*, p. 184.
[3] *Ibid.*, pp. 185-186.
[4] *Ibid.*, p. 187.

isted of the wisdom of engaging in radical forms of publicity and the anti-slavery committee refused to undertake the work. In consequence of this George Stephen was invited by James Cropper to attend a Quaker dinner where he explained his plans and after some discussion Cropper broke in with the practical question: " 'Friend S—, what money dost thou want?' 'I want £2,000 but I will begin if I can get one.' 'Then I will give thee £500,' said the noble fellow; and another, not a whit less nobly generous, Joseph Sturge, immediately followed with a promise of £250.' "[5] Wilberforce and James Stephen sanctioned the new campaign, Macaulay was harder to win over, but finally gave it his whole hearted approval.[6]

The agency committee soon fell into the hands of George Stephen and two Quakers, Emanuel and Joseph Cooper. These three able men roused England by sending out speakers and by posting lists of approved anti-slavery candidates for parliamentary elections. The creed adopted and accepted by their agents and lecturers was an uncompromising one: "To uphold slavery is a crime before God, and the condition must therefore be immediately abolished."[7] The demand was made for immediate emancipation and the complete enjoyment of civil rights by the freedmen. For the lecturers an address was outlined; a series of references on slavery was suggested for study; and even the general tone of the lecture

5 Sir George Stephen, *Antislavery Recollections*, pp. 130-131.

6 *Ibid.*, p. 131.

7 *Ibid.*, pp. 132-134. The influence and power of the Quakers was well stated by Sir George Stephen: "In any honest cause there is no agitator like a Quaker; they will give labour, time, money, courage, shrewdness, and perseverance, as if each were in himself a bank that was inexhaustible in such commodities. I have found them at times as obstinate as mules, and sometimes as wrong headed; but to back a man up in a good, honest, moral fight, commend me to a Quaker; they are as invulnerable as Achilles, and will never cry 'enough.' " *Ibid.*, pp. 65-66.

was prescribed. Numbers of volunteer lecturers and other workers were used and six paid lecturers were hired, one of whom, George Thompson, later visited the United States.[8] The agents were carefully routed and instructed to send in frequent reports to headquarters. Special problems, such as the breaking up of meetings by opponents, were taken care of by Stephen himself. So intense and successful was this campaign that within one year the number of affiliated societies increased from two hundred to thirteen hundred.[9]

This new campaign placed Buxton in a difficult situation, because he had to please both the old and the new groups of abolitionists. Besides, the uncompromising nature of the demands of the new men threatened the independence of action of such men as Buxton and Macaulay in their parliamentary battle. Both men were on record as favoring some kind of compensation for the planters and were unable to imagine a successful freeing of the slaves without such a concession. The intensive campaign increased the danger that the people of the British Isles might become so wrought up over this question that a satisfactory measure could not be passed through parliament. If the West Indians were depicted as mere promoters of a crime, who had for many years held men in a slavery unlawful in the sight of God, it might be difficult to gain any kind of compensation for the planters. Thus the question of compensation, as we shall see a little later, for a time threatened to break up the anti-slavery party. On the other hand, the agency committee devoted itself to the public campaign and left the parliamentary battle to Buxton, Lushington, Suffield, and their chief adviser, Macaulay. Moreover, George Stephen was probably right when he said that the mining and sapping

---

[8] Sir George Stephen, *Antislavery Recollections*, p. 139 ff.
[9] *Ibid.*, p. 158.

operations of the preceding eight or ten years would never have been successful without a storming party at the end.[10] The activity of the West Indians was almost equally intense. Threatened with what seemed to be the loss of a vast property, they made it plain to the country and to the ministers that compensation and some assurance in regard to continuity of labor in the islands were absolutely essential, even for the discussion of this difficult problem.[11]

The final battle will now be taken up in some detail. The large vote which Buxton had obtained in favor of his motion during the last session of the unreformed House of Commons, when the attention of parliament and the country was occupied with the question of electoral reform, caused the abolitionists to feel that they would have little difficulty in securing a satisfactory measure from the parliament which met in 1833. So absorbed, however, had the government been with the reform of parliament, that a number of questions, such as finance, the church, the -East India Company, and the state of Ireland, had been postponed for future settlement. The last of these questions demanded the attention of the government first, and with it parliament was largely concerned for several months. No question, however, had excited a wider and a deeper interest than that of negro slavery, and the country expected the ministry to take it up. Great was the surprise, therefore, when it was found that the king's speech contained no reference to slavery. The omission may be explained by the many problems pressing for solution, by the fact that William IV, like his family, was opposed to measures tending toward emancipation, by the constitution of the cabinet,

[10] Sir George Stephen, *Antislavery Recollections*, p. 245.

[11] *John Bull*, X, 382; XIII, 53-54; West India Standing Committee, *Minutes*, Jan. 16, 29, 31, Feb. 4, 1833.

in which Lord Goderich, a man of no particular originality and decision, was colonial secretary, and, lastly, by
the strength and vigorous exertions of the West India
planters and merchants, who were able to have the subject stricken from the king's speech.[12] But this omission
did not enable the government to dodge the question, for
Buxton hastened from the Lords to the House of Commons and on the speaker's return gave notice of a motion
on the subject for March 19.[13] On hearing of this,
Brougham and Goderich cautioned him to do nothing
hastily; but the notice had been given, and on the following evening he formally asked the government whether
they intended to initiate any measure themselves. They
replied that they would introduce a safe and satisfactory
measure.[14]

Two developments made emancipation possible. The better instincts of the nineteenth century were opposed to the
continuance of any cruel system. With every year cruelty
to man or beast became more and more unpopular. This
humanitarian movement manifested itself before and immediately after the Reform Bill of 1832, in a large number of reforms such as those dealing with the criminal
law, the prisons, the removal of Roman Catholic disabilities, and other measures. Secondly, a serious economic
decline of the West Indies actually and relatively reduced
the influence of the planters. During the Napoleonic wars,
the trade of the West Indies had formed one of the most
important branches of British commerce. The official
value of the imports from the British West Indies in 1814
was £9,022,309; this value decreased in 1830 to £8,599,100.
For the same years, the official value of the exports to the
islands was £6,282,226 and £3,749,799 respectively; and

12 West India Merchants Committee, *Minutes*, Feb. 1, 1833.
13 The London *Morning Chronicle*, Feb. 6, 1833.
14 *Ibid.*, Feb. 7, 1833. Buxton, *Memoirs*, p. 303.

the declared value £7,019,938 and £2,838,448, showing that there was some decline in the exports of the islands, but a far greater decline in their imports from Great Britain.[15] In other words, the purchasing power of the West India colonies was greatly reduced, proving that there was much distress in these sugar islands. This distress was caused chiefly by the large decline in the price of sugar in England, which in 1814 was seventy-three shillings per hundredweight, but had fallen, in 1831, to twenty-four shillings per hundredweight, in both cases exclusive of duty.[16] A select committee of the House of Commons, in 1832, reported that the distress was caused by over-production of sugar, and it is to be noted that the world production of sugar increased from 400,000 tons in 1814 to 570,000 tons in 1830, most of which increase was outside of the British West Indies, especially in Cuba, Brazil, and Mauritius.[17] The colonists claimed: first, that their sufferings were caused by the restrictive commercial policy of the mother country, which increased the cost of their production by not less than £1,392,000; secondly, that the prohibition of refining in the West Indies was a burden; and lastly, that the duties on sugar as well as on other articles of colonial produce were too high. Lower duties, it was declared, would increase the consumption and give some advantage to the colonists from the monopoly of the home market.[18] The committee refused to accept the high figure charged to the commercial system, and felt that the duties could not be lowered without impairing the revenue of Great Britain.[19] The colonists also complained of the tariffs of Austria and

15 ''Report from select committee on the commercial state of the West India colonies, with evidence, appendix, and index,'' *Parliamentary Papers*, 1831-1832, (381) XX, 657, appendix 2.

16 *Ibid.*, appendix 3.

17 *Ibid.*, p. 106. Much higher figures also given.

18 *Ibid.*, p. 7 ff.        19 *Ibid.*, p. 11 ff.

Russia. These high duties the committee thought might perhaps be removed by means of negotiations with those powers.[20] Certain other conditions which were practically non-remediable operated to depress the colonies. Among these was the acquisition of additional sugar islands by the peace of 1814. These islands had been admitted into the restrictive system of Great Britain, and their products helped to flood the markets of the home country. Moreover, the continuance of the slave trade to foreign colonies with a richer soil enabled those colonies to produce sugar at a lower cost.[21] Finally, most of the estates in the West Indies were mortgaged, and the money was advanced by merchants at a high rate of interest on condition that the produce be consigned to them and that all supplies be bought from them. Hurricanes and crop failures also added to the prevailing distress, while the system of slave labor made it practically impossible to raise anything but staple products, chiefly sugar, and the uncertainties attending the slavery agitation made the borrowing of money increasingly difficult.[22] Such, in brief, was the economic condition of the West Indies when the humanitarian sentiment, embodied in the anti-slavery party, forced the government to take up the question of the abolition of slavery and to promise a safe and satisfactory measure.

On March 19 Buxton rose to bring forward his motion,[23] but when Lord Althorp said that the ministers would explain their plan on April 23, Buxton announced

[20] *Parliamentary Papers*, 1831-1832, (381) XX, 657, p. 14.

[21] *Ibid.*, p. 15.

[22] *Ibid.*, pp. 18-21. I have simply mentioned what were considered the chief causes of West India distress, without making a critical estimate of the reasons given. All these causes have been mentioned before and are given here simply in summary.

[23] *Mirror of Parliament*, March 18, 1833; *Morning Chronicle*, March 19 and 20; Buxton, *Memoirs*, p. 309.

himself as satisfied.[24] This delay gave the ministers five weeks in which to perfect their scheme of emancipation; but, in the meantime, a change in the cabinet was made, by which Stanley became colonial secretary. He was eminently fitted for his new post, as he had shown unusual ability in the handling of the Irish question. He was a man of great energy and decision, the best debater, and the ablest man of business among the Whigs; he could, therefore, be counted on not only to draw up the best possible measure, but also to defend it when presented.[25] The problem which confronted him was one of the most difficult ever presented for solution, involving, as it did, the feelings of the abolitionists, the interests of the planters, and the welfare of the empire. It was manifestly impossible to reconcile all these conflicting claims, and Stanley had to make a choice of evils. He obtained an additional three weeks in which to complete his information, and on May 14 rose to explain the principles of the bill he had drafted for the abolition of slavery throughout the British colonies.[26]

The contending parties were neglecting no opportunity to influence the government. Soon after the ministers had pledged themselves to take up the question on April 23, Buxton heard that a plan was discussed for the negroes

---

[24] *Parliamentary Debates*, third series, XVI, 826; *Mirror of Parliament*, March 19, 1833.

[25] The reasons which caused the changes in the cabinet are to be found in George Macaulay Trevelyan, *Lord Grey of the Reform Bill*, p. 359; *Memoirs of the Courts and Cabinets of William IV and Victoria* (2 vols., 1861 edited by the Duke of Buckingham), II, 125. *The Greville Memoirs: a Journal of the Reigns of King George IV and King William IV* (3 vols.), II, pp. 352, 359, 366; and *The Life and Times of Henry, Lord Brougham, written by himself* (3 vols., New York, 1871), III, 166 ff.

[26] ''Sir James Stephen, upon whom the duty of supplying him [Stanley] with information devolved, always maintained that Lord Derby was the best recipient of *Cram* who had come within his experience.'' Viscountess Knutsford, *Macaulay*, p. 471.

to buy their own freedom. He hurried to Dr. Lushington, and they agreed to call a special meeting of the committee of the Anti-Slavery Society on the next day. The committee met and determined to rouse the people. They were aided in this by one Henry Whitely, who had just returned from Jamaica, where he had spent three months as a bookkeeper. In a most effective way, Whitely wrote down what he saw there, his account was printed, and two hundred thousand copies were distributed within a fortnight.[27]

The anti-slavery leaders had to meet an insurrection within their own party, for the radical members were opposed to compensation for the planters, which was an inherent part of the government scheme of emancipation. In order to conciliate their followers, therefore, the leaders determined to explain their views at an anti-slavery meeting on April 2. Buxton was the principal speaker, followed by Dr. Lushington, Joseph J. Gurney, and others.[28] A rather reluctant assent to compensation was secured.

Efforts to rouse public opinion were continued. Lectures were delivered to crowded meetings everywhere, and the newspapers and periodicals gave the cause hearty support. Many of the clergy and dissenting ministers preached on the sinfulness of slavery, and petitions were drawn up in all parts of England and signed by 1,500,000 persons. A circular letter was sent by the London committee to the friends of the anti-slavery movement in every considerable town, requesting them to appoint delegates to meet in London on April 18, to represent in person the anti-slavery crusade. More than

---

[27] Henry Whitely, *Three Months in Jamaica* (London, 1832); Buxton, *Memoirs*, pp. 311-312.

[28] *Anti-Slavery Reporter*, VI, 57-80, especially resolution on p. 65; Buxton, *Memoirs*, pp. 311-312.

three hundred delegates responded to this call, and an address was drawn up by Joseph J. Gurney for presentation to the prime minister. This address was carried by all the delegates in a body to Downing Street, where they were received by Althorp and Stanley.[29] Stanley said later that he was impressed by the delegation, though at the time he promised nothing, except that he would not again postpone his motion.[30]

Nor was the West India body negligent in its efforts to bring pressure to bear upon the government, and to present its cause publicly. As early as January 16, 1833, the standing committee of the West India body appointed a deputation to sound the government on its future policy in regard to the recent order in Council, on the reappointment of the committees by the houses of parliament, and on new policies.[31] On January 28, Grey and Goderich replied that the question was receiving the serious consideration of the cabinet and that the order in Council of November, 1831, would not be urged on the self-governing colonies.[32] Further meetings took place between Lord Goderich and the West India deputation, which the latter regarded as more or less unsatisfactory,[33] and on March 27 a government scheme of immediate and complete emancipation was transmitted to the deputation. This

29 *Morning Chronicle*, April 25, 1833.

30 Buxton, *Memoirs*, p. 318. This meeting was called largely to explain to the anti-slavery people over Great Britain the difficulties in the way of emancipation, particularly the compensation problem. Sir George Stephen wrote: ''It certainly was a sacrifice both of feeling and principle on the part of the Agency committee.'' He referred to compensation. Sir George Stephen, *Antislavery Recollections*, p. 196.

31 *The Proceedings and Resolutions of the West India Body, including Copies of their Various Communications with His Majesty's Government relative to the Measures of the Session 1833 for the Abolition of Slavery* (London, 1833, 8, 158 pages), p. 5.

32 *Ibid.*, p. 5.

33 *Ibid.*, pp. 6-16; *Morning Chronicle*, May 13, 1833.

scheme was explained by Goderich and commented on by the deputation, but Stanley regarded it as unsatisfactory and so developed one of his own.[34] The abandonment of the principle of an early and complete emancipation caused Lord Howick to resign and join the anti-slavery leaders. On April 23 the planters submitted to the colonial secretary a memorandum embodying their ideas on the subjects of compensation and emancipation. Stanley could not agree with their plan of compensation, based on the actual selling price of slaves in 1823, minus the percentage of decline in the price of West India produce, and insisted that the value of labor could only be obtained by determining the profit from it, and not by the gross produce. In addition he objected to the plan of keeping the slaves in contract for forty-one years, whereby a monopoly of the time and labor of the negroes was assured to their masters, though the latter were to receive the full price of the slaves at once.[35] His comment, written April 29, was answered on May 2 by the members of the deputation.[36] They objected to the secretary's basis of compensation and insisted on the loss and depreciation of land and buildings consequent on emancipation.[37] Meetings of the West India body, or its committee, were continued from day to day, and at these meetings the minister's plan was denounced as confiscatory.[38] After the government proposals had been explained in parliament, the colonists resolved to appeal to the country in behalf of their rights, and to petition the king and parliament.[39]

The most important meeting, however, and the one

[34] *The Proceedings and Resolutions of the West India Body*, pp. 17-53.
[35] *Ibid.*, pp. 55-73.
[36] *Ibid.*, pp. 73-77.
[37] *Morning Chronicle*, May 13, 1833.
[38] *Ibid.*, May 9, 10, 11, 13.
[39] *Ibid.*, May 20.

whose resolutions are worthy of notice, as containing the claims of the colonists on the mother country, took place on May 27, when fifteen hundred planters, merchants, and others connected with the West Indies assembled. A member of almost every banking and commercial house in London was present, and in the course of the day fully five thousand persons were said to have attended. The resolutions mentioned above were adopted, and each adoption was accompanied by long speeches from the mover, the seconder, and a third party, so that everybody had a chance to express his sentiments, or to hear them expressed. It was argued that the petitions of the abolitionists were "gotten up" in the most shameful manner, that the evils of slavery had been much exaggerated in the recent elections, and that emancipation would mean the ruin of the empire and would set an example of confiscation of property, which would be followed when other questions came up for settlement.[40]

Under such pressure from both parties, Stanley matured the ministerial scheme of slave emancipation, which he explained to the Commons in a committee of the whole house on May 14.[41] Beginning with the declaration that the increasing force of public opinion rendered it impossible to delay longer the consideration and settlement of the question, he entered at great length into a comparison of what parliament had recommended and resolved at various times, with what the colonial legislatures had done, arriving at the conclusion that the latter had manifested no disposition to carry into effect the wishes and determinations of the mother country, and that if ever a case justified the exercise of the paramount authority of parliament, it was when, as in the present instance, every

[40] Speeches and Resolutions found in *Morning Chronicle*, May 28; resolutions in *Proceedings and Resolutions of the West India Body*, p. 120 ff.
[41] *Parliamentary Debates*, third series, XVII, 1193-1231.

means of remonstrance and warning had been used in vain.[42] Government, therefore, had resolved to propose a plan which would insure the extinction of slavery, and free not only future generations of slaves, but also the existing generation, while it would prevent the dangers of immediate emancipation.[43] The plan was to place the slaves for a limited time in an intermediate state of apprenticeship. They would be made to enter into a contract by which their masters would be bound to give them food and clothing, and such other allowances as were then authorized by law, or to compound the whole for a money payment. In return for this consideration, the slaves would be called upon to work for their masters three-fourths of their time, leaving it to be settled between master and slave whether the period should be for three-fourths of the week or for three-fourths of each day. During the remaining fourth of their time, allowed them for purchasing their absolute freedom, they would be at liberty to transfer their labor elsewhere, if they so desired; but if they were inclined to give it to their masters, their masters would be obliged to find them employment according to a fixed rate of wages. It was impossible to leave the negro to do as he pleased, that is to work or not; for a man in a tropical climate like the West Indies, where the quantity of unoccupied land was as great as its fertility, would not need to work diligently to make a living. To remove the slave suddenly from labor and to place him in a situation in which he would be called upon to provide for nothing more than the necessities of life, would be to extinguish civilization and permit negroes to revert to savagery. One of the great difficulties, Stanley said, was how to fix a rate of wages for free labor applicable to all the islands. The system devised called on

---

[42] *Parliamentary Debates,* third series, XVII, 1205.
[43] *Ibid.,* 1221 ff.

the planter to put a valuation on his slaves at the time of their entering into a state of apprenticeship. Then the annual wages paid by the master were to be one-twelfth of the price of the negroes. If the master fixed a high price for his negro, he would have to pay that negro proportionately high wages. If, on the other hands, the master put a low valuation on his negro, the negro would, of course, receive low wages. To guard against too low wages, the stipulation was made that if the master fixed a low price, upon the payment of that price by any other person, the negro would be free.[44] The government thus divided the price for the slave's freedom into installments, so that at the end of twelve years the full price put on the slave by the master would be paid out of the proceeds of the slave's industry.[45] So much for the freedom of the slave.

Turning from the question of apprenticeship to that of compensation, Stanley outlined his plan, which called for a transaction in the nature of a loan. Slavery, he said, was a national wrong, for which the whole nation was responsible; therefore, the nation ought to help bear the burden of its extermination and not to throw that burden either on the West Indies or on the slaves. From the returns of West Indian property made to the Board of Trade, the net profits arising from the cultivation of sugar, rum, and coffee amounted to £1,500,000 annually. The ministers proposed to advance to the West India body a loan to the amount of ten years' annual profit, that is, a loan of £15,000,000. The conditions under which the loan should be repaid would remain open for further consideration by parliament. The sum thus advanced might be considered equal in value to the one-fourth of the slave's time, for which time the slave was to receive

[44] *Parliamentary Debates*, third series, XVII, 1225 ff.
[45] *Ibid.*, 1225 ff.

wages with which to buy his freedom. With that sum and the other three-fourths of the negro's labor, the planter, at the end of twelve years, would have received a just compensation for the price of his, slave and for all the expense to which the slave might have put him for food and clothing. During that time, however, the planter would have to pay interest upon his loan, and to that extent he might perhaps be considered a loser. The loss of interest by the planter would have to be borne either by the produce of negro labor or by the revenue of the mother country, as it could not, in fairness, be charged to the planters.[46]

Stanley vigorously defended the policy of taking something from the profits of negro labor, arguing that by taking a portion of their wages from them for the purpose of purchasing their freedom, the negroes would be induced to save some part of their wages when they became free and would be taught those habits of prudence and forethought which would tend to their moral improvement.[47] Stipendiary magistrates, moreover, were to be appointed by the crown, uninfluenced by the local assemblies, free from local passions and prejudices, who should dispense equal justice to the rich and the poor, the black and the white, who should watch over and protect the negro in his incipient state of freedom, and who should aid and direct his inexperience in forming a contract which might have so material an effect on his later life. As an aid to the moral advancement of the negro, schools were to be established in the colonies for his religious and moral instruction, if possible with the assistance of the local legislatures.[48] He concluded by moving the following resolutions:

46 *Parliamentary Debates,* third series, XVII, 1226-1227.
47 *Ibid.,* 1227.
48 *Ibid.,* 1228-1229.

1. That it is the opinion of this committee, that immediate and effectual measures be taken for the entire abolition of slavery throughout the colonies, under such provisions for regulating the condition of the negroes as may combine their welfare with the interests of the proprietors.

2. That it is expedient, that all children born after the passing of any act, or who shall be under the age of six years at the time of passing any act of parliament for this purpose, be declared free—subject, nevertheless, to such temporary restrictions as may be deemed necessary for their support and maintenance.

3. That all persons, now slaves, be entitled to be registered as apprenticed labourers and to acquire thereby all the restrictions of labouring under conditions, and for a time to be fixed by parliament, for their present owners.

4. That to provide against the risk of loss which proprietors in His Majesty's colonial possessions might sustain by the abolition of slavery, His Majesty be enabled to advance by way of loan, to be raised, from time to time, a sum not exceeding, in the whole, £15,000,000, to be repaid in such manner, and at such rate of interest, as shall be prescribed by parliament.

5. That His Majesty be enabled to defray any such expense as he may incur in establishing an efficient stipendiary magistracy in the colonies, and in aiding the local legislatures in providing for the religious and moral education of the negro population to be emancipated.[49] No vote was that day taken on the resolutions, and after some discussion the debate was adjourned to May 30.[50]

The contentions of the two parties now call for some consideration. The anti-slavery party struggled for immediate emancipation of the slaves, or, failing in that, for

[49] *Parliamentary Debates,* third series, XVII, 1230-1231.
[50] *Ibid.,* 1260.

a very short period of apprenticeship. The West India body fought for the largest possible compensation for the loss of the slaves, and was determined to keep the period of negro apprenticeship at twelve years. The leaders of the former party in parliament were anxious to see the government and parliament fully committed to the emancipation measure, and consequently did not have a division of the house taken during the consideration of the resolutions, although they protested vigorously against such a long period of apprenticeship.[51] The West India leaders, on the other hand, made their main fight during the consideration of the resolutions, and succeeded in obtaining resolutions providing for a long apprenticeship and a fair compensation[52] of one-half the slaves' value.

When the discussion was resumed, the first resolution was agreed to without a division. Some, however, defended the planters from the imputations of cruelty which had been cast upon them, others justified the compensation to be given, but still others demanded immediate emancipation without the intervention of any forced apprenticeship.[53] When the second resolution was under consideration, Hume moved an amendment, that before proceeding further committees be appointed to enquire into the probable efficiency of free labor in the colonies. He maintained that the ministers were acting rashly and that the house had no trustworthy information regarding the effect which these changes might produce on the welfare and productiveness of the colonies. This and other amendments were voted down and the original resolution agreed to.[54]

---

[51] Buxton, *Memoirs*, p. 325. *Mirror of Parliament*, June, 1833.

[52] *Proceedings and Resolutions of West India Body*, May 27.

[53] Debate, May 30, *Parliamentary Debates*, third series, XVIII, 112-166; May 31, pp. 204-236; June 3, pp. 308-360.

[54] Admiral Fleming, on the other hand, made a vigorous speech to prove

The third resolution, which involved the principle of
compulsory apprenticeship, was opposed by Buxton on
the ground that a period of apprenticeship was unnecessary and impracticable.[55] The resolution was founded, he
contended, on the assumption that emancipated negroes
would not work, or at least, would not work more than
was necessary to supply the mere wants of life. That assumption he denied, and cited instances in support of his
contention. Free labor, he said, had been tried with success in Trinidad, in the Bahamas, and in Cuba. Negroes
had a passion for the luxuries of life, and would come to
a ball dressed in all the finery of India and all the colors
of the rainbow.[56] Lord Howick, former under-secretary
for the colonies, as well as Buxton, felt that the plan of
apprenticed negroes must fail altogether. The latter argued that if slavery and its accompaniment, the whip,
were to be done away with, and if the hope of wages was
not to be substituted, the plan must fail, for the apprentices would not work.[57] Lord Howick contended that the
amelioration policy of government had really increased
the gross cruelty of the system of slavery, and that the
more absolute and despotic the master, the better was the
condition of the slave.[58] To place the power of punishment in the hands of magistrates would make it so remote
that obedience could only be enforced by the severest punishments. Jamaica was managed better than Trinidad, as the slaves generally suffered less cruelty in the
former, though, indeed, there were isolated cases of

the value of free labor, citing his own experiences and observations in
Venezuela and the West Indies. A number of amendments were proposed but
negatived, and the original resolution carried. *Ibid.*, pp. 458-509.

[55] *Ibid.*, pp. 515-524, June 10.

[56] *Ibid.*, pp. 522-523.

[57] *Ibid.*, p. 524.

[58] *Ibid.*, pp. 541-543, June 10; also, *ibid.*, XVII, pp. 1231-1259, where
Lord Howick developed his point at great length.

greater cruelty. In brief, his opinion was that labor, under an apprentice system, just as in a state of slavery, would have to be obtained by compulsion, and that consequently the condition of the negroes would be worse at the termination of the period than at the beginning. To these arguments Stanley, Lord Althorp, and Thomas Babington Macaulay replied that it was not merely a question of gradual or immediate emancipation. No matter what might be the period of apprenticeship, from the moment the bill passed, slavery in the British colonies, in its worse features, would be at an end. The contemplated bill recognized the rights of property and diminished the power of the master to inflict corporal punishment; it respected the domestic ties of the negro and insured to him some of the fruits of his labor. Moreover, proof was wanting that free labor would assure to the master the continuous work which was essential to his property. The ministers felt that the measure would essentially improve the condition of the slave, emancipate him completely at a certain period, and earlier if he proved himself fit, while at the same time guarding the interests of the master.[59] Buxton, on being assured that the question of the period of apprenticeship was not before the house, withdrew his motion and proposed that the labor should be "for wages."[60] This motion he also withdrew, but O'Connell insisted on dividing the house on those words, when the original resolution was carried three hundred and twenty-four to forty-two.[61]

The fourth resolution, dealing with the amount and mode of compensation to the planters, introduced perhaps the most difficult problem of all. The original proposal had been to give the planters a loan of £15,000,000, on

[59] *Parliamentary Debates*, third series, XVIII, pp. 532-537, 543, 544.
[60] *Ibid.*, p. 545.
[61] *Ibid.*, p. 547. List of minority given.

which they were to pay interest. To this proposal the West Indian party had refused to listen, and at a meeting held on May 27, by representatives of "Proprietors, Merchants, Bankers, Shipowners, Manufacturers, Traders, and others interested in the preservation of the West-India Colonies," vigorous resolutions were passed. The ministers were compelled to yield, and agreed to convert the loan of £15,000,000[62] into a gift, and to pay it to the planters absolutely, as the price of the emancipated slaves and other losses. The planters answered that this concession was insufficient, but that they would accept £20,000,000. This ultimatum was agreed to.[63]

Although Stanley a few weeks before had regarded a loan of £15,000,000 as sufficient, he now declared £20,000,000 was not, after all, too great a sum. The Emancipation Act, he said, would take away from the proprietors one-fourth of the value of the slaves immediately[64] and the whole of their property at the expiration of a limited period. In the meantime, they had to support the slaves. The value of the land would probably depreciate, a fact that had to be taken into account. According to the best information available the slaves were worth at least £40 per head, which totaled £30,000,000. The value of the slave's time which was taken from the proprietor he could not estimate at a lower sum than £15,000,000.[65] Allowing for a deterioration in the value of the slaves during a period of twelve years, and not allowing, on the other hand, for the value of the children thereafter born, who would be free, he arrived at the aforesaid sum. But the real reason which induced him and the government

---

[62] *Parliamentary Debates*, third series, XVIII, p. 496.

[63] *Ibid.*, pp. 549, 573.

[64] With a gift of £20,000,000 the slave was given one-fourth of his time free. *Ibid.*, p. 586.

[65] *Ibid.*, pp. 584-588.

to propose a larger sum than that which had first been mentioned was this: all those connected with the West Indies in mercantile lines had assured him that if parliament would consent to vote £20,000,000 to the proprietors as compensation for the loss of their property, this great interest would give its full concurrence to the government plan and would use its influence over the colonial legislatures in order to induce them to coöperate in the extinction of slavery.[66] He therefore moved that ''Towards the compensation of the West-Indian proprietors his majesty be enabled to grant a sum not exceeding £20,-000,000 to be appropriated as Parliament may hereafter think fit.''[67]

There was much opposition. Some objected to the amount, because it was more than the slaves were worth; because the British people were already over-burdened with taxes. Still others held that if free labor was such a great boon as the anti-slavery party contended, the West Indians ought to pay the mother country for the privilege of emancipation. Briscoe moved to reduce the sum from £20,000,000 to £15,000,000, but his motion was lost by three hundred and four to fifty-six.[68] Buxton wished to withhold half the amount as a pledge of good faith, until after the apprenticeship period was over, thinking thereby to induce the planters to have more interest in the negroes. A motion to that effect was lost by two hundred and seventy-seven to one hundred and forty-two.[69] Two other amendments were proposed in the attempt to prevent compensation from becoming a burden on the mother country. One of them proposed to give the compensation in the shape of a reduction of the duties on

[66] *Parliamentary Debates*, third series, XVIII, pp. 584-588.
[67] *Ibid.*, p. 550.
[68] *Ibid.*, pp. 597-598. List of minority given.
[69] *Ibid.*, p. 597.

West Indian produce. The other proposed to reduce the duty on sugar by one-half, and to impose a property tax on the colonies. Both were rejected by large majorities, and the original resolution passed by two hundred and eighty-six to seventy-seven.[70] The last of the resolutions, providing for stipendiary magistrates and moral and religious instruction, was carried without a division. The resolutions were then carried up for the concurrence of the Lords, who after long debate agreed to them on June 25.[71]

From June 25 to July 24, that is, from the passing of the resolutions by the Lords to the bringing in of the formal bill in the Commons, both the contending parties were active in furthering their respective causes. The planters had fared well so far and only needed to keep what they had gained. But with this advantage they were not content. They strove to obtain the execution of the act as far as possible by the colonial legislatures. The anti-slavery leaders, on the other hand, were determined to prevent such a result and also prepared themselves to play off the £20,000,000 against immediate emancipation, when the bill should come up for consideration. In other words, they were willing to grant the planters this large sum, provided the slaves were freed at once.[72]

A deputation of thirty-three members of parliament led by Buxton, with George Stephen as spokesman, attempted to get Stanley to agree to a reduction of the length of the period of apprenticeship. In a long interview Stanley explained that he was absolutely pledged to fight for the twelve year period, and refused to "abate an hour of the apprenticeship." To threats of appeals to the country, he replied that "the apprenticeship must

[70] *Parliamentary Debates*, third series, XVIII, p. 597. List of minority given. Buxton and Lushington voted with the majority.
[71] *Ibid.*, pp. 1163-1228.          [72] Buxton, *Memoirs*, p. 331.

stand, or the bill must go with it." Stephen had foreseen this contingency and had made full preparations to summon a special anti-slavery meeting at Exeter Hall, and instantly released the call. This so pleased O'Connell that he said to Stephen, "I have served a long apprenticeship to agitation, my young friend, but you are my master." So great was the pressure put upon members of parliament by the anti-slavery societies of the country that sixty-six members appeared on the platform at the Exeter Hall meeting and agreed to vote as directed by that body.[73]

When the bill was introduced in the Commons, a long debate took place on its provisions. Buxton raised objections to the clauses which the anti-slavery leaders found contrary to their ideas. Too much power, he said, was given to the colonial legislatures. He pointed out one clause whereby twenty-nine articles, such as food, clothing, lodging, maintenance, and regulations of the slaves, were all made dependent on the action of the colonial assemblies. He found another clause whereby it was left to these same legislative bodies to make laws necessary to establish such regulations of the slaves without any restriction whatever.[74] Moreover, the proposed grant of £20,000,000 had already proved a great boon to the West Indies, so that debts considered worthless a few weeks before had become perfectly sound. In return for such a large compensation by the mother country to the planters, he felt there should be immediate emancipation, especially because the apprenticeship system would be unsatisfactory. There would be neither the hope of wages, which induced white men to work, nor the immediate fear of the whip, which compelled slaves to labor.[75]

[73] Sir George Stephen, *Antislavery Recollections*, pp. 203-206.
[74] *Parliamentary Debates*, third series, XIX, pp. 1184-1185.
[75] *Ibid.*, p. 1188.

In slavery the labor was performed in the field under the vibration of the lash; but under the proposed change of system the offending negro must be taken out of the parish. A species of judicial proceedings had to be instituted against him with a consequent delay, which robbed the whip of half its terrors and hence made it necessary to apply it all the more severely.[76] He concluded by moving "that it be the instruction to the committee, that they shall not, for the sake of the pecuniary interests of the masters, impose any restraint or obligation on the negro which shall not be necessary for his own welfare and for the general peace and order of society; and that they shall limit the duration of any temporary restrictions which may be imposed upon the freedom of the negroes to the shortest period which may be necessary to establish, on just principles, the system of free labor for adequate wages."[77]

Buxton was supported by Lord Howick and Thomas Babington Macaulay. The determination of Macaulay to argue and vote for a short period of apprenticeship made it necessary for him to hand in his resignation as a member of the Whig government at a time when the family was in acute financial distress. Sir George Otto Trevelyan has given an account of the delicate situation. "Macaulay's colleagues, who, without knowing his whole story, knew enough to be aware that he could ill afford to give up office, were earnest in their remonstrances; but he answered shortly, and almost roughly; 'I can not go counter to my father. He has devoted his whole life to the question, and I can not grieve him by giving way when he wishes me to stand firm.' "[78] His colleagues, however,

[76] *Parliamentary Debates*, third series, XIX, pp. 1189, 1190-1192.

[77] *Ibid.*, p. 1192.

[78] Sir George Otto Trevelyan, *The Life and Letters of Lord Macaulay*, I, 274-275.

permitted him to take his own line in the debate and to
continue in office.

Macaulay objected to the transition state from slavery
to freedom through a period of apprenticeship, the chief
object of which was compensation to the planters.[79] He
could not justify a system under which twelve years'
labor would be compelled by magistrates, who would be
"run after" by both master and slave. Before the twelve
years were over, the system would be in utter decay, or at
least the negroes would be less fit for liberty than at the
beginning. It was, moreover, especially cruel to subject
artificers, carpenters, coopers, and the like, to an apprenticeship for seven years when they were fit for instant
liberty.

To these arguments Stanley replied that he proposed
to consider apprenticeship as part of the compensation
to the owner, though the term of its duration was open to
discussion and was capable of modification as long as the
principle of the bill was not abandoned. The planter, he
said, immediately lost the service of one-fourth of the
negro's time; and of all of it at the end of twelve years.
In the meantime, he had to support the negroes on three-
fourths of their labor, from which he derived certain advantages, which he would lose in case of short term emancipation.[80] Stanley denied, moreover, that government
intended to leave the abolition of slavery to the colonial
legislatures. On August 1, 1834, slavery would be entirely
abolished throughout the territories of Great Britain, but
the difficulties were so great of legislating in England
upon a subject of such extent, with imperfect knowledge,
in climates so various, with laws so different, that it was
thought best to leave the matter to be carried into effect

[79] *Parliamentary Debates*, third series, XIX, pp. 1202-1209.
[80] *Ibid.*, pp. 1196-1202.

by the colonies, which, however, knew that they would have to carry into effect the provisions of the bill.[81]

On the division Buxton's amendment was lost by a vote of one hundred and fifty-eight to one hundred and fifty-one.[82] This vote convinced the government that they must make some concession in regard to apprenticeship, and accordingly, the next day, Stanley stated that the ministers had resolved to reduce the period of predial apprenticeship from twelve years to seven, and of non-predial from seven to five.[83] As the government had often admitted that the period of apprenticeship formed part of the compensation to be given to the owners, the West Indians expressed strong displeasure at this alteration, which took away part of the compensation allowed. They complained of the change as an open breach of faith on the part of the government, and as a failure to carry out a contract which had been entered into for the purpose of obtaining their coöperation.[84] The ministers admitted that their negotiations with that body as to the precise periods of twelve and seven years, were undoubtedly binding on them, but bound them only to propose those periods to the house. The close division of the house made a change necessary.[85] Even with this change it was later moved, by Buxton, to reduce the apprenticeship period to three years (1834-1836), a motion which was lost by two hundred and six to eighty-nine.[86] He also moved to reduce £20,000,000 to £15,000,000, but the proposition was supported by only a small minority.[87] Clauses were added empowering the commissioners for the management of

[81] *Parliamentary Debates*, third series, XIX, 1194-1195.
[82] *Ibid.*, pp. 1218-1220. List of minority given.
[83] *Ibid.*, pp. 1238-1239. "Predial" has reference to field slaves.
[84] *Ibid.*, pp. 1239-1241.
[85] *Ibid.*, pp. 1239-1241.
[86] *Ibid.*, pp. 1269-1270. List of minority given.
[87] *Ibid.*, p. 1270; XX, p. 206.

the national debt to raise the money by a loan, and specifying the manner in which the operation was to be conducted.[88] The interest on the loan remained to be provided for, and the chancellor of the exchequer stated that the mode of raising it which he contemplated was by a tax on colonial produce.[89] The bill passed the Commons and was sent to the Lords where it was passed with some amendments which did not affect its substance and which were readily agreed to by the Commons.[90]

The emancipation victory was naturally an occasion for rejoicing. Only two of the great leaders were dead. James Stephen died in 1832, after having presided at an anti-slavery meeting in May of that year. But his two sons, James Stephen and George Stephen, carried on the work with redoubled vigor. The former had drafted the bill in record time and the latter, as has been seen, had given the work much help as solicitor of the Anti-Slavery Society, as chief investigator of the Mauritius case, and as organizer of the agency committee. William Wilberforce lived long enough to know that emancipation was assured and remarked: ''Thank God that I should have lived to witness a day in which England is willing to give twenty millions sterling for the Abolition of Slavery.''[91] There is no better illustration of the completeness of the emancipation victory than his triumphal funeral procession and burial in Westminster Abbey near the tombs of Pitt, Fox, and Canning.

The man who had made the greatest sacrifices, Zachary Macaulay, broke down in health and left London before the bill became a law. To him Buxton wrote: ''I look back

[88] *Parliamentary Debates,* third series, XX, pp. 290, 293.

[89] *Ibid.,* p. 340.

[90] *Ibid.,* pp. 503, 587, 628, 753, 783; *House of Commons Journals,* LXXXVIII, 711-712.

[91] R. I. and S. Wilberforce, *Life of Wilberforce,* V, 370.

to the letter which you and I wrote to Lord Bathurst in 1823, containing our demands, twelve in number. Bad as the bill is, it accomplishes every one of these, and a great deal more. Among the rest, the day is fixed after which slavery shall not be!" "Surely you have reason to rejoice. My sober and deliberate opinion is, that you have done more towards this consummation than any other man. For myself, I take pleasure in acknowledging that you have been my tutor all the way through, and that I could have done nothing without you."[92]

A little later Buxton wrote Clarkson also. "I trust you are really cheered and happy in the contemplation of the *Abolition* of Slavery! It is a mighty experiment at best; but we must trust that it will answer to the full, and be as it were the pulling away of the cornerstone of slavery throughout the world."[93] The extent of the sacrifice which many men had made for the emancipation of the slaves can perhaps be best seen in the brief statement of Emanuel Cooper: "My work is over. I go back to business in the hope that it may come back to me."[94]

A more hilarious celebration of the victory occurred at the dinner managed by George Stephen. The Quakers promised to attend if there were to be no toasts, and Daniel O'Connell agreed to come on condition that there would be no music. Stephen, however, started the toasting by the proposal that the king's health should be drunk, to which not even the Quakers objected. Then one toast followed another in rapid succession. O'Connell was kept from making a set speech by the band of the Guards, who played him down from behind some shrubbery where Stephen had carefully concealed them. The tact of Buxton and the natural good humor of such an

92 Buxton, *Memoirs*, p. 337, Aug. 20, 1833.
93 *Ibid.*, p. 338, Sept. 22, 1833.
94 Sir George Stephen, *Antislavery Recollections*, p. 213.

occasion made the Quakers and O'Connell forgive Stephen for the tricks that he had played on them.[95] Across the Atlantic, the royal governors were soon engaged in explaining to the negroes the intricate emancipation act. A fine tone was struck by Sir James Carmichael Smith, governor of British Guiana, who, after expounding the details of the law, made a concluding appeal. ''I have now made you acquainted with the King's order,'' he said, ''and with everything that is to be done with respect to you. I trust you will all return to your work quietly, happily, and cheerfully; and that in your prayers you will not fail to return your humble and sincere thanks to the Almighty God, in whose hands are the hearts of kings, for having thus opened the door, and prepared to lead you from the house of bondage. The wisest and ablest men never anticipated that such a great and blessed change could have been effected in your favour but at a remote period, and even then accompanied with bloodshed. Let me urge you for your own sakes, now that you are aware of all the good that is intended for you, to prove yourselves worthy of the blessing of freedom; and in all matters, and upon all occasions, to show yourselves loyal and obedient subjects of that truly paternal Government to which you owe so much.'' [96]

[95] Sir George Stephen, *Antislavery Recollections*, pp. 207-208.
[96] *Anti-Slavery Reporter*, VI, 230, Dec. 26, 1833.

# CONCLUSION

The anti-slavery movement in England was one of the decisive contests of modern times. As Buxton stated in his letter to Clarkson, it sounded the death knell of the slave system over the whole world. It destroyed Africa as a game preserve; it prevented that continent from becoming a slave farm; it revolutionized the social order in the West Indies and contributed to their decay by destroying their assured labor supply: it helped move the centre of the British possessions from the West Indies to India; and it intensified the ill feeling of the Boers against the British.[1]

Results more profound than those gained in great wars were here obtained with incessant toil and intense religious and philanthropic devotion. Energies and abilities which could have founded an empire were thrown into this attempt at human betterment. Well known characters from the gallery of English history contributed of their genius to strike the shackles from the black man. The active religious leader, John Wesley; the outstanding literary figure, Samuel Johnson; the successful law reformer, Jeremy Bentham; the leading economist, Adam

---

[1] The results of emancipation in South Africa are stated as follows: "For two centuries they [the Boers] had practiced a system of domestic slavery widely different from the cruel plantation-slavery of the West Indies; and they regarded the system as both natural and of divine ordinance. What increased their anger was that the compensation offered them was quite inadequate: the value of the South African slaves was estimated at £3,000,000; the compensation available was only £1,250,000. And the freed slaves drifted into vagrancy, could not be got to work, and became a nuisance and a danger." Ramsay Muir, *A Short History of the British Commonwealth*, II, 428-429.

Smith; the conservative political thinker, Edmund Burke; the hated radical, Thomas Paine; the able prime minister, William Pitt; the great foreign secretaries, Castlereagh and Canning; the victor at Waterloo, Wellington; and the caustic lord chancellor, Henry Brougham, were but a few of the men entering into the struggle of the first half century. The abolition party became so powerful that Castlereagh, Wellington, and Canning did its bidding. The anti-slavery crusade suggests a study of the influence of humanitarianism in international diplomacy. Statesmen have not always followed the wishes of investors nor have they always been the instruments of economic imperialism.

Other men, who might be called the general staff of slavery experts, gave their lives to the championship of the African race. Unwilling to trust the backward peoples of the tropics to the resident white men, they tied the colonies closer to the mother country. Partly through their efforts the half dozen recently conquered colonies were refused self-government with colonial legislatures and were organized as crown colonies. Their laws were made by the executive in London and enforced by the royal governors. During the height of the slavery controversy one man in the colonial office, James Stephen, exercised a powerful influence. In consequence, he became a conspicuous permanent official in the British service. The thirteen legislative colonies defied the executive until the emancipation act was passed.[2]

[2] Professor Paul Knaplund has thrown much light on the operation of the British government as it affected the colonies about the time the slaves were freed. He shows that Sir James Stephen was less powerful than has usually been assumed. Stephen was blamed for whatever was deemed wrong in the colonial administration. Authority was divided and long delays in making decisions were common. See Paul Knaplund, ''Sir James Stephen and British North American Problems, 1840-1847,'' in *The Canadian Historical Review*, March, 1924.

Two great judicial decisions destroyed slavery in the British Isles but the slave trade interests were so powerful that they resisted abolition successfully for twenty years. The humanitarian party was aided by the fact that the English slave trade partly supplied the French, Dutch, and Spanish islands with slaves. Only about one-half of the negroes carried in British ships were destined for the British planters.[3] The West Indians, therefore, were not willing for the trade to build up the more fertile French and other foreign islands against their own interests. This selfish argument was a powerful one and finally made West Indian opinion in large part support the abolition of the slave trade. The Guinea merchant in England, on the other hand, got his slave trade profits from the traffic regardless of who bought the slaves. Economic support for emancipation came partly from the general attack on monoplies which made people in England object to the monopoly which the West Indian planters had of the English market, the argument being that it raised the price of sugar. This hostility against monopolies was aided by the active interest of those engaged in the East India trade who wished to share the sugar monopoly.

The slave system showed amazing vitality. Pronounced dead in the British empire, it lived on elsewhere in the world, particularly in Brazil, Cuba, and the United States. However, the English anti-slavery contest gave a powerful stimulus to that of the United States. Some Englishmen came to this country to propagate their views but much more important was the vast outpouring of British anti-slavery literature into America. Libraries and old houses are still filled with it. Such leaders as Gar-

---

[3] Franz Hochstetter, *Abschaffung des britischen Sklavenhandels*, p. 49, reckons that during three specific years only 47% of the British slaves were disposed of in British islands.

rison, Sumner, and Mrs. Stowe drew inspiration from the success of the English effort. Brougham repeatedly stated the "higher law" doctrine before it was taken up by Americans. American anti-slavery leaders, in turn, helped maintain English anti-slavery feeling. During the first year of its publication one hundred and fifty thousand copies of *Uncle Tom's Cabin* were sold in the United States, while over one million copies were sold in Great Britain. The British anti-slavery public was largely responsible for British neutrality during our Civil War.

A few comparisons with American history suggest themselves. The decline of British West Indian sugar culture is to be contrasted with the rapid growth of American cotton growing; the sixty thousand white people of the islands with the six millions of the Southern states. The omnipotent power of the imperial parliament was strikingly different from the divided counsels of a country half slave and half free. The West Indians had to obey the home government in the end and took what compensation they could get. The Southerners resorted to defiance and fought for what they deemed their constitutional rights.

The concentration of power in the British government made it possible to attempt to abolish slavery by means of ameliorative measures. The hope was that the slave might pass rapidly through the stages of serfdom into freedom, thus condensing the one thousand years of mediaeval history of the white man into a generation or two. The favorite plan was to prepare him for freedom in advance, a course viewed with all but unanimous approval by all parties in Great Britain. It was only after almost ten years of work that even the anti-slavery party saw that negroes must be either freemen or slaves, that a man could not be half slave and half free. The determination of the government to prepare the negro for his freedom and the resolution of the planter to be certain of his labor supply resulted in a compromise, the apprenticeship system. This T. B. Macaulay attacked in parliament as unjust and absolutely without any historical precedent. With true foresight he predicted its early failure.[4]

The experiment of attempting to abolish slavery gradually was a most interesting one and stands as unique. Consequently, a detailed account has been given of the different slave codes drawn up by the colonial office and promulgated as orders in Council. The active or passive resistance of the planters in the sugar islands made the experiment a failure. In the end Lord Howick pronounced the whole attempt unwise and tending to aggravate the lot of the slaves by interfering with the power of the master.[5]

The emancipation of the eight hundred thousand negroes in the British empire was a remarkable triumph for the reformers. The first big body of negro slaves in the world were freed. The many compromises on compensation and apprenticeship remained to be applied. The effects of freedom on the slaves and on the property of the West Indians were anxiously awaited. Fifty years of agitation, discussion, diplomatic negotiation, and legislation

[4] *Parliamentary Debates*, third series, XIX, pp. 1202-1209. ''There had been no practical experience on this matter. Indeed, they might as well talk of practical experience of a nation of Amazons. There had been no example of such apprenticeships.''

[5] *Ibid.*, XVII, pp. 1240-1241. ''I adopted the opinion . . . that it is impossible suddenly to abolish slavery, and that the yoke imposed upon the negroes should not at once be removed, but that the weight should be gradually diminished, so that they might pass, as it were, insensibly from slavery to freedom. . . . I have been at length convinced, that, if the system is to be maintained at all, it had better be so altogether, and that, if labour is to be obtained by force, and not by acting upon the will of the labourer, it is better for all parties that the master should be a completely irresponsible despot.''

had reorganized the life of a million people without European war or race conflict.

George Macaulay Trevelyan has stated the influence of emancipation on Africa: "On the last night of slavery, the negroes in the West Indian Islands went up on the hilltops to watch for the sun to rise, bringing them freedom as its first rays struck the waters. But far away in the forests of Central Africa, in the hearts of darkness yet unexplored, none understood or regarded the day. Yet it was that continent whose future was most deeply affected. Before its exploitation by Europe had well begun, it had been decided by the most powerful of its future masters that slavery should not be the relation of the black man to the white.'"[6]

The freeing of the British slaves was more than a triumph for the humanitarian leaders. It was a victory of world-wide importance in the conflict between humanity and savagery. It was a great step in the reconciliation of the white man with the colored man: the European with the non-European. At times the progress of man seems slow. As the orators in parliament frequently stated, Britain in her slave catching was comparable to the Roman Empire many centuries before. Now in the course of a few decades the cumulative power of man's humanity to man made certain the emancipation of the black man throughout the world.

[6] George Macaulay Trevelyan, *British History in the Nineteenth Century*, pp. 254-255.

# BIBLIOGRAPHICAL NOTE

A comprehensive bibliography of the Anti-Slavery Movement in England would involve the citation of an enormous number of titles. The works noted below are those only which have been found most useful and suggestive and are illustrative of the different kinds of material on which this study is based.

## BIBLIOGRAPHICAL AIDS

Very useful for the student are the excellent critical essays upon authorities in Hunt and Poole, *Political History of England,* IX, 1702-1760, by I. S. Leadam, X, 1760-1801, by William Hunt, and XI, 1801-1837, by George C. Brodrick and J. K. Fotheringham. Other good bibliographies are given in Sir Charles Oman, *History of England,* VI, 1714-1815, by C. Grant Robertson, and VII, *England Since Waterloo,* by J. A. R. Marriott. Additional bibliographical information is to be found in vols. VIII, IX, X, of the *Cambridge Modern History,* and in vols. I and II of the *Cambridge History of British Foreign Policy.* The bibliographies at the close of the articles in the *Dictionary of National Biography* are generally of much value, and those in the *Cambridge History of English Literature* are helpful for the literary side. Hilda Vernon Jones, *Catalogue of Parliamentary Papers,* 1801, 1900 (London, 1904), is of value. Much aid may be derived from Frank Cundall, *Bibliotheca Jamaicensis, Supplement to Bibliographia Jamaicensis,* and *Bibliography of the West Indies* (excluding Jamaica). The catalogue of the British Museum has many references to the slavery question and the leading libraries of America are often rich in literature on British slavery. The anti-slavery material was printed in great quantities and found its way into many countries. In addition to the British Museum much valuable material is to be found in the library of the West India Committee, in the Public Record Office, and in the Anti-Slavery and Aborigines Protection Society library.

BRITISH OFFICIAL DOCUMENTS, PRINTED

While much was accomplished by public propaganda and agitation both anti-slavery leaders and West Indian defenders felt that their chief efforts had to be concentrated on persuading the House of Commons and the executive government. Consequently, the mass of official printed sources is almost overwhelming and the whole question can be studied in its main outlines in these documents. It was not what remained hidden in manuscript but what appeared in print that was decisive in the British anti-slavery struggle. Among the most useful of the printed sources for my purpose is Cobbett-Hansard, *The Parliamentary History of England from the Earliest Period to the Year 1803*. After 1803 Cobbett, *Parliamentary Debates*, began to appear, and after 1812 the work was continued under the superintendence of T. C. Hansard. *The Annual Register* is a most useful authority for the years 1758 to 1833. In addition to general information, it contains a very full report of important parliamentary debates and many treaties and other state papers. It supplements the information given in Cobbett and Hansard.

Numerous *Parliamentary Papers and Reports* were issued on slavery and on the economic condition of the West Indies. West Indian distress was chronic and committees were appointed to examine into the causes and to suggest remedies. Negotiations with foreign powers, correspondence with the colonial governors, and orders in Council bulk large in the *Parliamentary Papers*. Some of the most important ones are referred to in the footnotes. Valuable information can also be gathered from the *Journals of the House of Commons* and the *Journals of the House of Lords*. British laws may be found in *Statutes at Large of England and of Great Britain, from Magna Carta to the Union of the Kingdoms of Great Britain and Ireland* (London, 1811); *Statutes of the United Kingdom of Great Britain and Ireland*, 1801-1832 (London, 1804-1832); and *Collection of the Public Statutes . . . 1833-1867*, (London, 1832-1867). Important trials are recorded in Cobbett's *Complete Collection of State Trials and Proceedings for High Treason and Other Crimes and Misdemeanors, from the Earliest Period to the Present Time*, ed. by T. B. and T. J.

Howell (London, 1809-1826). *British and Foreign State Papers,* compiled by the librarian and keeper of the papers, foreign office and others (vols. I-XCI, 1812—, London, 1841—).

## AMERICAN OFFICIAL DOCUMENTS, PRINTED

*American State Papers: Documents, Legislative and Executive* (38 vols., Washington, 1832-1861). [*Annals of Congress.*] *Annals of the Congress of the United States* (42 vols., Washington, 1834-1856). *Journal of the House of Representatives of the United States. Journal of the Senate of the United States.* W. M. Malloy, *Treaties, Conventions, International Acts, Protocols, and Agreements between the United States and other Powers* (2 vols., Washington, 1910). J. D. Richardson, *Compilation of the Messages and Papers of the Presidents* (10 vols., Washington, 1896-1899).

## CORRESPONDENCE, MEMOIRS AND COLLECTED WORKS

*The Dispatches of the Duke of Wellington during his various Campaigns . . . from 1799 to 1818* (12 vols., London, 1844-1847), compiled by Lieut.-Colonel Gurwood. *Supplementary Despatches, Correspondence, and Memoranda of the Duke of Wellington* (15 vols., 1858-1872), edited by his son. *Despatches, Correspondence, and Memoranda of the Duke of Wellington* (8 vols., 1867-1880), edited by his son. The material in these collections consists of not only the duke's dispatches, but includes a great mass of political correspondence which passed through his hands. These collections are an invaluable source for the account of the universal abolition of the slave trade. The *Memoirs and Correspondence of Viscount Castlereagh* (12 vols., 1850-1853), edited by his brother, contains valuable material on slave trade negotiations. *Memoirs of Sir Thomas Fowell Buxton* (London, 1848), edited by his son, Charles Buxton, is a valuable source for the anti-slavery conflict. Historical Manuscripts Commission, *Report on the Manuscripts of Earl Bathurst* (London, 1923) contains information from the minister in charge of colonial affairs from 1812 to 1827. *The Works of Jeremy Bentham* (11 vols., Edinburgh, 1859), published under the superintendence of his executor, John Bowring. Mrs. Aphra Behn, *Histories and Novels* (2 vols., eighth edition, London, 1735). *The Poetical Works of William Blake* (London, 1914), edited by John Sampson. *The Critical and Miscellaneous Writings of Henry Lord Brougham* (2 vols., Philadelphia, 1841). *The Speeches of Henry Lord Brougham* (Edinburgh, 1838). *The Works of The Right Honorable Edmund Burke* (12 vols., seventh edition, Boston, 1881). [Condorcet, Marie Jean Antoine Nicolas Caritat], *Réflexion sur l'esclavage des nègres* (1781). *The Correspondence of William Cowper* (4 vols., London, 1904), arranged in chronological order, with annotations, by Thomas Wright. *The Poems of William Cowper* (London, 1905), edited by J. C. Bailey. *The History of the Life of Thomas Ellwood . . . Written by his Own Hand* (London, 1900), edited by C. G. Crump. *The Farington Diary* by Joseph Farington (third edition, New York, 1923), edited by James Greig. *The Speeches of the Right Honourable Charles James Fox in the House of Commons* (6 vols., London, 1815). George Fox, *A Journal or Historical Account of the Life, Travels, Sufferings, Christian Experiences, and Labour of Love, in the Work of the Ministry, of that Ancient, Eminent, and Faithful Servant of Jesus Christ* (Philadelphia, n. d.). Boswell's *Life of Johnson,* including Boswell's ''Journal of a Tour to the Hebrides and Johnson's Diary of a Journey into North Wales'' (6 vols., New York, 1891), edited by George Birkbeck Hill. The editor has collected Johnson's opinions on various phases of the slavery question. *Memoirs of Sir James Mackintosh* (2 vols., London and Boston, 1853). M. De Secondat, Baron de Montesquieu, *The Spirit of Laws* (2 vols., Cincinnati, 1873), translated from the French by Thomas Nugent. *The Works of the Rev. John Newton, Late Rector of the United Parishes of St. Mary Woolnoth and St. Mary Woolchurch Haw, London* (4 vols., New Haven, 1824). *Lady Nugent's Journal: Jamaica One Hundred Years Ago* (published for The Institute of Jamaica by Adam and Charles Black, 1907), edited by Frank Cundall. *The Writings of Thomas Paine* (3 vols., New York, 1894-1895), edited by Moncure Daniel Conway. William Paley, *Complete Works* (New York, 1824). Mungo Park, *Travels in the Interior Districts of Africa* (London, 1814). *The Life of Sir Samuel Romilly* (2 vols.,

London, 1842), written by himself, with a selection of his correspondence, edited by his sons. Prince Hoare, *Memoirs of Granville Sharp* (1 vol., London, 1820; another edition, 2 vols., 1828). *The Works of Adam Smith;* With an Account of his life and Writings by Dugald Stewart (5 vols., London, 1811-1812). Thomas Southern "Oronooko" in *Bell's British Theatre* (London, 1730). *Talleyrand's Briefwechsel mit König Ludwig XVIII während des Wiener Congresses. The Poetical Works of James Thomson* (2 vols. in 1, Boston, 1863). Horace Walpole, *The letters of Horace Walpole, fourth earl of Oxford* (16 vols., Oxford, 1903-1905), edited by Mrs. Paget Toynbee. *The Works of the Rev. John Wesley* (7 vols., third edition, New York, 1825). *Memoirs of the Life and Character of the late Rev. George Whitefield* (Boston, 1813), edited by the Rev. John Gillies and Aaron C. Seymour. William Wilberforce, *Correspondence* (2 vols., London, 1840), edited by his sons, R. I. and S. Wilberforce. *Private Papers of William Wilberforce* (London, 1897), collected and edited, with a preface, by A. M. Wilberforce.

## HISTORIES AND BIOGRAPHIES

Only a few of the many histories covering the period of the anti-slavery struggle can be mentioned. William Cunningham, *Growth of English Industry and Commerce* (2 vols., fifth edition, Cambridge, 1910, 1912), is invaluable for general economic history. Frank Wesley Pitman, *The Development of the British West Indies, 1760-1763,* is the standard account of the British islands. It is a work of high quality. Edward Long, *History of Jamaica* (London, 1774), and Bryan Edwards, *The History, Civil and Commercial of the British Colonies in the West Indies* (2 vols., second edition, London, 1794), are still works of value. Captain Thomas Southey, *Chronological History of the West Indies* (3 vols., London, 1827), contains documentary material. Sir Charles P. Lucas, *A Historical Geography of the British Colonies,* vol. II, *The West Indies* (second edition, Oxford, 1905), is an authoritative account. James Williamson, *A Short History of British Expansion* (London, 1922), is an excellent recent summary. Ramsay Muir, *A Short History of the British*

*Commonwealth* (2 vols., Yonkers-on-Hudson, New York, 1922-1923), outlines the humanitarian movement. Williamson and Muir contain bibliographies. W. E. H. Lecky, *History of England in the Eighteenth Century* (8 vols., New York, 1878), is a standard account. Harriet Martineau, *History of the Peace: being a History of England from 1816 to 1854, with an introduction*, 1800-1815 (4 vols., London, 1877). Sir Spencer Walpole, *A History of England from the Conclusion of the Great War in 1815* (6 vols., London, 1902-1905), is the best single treatment of this period.

The best biography of an anti-slavery leader is that of R. Coupland, *Wilberforce: A Narrative* (Oxford, 1923). Professor Coupland found that the sons of Wilberforce had made full use of all the manuscript material left by their father. He has written an admirable biography, giving excellent interpretations. The older account of Robert Isaac and Samuel Wilberforce, *The Life of William Wilberforce* (5 vols., London, 1838), is rich in source materials and is one of the foundations for any study of the anti-slavery crusade. A good short biography is that of John Stoughton, *William Wilberforce* (London, 1880). J. C. Colquhoun, *William Wilberforce, his friends and his times* (London, 1866), is an older account. The other anti-slavery leaders have not been equally fortunate in their biographies. Two only may be mentioned: Viscountess Knutsford, *Life and Letters of Zachary Macaulay* (London, 1900) and Caroline Emelia Stephen, *The Right Honourable Sir James Stephen* (London, 1906).

Sir Archibald Alison, *Lives of Lord Castlereagh and Sir Charles Stewart, the Second and Third Marquesses of Londonderry* (3 vols., 1861). H. W. V. Temperley, *Life of Canning* (London, 1905). Temperley, *The foreign policy of Canning, 1822-1827* (London, 1925), and C. K. Webster, *The foreign policy of Castlereagh, 1815-1822* (London, 1925), appeared while this study was in the press. Carl Becker, *The Declaration of Independence* (New York, 1922). Frank Cundall, *Historic Jamaica* (London, 1915). Daniel Defoe, *The History and Remarkable Life of the truly Honourable Colonel Jacque commonly called Colonel Jack* (2 vols., London, 1895), edited by George A.

Aitken. C. Washington Eves, *The West Indies* (fourth edition, London, 1897). J. W. Fortescue, *A History of the British Army* (10 vols., London, 1899—), covers much more than the army. A very valuable work. James Anthony Froude, *The English in the West Indies or the Bow of Ulysses* (new edition, London, 1888). W. J. Gardner, *History of Jamaica* (London, 1873). G. R. Gleig, *Life of Wellington* (4 vols., London, 1858-1860). J. L. Le B. Hammond, *Charles James Fox: A Political Study* (London, 1903). J. L. and Barbara Hammond, *Lord Shaftesbury* (New York, 1923). John Hawkins, *Life of Samuel Johnson* (Dublin, 1787). C. C. S. Higham, *The Leeward Islands, 1660-1668* (Cambridge, 1921). Thomas Hodgkin, *George Fox* (second edition, Boston, 1898). Paul Leroy-Beaulieu, *De la Colonisation chez les Peuples Modernes* (sixième édition, Paris, 1908), a standard history of modern colonization. David Macpherson, *Annals of commerce, manufactures, fisheries, and navigation . . .* (4 vols., London, 1805), valuable for statistical information. William Law Mathieson, *England in Transition, 1789-1832* (London, 1920), contains suggestive material. Cecil A. Moore, ''Shaftesbury and the Ethical Poets in England, 1700-1760,'' *Publications of the Modern Language Association* (vol. 31, 1916). The best account of the origin of the humanitarian philosophy. Ramsay Muir, *A History of Liverpool* (London, 1907). Lillian M. Penson, *The Colonial Agents of the British West Indies* (London, 1924). R. E. Prothero (Lord Ernle), *English Farming Past and Present* (third edition, London, 1922). Abbé Raynal, *A Philosophical and Political History of the Settlements and Trade of the Europeans in the East and West Indies* (8 vols., revised edition, London, 1788), translated from the French by J. O. Justamond. J. Holland Rose, *William Pitt and National Revival* (London, 1911). J. Holland Rose, *William Pitt and the Great War* (London, 1911). This and the preceding volume are the best biography of the prime minister. William Robertson, *The History of the Reign of the Emperor Charles the Fifth* (3 vols., William H. Prescott edition, Philadelphia, 1902). William Robertson, *The History of the Settlement and Discovery of America* (Aberdeen, 1848). J. Holland Rose, *Pitt and Napoleon: Essays and Letters* (London, 1912). G. W. Surface, *The Story of Sugar*

(New York, 1910). Adam Smith, *An Inquiry into the Nature and Causes of the Wealth of Nations* (2 vols., London, 1904), edited by Edwin Cannan. Earl Stanhope, *Life of William Pitt* (4 vols., second edition, 1862). Leslie Stephen, *The English Utilitarians* (3 vols., London, 1900)'. Sir James Stephen, *Essays in Ecclesiastical Biography* (second edition, 2 vols., London, 1850), contains an invaluable interpretation of the Evangelical movement. Leslie Stephen, *English Literature and Society in the Eighteenth Century* (New York, 1904), and *History of English Thought in the Eighteenth Century* (third edition, 2 vols., London, 1902). T. Lothrop Stoddard, *The French Revolution in San Domingo* (Boston, 1914). S. H. Swinny, ''The Humanitarianism of the Eighteenth Century,'' in *The Western Races and the World* (edited by F. S. Marvin, Oxford, 1922). Joseph Texte, *Jean-Jacques Rousseau and the Cosmopolitan Spirit in Literature*, translated by J. W. Matthews (New York, 1899). Chauncey Brewster Tinker, *Nature's Simple Plan:* a phase of radical thought in the mid-eighteenth century (Princeton, 1922). A very valuable and suggestive study. An excellent book review by Professor R. S. Crane in *Modern Language Notes* (vol. 29, no. 5, May, 1924) gives many bibliographical references, particularly to the American Indian. George Macaulay Trevelyan, *British History in the Nineteenth Century* (London, 1922), and *Lord Grey of the Reform Bill* (New York, London, 1920). Sir George Otto Trevelyan, *The Life and Letters of Lord Macaulay* (2 vols., London, 1876), contains a brief account of Zachary Macaulay. Rev. L. Tyerman, *The Life of the Rev. George Whitefield* (2 vols., New York, 1877). W. C. Westergaard, *The Danish West Indies, 1671-1917* (New York, 1917). An excellent account. Lois Whitney, ''English Primitivistic Theories of Epic Origins,'' *Modern Philology* (vol. 21, May, 1924), a valuable study of the origin of the ideas of primitive man current in Scotland and England in the mid-eighteenth century.

BOOKS AND PAMPHLETS ON THE SLAVE TRADE AND SLAVERY

The following list is merely suggestive. Thomas Clarkson, *History of the Rise, Progress, and Accomplishment of the Abolition of the African Slave Trade by the British Parliament* (new edition, London, 1839). The first edition appeared in two vols. in 1808. This account is very valuable. It tends to make Clarkson the hero of the struggle and a controversy with the sons of Wilberforce resulted. *Id., An Essay on the Slavery and Commerce of the Human Species, particularly the African, translated from a Latin Dissertation, which was honoured with the First Prize in the University of Cambridge, for the year 1785; with Additions* (London, 1786). *Id., Thoughts on the Necessity of Improving the Condition of the Slaves in the British Colonies, with a View to their Ultimate Emancipation; and on the Practicability, the Safety, and the Advantages of the Latter Measure* (London, 1823). James Stephen, *The Slavery of the British West India Colonies Delineated, as it exists Both in Law and Practice, and compared with The Slavery of other Countries, Antient and Modern* (2 vols., London, 1824, 1830). This is the standard anti-slavery treatise. The chief reply to vol. I was made by Alexander Barclay, *A Practical View of the Present State of Slavery in the West Indies* (second edition, London, 1827). Hubert H. S. Aimes, *A History of Slavery in Cuba* (New York, 1907). James Bandinel, *Some Account of the Trade in Slaves from Africa, as connected with Europe and America* (London, 1842). *Speeches of Mr. Barrett and Mr. Burge, at a General Meeting of Planters, Merchants, and others interested in the West India Colonies* (1833). *British Colonial Slavery* [Documents submitted to the British Public by the Committee of the West India Planters and Merchants.] (London, 1833). *The Proceedings and Resolutions of the West India Body, including Copies of their Various Communications with His Majesty's Government relative to the Measures of the Session 1833 for the Abolition of Slavery* (London, 1833). Sir Thomas Fowell Buxton, *The African slave trade and its remedy* (London, 1840). Dr. Collins, *Practical Rules for the Management of Negro Slaves in the Sugar Colonies* (London, 1803). J. Cropper, *Letters to Mr. Wilberforce, M.P., recommending the Encouragement of the cultivation of Sugar in the East Indies, as a certain and natural means of effecting the total Abolition of the Slave Trade* (1822). J. Cropper, *Relief for West-Indian Distress, showing the Inefficiency of Protecting Duties on East India Sugar* (1823). Jerome Dowd, *The Negro*

*Races, a sociological study* (2 vols., New York, 1907-1914). W. E. Burghardt Du Bois, *The Suppression of the African Slave-Trade to the United States of America* (New York, 1896). The standard work on this subject. Sir Edward Hyde East, *Short Review of leading and operating causes of the Distress of the British West India Colonies* (1832). *Emancipation of the Negro Slaves in the West India Colonies considered, in answer to Mr. Wilberforce's Appeal* (1824). T. Fletcher, *Letter in Vindication of the Rights of the British West India Colonies, in answer to Mr. Cropper's letters to Mr. Wilberforce* (1822). Gentlemen of Barbadoes to his Friend in London, *The Present State of the British Sugar Colonies considered* (1831). Reverend Benjamin Godwin, *Lectures on British Colonial Slavery* (London, 1830). Morgan Godwyn, *The Negro's and Indian's Advocate, suing for their admission into the Church* (1680). Charles Oscar Hardy, *The Negro Question in the French Revolution* (Menasha, Wisconsin, 1919). Franz Hochstetter, *Die wirtschaftlichen und politischen Motive für die Abschaffung des britischen Sklavenhandels in Jahre 1806-1807* (Leipzig, 1905). Adam Hodgson, *Letter to Mr. Jean-Baptiste Say, on the Comparative Expense of Free and Slave Labour* (second edition, Liverpool, 1823). J. M. Hogg, *Brief View of Colonial Slavery* (1827). Sir Robert John Wilmot Horton, *First Letter to the freeholders of the County of York on Negro Slavery: being an Enquiry into the claims of the West Indians for equitable compensations* (London, 1830). *Impartial Review of the Question between Great Britain and her West Indian Colonies, respecting the Abolition of Negro Slavery* . . . by a Resident and Proprietor in the West Indies (1824). *Impolicy and Injustices of Emancipating the Negro Slaves in the West Indies* (1824). John Jeremie, *Four Essays on Colonial Slavery* (1831). [Zachary Macaulay] *Negro Slavery; or A View of Some of the More Prominent Features of That State of Society as it Exists in the United States of America and in the Colonies of the West Indies especially in Jamaica* (fourth edition, London, 1824). [*Id.*], *East and West India Sugar; or, A Refutation of the Claims of the West India Colonists to a Protecting Duty on East India Sugar* (London, 1823). [*Id.*], *East India Sugar, or an Inquiry Respecting the Means of Improving the Quality and Reducing the Cost of Sugar Raised by Free Labour in The East Indies* (London, 1824). Alexander Macdonnell, *Colonial Commerce; Comprising an Inquiry into the Principles upon which Discriminating Duties Should be Levied on Sugar, The Growth Respectively of the West India British Possessions of the East Indies, and of Foreign Countries* (London, 1828). *Id., Letter to T. F. Buxton, in refutation of his allegation respecting the decrease of the slaves in the British West India Colonies* (London, 1833). James M'Queen, *The Colonial Controversy, containing a Refutation of the Calumnies of the Anti-colonists in the State of Hayti, Sierra Leone, India* (1825). *Id., The West India Colonies, the calumnies and misrepresentations circulated against them by the Edinburgh Review, Mr. Clarkson, Mr. Cropper, etc., examined and refuted* (London, 1824). Joseph Marryat, *A Reply to the Arguments Contained in Various Publications Recommending An Equalization of the Duties on East and West Indian Sugar* (London, 1823). H. J. Nieboer, *Slavery as an Industrial System* (The Hague, 1900). Ulrich Bonnell Phillips, *American Negro Slavery* (New York, 1918). This is the first authoritative treatment of this topic. Reverend James Ramsay, *An Essay on the Treatment and Conversion of African Slaves in the British Sugar Colonies* (Dublin, 1784). Granville Sharp, *Extract from A representation of the injustice and dangerous tendency of tolerating slavery, or admitting the least claim of private property in the persons of men in England* (London, 1769). Sir George Stephen, *Antislavery Recollections: in a Series of Letters addressed to Mrs. Beecher Stowe written by Sir George Stephen at her Request* (London, 1854). [James Stephen], *Reasons for Establishing a Registry of Slaves in the British Colonies* (London, 1814). [*Id.*], *The History of Toussaint Louverture,* a new edition with a dedication to His Imperial Majesty The Emperor of all the Russias (London, 1814). Edward Raymond Turner, *The Negro in Pennsylvania* (Washington, 1911). Henry Whiteley, *Three months in Jamaica* (London, 1833). Gomer Williams, *History of the Liverpool Privateers and Letters of Marque with an Account of the Liverpool Slave Trade* (London, 1897).

NEWSPAPERS AND PERIODICALS

*Gentlemen's Magazine*, 1731—. *Edinburgh Review*, 1802—. *Quarterly Review*, 1809—. *Westminster Review*, 1824—. *The Anti-Slavery Monthly Reporter*, June, 1825, to December, 1833. *The West Indian Reporter*, Jan., 1827, to Mar., 1831. *The Morning Chronicle*, 1769—. *The Morning Post*, 1772—. *The Times*, 1788—. Cobbett's *Weekly Political Register*, 1802-1836. *The Examiner*, 1808—. *John Bull*, 1820—. *John Bull* was the bitterest opponent of the anti-slavery party. *The Anti-Slavery Monthly Reporter* was the chief opponent of slavery, founded and edited by Zachary Macaulay. One hundred and eleven numbers were issued by the end of 1833. *The West Indian Reporter* was a smaller publication and appeared irregularly. Forty-one numbers were issued.

# APPENDIX A

## EDMUND BURKE, SKETCH OF A NEGRO CODE

A Letter to The Right Hon. Henry Dundas, . . . with the Sketch of a Negro Code. 1792.[1]

This code was submitted with a letter of apology for its having remained unmatured and unexhibited to the public for twelve years. This letter and code were well known to all parties, and Mr. Stanley made a study of it, as his speech in presenting his own plan shows.[2] Mr. Burke wrote that "he was convinced the true origin of the slave trade was not in the place it began at, but in the place of its final destination,"[3] and that the slave trade and slavery ought to be abolished together and gradually. He continued,[4] "Whenever, in my proposed reformation, we take our *point of departure* from a state of slavery, we must precede the donation of freedom by disposing the minds of the objects to a disposition to receive it without danger to themselves or to us. The process of bringing *free* savages to order and civilization is very different. When a state of slavery is that upon which we are to work, the very means which lead to liberty must partake of compulsion. The minds of men, being crippled with that restraint, can do nothing for themselves: everything must be done for them. The regulations can owe little to

---

[1] *The Works of the Right Honorable Edmund Burke* (12 vols., seventh edition, Boston, 1881), VI, 257-289.

[2] *Parliamentary Debates*, third series, XVII, 1196 ff.

[3] *Ibid.*, 1196; Burke, *Works*, VI, 259.

[4] *Ibid.*; Burke, *Works*, VI, 260.

consent. Everything must be the creature of power. Hence it is that regulations must be multiplied, particularly as you have two parties to deal with. The planter you must at once restrain and support, and you must control at the same time that you ease the servant. This necessarily makes the work a matter of care, labor, and expense. It becomes in its nature complex. But I think neither the object impracticable nor the expense intolerable . . .''

He expected little from the West Indians. ''I have seen what has been done by the West Indian Assemblies. It is arrant trifling. They have done little; and what they have done is good for nothing,—for it is totally destitute of an *executory* principle. This is the point to which I have applied my whole diligence. It is easy enough to say what shall be done: to cause it to be done,—*hic labor, hoc opus.*''[5]

(PREAMBLE)

Whereas it is expedient, and conformable to the principles of true religion and morality, and to the rules of sound policy, to put an end to all traffic in the persons of men, and to the detention of their said persons in a state of slavery, as soon as the same may be effected without producing great inconveniences in the sudden change of practices of such long standing, and during the time of the continuance of the said practices it is desirable and expedient by proper regulations to lessen the inconveniences and evils attendant on the said traffic and state of servitude, until both shall be gradually done away.[6]

.    .    .    .    .    .    .

And whereas the condition of persons in a state of slavery is such that they are utterly unable to take ad-

5 *Parliamentary Debates*, third series, XVII, 1196; *Burke, Works*, VI, 261.

6 *Ibid.; Burke, Works*, VI, 262.

vantage of any remedy which the laws may provide for their protection and the amendment of their condition, and have not the proper means of pursuing any process for the same, but are and must be under guardianship: and whereas it is not fitting that they should be under the sole guardianship of their masters, or their attorneys and overseers, to whom their grievances, whenever they suffer any, must ordinarily be owing:

(Attorney-General to be protector of negroes. To inquire and file informations *ex officio*.) 1. Be it therefore enacted, that his Majesty's Attorney-General for the time being successively shall, by his office, exercise the trust and employment of protector of negroes within the island in which he is or shall be Attorney-General to his Majesty, his heirs and successors: and that the said Attorney-General, protector of negroes, is hereby authorized to hear any complaint on the part of any negro or negroes, and inquire into the same, or to institute an inquiry *ex officio* into any abuses, and to call before him and examine witnesses upon oath, relative to the subject-matter of the said official inquiry or complaint: and it is hereby enacted and declared, that the said Attorney-General, protector of negroes, is hereby authorized and empowered, at his discretion, to file an information *ex officio* for any offences committed against the provisions of this act, or for any misdemeanors or wrongs against the said negroes, or any of them.

(Power to challenge jurors.) 2. And it is further enacted, that in all trials of such informations the said protector of negroes may and is hereby authorized to challenge peremptorily a number not exceeding —— of the jury who shall be impanelled to try the charge in the said information contained.

(To appoint inspectors of districts, who are to report to him twice in the year the number and condition of the slaves.) 3. And be it enacted, that the said Attorney-General, protector of negroes, shall appoint inspectors, not exceeding the number of ——, at his discretion; and the said inspectors shall be placed in convenient districts in each island severally, or shall twice in the year make a circuit in the same, according to the direction which they shall receive from the protector of negroes aforesaid: and the inspectors shall and they are hereby required, twice in the year, to report in writing to the protector aforesaid the state and condition of the negroes in their districts or on their circuit severally, the number, sex, age, and occupation of the said negroes on each plantation: and the overseer or chief manager on each plantation is hereby required to furnish an account thereof within [ten days] after the demand of the said inspectors, and to permit the inspector or inspectors aforesaid to examine into the same; and the said inspectors shall set forth, in the said report, the distempers to which the negroes are most liable in the several parts of the island.

(Instructions to be formed for inspectors.) 4. And be it enacted, that the said protector of negroes, by and with the consent of the governor and chief judge of each island, shall form instructions, by which the said inspectors shall discharge their trust in the manner the least capable of exciting any unreasonable hopes in the said negroes, or of weakening the proper authority of the overseer, and shall transmit them to one of his Majesty's principal secretaries of state: and when sent back with his approbation, the same shall become the rule for the conduct of the said inspectors.

(Registry.) 5. And be it enacted, that the said Attorney-General, protector of negroes, shall appoint an office for registering all proceedings relative to the duty of his place as protector of negroes, and shall appoint his chief clerk to be registrar, with a salary not exceeding ——.

(Ports where negroes are to be landed. Vessels to be inspected. Masters or officers offending to be fined.) 6. And be it enacted, that no negroes shall be landed for sale in any but the ports following: that is to say, ——. And the collector of each of the said ports severally shall, within —— days after the arrival of any ship transporting negroes, report the same to the protector of negroes, or to one of his inspectors: and the said protector is hereby authorized and required to examine, or cause to be examined by one of his inspectors, with the assistance of the said collector, or his deputy, and a surgeon to be called in on the occasion, the state of the said ship and negroes: and upon what shall appear to them, the said protector of negroes, and the said collector and surgeon, to be a sufficient proof, either as arising from their own inspection, or sufficient information on a summary process, of any contravention of this act, or cruelty to the negroes, or other malversation of the said captain, or any of his officers, the said protector shall impose a fine on him or them, not exceeding ——: which shall not, however, weaken or invalidate any penalty growing from the bond of the said master or his owners. And it is hereby provided, that, if the said master, or any of his officers, shall find himself aggrieved by the said fine, he may within —— days appeal to the chief judge, if the court shall be sitting, or to the governor, who shall and are required to hear the said parties, and on hearing are to annul or confirm the same.

(Rates respecting the sales of negroes.) 7. And be it enacted, that no sale of negroes shall be made but in the presence of an inspector, and all negroes shall be sold severally, or in known and ascertained lots, and not otherwise: and a paper containing the state and description of each negro severally sold, and of each lot, shall be taken and registered in the office aforesaid: and if, on inspection or information, it shall be found that any negroes shall have, in the same ship, or any other at the same time examined, a wife, an husband, a brother, sister, or child, the person or persons so related shall not be sold separately at that or any future sale.

(Every island to be divided into districts. A church to be built in each.) 8. And be it enacted, that each and every of his Majesty's islands and plantations, in which negroes are used in cultivation, shall be, by the governor and the protector of negroes for the time being, divided into districts, allowing as much as convenience will admit to the present division into parishes, and subdividing them, where necessary, into districts, according to the number of negroes. And the said governor and protector of negroes shall cause in each district a church to be built in a convenient place, and a cemetery annexed, and an house for the residence of a clergyman, with ―― acres of land annexed: and they are hereby authorized to treat for the necessary ground with the proprietor, who is hereby obliged to sell and dispose of the same to the said use: and in case of dispute concerning the value, the same to be settled by a jury, as in like cases is accustomed.

(Appointment of a priest and clerk.) 9. And be it enacted, that in each of the said districts shall be established a presbyter of the Church of England as by law established, who shall appoint under him one clerk, who shall be a free negro, when such properly qualified can be found (otherwise, a white man), with a salary, in each case, of ――; and the said minister and clerk, both or one, shall instruct the said negroes in the Church Catechism, or such other as shall be provided by the authority in this act named: and the said minister shall baptize, as he shall think fit, all negroes not baptized, and not belonging to Dissenters from the Church of England.

(Owner to deliver a list of negroes to the minister, and

to cause them to attend divine service.) 10. The principal
overseer of each plantation is hereby required to deliver
annually unto the minister a list of all the negroes upon
his plantation, distinguishing their sex and age, and shall,
under a penalty of ——, cause all the negroes under his
care, above the age of —— years, to attend divine service
once on every Sunday, except in case of sickness, infirmity, or other necessary cause, to be given at the time,
and shall, by himself or one of those who are under him,
provide for the orderly behavior of the negroes under
him, and cause them to return to his plantation, when
divine service, or administration of sacraments, or catechism, is ended.

(Minister to direct punishment for disorderly conduct.) 11. And be it enacted, that the minister shall have
power to punish any negro for disorderly conduct during
divine service, by a punishment not exceeding (ten)
blows to be given in one day and for one offence, which
the overseer or his under agent or agents is hereby directed, according to the orders of the said minister, effec-
tually to inflict, whenever the same shall be ordered.

(Spirituous liquors not to be sold.) 12. And be it enacted, that no spirituous liquors of any kind shall be sold,
except in towns, within —— miles distance of any church,
nor within any district during divine service, and an hour
preceding and an hour following the same: and the minister of each parish shall and is hereby authorized to act as
a justice of the peace in enforcing the said regulation.

(Register of births, burials, and marriages.) 13. And
be it enacted, that every minister shall keep a register of
births, burials, and marriages of all negroes and mulattoes in his district.

(Synod to assemble annually, and to form regulations.)
14. And be it enacted, that the ministers of the several
districts shall meet annually, on the —— day of ——,

in a synod of the island to which they belong: and the said synod shall have for its president such person as the Bishop of London shall appoint for his commissary: and the said synod or general assembly is hereby authorized, by a majority of voices, to make regulations, which regulations shall be transmitted by the said president or commissary to the Bishop of London: and when returned by the Bishop of London approved of, then, and not before, the said regulations shall be held in force to bind the said clergy, their assistants, clerks, and schoolmasters only, and no other persons.

(And to report to the Bishop of London.) 15. And be it enacted, that the said president shall collect matter in the said assembly, and shall make a report of the state of religion and morals in the several parishes from whence the synod is deputed, and shall transmit the same, once in the year, in duplicate, through the governor and protector of negroes, to the Bishop of London.

(Bishop of London to be patron of the cures.) 16. And be it enacted and declared, that the Bishop of London for the time being shall be patron to all and every the said cures in this act directed: and the said bishop is hereby required to provide for the due filling thereof, and is to receive, from the fund in this act provided for the due execution of this act, a sum not exceeding —— for each of the said ministers, for his outfit and passage.

(And to have power of suspending and removing ministers.) 17. And be it enacted, that, on misbehavior, and on complaint from the said synod, and on hearing the party accused in a plain and summary manner, it shall and may be lawful for the Bishop of London to suspend or to remove any minister from his cure, as his said offences shall appear to merit.

(Schools for young negroes.) 18. And be it enacted, that for every two districts a school shall be established for young negroes to be taught three days in the week, and to be detained from their owner four hours in each day, the number not to be more or fewer than twenty males in each district, who shall be chosen, and vacancies filled, by the minister of the district: and the said minister shall pay to the owner of the said boy, and shall be allowed the same in his accounts at the synod, to the age of twelve years old, three-pence by the day, and for every boy from twelve years old to fifteen, five-pence by the day.

(Extraordinary abilities to be encouraged.) 19. And it is enacted, that, if the president of the synod aforesaid shall certify to the protector of negroes, that any boys in the said schools (provided that the number in no one year shall exceed one in the island of Jamaica, and one in two years in the islands of Barbadoes, Antigua, and Grenada, and one in four years in any of the other islands) do show a remarkable aptitude for learning, the said protector is hereby authorized and directed to purchase the said boy at the best rate at which boys of that age and strength have been sold within the year: and the said negro so purchased shall be under the entire guardianship of the said protector of negroes, who shall send him to the Bishop of London for his further education in England, and may charge in his accounts for the expense of transporting him to England: and the Bishop of London shall provide for the education of such of the said negroes as he shall think proper subjects, until the age of twenty-four years, and shall order those who shall fall short of expectation after one year to be bound apprentice to some handicraft trade: and when his apprenticeship is finished, the Lord Mayor of London is hereby authorized and directed to receive the said negro from his master, and to transmit him to the island from which he came, in the West Indies, to be there as a free negro, subject, however, to the direction of the protector of negroes, relatively to his behavior and employment.

(Negroes of Dissenters; their marriages, &c., to be registered.) 20. And it is hereby enacted and provided, that any planter, or owner of negroes, not being of the Church of England, and not choosing to send his negroes to attend divine service in manner by this act directed, shall give jointly or severally, as the case shall require, security to the protector of negroes that a competent minister of some Christian church or congregation shall be provided for the due instruction of the negroes, and for their performing divine service according to the description of the religion of the master or masters, in some church or house thereto allotted, in the manner and with the regulations in this act prescribed with regard to the exercise of religion according to the Church of England: provided always, that the marriages of the said negroes belonging to Dissenters shall be celebrated only in .the church of the said district, and that a register of the births shall be transmitted to the minister of the said district.

(Regulations concerning marriage.) 21. And whereas a state of matrimony, and the government of a family, is a principal means of forming men to a fitness for freedom, and to become good citizens: Be it enacted, that all negro men and women, above eighteen years of age for the man and sixteen for the woman, who have cohabited together for twelve months or upwards, or shall cohabit for the same time, and have a child or children, shall be deemed to all intents and purposes to be married, and either of the parties is authorized to require of the ministers of the district to be married in the face of the church.

(Concerning the same.) 22. And be it enacted, that,

from and after the —— of ——, all negro men in an
healthy condition, and so reported to be, in case the same
is denied, by a surgeon and by an inspector of negroes,
and being twenty-one years old, or upwards, until fifty,
and not being before married, shall, on requisition of the
inspectors, be provided by their masters or overseers
with a woman not having children living, and not exceeding the age of the man, nor, in any case, exceeding the age
of twenty-five years: and such persons shall be married
publicly in the face of the church.

(Concerning the same.) 23. And be it enacted, that, if
any negro shall refuse a competent marriage tendered to
him, and shall not demand another specifically, such as it
may be in his master's power to provide, the master or
overseer shall be authorized to constrain him by an increase of work or a lessening of allowance.

(Adultery, &c., how to be punished.) 24. And be it enacted, that the minister in each district shall have, with
the assent of the inspector, full power and authority to
punish all acts of adultery, unlawful concubinage, and
fornication, amongst negroes, on hearing and a summary
process, by ordering a number of blows, not exceeding
——, for each offence: and if any white person shall be
provided, on information in the supreme court, to be exhibited by the protector of negroes, to have committed
adultery with any negro woman, or to have corrupted
any negro woman under sixteen years of age, he shall be
fined in the sum of ——, and shall be forever disabled
from serving the office of overseer of negroes, or being
attorney to any plantation.

(Concerning marriage.) 25. And be it enacted, that no
slaves shall be compelled to do any work for their masters for [three] days after their marriage.

(Concerning pregnant women.) 26. And be it enacted,
that no woman shall obliged to field-work, or any other

laborious work, for one month before her delivery, or for six weeks afterwards.

(Separation of husband and wife, and children, to be avoided.) 27. And be it enacted, that no husband and wife shall be sold separately, if originally belonging to the same master: nor shall any children under sixteen be sold separately from their parents, or one parent, if one be living.

(Concerning the same.) 28. And be it enacted, that, if an husband and wife, which before their intermarriage belonged to different owners, shall be sold, they shall not be sold at such a distance as to prevent mutual help and cohabitation: and of this distance the minister shall judge, and his certificate of the inconvenient distance shall be valid, so as to make such sale unlawful, and to render the same null and void.

(Negroes not to work on Saturday afternoon or Sunday.) 29. And be it enacted, that no negro shall be compelled to work for his owner at field-work, or any service relative to a plantation, or to work at any handicraft trade, from eleven o'clock on Saturday forenoon until the usual working hour on Monday morning.

(Other cases of exemption from labor.) 30. And whereas habits of industry and sobriety, and the means of acquiring and preserving property, are proper and reasonable preparatives to freedom, and will secure against an abuse of the same: Be it enacted, that every negro man, who shall have served ten years, and is thirty years of age, and is married, and has had two children born of any marriage, shall obtain the whole of Saturday for himself and his wife, and for his own benefit, and after thirty-seven years of age, the whole of Friday for himself and his wife: provided that in both cases the minister of the district and the inspector of negroes shall certify that they know nothing against his peaceable, orderly, and industrious behavior.

(Huts and land to be appropriated.) 31. And be it enacted, that the master of every plantation shall provide the materials of a good and substantial hut for each married field negro: and if his plantation shall exceed —— acres, he shall allot to the same a portion of land not less than ——: and the said hut and land shall remain and stand annexed to the said negro, for his natural life, or during his bondage: but the same shall not be alienated without the consent of the owners.

(Property of negroes secured.) 32. And be it enacted, that it shall not be lawful for the owner of any negro, by himself or any other, to take from him any land, house, cattle, goods, or money, acquired by the said negro, whether by purchase, donation, or testament, whether the same has been derived from the owner of the said negro, or any other.

33. And be it enacted, that, if the said negro shall die possessed of any lands, goods, or chattels, and dies without leaving a wife or issue, it shall be lawful for the said negro to devise or bequeath the same by his last will: but in case the said negro shall die intestate, and leave a wife and children, the same shall be distributed amongst them, according to the usage under the statute, commonly called the Statute of Distributions: but if the said negro shall die intestate without wife or children, then, and in that case, his estate shall go to the fund provided for the better execution of this act.

34. And be it enacted, that no negro, who is married, and hath resided upon any plantation for twelve months, shall be sold, either privately or by the decree of any court, but along with the plantation on which he hath resided, unless he should himself request to be separated therefrom.

(Of the punishment of negroes.) 35. And be it enacted, that no blows or stripes exceeding thirteen shall be inflicted for one offence, upon any negro, without the order of one of his Majesty's justices of peace.

(Of the same.) 36. And it is enacted, that it shall be lawful for the protector of negroes, as often as on complaint and hearing he shall be of opinion that any negro hath been cruelly and inhumanly treated, or when it shall be made to appear to him that an overseer hath any particular malice, to order, at the desire of the suffering party, the said negro to be sold to another master.

37. And be it enacted, that, in all cases of injury to member or life, the offences against a negro shall be deemed and taken to all intents and purposes as if the same were perpetrated against any of his Majesty's subjects: and the protector of negroes, on complaint, or if he shall receive credible information thereof, shall cause an indictment to be presented for the same; and in case of suspicion of any murder of a negro, an inquest by the coroner, or officer acting as such, shall, if practicable, be held into the same.

(Of the manumission of negroes.) 38. And in order to a gradual manumission of slaves, as they shall seem fitted to fill the offices of freemen, be it enacted, that every negro slave, being thirty years of age and upwards, and who has had three children born to him in lawful matrimony, and who hath received a certificate from the minister of his district, or any other Christian teacher, of his regularity in the duties of religion, and of his orderly and good behavior, may purchase, at rates to be fixed by two justices of peace, the freedom of himself, or his wife or children, or any of them separately, valuing the wife and children, if purchased into liberty by the father of the family, at half only of their marketable values: provided that the said father shall bind himself in a penalty of —— for the good behavior of his children.

(Of the same.) 39. And be it enacted, that it shall be lawful for the protector of negroes to purchase the freedom of any negro who shall appear to him to excel in any mechanical art, or other knowledge or practice deemed liberal, and the value shall be settled by a jury.

(Free negroes how to be punished.) 40. And be it enacted, that the protector of negroes shall be and is authorized and required to act as a magistrate for the coercion of all idle, disobedient, or disorderly free negroes, and he shall by office prosecute them for the offences of idleness, drunkenness, quarrelling, gaming, or vagrancy, in the supreme court, or cause them to be prosecuted before one justice of peace, as the case may require.

(Of the same.) 41. And be it enacted, that, if any free negro hath been twice convicted for any of the said misdemeanors, and is judged by the said protector of negroes, calling to his assistance two justices of the peace, to be incorrigibly idle, dissolute, and vicious, it shall be lawful, by the order of the said protector and two justices of peace, to sell the said free negro into slavery: the purchase-money to be paid to the person so remanded into servitude, or kept in hand by the protector and governor for the benefit of his family.

(Governor to receive and transmit annual reports.) 42. And be it enacted, that the governor in each colony shall be assistant to the execution of this act, and shall receive the reports of the protector, and such other accounts as he shall judge material, relative thereto, and shall transmit the same annually to one of his Majesty's principal secretaries of state.[7]

[7] *Burke, Works*, VI, 275-289.

## APPENDIX B

### BATHURST LETTERS

#### COPY OF A LETTER ADDRESSED TO THE GOVERNORS OF DEMERARA AND BERBICE.[1]

Colonial Office, Downing-Street, 28th May 1823.

Sir,

I TAKE the earliest opportunity of communicating to you the resolutions which were unanimously agreed to by the House of Commons on the 15th instant, and in order that you may better understand not only the general impression of the House in coming to these resolutions, but more particularly the principles which have guided His Majesty's Government in proposing them, and which will continue to guide them in the measures to be adopted for the furtherance of the important objects to which they relate, I have inclosed the best report that I can procure, although it may not be altogether a correct one, of the speech of Mr. Secretary Canning.

I do not propose in this despatch to call your immediate attention to all the subjects to which that speech refers, but to confine myself to one of those points on which I have not found that any difference of opinion exists, and which, being simple in its nature, may be at once adopted, viz. an absolute prohibition to inflict the punishment of flogging, under any circumstances, on female slaves.

The system of meliorating the condition of slaves, to which His Majesty's Government stands pledged by those resolutions, cannot better commence than by the

---

[1] "Papers in explanation of measures adopted by His Majesty for amelioration of the condition of the slave population in the West Indies," *Parliamentary Papers*, 1824, XXIV, 427, schedule 1, pp. 3-4.

adoption of a principle which, by making a distinction of treatment between the male and female slaves, cannot fail to raise this unfortunate class generally above their present degraded level, and to restore to the female slaves that sense of shame which is at once the ornament and the protection of their sex, and which their present mode of punishment has tended so unfortunately to weaken if not to obliterate.

I should therefore have communicated to you His Majesty's commands that the punishment of flogging should for the future cease with respect to females, had I not been desirous that the prohibition should proceed from the Court of Policy, as I am unwilling to deprive them of the satisfaction which I am sure they will feel in originating and supporting a measure which has been approved by all classes.

With respect to the practice of driving slaves to their work by the sound of the whip, and to the arbitrary infliction of it by the driver as a stimulus to labor, I am equally disposed to trust to the Court of Policy to originate measures for the cessation of this practice, which I need not to state must be repugnant to the feelings of every individual in this country. I am aware that a necessity may exist for retaining the punishment of flogging with respect to males, though at the same time it should be subjected to defined regulations and restrictions: but as an immediate measure, I cannot too strongly recommend that the whip should no longer be carried into the field, and there displayed by the driver as the emblem of his authority, or employed as the ready instrument of his displeasure.

I have the honour to be, &c.

(Signed)

BATHURST.

COPY OF A LETTER ADDRESSED TO GOVERNORS OF
COLONIES HAVING LOCAL LEGISLATURES[2]

Colonial-Office, Downing-Street, 9th July 1823.
(Circular.)

IN my despatch of the 12th ultimo, I apprized you that it
was my intention to communicate to you by the first
packet in the present month, further instructions respecting those improvements in the slave code of the Colony
under your Government, which, in conformity with the
recent resolution of the House of Commons, it is the
earnest desire of His Majesty's Government to carry into
effect.

The suggestions which I am about to make, are not to
be understood as affording a full development of what
His Majesty's Government have in contemplation on
this important subject: it is my purpose rather to point
out such changes in the law as may be conveniently
adopted at present, and which will (it is hoped), lay the
foundation for a further and more effectual reformation. I am therefore to direct you to lay before the Colonial Legislature of —— the following remarks and
propositions, and you will not fail to press upon that
body the importance of directing their immediate and
most serious attention to them.

It would be superfluous to insist upon the indispensable
necessity of religious instructions as the foundation of
every beneficial change in the character and future condition of the slaves; so deeply, indeed, is His Majesty's
Government impressed with this truth, and with the
necessity of maintaining an adequate number of Clergymen and Teachers throughout the West Indies, under
Episcopal controul, that, if it shall appear that the reve-
nues of the Colonies are insufficient for this purpose, they

---

[2] *Parliamentary Papers*, 1824, XXIV, 427, schedule 1, pp. 8-13.

will not hesitate to apply to Parliament for such pecuniary grants as may be necessary for supplying the deficiency; nor can they doubt that the anxiety which has been manifested by the Legislature, and by the public at large, for the welfare of the slave population, will induce Parliament cheerfully to contribute such funds as may be required for effecting this important object; but this disposition must be met on the part of the Assembly by a Legislative provision for the abolition of markets on the Sunday, and the substitution of some other time for that purpose, so that the Sabbath may be appropriated to the purposes of rest from labour, and of moral and religious instruction. Unless the time withdrawn from the market were employed in the more becoming occupations of the day, it would too probably be passed by the slaves without benefit to themselves, and perhaps with material detriment if not danger to the Community. The immediate abolition of Sunday markets, is not insisted upon until the means of religious instruction shall have been provided. But His Majesty's Government will not recommend to Parliament the grant of any pecuniary assistance towards the expence of a religious establishment, in any case in which the abolition of Sunday Markets and the substitution of some other day for that purpose, shall not have been prospectively secured.

Religious instruction is also a necessary preliminary to another important improvement in the condition of the slaves, the admission of their evidence in courts of justice. The permanent exclusion of the testimony of slaves must essentially interfere with the provisions adopted for their protection. On the other hand, to declare that all slaves shall be qualified to give evidence, would be a change in the system of administering justice in the Colonies too momentous to be introduced suddenly; it can only be consequent upon the moral and religious improvement of the slave population. It is highly expedient, therefore, that in furtherance of the resolutions unanimously adopted by the House of Commons, a law should be passed, declaring that the evidence of a slave shall be received in all, except perhaps certain cases, if upon his appearing in Court to give testimony, he shall produce, under the hand of some of the parochial Clergymen, or of the religious Teacher authorized by the master or overseer to instruct him, a certificate, stating that the proposed witness has been so far instructed in the principles of religion as, in the judgment of the party certifying, adequately to understand the obligation of an oath. The cases to be considered must be those in which the master of the slaves is directly concerned, and such as would affect the life of a white person. For the better preventing the fabrication of certificates, it may be necessary to keep parochial registers of the persons whose competency to give evidence shall from time to time have been certified by the proper authority, and the being enrolled in such a list may be made an object of laudable ambition, and a stimulus to attention and good conduct. Perhaps such certificate should not of itself be an absolute qualification to be received as a witness, but it might be regarded as raising such a presumption of competency, that the party producing it should be taken and adjudged to be competent, unless he should be proved to labour under some such disability, as would, according to the law and usage of English courts of justice, disqualify a free person.

Religious instruction is not less necessarily the foundation of that relation, the want of which in the system of Colonial slavery excites a deep and general commiseration in this country, that of marriage. Where the conjugal and parental rights of the father of a family cannot be maintained, it would be vain to expect from this institution that infinite variety of salutary consequences which naturally belong to it in civilized society. The present want of religious teachers in the Colonies presents another difficulty, for without their instrumentality it will scarcely be possible to impress the mind of a slave with a due sense of the sacred obligations of matrimony, or even to celebrate the mere ceremonial of marriage with any proper and impressive solemnity.

Advantage cannot be too soon, or too anxiously taken of the opportunity of establishing this salutary institution; in doing so, care must be taken to encourage, as far as possible, marriages between slaves attached to the same estates, since the insecurity of conjugal and parental rights is manifestly increased by distant connections, which moreover tend to withdraw the interest and attachment of the slave from the plantation to which he belongs. As part of this system, provision ought to be made by law for exempting from future labour in the field the mother of a given number of children born in lawful wedlock. Until the religious establishment shall be completed, the solemnization of marriages by persons who are not in holy orders might be permitted, and any Minister of religion not engaged in any secular calling might be employed, in cases where the attendance of a Clergyman of the Church of England cannot be procured. Care however should be taken that all marriages should ultimately be registered at the parish church, and none celebrated without the consent of the master given in writing; but in the event of the master feeling it necessary to object to the marriage, he should be called upon to communicate the cause of his resistance to the Clergyman of the parish to which the parties belong.

The next subject to which I must draw your attention is the manumission of slaves, every unnecessary obstacle to which must be removed. Although it appears from the recent returns that taxes have in almost every Colony been imposed on manumissions, I am gratified to learn that they have in practice been generally discontinued. No difficulty can therefore be anticipated in obtaining the concurrence of the Colonial Legislature in the final repeal of all such charges, and in this I include all official fees which may have been collected either by usage or under positive enactment. The first obstacle to manumission arises from the apprehension of this being resorted to by the owner for the purpose of relieving himself from the burden of maintaining infirm or aged slaves. I conceive it would be necessary to require the appearance of the person to be manumitted at the office, either of the Colonial Secretary or Treasurer, whose duty it should be, before registering the deed of manumission, to satisfy himself that the slave was not less than six nor more than fifty years of age, and that he did not labour under any permanent sickness or infirmity. In cases of slaves below six or above fifty years of age, or labouring under sickness or infirmity (but in whose cases only) the Secretary or Treasurer should be required before recording the manumission, to take from the owner a bond to the King, with a condition that the penalty should not be enforced, unless the manumitted slave should, within ten years in the case of the child and fourteen in the case of the adult, become incapable of earning his own subsistence. A second obstacle to manumission seems to arise from a presumed legal difficulty. It has been urged that a slave not being capable of making contracts, cannot legally contract for, or become the purchaser of his own freedom; now as this is plainly a difficulty of form only, and not of substance, a remedy may of course be readily devised. Either the competency of the slaves to make contracts respecting his freedom might be acknowledged by a declaratory act, or it might be provided that all such con-

tracts should be made in the name of the King, in whose
name also all actions might be brought to enforce the
performance of it. A third and much more serious obstacle to manumission arises out of the legal limitations under which slaves are legally held. Thus, for example, a
slave and his issue may have been made the subject of
entails or of family settlement, or may be held under two
or more successive mortgages, &c. and his manumission
cannot be effected without the concurrence of a series of
reversioners, remainder men, mortgagees or mortgagers,
some of whom may be infants, and others who may not
even be in existence during the life of the slave. A difficulty analogous to this arises from the case of doubtful
or disputable titles, and from the circumstance of a slave
being regarded as assets for the payment of the debts of
a deceased owner, since in either of these cases it is impossible for the individual prepared to emancipate such
slave to know in whom the legal right to the slave is
vested. The pendency of a suit or action involving the
question of the title of the two litigant parties to a slave,
imposes on the latter the necessity of waiting the determination of the controversy before he can safely pay to
either the price of his freedom.

To remove all the preceding obstacles to manumission
you will therefore propose to the Legislature of ——
to pass a law to the following effect: Permanent Commissioners should be appointed, who (on application being made by or on behalf of any slave with his master's
consent), should ascertain the names and places of abode
of every person having any interest or probable interest
in him, either as tenant for years or for life, as reversioner, remainder-man, mortgagee, mortgager, trustee,
executor, receiver or creditor of any deceased owners or
their agents; all these persons should be summoned, by
personal notice if possible, and if not, then by public ad-

vertisement, to attend at the time and place of the appraisement of the slave. The appraisement should take place at the time and place to be thus appointed, in the presence of at least one Commissioner, and by at least one sworn appraiser, and the Commissioners should have authority, on application made within one month by any of the parties interested, to direct a new appointment in case there should seem reason to dispute the justice of the original valuation. The second appraisement should be final. The appraised value should then be paid into the Colonial Treasury. The Treasurer should invest the amount of good security, and every right which formerly existed in the slave should thenceforward exist, not in him, but in the fund to be thus purchased by the appraised price of his freedom.

The last topic relating to manumission, to which I think it necessary at present to advert, is the loss of the deed of manumission. It will be expedient that provision should be made for the registration of all manumissions, and that to secure punctuality in this respect, a simple form of manumission should be prescribed by legislative authority, and that the appearance of the party before the Registrar, or one of his deputies, should be an essential part of every act of manumission.

I have next to advert to the subject of the sale of slaves in satisfaction of the debts of their owners. Among the whole range of projected improvements in the Colonial system, there is, perhaps, none which, on an attentive consideration, will be found to present more difficulties than this.

As far as the rules of Colonial law, respecting the sale of slaves, are to be collected from the documents in this office, they may, I conceive, be stated, without any material inaccuracy, as follows:

First, it appears to be a general maxim in our Colonial

jurisprudence, that the whole property of the debtor, whether real or personal, and all his interest in real estates, whether legal or equitable, may be taken in execution, and sold in satisfaction of any judgment against him. I further collect that in the order of sale, the executive Officer of the Courts (the Sheriff or Provost Marshall) is bound to seize and sell such property in the following order:—that is,—he is first to take the severed crops; then the moveable goods; then the debts due to the defendant; then his plantation utensils; then his slaves; and lastly his land; resorting to the two latter descriptions of property only in case of a deficiency in the former. It also seems that in every one of the Colonies, a judgment has the effect of a mortgage upon all the immovable property, and upon all the interests in such property which were vested in the debtor when the judgment was entered against him; lastly,—it seems that an earlier judgment will, in the order of payment, take precedence of a later mortgage.

A judgment having so much greater effect in the Colonies than in England, the number entered in the West Indies bears a most unusual proportion to the number of the free inhabitants, and to the extent of their pecuniary transactions. Another result has been, that mortgagees have usually taken judgments as a collateral security for the advances they have made. There is, therefore, a large body of persons holding charges on the slaves throughout the Colonies, which they have acquired on the faith of laws passed by the Assemblies, and subsequently approved by the Crown. Now, if a law were introduced by which the sale of slaves, under legal process, in satisfaction of the debts of the proprietor, were prohibited absolutely and without qualification, the rights thus acquired under acts of Assembly would be subverted, and I am not prepared to recommend a measure trenching so largely on the rights of private property. Supposing that the prohibition were prospective only, and that it therefore should affect merely those debts which might subsequently be contracted, still the Provost Marshall might put up the utensils and the land itself to sale; and it is obviously immaterial to the present question, whether the slaves are sold without the land, or the land without the slaves; supposing further, that both the land, the slaves, and the utensils, were withdrawn from legal process, if the proprietor still retained the power of voluntary sale, the practical result would be this,—that men would then relieve their necessities by selling their slaves as they could find purchasers, instead of borrowing money on the credit of them as at present. It seems then to follow, that the absolute prohibition of the sale of slaves, in satisfaction of the debts of the proprietor, would not have the effect of preventing the forced separation of the slave from his home, unless the right of voluntary sale were also taken away. But a prohibition thus extensive is a more considerable innovation than I am prepared to recommend.

It is satisfactory, however, to remark, that although the theory of the law allows the sale of slaves to pay the debts of the owner, yet in practice such sales can only take place where the owner has the fee simple of the land and slaves (which, from the practice of strict entails, in the West Indies, is, in many of the Colonies unusual) and has also not contracted any mortgage debt, which (I am afraid) is, in most of them still more uncommon. The land and the slaves being almost universally settled, or mortgaged as one consolidated property, the rights of the reversioner, or remainder man in the one case, and of the mortgagee in the other, necessarily prevent the creditor from selling the slaves apart from the land. I am, therefore, disposed to infer that the great majority of slaves who are brought to sale for payment of their masters debts, whether under the Old English Writ of *Venditioni exponas* in Jamaica, or under the general Executions directed by the Court Acts of the smaller Islands, are sold with the land, and suffer no other alteration from the transaction than that of a change of masters. The slaves who are sold separately, are therefore, in all probability (for the returns give no accurate information on this point) for the greater part, those who are not habitually worked upon the plantations and are in general the domestic servants of their owners, or are employed by the lower classes of freemen in various menial occupations for the profit of their masters—slaves thus circumstanced are not perhaps materially injured by a compulsory sale, since their employments are not such as to create strong local attachments.

Still to whatever degree the removal of slaves from their homes to satisfy the debts of their owners, may occur, it is obviously fit that it should if possible be prevented, and that precaution should be taken against the more frequent occurrence of such removals hereafter. I am, therefore, with reference to the preceding remarks, to direct you to call the attention of the Legislature of the Colony of —— to the following amendments of the law upon this subject, without infringing on the rights of any judgment creditors, who may at present hold unsatisfied judgments, provision might be made for preventing the keeping of such judgments alive after the debts for which they may have been obtained shall have been really satisfied. A time should also be fixed beyond which no existing judgment should be capable of being enforced. With reference to judgments which may be hereafter obtained, the executions to issue on them, might perhaps be, both in form and effect a sequestration rather than a sale, that is to say, the creditor to hold them together until his claims were satisfied by the proceeds, or the rents and profits of the land, slaves, and utensils, might be put up to sale as one entire lot, without removing them, one from the other. If, however, the substitution of a sequestration for a sale, should not be practicable, the only other plan which I can suggest, is that of directing, that the land slaves and plantation utensils, shall always be sold together in one entire lot. It may, also be expedient to provide, that slaves shall not in future be considered as separate assets for the payment of debts of the deceased owner, but that the land, and slaves, and plantation stock, shall always be sold together.

With regard to all slaves, whether attached to estates, or not, you will propose an enactment prohibiting their being sold apart from their husbands, or wives, or apart from any child, who may be under the age of 14. As unhappily the disuse of marriage has prevented the growth of any legal relationship between the slaves, the prohibition must extend to the case of *reputed* husbands, wives or children. I have, also to suggest, that if the debtor should not be the proprietor both of the husband and wife, or of the parents and children, an appraisement should be made of the value of such members of a family as are the property of the debtor, and they should be offered at something below such appraised value to the proprietor of the other members of the family.

On the subject of the punishment of slaves, I have already in some degree anticipated the object of the present dispatch, by directing that Legislative measures should be proposed for preventing the punishment of flogging in every case where the offender is a woman, I also pointed out the necessity of prohibiting the use of the whip in the field; I have now in addition to those instructions, to direct that you will cause some effectual law to be submitted to the Legislature, for preventing any domestic punishment whatever, until the day following that on which the offence may have been committed, and even then, except in the presence of one free person, besides the person under whose authority the punishment may be inflicted. If the punishment should exceed three lashes, it should be provided that a regular entry should be made in a plantation-book to be kept for that purpose. First, of the nature of the offence; secondly of the time when, and of the place where it was committed; thirdly, of the names of the free persons present at the punishment, and fourthly, of the number of lashes received. The accuracy of the entries in this book should be certified quarterly by an oath to be taken by the owner, manager, or overseer, before a magistrate. As the offence of punishing a slave in the absence of any free person, would not be susceptible of direct proof if it should happen, that the slaves themselves were not among that class, whose evidence it is proposed to admit, to ensure as far as possible the detection of any such counteraction of the law, it should be enacted, that if the person of a slave should exhibit marks of recent flogging or mutilation, which he or any other slave should state to be the traces of punishment not duly registered, such appearances should be considered sufficient to raise a presumption of the law having been broken, and the manager or overseer should be condemned to suffer a given penalty to be enacted, unless he could repel that presumption by sufficient evidence.

The last subject to which I propose at present to advert, is the necessity of insuring to the slave the enjoyment of whatever property he may be able to acquire. For this purpose, *Savings Banks* should be established under Legislative Authority, upon the model of those in England; but, with this alteration, viz. that the depositor should at the time of first becoming a subscriber, state to whom, in the event of his own death, the fund is to devolve. An entry of this declaration being duly registered at the Bank, should be declared equivalent to a will in the absence of any other.

In conclusion, I have most earnestly to impress upon you the necessity of proceeding to carry these improvements into effect, not only with all possible dispatch, but in the spirit of perfect and cordial co-operation with the efforts of His Majesty's Government. More particularly, you will be attentive to have the necessary laws framed with such precaution and foresight, as, if possible, to provide an effectual security for the faithful observance of them. To this end, you will consult with the legal advisers of the crown on the frame of the necessary bills, and you will from time to time communicate with me upon the progress you make in this work, or upon the difficulties which may obstruct its completion, and if (what I am unwilling to imagine) you should meet with any serious opposition, you will lose no time in transmitting to me the necessary communication, in order that I may take the earliest opportunity of laying the matter before Parliament, and submitting for their consideration such measures as it may be fit to adopt in consequence.

I have the honour to be, your obedient servant,

(Signed) BATHURST.

## APPENDIX C

*An Abstract of an Order of the King in Council for consolidating the several laws recently made for improving the condition of the slaves in His Majesty's Colonies of Trinidad, Berbice, Demerara, St. Lucia, the Cape of Good Hope, and Mauritius.*[1] (*Feb. 2, 1830.*)

Section 1 repeals all the laws for improving the condition of the slaves in the crown colonies of Trinidad, Berbice, Demerara, St. Lucia, the Cape of Good Hope, and the Mauritius, passed since March 1824.

Sections 2-4 provide that his Majesty shall appoint in each of these colonies a protector of slaves, who shall take an oath faithfully to perform the duties of his office, without fear, favour, or partiality, and shall keep and preserve all records, books and papers connected with those duties.

Section 5 enacts that no protector of slaves shall himself be the owner of any slaves, nor have any share or interest in, or any mortgage or security upon any slave; nor be the proprietor of, nor have any interest in any land cultivated by slaves; nor be competent to act as manager, or agent of any plantation or estate in the colony to which he is appointed. And if he shall acquire or possess in his own or his wife's right, or as guardian, trustee, or executor of others, any slave or any land cultivated by slaves, or any share or interest in such land or slaves, or shall act as manager, agent, or attorney for

[1] This abstract is taken from the *Anti-Slavery Reporter*, III, 129-133. The complete order in Council may be found in *Parliamentary Papers*, 1830, XXXIII, 1, pp. 1-19, and in *Parliamentary Debates*, second series, XXII, 179-210. The order is very minute in its provisions and so is of great length.

such property, he shall henceforth *de facto* cease to be such protector, and some other fit person shall be forthwith appointed in his place. The protector, however, may *hire* slaves for domestic purposes, provided he shall first make it appear to the satisfaction of the Governor that he cannot hire free persons to perform such services.

Sections 6-8 empower the Governor to provide temporarily for the necessary absence from ill health, or for the removal, resignation, or death of the protector; and also to appoint assistant protectors in each district into which the colony may be divided, to aid under the protector's instructions in executing the duties of his office.

Sections 9-11 prohibit protectors or their assistants from acting "as magistrates or otherwise," in deciding any complaint made by or against a slave, or in punishing any offence committed by or against a slave; and require that in the case of all prosecutions of slaves for capital or transportable offences, or of other persons for the murder of a slave, or for any offence against the person of a slave; and in the case of all suits affecting the freedom of any alleged slave, or the rights of property of any slave; the same notices shall be given to the protector or his assistant as by law are given to persons of free condition. It is further required that the protector or his assistant shall be present, on behalf of the slave, at the trial and other proceedings in such suits and prosecutions; and also that if any complaint is made to the protector or any of his assistants, of any injury done to a slave, or if the protector or his assistant shall know of such injury, it shall be their duty to inquire into the case, and, if he shall see it expedient so to do, to bring a civil action or institute a prosecution, as the case may be, and shall conduct such proceeding to its close by himself or by an advocate or solicitor.

Sections 12-20 respect Sunday markets and Sunday

labour. Sunday markets are henceforth abolished, and are absolutely to cease and determine, and persons holding such markets or exposing goods for sale on Sunday, shall be fined from five shillings to twenty. Another day in each week shall be appointed by the Governor for the market, on which day slaves shall be free from arrest on any civil process whatever.

No slave shall be liable to labour for the benefit of his owner or of any other person on a Sunday, and any one compelling, hiring or inducing him to do so may be fined from one to three pounds. From this prohibition are excepted domestic labour, and labour in tending cattle, and "works of necessity"; such "works of necessity" to be previously defined and regulated by the Governor's proclamation, and not to be required of the slave without previous notice to the protector or his assistant. If, however, the necessity be so urgent as not to admit of notice previously, it must be given within forty-eight hours after, otherwise the fine will be levied; it being always provided that the necessity shall be such as had been defined and specified beforehand in the Governor's proclamation.

Section 21 makes it "henceforth illegal" for any person "while superintending the labour of a slave or slaves in any agricultural or manufacturing operation, to carry any whip, cat, or other instrument usually employed in the punishment of slaves," or to "exhibit it as an emblem of authority," or to strike, beat, or scourge a slave with any such whip, &c., except for the punishment of some fault previously committed; and any person offending in any of these instances, or who shall direct, authorize, or procure, or assist in, the commission of such offence, shall be deemed guilty of a misdemeanor.

Sections 22-24 prohibit entirely the flogging of females, except under ten years of age, and in the manner and degree in which children of that age are punished at school;

and, leaving the infliction of severer punishments to competent courts, permit owners to flog males to the extent of twenty-five stripes for any offence and on the same day, provided no unhealed laceration from former punishment shall remain on the person of the slave, and provided also that one free person, or, if no free person can be procured, six adult slaves, besides the person inflicting or authorizing the punishment, shall be present to witness it. The violation of this clause is punishable as a misdemeanour.

Section 25 authorizes the Governor by proclamation to prescribe, with all practicable precision, the mode in which offences of female slaves, heretofore punishable by whipping, shall thenceforward be punished, either by imprisonment or the stocks, or in such other mode as may be specially authorized in the proclamation, which shall also contain rules for preventing and punishing abuses in the infliction of such substituted modes of punishment.

Sections 26-36 require masters and managers to keep, in a prescribed form, a regular record of all arbitrary punishments inflicted by them on slaves employed in any agricultural or manufacturing labour, and to make a half-yearly return of such record to the protector, in which every required particular shall be specified, the neglect or non-performance being punishable as a misdemeanour.

Sections 37-41 regulate the marriages of slaves and require them to be recorded, and declare them, when solemnized, under the protector's license, by any clergyman, or other religious teacher not carrying on any secular trade except that of schoolmaster, to be valid and effectual in law. A proviso is added that marriage shall not invest slaves or their progeny with any rights at variance with the legal title of the owners to the service of such slaves or their progeny, or with the duties slaves are bound to render to their owners.

Sections 42-44 declare that no slave shall be incompetent to purchase, acquire, possess, enjoy, alienate, or bequeath property of any amount or description whatsoever (excepting slaves, boats or vessels, gunpowder and military weapons); or to bring, prosecute and defend any action in any court of justice, in respect to such property, in the same manner as if he were free; it being provided, however, that no slave shall be liable to be taken in execution in any civil suit or process to which he is himself a party.

Sections 45-51 prohibit the separation of husband and wife, parent and child under sixteen years of age, or such relations by repute, either by judicial sale, or by private contract, or by conveyance, or by will; and prescribe the measures to be taken, in doubtful cases, to ascertain the relationship by repute of husband and wife, parent and child. All sales whatever in violation of this law shall be null and void; it being provided, however, that if persons in the relation of parent and child shall fully and freely consent to a separation, and the protector is satisfied as to such consent, and also that the separation will not be injurious to the parties, then he may authorise such separation.

Section 52 abolishes all fees and all duties on acts of manumission, except a fee of twenty shillings, to be paid from the public revenue, for the enrolment of each of such acts.

Sections 53-56. The manumission of slaves with the master's consent may be effected either by will or by deed at pleasure. When done gratuitously by deed, if the slave be under six or above fifty years of age, or infirm or diseased in mind or body, the owner shall enter into a bond for £200 to secure that such child shall be properly maintained till the age of fourteen, and such adult for life; but when done gratuitously by will, no bond shall be required, but instead thereof the testator's estate shall continue chargeable for maintenance as aforesaid. When owners are willing to contract with a slave for his freedom, at a price to be agreed upon between them through the agency of the protector, the protector is required to take certain measures, and to give certain public notices, in order to ascertain the right of the alleged owner to manumit the slave, and having done so, he shall proceed to prepare, and execute, and enrol the deed of manumission.

Sections 57-69. When the owner or other person interested in a slave is unwilling, when applied to, to manumit him, or unable from mortgage, minority, idiocy, absence or other cause to do so; or when the slave seeking to be manumitted is the subject of a pending suit; or when a higher price is demanded for the slave's freedom than to the protector appears just; then and in all these cases, after certain prescribed notices, the protector and owner or manager shall be required by the chief civil judge to nominate each an appraiser, the judge himself nominating an umpire, and also the appraiser on behalf of the owner or manager if he shall refuse or omit to do so; and the persons so named, being duly sworn, shall make a fair and impartial appraisement of the slave within seven days, and within seven days more shall certify the same to the chief judge; and the award so made shall be conclusive; it being provided, however, that should it be made to appear to the judge within one month that the valuation had been unjustly or fraudulently, or improperly made, then he may set it aside, and appoint new appraisers and a new umpire, and so on *toties quoties,* while there remains any just ground to complain of injustice or fraud; and it being also provided that if the price of the slave to be manumitted is not paid within three months after enrolment, the enrolment shall be cancelled, and no proceedings for the manumission of the same slave shall be again instituted till after twelve months. When the enrolment shall have been made and the money paid into the hands of the treasurer of the colony, the slave shall be declared and adjudged free, and the money shall either remain in the hands of the treasurer, bearing an interest of 5 per cent, or be laid out in purchasing another slave, or be invested in the public funds of Great Britain, subject to all the uses, trusts and claims to which the manumitted slave was liable. The Governor shall frame a moderate table of fees on these proceedings, to be paid in certain specified cases by the slave, and in certain others by the owner; and the chief judge shall make rules for the due exercise of his jurisdiction in these matters. ———The following three rules are prescribed in the Order itself. 1. The appraisers shall consider the qualities of the slave proposed to be manumitted, and his skill in domestic service or in other labour whatsoever, with any other facts or circumstances which ought to influence their judgment as to the price to be paid by such slave. 2d. If it shall be alleged by or on behalf of the master, that the money to be paid for the freedom of a slave, or any part of it has been acquired, by such slave, by means of a donation *inter vivos* made to enable such slave to purchase freedom, the chief judge may stay the enrolment till he shall have inquired into the truth of the allegation, and if found true, then the judge shall stay further proceedings, but without prejudice to the future renewal of them; but if not proved, the chief judge shall proceed to record the slave's freedom. 3d. If the owner or manager of a slave proposed to be manumitted, shall allege that such slave had, within the five preceding years, committed any robbery or theft, and the allegation be proved, the judge is required to order all further proceedings, with a view to the manumission of the slave, to be stayed till the expiration of five years from the date of such theft or robbery.

Section 70 enacts that no person shall henceforth be deemed incompetent to give evidence in any civil or criminal court, or in any proceeding whatever, by reason that such person is in a state of slavery; but that the evidence of slaves shall, in all courts and for all purposes, be received in the same manner as the evidence of free persons; Provided that this shall not prevent any court or jury, judge or magistrate, from adverting to the servile condition of any witness, or to the relation in which he may stand to any other person, in estimating the credit due to his testimony.

Section 71. If any person shall be convicted, of having inflicted or authorized an illegal and cruel punishment, or of any cruelty towards his slave, it shall be in the discretion of the court to declare the interest of the person so convicted in such slave forfeited to His Majesty, in addition to any other punishment that may be pronounced on the offender; it being provided that no other person than the party offending shall be deprived of any right or interest he may have in such slave.

Section 72. No slave shall be liable to be punished for preferring, and failing' to establish, any complaint against his owner or manager, unless such complaint shall have originated in some malevolent or culpable motive; and in any such case, such slave shall be liable to be punished, under the authority of any court or magistrate, upon proof being made in a summary way before such court or magistrate, that the complaint was without foundation, and originated in a malevolent and culpable motive.

Section 73. Erasures, interlineations, falsifications, or the destruction of books or records connected with this Order, are punishable as misdemeanours.

Section 74. Misdemeanours are punishable by fine of from £10 to £500, or by imprisonment from one to twelve months, or by both fine and imprisonment.

Section 75. Perjuries are punishable as other perjuries are punishable by the laws of the particular colony.

Section 76. The protector is to prosecute for fines and forfeitures, one third of which shall go to himself, and two thirds to His Majesty.

Section 77. The courts, judges, and magistrates, who are to have jurisdiction in the matters contained in this Order; and the manner in which penalties shall be sued for, and the protector shall execute the duties of his office; shall be pointed out in a proclamation of the Governor comformably to the laws and usages existing in the colonies respectively.

Section 78. The fines, &c., shall be taken to be sterling money.

Section 79. All proclamations of Governors, and all rules of court, authorized by this Order, shall be consistent with and not repugnant to it, and, till disallowed by His Majesty, shall have the force of law.

Section 80. The protectors are, on the first Mondays after the 24th of June and 25th of December in each year, to make a written report, on oath, to the Governor, of the manner in which their various duties have been performed, and then and not before shall be paid their salary; such report to be transmitted to the Colonial Secretary of State by the first opportunity.

Section 81. Explains the meaning to be affixed to various terms in this Order.

Section 82. The Governor of each colony shall make known this Order, by proclamation, within one month after it shall be received by him; and it shall be in force in fourteen days after the date of such proclamation, and not before.

## APPENDIX D

*Circular Dispatch addressed by Viscount Goderich to the Governors of the West Indian Legislative Colonies, dated 10th December 1831.*[1]

Downing Street, 10th December 1831.

Sir,

I HAVE the honour to enclose to you herewith, for your own information and for that of the Legislative bodies of the Colony under your Government, a copy of an amended Order made by His Majesty in Council on the 2d Ultimo, for improving the Condition of the Slaves in British Guiana, Trinidad, St. Lucia, Mauritius, and the Cape of Good Hope. The grounds upon which His Majesty's confidential servants have felt it their duty to advise the making of this Order, and the views by which they have been guided in resisting the opposition made to several of its provisions, are fully set forth in a Circular Dispatch which I addressed to the Governors of the above-mentioned Colonies on the 5th ultimo; and I enclose certain printed papers, which have been presented to the House of Commons by His Majesty's Command, wherein you will find a copy of that document, as well as of others relating to the Order in Council. The

---

[1] This and the other dispatches referred to are found in *Parliamentary Papers*, 1831-1832, (279) XLVI, 1, 191. The order in Council: schedule no. 4, pp. 93-138. Letter, 5 November: schedule no. 4, pp. 59-88. Letter, 14 November: schedule no. 5, pp. 183-187. The letters are too long for insertion. They defend the policy of the government and give the genesis of the order in Council. See also ''Report of select committee of the House of Lords on the state of West India Colonies,'' *House of Lords Journals*, LXIV, appendix no. 2, pp. 769-770.

further object of my present Dispatch is to enable you, at the same time that the measures in favour of the Slaves which have thus been enforced in the Crown Colonies are brought to the knowledge of the Council and Assembly within your Government, to communicate also to those bodies the course which His Majesty's Government have resolved to adopt, with a view to induce the extension of these measures to the colonies having local Legislatures; and it is my anxious desire, not only that the intentions of His Majesty's Government should be made known to the Legislative bodies at the earliest possible moment, but that our motives should be fully explained to them. I am most desirous to satisfy them, if not that our measures are, as we consider them, necessary for the well-being of the Slaves, at least that they are dictated by a conscientious sense of duty. I am anxious to convey to them an adequate impression of the necessity which exists for us to take at length some effective step towards the redemption of the pledges given with the concurrence of the West India body in 1823, and of the solicitude which we have felt to consult the Interests of the Planters simultaneously with those of the Slaves, and to accomplish by such means as should be the least unacceptable to the owners of West Indian property an object which it has become impossible to postpone without compromising the dignity and consistency of the Imperial Legislature, and occasioning danger to all parties concerned.

When I look back in the records of this Department to the many earnest appeals upon this subject which have been addressed since the year 1823 to the reason and discretion of the Colonial Legislatures, it may well seem superfluous to observe, that nothing has been further from the wish of those who have successively administered the affairs of this country since that period than to have recourse to any measures of a coercive character. The Circular Dispatches which were written from year to year, repeating the expression of hopes which had been in no instance fulfilled, and of confidence which had not been justified, evince with what extreme reluctance the Ministers of the Crown have been compelled to relinquish the expectations which were originally entertained that effectual Measures for the improvement of the condition of the Slaves would be at length spontaneously adopted by the Colonial Legislatures. The Dispatches which have been written to point out in detail the defects of such laws as were enacted in alleged fulfilment of the wishes of His Majesty's Government, or in partial compliance with them, bear further testimony to the patient and persevering endeavours which have been made by His Majesty's Government to impress upon the several Councils and Assemblies the necessity which existed for satisfying the feelings entertained in this country in favour of the Slaves, and the inadequacy of their legislation to effect that purpose. If His Majesty's present advisers have resolved to pursue no further this course of warning and entreaty, it is not that they are in any degree less anxious to conciliate the good-will, whilst they consult the real interests of the Colonists, but only because they feel that the language of admonition has been exhausted, and that any further attempt to produce an impression upon the Legislatures by the same means alone could add nothing to the respect of those bodies for the authority of the crown, whilst it would be in vain to expect that it could contribute any thing to the accomplishment of the object in view.

His Majesty's Government had thus before them the alternative; either of proposing some measure of a stronger character than mere injunction, or of desisting altogether from the promotion of an object to which

Parliament is not less justly than solemnly pledged, and the postponement of which is tending more and more every day to precipitate a powerful party in this country in the opposite extreme, and to produce dangers which, however ill they may be understood in a distant quarter of the world, no one who is conversant with the influence of public opinion in this country, and the direction of it upon the subject of Slavery, could fail to forsee.

At the same time that this alternative presented itself, the increasing commercial distress of the West India interest could not but attract the most anxious and painful attention of His Majesty's Government. Deeply as they have regretted the opposition of the Colonies to their measures in favour of the Slaves, neither that opposition, nor any thing that was ill-judged and intemperate in the manner of it, has prevented His Majesty's Government from entertaining the strongest feelings of sympathy and compassion for the distress under which all persons connected with West Indian property are indiscriminately suffering. His Majesty's Government were thus scarcely more anxious to secure the adoption of their measures for the protection of the Slaves than to find means, not incompatible with that object, of relieving the Planters from some portion of their commercial difficulties. In this view, as well as from its importance to the interests of humanity, it has been peculiarly gratifying to His Majesty's Government to have been enabled to conclude a Convention with France, which promises, more than any other practicable measure, to repress the Foreign Slave Trade; and this, at the same time that it militates against the dreadful atrocities of that traffic, will give some check to the competition of foreign sugar growers, so far as it is promoted by such iniquitous means. A measure of fiscal regulation, so devised as to be productive of real and substantial relief, has appeared to be the only additional

method within the power of His Majesty's Government
to propose, which would in some degree meet the exigen-
cies of the West Indian commercial interest; but to offer
such an Advantage to the Planters, without at the same
time taking any security for their acceptance of the measures in behalf of the Slaves, would be, if not directly inconsistent with the Parliamentary Resolutions of 1823,
at least an abandonment, and even reversal, of the policy
of the Executive Government resulting from those Resolutions. On the 16th of March 1824 the late Mr. Canning
announced in his place in parliament the several modes of
giving effect to the Resolutions of 1823, which were successively to be tried for the purpose of overcoming the
resistance to them which, it had appeared from the experience of the preceding year, was to be expected from
the Colonial Legislatures. He pointed out the course of
authoritative admonition as the most eligible in the first
Instance; and, should that be unavailing, he adverted to
the means which Parliament possesses of constraining
the Colonies by fiscal regulations and enactments adverse
to their navigation, as preferable to a more direct application of the powers of Parliament; of which more direct
exercise of power he nevertheless declared the necessity,
should all other means fail. The course of authoritative
admonition had been pursued for eight years, and has
been, as I have already observed, utterly unsuccessful.
Advice again and again tendered to the Colonial Legislatures has been but little listened to in any of the Colonies,
and in some of the most important and considerable has
been more than once rejected, without even the forms of
respect. Ceasing, therefore, to entertain hopes that their
admonitions will ever prove efficacious, it might, perhaps,
be expected of His Majesty's Government to propose at
once to Parliament the second mode of operating upon
the Legislatures which was contemplated by Mr. Can-

ning; but to use any endeavours to harass the Colonies by fiscal regulations, in their present circumstances of distress, would indeed be most repugnant to the feelings of His Majesty's Government. They could not at this moment, nor until a less painful experiment should have been tried, reconcile it to those feelings which the sufferings consequent upon commercial adversity must always excite, to propose any measures to which a character of unmixed severity could be attributed. Whilst, however, their feelings of concern for the difficulties of the West Indian proprietors and merchants withhold them from originating any measures in which their interests should not be considered, they are not less powerfully withheld by a sense of their duty to the great cause of Slave Melioration, and by a Consciousness of the obligations under which the government of this country has been placed by the Resolutions of Parliament, from propounding any measure of indulgence to the Planters in which the interests of the Slaves should be lost sight of. To propose a measure of fiscal relief, to take effect before the object of the Parliamentary Resolutions should be secured, would be a manifest dereliction of the only course of policy, short of the direct application of power, through which there has ever been a prospect of redeeming the pledges contained in those Resolutions. Such being the position of the question, and such the obligations incumbent upon His Majesty's Government, it only remained for them to combine the two great objects which they had to effect in a single measure, and thus to make the one contingent upon the other.

I have therefore to announce to you the fixed determination of His Majesty's Government to propose to Parliament in the present session, and so soon as the details of this, in common with their other financial operations for the Year 1832, can be arranged, a measure of substantial relief to the West Indian interests; and that this measure will be so framed as to take effect upon the produce of the Crown Colonies as a matter of course, and upon that of those only of the other Colonies in which the provisions, in their precise terms and in their entire extent, of His Majesty's Order in Council of the 2d ultimo, for improving the Condition of the Slaves in British Guiana, Trinidad, Saint Lucia, Mauritius, and the Cape of Good Hope, shall have acquired in perpetuity the force of law. It cannot be too distinctly explained, that the measure to be submitted to Parliament will be so framed that the indispensable condition of receiving the consequent benefit will be the fact of a statute having passed the Colonial Legislature, simply, and without qualification in terms of limitation of time, declaring the Order in Council to possess the force of law in the Colony.

The Language here used is by no means needlessly strict. The motives and sentiments of His Majesty's Government would be much mistaken, were it to be conceived that, in making the terms of the proposed alternative thus definite and precise, they had been actuated by any spirit of peremptory dictation. The whole efficacy of a law depends upon verbal distinctions and minute accuracies of expression. To leave the choice of the words to any body of men is to place the substance and essence of the law at their discretion; to do this would be nothing less than to resume and continue the fruitless correspondence of the last eight years upon the terms of Colonial Slave Acts. An interminable controversy would arise between His Majesty's Government and each of the Legislative Colonies, as to whether the required amendments in the laws relating to Slavery had or had not been enacted, and His Majesty's Government would be called upon to discharge the invidious and even impracticable office of determining constructively upon the words of thirteen different codes; while upon their decision it would depend to which of as many Colonies the benefit provided by Parliament should be dispensed, and to which it should be denied. Even if such a revision were possible, the experience of eight years has now placed beyond the reach of all rational doubt the fact, which, independently of such experience, might have been anticipated, that laws framed in the Colonies and passed by the Colonial Assemblies, for the improvement of the condition of Slavery, are deficient in that quality without which all such legislation must be nugatory. The compilation of acts passed during that period by thirteen different Assemblies (with the Exception of a few Enactments passed in some of the smaller Islands on the subject of Slave evidence, and of an Act of Grenada respecting the legal presumption in favour of freedom), does not contain a single statute which carries within itself any reasonable security for the faithful execution of its provisions. I am willing to give to the Colonial Legislatures the same credit for upright intentions which is claimed for those who discharge corresponding functions in this country; but I should sacrifice truth to an unmeaning and ill-timed compliment, were I to attribute to the members of those bodies that freedom from prejudice and dispassionate self-possession on the subject of Slavery, or that skill in the technical business of legislation, without which the most honest intentions are totally inadequate to the production of an effective law. Moreover, the opinion of the Assemblies has been too distinctly and repeatedly expressed to leave it doubtful what would be the result if the task of reconstructing the Order in Council were referred to them, instead of the option of unconditionally adopting or absolutely rejecting it.

You will lay this Dispatch and its enclosures before both branches of the Legislature in the Colony under your government; and I shall await, with feelings of deep and anxious interest, the result of the proposals here made. Should they not meet the views of the legislature, His Majesty's Government will have more than one cause for the most serious concern; they will then have to regret, not only the temporary postponement (for more than temporary it cannot be) of the benefits which are intended for the Slaves, but the failure also of their efforts to renew the prosperity or mitigate the distress of the Planters; and, above all, they will have to deplore the continuance, on the part of the West Indian Colonists, of that insensibility to the influence of public opinion in the Mother Country, by which they are daily bringing themselves more and more within the danger of calamities far more grievous than any which can be caused by commercial reverses, and of disasters from which it may be beyond the power of any Government to protect them.

I have, &c.

GODERICH.

# INDEX